Resisting McDonaldization

Resisting McDonaldization

edited by

Barry Smart

SAGE Publications
London • Thousand Oaks • New Delhi

First published 1999

 SAGE Publications Ltd
6 Bonhill Street
London EC2A 4PU

SAGE Publications Inc.
2455 Teller Road
Thousand Oaks, California 91320

SAGE Publications India Pvt Ltd
32, M-Block Market
Greater Kailash – I
New Delhi 110 048

British Library Cataloguing in Publication data

A catalogue record for this book is available
from the British Library

ISBN 0 7619 5517 8
ISBN 0 7619 5518 6 (pbk)

Library of Congress catalog card number 98–61886

Typeset by Mayhew Typesetting, Rhayader, Powys
Printed in Great Britain by The Cromwell Press Ltd,
Trowbridge, Wiltshire

Contents

Notes on Contributors   vii

1   Resisting McDonaldization:
Theory, Process and Critique   1
Barry Smart

2   Golden Arches and Iron Cages: McDonaldization and the
Poverty of Cultural Pessimism at the End of the Twentieth
Century   22
Christiane Bender and Gianfranco Poggi

3   Have You Had Your Theory Today?   41
John O'Neill

4   McDonaldization Enframed   57
Deena Weinstein and Michael A. Weinstein

5   Rich Food: McDonald's and Modern Life   70
Joanne Finkelstein

6   McCitizens: Risk, Coolness and Irony in Contemporary
Politics   83
Bryan S. Turner

7   Theme Parks and McDonaldization   101
Alan Bryman

8   The McDonaldization of Sport and Leisure   116
David Jary

9   McDonaldized Culture: The End of Communication?   135
Richard Münch

10   Art Centres: Southern Folk Art and the Splintering of a
Hegemonic Market   148
Gary Alan Fine

11   Dennis Hopper, McDonald's and Nike   163
Norman K. Denzin

12   Theorizing/Resisting McDonaldization: A Multiperspectivist
Approach   186
Douglas Kellner

13 The Moral Malaise of McDonaldization: The Values of
   Vegetarianism   207
   Keith Tester

14 McFascism? Reading Ritzer, Bauman and the Holocaust   222
   Peter Beilharz

15 Assessing the Resistance   234
   George Ritzer

Index   256

Notes on Contributors

Peter Beilharz is Professor of Sociology at La Trobe University, Australia. His books include *Transforming Labor* (1994), *Postmodern Socialism* (1994), *Imagining the Antipodes* (1997) and, with Chris Nyland, *The Webbs, Fabianism and Feminism* (1998). Co-founder of *Thesis Eleven*, he is 1999–2000 Professor of Australian Studies at Harvard. His next books are *Zygmunt Bauman: Modernity as Ambivalence* and *The Bauman Reader*.

Christiane Bender is Associate Professor of Sociology at the Institute of Sociology, University of Heidelberg, in Germany. Her research focuses on sociological theory, on sociology of religion and on industrial sociology. She has published empirical studies on women in the Catholic Church, on sociology of work organization and other workplace industrial developments. She is also the author of several articles concerning cultural theory, organization theory, theory of knowledge and basic sociological theory.

Alan Bryman is Professor of Social Research in the Department of Social Sciences, Loughborough University, UK. His main research interests lie in research methodology, leadership studies, organizational analysis and theme parks. He is the author and co-author of a number of books, including *Quantity and Quality in Social Research* (1988), *Charisma and Leadership in Organizations* (1992), *Disney and His Worlds* (1995), *Quantitative Data Analysis with SPSS for Windows: A Guide for Social Scientists* (1997) and *Mediating Social Science* (1988).

Norman K. Denzin is College of Communications Scholar, and Research Professor of Communications, Sociology, Cinema Studies, Criticism and Interpretive Theory at the University of Illinois at Urbana-Champaign, USA. His most recent book is *Interpretive Ethnography* (1997). He is editor of *The Sociological Quarterly*, and co-editor of *Qualitative Inquiry*.

Gary Alan Fine is Professor of Sociology at Northwestern University, USA. His books include *Kitchens: The Culture of Restaurant Work* (1996) and *Morel Tales: The Culture of Mushrooming* (1998). He is currently completing a research project on the development of a market for self-taught art.

Joanne Finkelstein currently teaches sociological theory and popular culture at the University of Sydney, Australia, and is the author of four monographs, including *Dining Out: A Sociology of Modern Manners* (1989) and *Slaves of Chic* (1994). Her research areas include fashion, consumerism and cultural studies.

David Jary is Professor of Sociology and Dean of the Graduate School at Staffordshire University in the UK. He has written extensively on social theory, including a number of recent volumes, with Christopher Bryant, on the work of Anthony Giddens. His writings on the sociology of sport and leisure have focused on soccer and on theories of sport and leisure. With Martin Parker, he has previously applied the concept of McDonaldization to higher education – the McUniversity – and his most recent edited book, *The New Higher Education* (also with Martin Parker, 1998) examines the many changes facing higher education, including tendencies to McDonaldization. He is currently exploring the rise of 'Karaoke culture', which he sees as both a continuation of and a counter-tendency to McDonaldization.

Douglas Kellner is George Kneller Chair in the Philosophy of Education at UCLA and is author of *Critical Theory, Marxism, and Modernity, Jean Baudrillard: From Marxism to Postmodernism and Beyond, Television and the Crisis of Democracy, The Persian Gulf TV War, Media Culture,* and, with Steven Best, *Postmodern Theory: Critical Interrogations* and *The Postmodern Turn.*

Richard Münch has been Professor of Sociology at the University of Bamberg, Germany, since 1995. He taught at the University of Düsseldorf from 1976 to 1995 and at the University of Cologne from 1974 to 1976. He has served several times as visiting professor at the University of California, Los Angeles, USA. He has published widely in the areas of social theory, historical-comparative sociology, and media communication. His most recent books are *Die Kultur der Moderne*, 2 vols (1986); *Dialektik der Kommunikationsgesellschaft* (1991); *Das Projekt Europa* (1993); *Sociological Theory*, 3 vols (1994); *Dynamik der Kommunikationsgesellschaft* (1995); *Risikopolitik* (1996); *Globale Dynamik, lokale Lebenswelten* (1998).

John O'Neill is Distinguished Research Professor of Sociology at York University, Toronto, Canada. He is also a Member of the Centre for Comparative Literature at the University of Toronto, and a Fellow of the Royal Society of Canada. He is also the co-editor of the international quarterly *Philosophy of the Social Sciences.* His most recent books are *The Communicative Body: Studies in Communicative Philosophy, Politics and Psychology* (1989), *Plato's Cave: Desire, Power and the Specular Functions of the Media* (1991), *Critical Conventions: Interpretation in the Literary Arts and Sciences* (1992), *The Missing Child in Liberal Theory* (1994) and *The Poverty of Postmodernism* (1995). Currently, he is working on the political economy of child suffering, welfare state theory and civic practice.

Gianfranco Poggi is Professor of Political and Social Theory at the European University Institute in Fiesole, Italy. He has previously held chairs in sociology of political science at the Universities of Edinburgh, Sydney and Virginia. Among his books are *The Development of the Modern State* (1978), *Money and the Modern Mind* (1993), and *Il gioco dei poteri* (1998). He is currently writing a book on Emile Durkheim.

George Ritzer is Professor of Sociology at the University of Maryland where he has been a Distinguished Scholar-Teacher and won a Teaching Excellence Award. He has served as Chair of two Sections of the American Sociological Association – Organizations and Occupations and Theoretical Sociology. In addition to *The McDonaldization of Society* (1993, 1996, translated into a dozen languages), his other efforts to apply social theory to the everyday realms of the economy and consumption include *Expressing America: A Critique of the Global Credit Card Society* (1995), *The McDonaldization Thesis: Explorations and Extensions* (1998), and *Enchanting a Disenchanted World: Revolutionizing the Means of Consumption* (1999). At the other end of the spectrum, his contributions to metatheorizing include *Sociology: A Multiple Paradigm Science* (1975), *Toward an Integrated Sociological Paradigm* (1981), and *Metatheorizing in Sociology* (1991). He is currently editing *The Blackwell Companion to Major Social Theorists* and co-editing (with Barry Smart) *The Handbook of Social Theory*.

Barry Smart is currently Research Professor of Sociology in the School of Social and Historical Studies at the University of Portsmouth. He has published widely in the field of social theory and his publications include *Michel Foucault* (1985), *Postmodernity* (1993) and *Facing Modernity* (1999). He is the editor of *Michel Foucault: Critical Assessments I* (3 vols, 1994) and *Michel Foucault: Critical Assessments II* (4 vols, 1995).

Keith Tester is Professor of Social Theory at the School of Social and Historical Studies, University of Portsmouth, UK. He is the author of a number of books including *Moral Culture* (1997). His first book, *Animals and Society*, won the British Sociological Association Philip Abrams Memorial Prize in 1992.

Bryan Turner is Professor of Sociology at the University of Cambridge. His recent publications include *The Body and Society* (1996) and *The Blackwell Companion to Social Theory* (1996). He is co-editor of *Body and Society* (with Mike Featherstone) and editor of *Citizenship Studies*.

Deena Weinstein, Professor of Sociology at DePaul University in Chicago, USA, is a cultural sociologist and cultural theorist, specializing in youth sub-cultures and rock music. She is the author of *Heavy Metal: A Cultural Sociology* (1991) and numerous other books and articles in sociology of organizations, sociology of science and sociological theory, as well as in her main fields of specialization. She is also a rock critic.

Michael A. Weinstein, Professor of Political Science at Purdue University in Lafayette, USA, is a political philosopher specializing in twentieth-century thought. He is the author of *Culture/Flesh: Explorations of Post-Civilized Modernity* (1996), among many other books and articles in the fields of sociological theory, cultural theory, literary criticism, ideology studies and philosophy, as well as political science. He is also a photography critic and a performance artist.

1 Resisting McDonaldization:
Theory, Process and Critique

Barry Smart

The signs of corporate life, the symbols, services and commodities associ-ated with large multinational corporations, are intruding into an ever-increasing number of areas of more and more people's lives. For example, Coca-Cola, McDonald's and Nike are probably known to most inhabitants of our planet, and Pepsi-Cola, Burger King and Reebok cannot be far behind. An increasing proportion of what we drink, eat, wear and come to want is currently provided, and is likely to be provided in the future, by global corporations competing to expand the market for their goods and services. Furthermore, with the extension of market principles to more and more areas of economic activity, how large commercial corporations rationalize the organization of production and consumption has increas-ingly become the model, frequently imposed by central governments trying to reconcile rising demand for 'public' provision with declining 'private' willingness to accept the necessity of increased levels of taxation (Bell, 1976), for delivering a wide range of other commodities and services, including public services like education, health and welfare. In most instances political and cultural boundaries, associated differences, and expressions of opposition constitute merely minor, or temporary, obstacles to the expansion of corporate interests. The globalization of capitalism, potentially, and increasingly in reality, brings everyone within the ambit of the economic empires of powerful enterprises eager to encourage us to develop a taste for their products, to acquire a need for their services, and to accommodate to their ways of doing things.

Most of the globally ubiquitous commodities have their roots in America; they are the products of the first mass consumer society. Brand names like Coca-Cola, McDonald's and Nike represent high-profile symbols which are (over)loaded with a series of complex cultural associations, and their continually growing global presence and appeal serve as evidence of the persisting presence, power and success of American commercial imperial-ism. As one analyst has remarked of Coca-Cola, assiduous promotion has meant that when you drink one 'you participate in the American Dream' (Bayley, 1986: 93). Another analyst has made reference to a process of 'Coca-colonization' as a metaphor for continuing American cultural imperialism (Pendergrast, 1993). Nike, a relative newcomer to the portfolio of cultural imperialism, has been described as 'a dream machine that seeks to redefine culture through the power of sports' (Katz, 1994, back cover), and from the proliferating signs in the street, and in particular the high-profile prevalence of the 'Swoosh' logo, the dream seems to have become a commercial, if not a cultural, reality.

The global expansion of the McDonald's Corporation through its franchised fast-food outlets constitutes yet another example of American economic and cultural imperialism. However, it might be argued that McDonald's is in a different league, for it has been suggested that the operating procedures adopted and employed in the production of its fast-food exemplify a form of economic organization which is increasingly evident in the delivery of a wider range of goods and services. Such a diagnosis has led American sociologist George Ritzer to make reference to a process of 'McDonaldization', and the thesis, outlined in a very popular and successful academic text – *The McDonaldization of Society* – and in a related series of papers, has undoubtedly captured the imagination of students and teachers around the world.

McDonaldization

Ritzer remarks in the preface to the first edition of his book, published in 1993, that he employs the term 'McDonaldization' to describe the process of rationalization – 'I have labeled the process of concern here "McDonaldization" because McDonald's was, and is, *the most important manifestation of this process*' (Ritzer, 1996: xix, emphasis added). This is a large and controversial claim, one which needs to be placed alongside Ritzer's admission a few lines later that, 'all the basic dimensions of McDonaldization . . . are part of what Weber called the rationalization process' (1996: xix). Such remarks invite the reader not only to question the terms on which McDonald's is deemed to be the most important manifestation of the process of rationalization, but also to ask what analytic value the notion of McDonaldization has, beyond rendering Weber's original thesis 'more timely' and appetizing for students attempting to achieve a better understanding of modern social theory and the world they inhabit. One question which needs to be asked, then, is what, if anything, the notion of McDonaldization adds to an understanding of the process of rationalization derived from Weber's work and that of generations of other social scientists who have subsequently sought to extend and develop Weber's insights. A number of the contributions to this volume, notably those by Christiane Bender and Gianfranco Poggi, John O'Neill, Deena Weinstein and Michael Weinstein, and Joanne Finkelstein direct their critical attention to the question of the analytic value the notion of a process of McDonaldization may have for our understanding of the rationalization of modern social life.

Is George Ritzer offering anything other than a discussion of some of the ways in which the process of rationalization analysed by Weber has been extended and elaborated? Clearly the process Weber identified has become increasingly more prominent as more areas of existence have been subjected to an intensification of formal rationality. For Weber bureaucracy was the most prominent expression of the institutionalization of formal rationality, a form of organization, of rules and regulations, which was considered to constitute an optimum means for realizing preordained ends. The large corporations represented for Weber a type of bureaucracy 'rivaled only by the state bureaucracy in promoting rational efficiency, continuity of operation, speed, precision, and calculation of results' (1970: 49). Since Weber wrote of the social and economic consequences of bureaucracy, the articulation with capitalism, and the extension of rationalization to other areas of existence, including education and training, and art and music, many other aspects have fallen under the seemingly irresistible influence of formal rationality.

Reflecting on contemporary conditions and the purchase Weber's notion of rationalization may offer, Martin Albrow remarks that '[a] computerized information system covering all individuals in a nation state and the regulation of the scientific control of human genetic material extend the frontiers of rationalization considerably beyond anything Weber conceived' (1987: 178). McDonald's-style fast-food production and some of the other instances discussed by Ritzer – health care, 'the "colonization" of birth and its antecedents, and death and its aftermath' (1996: 161), and the increasingly dehumanizing assembly-line processing of higher education, where the objective is to produce 'submissive, malleable students; creative, independent students . . . often [being], from the educational system's point of view, "messy, expensive, and time consuming"' (1996: 107) – clearly represent further examples of the extension of the frontiers of rationalization, but do they warrant the designation 'McDonaldization'? The question of the extension of the frontiers of rationalization, and the appropriateness of a notion of McDonaldization to describe such developments, is addressed by a number of other contributors to this volume, notably by Bryan Turner in a discussion of citizenship, Alan Bryman on theme parks, David Jary on sport and leisure, Richard Münch on culture and Gary Alan Fine on the art world.

The continuing growth of the fast-food industry is undoubtedly an interesting and important social, cultural, economic and environmentally consequential development. The fast-food industry is worthy of analytic attention in its own right, and in this context McDonald's fast-food chain is without doubt, as John Law has remarked, 'a big phenomenon' (1984: 180). It is to a critical analysis of the fast-food restaurant, and McDonald's in particular, that the bulk of Ritzer's analysis is directed, but not so much because of its intrinsic sociological significance. A bigger claim is made. Ritzer argues that the fast-food restaurant, and McDonald's in particular, now constitutes 'the model for rationalization', and that it has 'revolutionized not only the restaurant business, but also American society and, ultimately, the world' (1996: xvii).

Food Rationalization

In their corporate promotional material McDonald's makes much of its provision of 'Quality food, good Service, Cleanliness and good Value'. However, rather than serving millions of people each day through 'four easy letters: Q S, C and V', as the promotional material suggests, Ritzer argues that it is another four letters which represent the reality of rationalized fast-food production McDonald's-style, namely, E, C, P and C: Efficiency, Calculability, Predictability and Control. Where the emphasis in the corporate rationale is, somewhat predictably, placed upon the idea of providing what consumers want, the analytic emphasis in Ritzer's account falls upon the McDonald's fast-food restaurant as the 'culmination of a series of rationalization processes that had been occurring throughout the twentieth century' (1996: 31). The processes Ritzer has in mind are outlined in a discussion of rationalization from 'the iron cage to the fast-food factory'.

Proceeding from Weber and an account of the notion of bureaucracy, and the broader distinctive process of rationalization first associated with the modern Western world, Ritzer briefly discusses Taylorism and scientific management, Fordism and assembly-line and automated forms of production, and the Holocaust, the latter, as Peter Beilharz suggests in his contribution to this volume, serving to dramatically emphasize the dangers, costs and risks associated with the practice of formal rationality. For good measure reference is also made to the construction of 'highly rationalized homes' (1996: 27) and the shopping 'malling' of America. The McDonald's fast-food factory is represented as the end, in effect the fulfilment, of this particular series of rationalization processes. What is noticeably lacking from the discussion is any sustained analysis of the possible articulation between, on the one hand, the spread of formal rationality and, on the other, the relentless pursuit of capital accumulation, exemplified by accelerating technological innovation designed to reduce socially necessary labour time and strategies to increase existing markets and cultivate new global markets for goods and services. In short, there are other possible complementary routes from Weber's work which would allow for the marginalized political economy of rationalized fast-food production to be addressed analytically. There are also relevant and analytically profitable routes that stem from the work of Marx on the political economy of the modern capitalist mode of production which warrant reconsideration in this context.

There is undoubtedly a preoccupation with efficiency, calculability, predictability and control in the organization of the fast-food factory and other late modern economic enterprises. A good case can also be made for these features becoming an increasingly prominent part of more and more aspects of the lives of an increasing number of people, and one of the undoubted merits of Ritzer's ambitious thesis is that it does carefully document and discuss a number of examples of the rationalization of the modern everyday life-world. However, what lies behind the accelerating diffusion of strategies of formal rationality is another matter, one to which Ritzer really devotes scant attention. It is primarily in the context of an acknowledgement of the 'profound irrationalities', the risks and the costs, which are a corollary of the rationalization of modern every day life that Ritzer gives a belated, and brief, consideration to the issue of the 'factors that drive McDonaldization'. Three sets of factors are identified, namely 'material interests', a sense of intrinsic value, and compatibility and articulation with other transformations in the organization and constitution of social and cultural life.

In a series of notebooks written for the purpose of self-clarification almost 150 years ago, Karl Marx reflected on the process of development of the capitalist mode of production and remarked that,

> to the degree that large industry develops, the creation of real wealth comes to depend less on labour time and on the amount of labour employed than on the power of the agencies set in motion during labour time, whose 'powerful effectiveness' is itself in turn out of all proportion to the direct labour time spent on their production, but depends rather on the general state of science and on the progress of technology, or the application of this science to production. (1973: 704–5)

Marx was not making reference to any one particular industry but to the general way in which all the sciences are 'pressed into the service of capital' as business comes to rely more and more on invention, and invention itself 'becomes a business'. It is here in this complex process of rationalization in which specific modes of working are 'transferred from the worker to capital in the form of the machine' that the forefathers of the McDonald's operatives, who find themselves not acting as chefs or really cooking food but rather functioning, as Ritzer remarks, as 'human robots' (1996: 103), literally as appendages to a variety of machines, are to be found.

Marx made reference to the way in which the application of science to production was creating a situation in which 'the human being comes to relate more as watchman and regulator to the production process itself' (1973: 705). This is how Ritzer describes the series of simple operations required of the hamburger assemblers at McDonald's –

> the food . . . arrives at the restaurant preformed, precut, presliced, and 'pre-prepared', often by nonhuman technologies . . . there is usually no need for them to form the burgers, cut the potatoes, slice the rolls, or prepare the apple pie. All they need to do is, where necessary, cook or often merely heat the food and pass it on to the customer. (1996: 103)

Machines control the pouring of soft-drinks through sensors, preventing overflows arising from operator failure and 'french-fry machines . . . ring or buzz when the fries are done, or . . . shut themselves off and auto-matically lift the french-fry baskets out of the hot oil' (1996: 103). Marx probably would have been bemused if not repelled, by the sight of a 'Big Mac', fries and milkshake, undoubtedly he would have found very familiar the economic logic of the fast-food industry, operating as it does con-tinually to lower the costs of production and increase profitability. It is the pursuit of increasing capital accumulation which lies at the foundation of most, if not all, of the instances of rationalization considered by Ritzer to be an exemplification of McDonaldization.

The identification by Ritzer of 'material interests' as one of the factors driving McDonaldization constitutes a recognition of the possible signifi-cance of political economy to an understanding of the processes described; however, the precise respects in which 'economic factors lie at the root of McDonaldization' do not receive much clarification at all. Had more atten-tion been devoted to the political economy of fast-food, and McDonald's in particular, then the other forces identified as driving McDonaldization might have been recognized for what they are, namely closely articulated in the final instance with economic factors. The explanation of McDonaldiza-tion as an end in itself is provided through a series of empirical illustrations which are presented as indicative of the fact that efficiency, calculability, predictability and control come to be valued by individuals and represen-tatives of institutions independently of economic factors and associated outcomes. Ritzer remarks that 'eating in a fast-food restaurant, or having a microwave dinner at home, may be efficient but it is more costly than if people prepared the meal "from scratch"' (1996: 145). At issue here, but not considered in this context, are questions about changing ways of living that have lead to transformations in eating habits and the structure of meals. As one analyst has remarked, gastronomic habits – what, when and how we eat – are a 'product of our history' and they continue to change. For example, Americans tend now 'to snack rather than fast during the mid-morning and mid-afternoon, and the meals they do eat have become much more snack like' (MacClancy, 1992: 52). And in Britain, too, traditional meals are reported to be 'in decline as families grab quick takeaways' (Millar, 1997) or resort to 'ready-made meals' (Preston, 1997). Are such developments to be explained simply through a notion of 'efficiency' or in some other way? Are consumers choosing efficiency, or being constrained to respond to the increasing time pressures, distractions and powerful forms of consumer marketing that are a corollary of capitalist modernity?

Amongst other things, what is implicit in Ritzer's account is a continuing process of extension of commodity exchange relations into the very heart, perhaps stomach would constitute a more appropriate metaphor, of the household. In a household where the adult members are engaged in waged work outside the household, who has the time and inclination to choose ingredients, prepare them, cook and organize the serving, and then subsequently to deal with the clearing up? It is in this context, that people increasingly seem to be resorting to fast-food, pre-prepared, oven-ready or microwave dishes. Ritzer does subsequently acknowledge factors such as the impact of the increasing employment of women outside the household on the reorganization of domestic life and food preparation in particular, but only in the context of a relatively brief discussion of what is presented as a third explanation of 'the rush toward McDonaldization'. In short, the evidence offered, of both a sense of the intrinsic value of McDonaldization and its apparent compatibility with a range of other transformations in the organization of social and cultural life, in fact points to the underlying presence of powerful material interests and forces.

Reflecting on the proliferation of fast-food outlets Ritzer remarks that it is understandable that an individual entrepreneur may want to open 'another McDonaldized institution', but then he asks 'does it make economic sense at the societal level to have so many of them concentrated in given locales?' (1996: 145). The concentration identified is, however, readily understandable as soon as attention is directed to the nature of the economic system within which the developments discussed are to be found. Capitalism is an open, competitive, and now increasingly globalized economic system, one in which different enterprises compete vigorously for an increasingly larger share of the available market(s). There is currently no viable 'societal-level' economic planning rationale, merely the hegemonic economic logic of the 'free' market, modified by the possible influence of 'local' legal statute and planning restrictions. Moreover, the very notion of a 'societal-level' economic planning rationale has proven to be incompatible with 'transnational practices which transcend individual nation-states through generating immense flows of capital, money, goods, services, people, information, [and] technologies' (Lash and Urry, 1994: 280).

The advent of a globalized process of capitalist economic rationalization has been associated with more competitive and flexible forms of capital accumulation and more extensive labour-displacing computer-controlled technologies, and simultaneously an erosion of the sovereignty nation-states are able to exercise over their economies. In the context of a continuing process of capitalist globalization it is difficult to know how effective 'societal level' economic regulation or planning might be achieved. As Lash and Urry remark, with 'global interdependence there is a decrease in the effectiveness of policy instruments which would enable states to control activities which occur within their borders' (1994: 280). In short, contrary to Ritzer's hypothesis, it is precisely the economic or material interests of competing corporate capitals that gives rise to the phenomenon identified, namely the concentration of 'McDonaldized institutions . . . in given locales' (1996: 145). The rationalized consumer ghettos of fast-food restaurants, designer clothes emporia, shopping malls, and so on, do not signify that 'McDonaldization . . . has become valued in and of itself' (1996: 145), but rather that in its hyper-competitive, relatively unregulated, consumer phase contemporary capitalism constitutes a socio-economic system in which the pursuit of capital accumulation and the difficulty of maintaining and/or increasing profitability necessarily leads capital continually to seek new possibilities, to create new needs, desires and appetites, to produce new commodities and services, and to try to find new locations and markets for products, whatever the cost to competitors, and with relatively little, if any, consideration for the interests or wishes of the local communities likely to be affected.

The real forces driving the expansion of the fast-food industry – and notwithstanding Ritzer's wider thesis about a process of McDonaldization it is fast-food and McDonald's in particular to which the argument continually returns to affirm the intrinsic value, acceptance and articulation of rationalization processes with wider socio-economic transformations – are economic and cultural. A few mundane examples will serve to illustrate the point. The opening in 1997, in the face of strong local opposition, of a large McDonald's and a Planet Hollywood restaurant in close proximity to one another in the central area of Cannes demonstrates the persistence of American economic and cultural imperialism, rather than any intrinsic value, appreciation, or acceptance of McDonaldization for its own sake (French, 1997). Reactions to eating *vite* recorded in Paris, reactions which echo the sentiments of Italian and French chefs who founded the 'international "Slow Food" movement' in 1989 (MacClancy, 1992: 212), suggest that appreciation of the rationalization of food still remains very limited, notwithstanding the accumulating evidence of a growing number of diners coming to regard food and eating purely instrumentally, as a 'no-nonsense utilitarian' activity which exemplifies a 're-fuelling ethos' (Law, 1984: 185), rather than as an intrinsic source of pleasure to be anticipated, savoured and consumed at leisure in the company of significant others. For example, one dissatisfied Burger King customer is reported to have remarked 'This won't fill me up. You walk into fast food restaurants believing they will be cheaper, cleaner and somehow better because you help yourself. None of this is true because you get caught up in the illusion.' The same diner goes on to comment resignedly that 'We are all caught up in the McDonald–Disney–frozen-food culture' and that its only going to get worse given 'an increasingly high-speed approach to life' (Smith, 1996). But if there is a sense in which an increasing number of people are experiencing more intense time-space compression as a consequence of the 'transition from Fordism to flexible accumulation' (Harvey, 1989: 284), it is also clear that some people are not (as) caught up in the illusions of consumer capitalism. In short, it is important to recognize that the economic interests of global corporations like McDonald's can be, and are, resisted. I will turn in the final section to some issues of criticism and resistance as they arise in relation to Ritzer's thesis and the critical reflections of other analysts contributing to this volume.

The Burdens of Modernity

In a discussion of the ethos of modern capitalism at the beginning of the twentieth century, Max Weber argued that the modern economic order is 'bound to the technical and economic conditions of machine production which today determine the lives of all the individuals who are born into this mechanism, not only those directly concerned with economic acquisition' (1976: 181). Weber proceeds, in a subsequent paragraph, to express concern that the fate confronting the modern subject was to be burdened by 'material goods [which] have gained an increasing and finally inexorable power over the lives of men as at no period in history' (1976: 181). Weber's reference is to the modern economic order, to which it is necessary to accommodate, one which determines substantial aspects of our existence and might be regarded as constitutive of modern subjectivity itself. It is an economic order which no longer seeks justification in terms of religious or ethical meaning; it represents a form of life for Weber in which the pursuit of material wealth has seemingly become an end in itself.

In his reflections on the process of rationalization exemplified by the fast-food industry, an industry now argued to represent 'the model for rationalization', Ritzer invokes a metaphor attributed to Weber and refers to the 'iron cage of McDonaldization' (1996: 143ff.; see also Chapter 2). Ritzer wants to draw attention to the way in which modern social life has become increasingly subject to efficiency, calculability, predictability and control, and to argue that it has become increasingly difficult to escape from the 'rational systems of a McDonaldized society' (1996: 143). There are a number of issues here which warrant further reflection, and they are all connected to the question of the appropriateness of the 'iron cage' metaphor for making sense of the complex conditions and consequences identified with McDonaldization by Ritzer.

There are two related relevant contexts in which Weber comments on the constraints to which modern forms of life are subject as a consequence of an increasing rationalization of conduct. One, noted above, concerns the consequences for modern subjectivity of what Weber presciently termed 'victorious capitalism'. The other involves the features of formal rationality exemplified by modern bureaucratic organization. In his discussion of the development of an increasingly '"rationalist" way of life', Weber places emphasis upon the 'advance of the rational bureaucratic structure of domination' (Weber, 1970: 240). It is the technical superiority of bureaucratic rationality which accounts for its advance and its indispensability in a complex modern community. There is, Weber argues, no question of being able to

> dispense with or replace the bureaucratic apparatus of authority once it exists. For this bureaucracy rests upon expert training, a functional specialization of work, and an attitude set for habitual and virtuoso-like mastery of single yet methodically integrated functions. If the official stops working, or if his work is forcefully interrupted, chaos results. . . . This holds for public administration as well as for private economic management. More and more the material fate of the masses depends upon the steady and correct functioning of the increasingly bureaucratic organization of private capitalism. The idea of eliminating these organizations becomes more and more utopian. (Weber, 1970: 229)

It is clear that for Weber there is really little question of choice; the material, technical and functional complexity of the modern world is constitutive of our subjectivity, it gives form to our desires, shapes our tastes and sets the parameters from which it is difficult, some might say impossible, to escape, even if we wished to do so.

After describing the process of bureaucratic rationalization as a precursor of McDonaldization, Ritzer proceeds to draw parallels between what is described as Weber's view of bureaucracies as 'cages in the sense that people are trapped in them, their basic humanity denied' (1996: 21), and the organizational reality of the fast-food industry and other institutions considered to be subject to McDonaldization. Attributing to Weber a concern with the 'iron cage of rationality' and its consequences, Ritzer goes on to talk about the 'iron cage of McDonaldization'. There are two problems with this. The first concerns the adequacy of the 'iron cage' metaphor itself for conveying an understanding of the problematic cultural consequences Weber had in mind. The second concerns the appropriateness of the metaphor for describing the more negative consequences of the complex processes and relationships (rationalization, commodification, American economic and cultural imperialism, and globalization) for which Ritzer has coined the term 'McDonaldization'.

The context in which the 'iron cage' metaphor appears in Weber's work is where the effects of an increasingly secularized early twentieth-century modern economic order are being considered. Weber, reflecting on the cultural and historical context in which the ethos of capitalism was formed, notes that while the seventeenth-century Protestant theological moralist Richard Baxter had preached that 'external goods should only lie on the shoulders of the "saint like a light cloak, which can be thrown aside at any moment"', the secular reality of modern economic life was that the cloak had 'become an iron cage' (1976: 181).

In a reconsideration of the respective works of Marx and Weber on capitalism and modernity, Derek Sayer has questioned the adequacy of the interpretation which has given us the 'iron cage' metaphor and has proposed instead that the constraining consequences of the modern economic ordering of life, to which we are increasingly subject, be thought of in a different and more appropriate way. Rather than 'iron cage', Sayer suggests that a better metaphorical translation of Weber's reference to the cloak 'turning into *ein stahlhartes Gehause*: a casing, or housing, as hard as steel . . . might be the shell (also *Gehause*) on a snail's back: a burden perhaps, but something impossible to live without, in either sense of the word' (1991: 144). It is precisely this complex condition and experience that modernity promotes and represents. It provides our 'home' or shelter – the only one with which we are familiar, it is literally where and how we live our lives – and yet it is also experienced, at times, as a constraint or burden from which there seems to be no prospect of escape, to which there appears to be no realistic alternative. There are clearly benefits, but there are also burdens, such is the condition of ambivalence increasingly associated with modernity (Bauman, 1991). We now understand that many of the difficulties which we continue to encounter, the discontents which we feel and suffer, are part and parcel of modernity, and that as such difficulties are alleviated or overcome their place is destined to be taken by other, as yet unanticipated, problems. As Bauman has remarked, 'There are no gains without losses, and the hope of a wonderous purification of gains from losses is as futile as the proverbial dream of a free lunch' (1997: 4).

The metaphor of the 'iron cage' inappropriately suggests containment through external constraint. The reality of the forms of subjectivity constituted through various processes of modern rationalization and considered, in some of their manifestations, by Weber is quite different. The emphasis in Weber's discussion of the development of modern forms of life is placed on the cultivation of rational forms of conduct achieved through the cultural constitution of predispositions to act in particular ways. For example, the objective of Protestant asceticism outlined by Weber was not to externally constrain, but rather to positively nurture and support a particular form of self-disciplined subjectivity, which would voluntarily engage in 'continuous systematic work in a worldly calling' and simultaneously exercise a 'limitation of consumption', a significant consequence of which was to be capital accumulation (1976: 170–2). The 'iron cage' metaphor is not only inadequate for figuring out what Weber thought about the uneven impact of modern rationality, it is also questionable, as Doug Kellner, another of the contributors to this volume, argues, whether it is appropriate for understanding the complex processes which Ritzer has designated as 'McDonaldization'.

Weber was writing at the beginning of the twentieth century and he described how the Puritan ascetic attitude of 'sober utility' constituted a 'powerful tendency toward uniformity of life, which today so immensely aids the capitalistic interest in the standardization of production' (1976: 169). Clearly much has changed. Rather than a limitation of consumption and a recommendation of sober utility, it is the promotion of ever-increasing levels of consumption and the pursuit of hedonistic individualism which are intrinsic to the ethos of contemporary capitalism. And in contrast to a uniformity of life, articulated with a standardization of production, it is diversity and difference that are increasingly cultivated within late modern capitalism and the culture of individualism. The emphasis now in economic production is not so much on standardization as flexibility and reflexivity (Lash and Urry, 1994).

In the early decades of the twentieth century, standardized mass production and consumption represented a new regime of capital accumulation, one sometimes designated 'Fordism' because, perhaps not unlike the thesis under discussion, a particular form of economic rationalization, introduced by Henry Ford in his Michigan factory in 1913, involving organizational and technological innovations which made automated car assembly-line production possible, was argued to be, and indeed came to be regarded as, a model for economic rationalization in general (Harvey, 1989). Ritzer discusses how the fast-food industry has embraced F.W. Taylor's conception of 'scientific management', which involved breaking down the 'labour process into component motions and organizing fragmented work tasks according to rigorous standards of time and motion study' (Harvey, 1989: 125), and has adopted the assembly-line processing of production associated with the name of Ford. These production innovations, along with suburban development, facilitated by the increasing availability of private car ownership, and the growth of enclosed shopping malls, are presented by Ritzer as precursors of McDonaldization. Without doubt they constitute some of the necessary preconditions for the successful development of the fast-food industry and the McDonald's fast-food franchised restaurant chain in particular, but is it appropriate to now regard such enterprises as representing the model for rationality? And is the metaphor of the iron cage helpful for understanding the consequences of McDonaldization?

In response to the argument that a transition from Fordism to more flexible forms of accumulation has been underway since the early 1970s, a transition in which the emphasis shifts from standardized forms of production and consumption to more specialized products, niche marketing and 'differentiated commodities, life-styles, and cultural outlets', Ritzer remarks that 'it is equally clear that elements of Fordism persist and show no signs of disappearing' (1996: 152). There is no doubt that standardization, routinization, de-skilling, and the homogenization of production and consumption remain significant features of some forms of economic activity, and the fast-food industry and McDonald's in particular, but recognition of the emergence of post-Fordist, more flexible and reflexive forms of production and consumption calls into question the idea that McDonaldization now represents *the model* of rationalizaton.

In his discussion of the forces considered to be driving McDonaldization, Ritzer alludes, again briefly, to the powers of persuasion employed to create a demand for rationalized, highly processed food. The means by which a substantial level of demand has been achieved and reproduced, if not increased, are not, however, considered, and the possibility that it is not efficiency, or at least not always or primarily efficiency, which leads people to consume McDonaldized commodities, and fast-food in particular, is not really explored. The question 'Why McDonald's?' has been addressed briefly by Arthur Kroker et al. (1989) and at greater length by John Law (1984), and the explanations they advance suggest that the consequences of McDonaldization are far more complex than the metaphor of the iron cage allows. People are not so much 'trapped' or 'imprisoned' as powerfully seduced by the signs and promised prospect of pleasure, economy and sociability promoted by marketing departments and persuasively portrayed in advertising copy. Reflecting on the way in which McDonald's markets it primary product line, Arthur Kroker et al. argue that

Hamburgers . . . have been aestheticized to such a point of frenzy and hysteria that the McDonald's hamburger has actually vanished into its own sign. Just watch the TV commercials. Hamburgers as *party time* for the kids; . . . as *nostalgia time* for our senior citizens; . . . as *community time* for small town America; and, as always, hamburgers under the media sign of *friendship time* for America's teenagers. Thus processed hamburgers for a society where eating is *the* primary consumptive activity. (1989: 119)

It is to the issue of the nurturing of a market for McDonaldized commodities through advertising campaigns which rationalize 'the emotional, and the personal' that Norman Denzin's contribution to this volume is directed.

There is reference by Ritzer to the fact that McDonald's and many other companies have 'invested enormous amounts of money and effort' convincing people of the value of their wares, and the success they have had in creating 'a large number of highly devoted customers' (1996: 145) is noted, but how this has been achieved is not really explored. What is missing is an analysis of the formation of 'McDonaldized' cultures of consumption – how consumer subjects are constituted, tastes cultivated and desires stimulated. As Alan Warde has observed, 'Many forces operate together to provide collective orientations towards selecting food [or whatever]. Socio-cultural forces, media representations of taste, and socio-demographic circumstances predispose people to similar consumption patterns' (1997: 189–90). Where issues of consumption are addressed in Ritzer's account it tends to be in terms of a consideration of the way in which the process of rationalization of productive forces has been increasingly extended in the course of the development of late capitalism to the sector of consumption. But apart from a discussion of the ways in which customers are put to work in the fast-food restaurant – standing in line to place an order, carrying food to the table, disposing of waste and stacking trays, features common to many earlier self-service establishments – and also in other 'McDonaldized' establishments in the health, telecommunications and banking industries, no analytic consideration is given to the activity of consumption itself, to the question of what it is to consume, and indeed what it is that is being consumed, or for that matter how, or through which mechanisms, the consumer subject is constituted. The 'individual consumer' has become necessary and irreplaceable as the centre of gravity of contemporary capitalism has shifted from production to consumption and, simultaneously, the object of consumption has taken on the value of a sign and now responds not so much to a utilitarian calculus of 'need' as a cultural logic of 'desire for social meaning' (Baudrillard, 1997). In short, consideration needs to be given to the complex process by which the power of seduction, rather than the force of repression which is implied by the 'iron cage' metaphor, has become paramount in consumer capitalist society (Bauman, 1992).

The central objective of the processes of rationalization described by Ritzer is effectively to achieve an ordering (or reordering) of conduct. To put this another way, it might be argued that the aim is to achieve an accommodation of conduct to particular ways of organizing production and consumption practices. In the particular case of McDonald's it has been argued that although people might accommodate 'to the McDonald's version of social structure', this does not necessarily mean that they subscribe to it, or that they value it, or 'that they all subscribe to the *same* version of the social order' (Law, 1984: 181). A variety of reasons have been advanced to account for McDonald's success, ranging from Kottak's attempt to liken the experience to a 'religious ritual', the secular institution being held to possess some of 'the attributes of a sacred place' (1978: 75), to Vidal's identification of the scale of the corporation's global advertising campaign, around $20,000 million having been spent on promotion in the last 20 years, which has made it 'one of the world's biggest advertisers' and, in turn, has led to the 'Golden Arches of McDonald's . . . [overtaking] the Christian cross as the second most widely recognized symbol in the world' (1997: 135). However, while some people subscribe to the McDonald's version of social order and appear to enjoy the experience, others have criticized and resisted it.

Critique and Resistance

The analysis presented by Ritzer identifies both benefits and costs associated with 'McDonaldized' processes of rationalization. Benefits identified include the easier availability of a greater number and range of goods and services, which are deemed to be more uniform in quality, if not in some cases of a higher standard than before McDonaldization. There is the suggestion of a more 'convenient' access to goods and services, as well as other benefits, such as safety and security which are assumed to be a feature of the 'environment of a McDonaldized system'; the prospect that people are 'more likely to be treated similarly, no matter what their race, gender, or social class'; and finally that the 'products of one culture are more easily diffused to others' (Ritzer, 1996: 12).

Some of the benefits identified are open to question. For example, if there appears to be 'comfort in the comparatively stable, familiar, and safe environment of a McDonaldized system' (1996: 12), we now appreciate, given a knowledge of the risks associated with modernity (Beck, 1992; Lash et al., 1996), that it may well be false comfort. For a good example of the rapidity with which the falsity of comfort and confidence in a quite literally highly McDonaldized environment can be exposed, we have to go no further than the events of 1996 concerning the beef industry in Britain, an industry which provided the fast-food burger restaurant business, and the McDonald's Corporation in Britain in particular, with the key ingredient for its primary product. After much prevarication, the British government finally had to acknowledge that evidence existed of a possible link between bovine spongiform encephalopathy (BSE) in cattle and Creutzfeldt–Jakob disease (CJD) in humans. There was little comfort to be had from the fact that the McDonald's Corporation had already moved earlier in the same year to remove British beef from its product lines because of growing public concern about a possible link between BSE and CJD, for the emerging evidence of a new strain of CJD in humans was believed to be related to exposure to BSE before an offal ban had been introduced in 1989 (Smart, 1999).

Furthermore, when consideration is given to some of the consequences of an extension of 'McDonaldized' processes of rationalization, particularly economic rationalization, to public services and institutions, notably the extension of what are called 'free-market' principles to education, health and welfare, it is clear that the outcome has been not a reduction in differences in treatment, but rather a pronounced widening of the quality gap between those dependent on public provision and those able to afford private provision. And, as I will show below, the notion that an increase in the ease with which the products of one culture can be diffused to others constitutes a benefit is, in its turn, a contentious matter, as ironically Ritzer's own reference to a French politician's protest at the opening of Euro Disney, namely that 'it will "bombard France with uprooted creations that are to culture what fast food is to gastronomy"', clearly indicates (1996: 14). Certainly, the global proliferation of McDonald's fast-food outlets has been of financial benefit to the Corporation, but, as John Vidal comments, the 'diet that McDonald's exports is alien to most cultures. McDonald's learned that globalization did not mean having to diversify or take account of indigenous foods or tastes and that through television and strong marketing they could "teach" people, especially the young, that the diet they were promoting was good' (1997: 42–3). We now know that the quality and benefit of such a diet is, to say the least, 'nutritionally questionable', for as Ritzer subsequently notes, fast-food poses a danger in so far is it contains 'a lot of fat, cholesterol, salt, and sugar' (1996: 129, 130).

Ritzer outlines a number of criticisms of McDonaldization in a critique of the 'irrationality of rationality'. The argument advanced is that the irrationality of rationality constitutes a 'fifth dimension of McDonaldization'. The basic thesis is that, however rational the system, there is a strong possibility, virtually a certainty, that there will be unanticipated irrational consequences. The outcomes Ritzer identifies include 'adverse effects on the environment' associated with the fast-food industry in particular. For example, the 'need to grow uniform potatoes to create those predictable french fries' is associated with huge farms making extensive use of chemicals, which subsequently contaminate underground water supplies (Ritzer, 1996: 13). Other 'irrationalities' identified in this context include the destruction of forests to produce paper, 'the damage caused by polystyrene' and the disproportionate quantity of 'food needed to produce feed cattle' (Ritzer, 1996: 13). It is worth adding that such consequences also undermine the idea that a McDonaldized system brings the benefit of safety.

Safety and security may well be part of the corporate rhetoric and may in particular feature large in the marketing of commodities and services, but we should not allow our attention to be deflected from the reality of corporate life and the consequences increasingly associated with it, consequences which have led analysts such as Ulrich Beck to identify the emergence of a society in which recognition of risks and experiences of insecurity and uncertainty 'threaten to become the norm' (1992: 24). Interestingly many of the examples of irrationality discussed by Ritzer involve the fast-food industry – restaurants are described as 'dehumanizing' places in which to eat and work and customers are said to feel as though they are on an 'assembly-line', which is precisely what Kroker et al. have in mind when they refer to processed food and processed crowds, and McDonald's as 'a phasal eating station . . . a whole apparatus of processed eating . . . [designed] to speed the way from secretion to excretion' (1989: 119).

However, there is a wider discussion of the costs associated with organizational forms of rationality, that is, other manifestations of what Ritzer terms the 'irrationality' of McDonaldization. While processes of rationalization may be promoted in terms of a promised yield of efficiency, predictability, calculability and control, Ritzer remarks that such processes can be viewed as leading to the opposite. What Ritzer has in mind includes a number of 'inefficiencies' experienced or suffered by consumers in the form of lengthy queues of people/cars at counters/windows at McDonald's restaurants/drive-throughs; the 'labour' involved in using automated cash machines at banks; and the time spent and frustration incurred responding to computerized switchboards which request and dispense a menu of information as they distribute and channel telephone enquiries.

However, such consequences of economic rationalization do not so much constitute 'irrationalities' as a logical outcome of the development of the capitalist mode of production as it pursues increasing capital accumulation. Many of the examples given concern consumers becoming involved in unpaid self-servicing work, which is a direct corollary of the displacement of living labour from productive activity, following the increasing application of science and technology to production anticipated by Marx (1973). In such a setting it is indeed, as Ritzer recommends, appropriate and necessary to ask 'Efficient for whom?'(1996: 123). The answer is not difficult to determine, if the analysis is adequately focused on the mode of production which has promoted increasing economic rationalization, and in the case of McDonald's fast-food it is the Corporation with its '$30 billion a year turnover' (Vidal, 1997: 243).

While Ritzer identifies a number of significant costs and problems which follow from processes of McDonaldization, little attempt, as I have noted, is made to analyse the complex and costly mechanisms which are routinely employed to continually persuade people of the virtue, or necessity, of rationalization, or to seduce them into pursuing the McDonald's illusion of 'food, folks and fun' as a potentially realizable and enjoyable, if not

beneficial, objective. Although some broader negative effects of McDonaldization on the dehumanization of human relationships are considered,
and not only in respect of the production and consumption of fast-food,
but also in relation to health care and education, the source of the
continuing power of 'the illusion', as Ritzer describes it, is not really
explored. In short, as Doug Kellner argues in his contribution, 'the cultural
side of the McDonald's phenomenon' is somewhat neglected.

However, as powerful as the 'illusion' might be, it is nevertheless clear
that not everyone buys into it. There is resistance to McDonaldization and
it has assumed a number of different forms. Addressing the issue of critical
responses to rationalization processes, Ritzer once again offers examples
from the fast-food industry. Ritzer notes how American communities like
Saugatuck in Michigan offered resistance to McDonald's attempt to take
over and convert an old café, and how outside the USA opposition has
arisen to the siting of several fast-food restaurants, as well as to the
negative nutritional and cultural consequences attributed to existing
outlets. Such examples are interesting, but they simultaneously invite the
question 'What precisely is being resisted?'. Is it rationalization *per se*
which is the issue, or is it the entry of a powerful global corporation into a
local environment, bringing with it the threat of an erosion of the
distinctiveness of a local culture? When the owner of a local Saugatuck inn
remarks that, 'It's . . . the McDonald's, the malls of the world that we're
fighting against. . . . You can go to a mall and not know what state you're
in. We're a relief from all that' (quoted in Ritzer, 1996: 180), it is the
corporate power to impose particular forms of economic rationalization
that is being opposed. Likewise, resistance to McDonald's in Barbados,
France and Italy (Smart, 1994), to mention but a few locations, has
primarily involved opposition to the threat posed by American economic
and cultural imperialism to indigenous cultural values and practices, rather
than an opposition to rationality *per se* and/or an embrace of irrationality.

The problem identified above arises from conceptual slippage, from
Ritzer's failure to adequately differentiate between complex processes of
modern rationalization and their uneven consequences, and from a parallel
tendency to conflate discussion of McDonald's the fast-food business with
'McDonaldization' as a complex social and economic process. It is worth
adding that these conceptual difficulties continue to present a problem in
Ritzer's subsequent reflections on his thesis, as the following statement
reveals:

> McDonaldization as a form of Americanization, *does* represent something unique
> . . . it brings together in one package a threat to both European business *and*
> cultural practices. . . . In contrast, the coming of MTV, Coca-Cola and Disney
> threaten to homogenize culture, but they do not greatly affect European business
> practices. McDonaldization involves *both* a revolutionary set of business prac-
> tices *and* a revolution in one absolutely key element of culture – the way in which
> people eat. (1998: 74)

There are two parallel theses in Ritzer's text, the more modest and sustainable one is about the development and impact of McDonald's the fast-food business on the social rituals, culture and economy of eating, the other, much grander, more innovative and ambitious, yet simultaneously more questionable, argues that the fast-food industry, and McDonald's in particular, has become the model of rationalization.

There are many examples of local resistance to McDonald's and its rationalization of food production and consumption. For example, Ritzer makes reference to the critical reaction which followed the opening of a new McDonald's in Jerusalem and quotes a kosher restaurant inspector who was moved to comment that 'McDonald's is contaminating all of Israel and all of the Jewish people' (1998: 18). Numerous journalists have reported on the ways in which local communities opposed to McDonald's have fought the global corporation's plans to open restaurants in their neighbourhoods. For example, for 12 years the London suburb of Hampstead successfully resisted the fast-food chain's attempts to open a restaurant, but finally had to accept defeat in 1993 when a small 40-seat outlet opened (Pearman, 1993), and there have been several comparable examples of community resistance to the McDonald's Corporation in Paris and elsewhere in France (Webster, 1996). Criticism and resistance may also extend to alternative dietary practices such as vegetarianism. However, as Keith Tester argues in his contribution to this volume, the value of vegetarianism needs to be reconsidered in the light of the 'moral malaise of McDonaldization'.

Perhaps the most significant widely publicized sign of resistance to McDonald's and its rationalization of food production and consumption has been what has come, very aptly, to be known as 'McLibel', a term signifying a legal process, an associated global social movement, and a website ('McSpotlight'). As George Ritzer remarks in a subsequent collection of essays on his thesis, McDonald's has become a 'negative symbol' to a number of global social movements concerned about 'ecological hazards, dietary dangers, the evils of capitalism and the dangers posed by Americanization' (1998: 175). Certainly between 1990 and 1997 the trial in London of two individuals, Helen Steel and David Morris, who had been issued with writs for libel by the McDonald's Corporation – hence 'McLibel' – became a powerful focus for the expression of criticism and resistance.

Although Ritzer warns that 'we must not confuse threats to McDonald's with dangers to the process of McDonaldization' (1998: 176), there is a strong connection between the campaign against McDonald's, which involved the circulation of a 10-page 'What's Wrong with McDonald's?' leaflet and which led to the writs for libel being issued, and wider concern, criticism and resistance to particular forms of rationalization. The full libel trial began on 28 June 1994, the last day for final submissions was 13 December 1996, and a ruling was finally given by the judge, Mr Justice Bell, on 19 June 1997. The civil trial, the longest in English legal history, reputedly cost McDonald's £10 million and, although the ruling was ultimately in the Corporation's favour, the judge upheld several damaging charges made by the campaigners against the Corporation, including the cruel treatment of animals used in its food products and the exploitation of children in its advertising campaigns (Vidal, 1997), and in addition there was criticism of the company for 'misleading publicity involving the recycled content of its packaging and false nutritional claims' (*The Guardian* editorial, 20 June 1997).

The factsheet, 'What's Wrong with McDonald's?', prophetically subtitled 'Everything they don't want you to know', contained a number of criticisms of the Corporation for the way it treated animals, produced food of questionable nutritional value, damaged the environment, and promoted exploitative employment practices (Vidal, 1997). In seeking legal redress McDonald's Restaurants (UK) and the parent company the McDonald's Corporation, based in Oakbrook, Illinois, inadvertently drew greater attention to the allegations contained in the offending factsheet. The 315-day McLibel trial understandably attracted a great deal of media attention and the McSpotlight website with its '2,500 files on McDonald's: a hundred megabytes of information including videos, interviews, discussion groups, [and] transcripts from the trial', not to mention the factsheet 'ready to print off the screen in a dozen languages', is reported to have had 'more than 7 million "hits"' by the end of the trial (Vidal, 1997: 177–8). However, while McDonald's was the immediate focus of concern during the trial, the issues raised by the campaigners, their witnesses and supporters, had a wider relevance and might be argued to simultaneously constitute criticism of broader processes of economic rationalization, processes for which Ritzer employs the term 'McDonaldization'.

As John Vidal remarks in his discussion of the McLibel trial, it is not just about McDonald's, it is about the social cultural and economic consequences of market globalization. McDonald's represents an example of 'market globalism', of how to 'manage the globalization of corporations' (Vidal, 1997: 237), but the bigger issue, to which the McLibel trial and George Ritzer's thesis on the McDonaldization of social life directs our attention, is that of the consequences of the concentration of power in the hands of a few transnational corporations. It has been suggested that the flow of events still favours the transnational corporations, 'those who would homogenize, standardize and globalize', and that 'corporate culture is now the bedrock of . . . Western political culture', but there is also accumulating evidence of increasing disquiet about, and resistance to, 'McWorld' (Vidal, 1997: 255, 266, 272). It is precisely here that the value of Ritzer's thesis lies, namely in the provision of a popular and accessible critical analysis of key aspects of the processes of rationalization, commodification, American economic and cultural imperialism, and globalization associated with an industry familiar to virtually everyone.

Forty years ago another American sociologist, C. Wright Mills (1970 [1959]), wrote of the responsibilities of the analyst, of the need to focus critically on the preoccupations and concerns of the present, and of the importance of nurturing the sociological imagination to allow us to achieve an appropriate and effective understanding of the conditions in which we find ourselves living, so that we can act to do something about them. George Ritzer, like C. Wright Mills, evidently finds the consequences of increasing rationality to be uneven, and in some important respects problematic, and it is to an analysis of the associated complex conditions and circumstances in which we now find ourselves living that his McDonaldization thesis is directed. The analysis provided of modern rationality and related preoccupations and concerns has, as the chapters in this volume demonstrate, simultaneously stimulated the sociological imagination and provoked strong criticism. But whether the thesis is adopted and endorsed, or criticized and rejected, there is no denying its powerful impact.

References

Albrow, M. (1987) 'The application of the Weberian concept of rationalization to contemporary conditions', in S. Whimster and S. Lash (eds), *Max Weber, Rationality and Modernity*. London: Allen & Unwin.

Baudrillard, J. (1997) *The Consumer Society: Myths and Structures*. London: Sage.

Bauman, Z. (1991) *Modernity and Ambivalence*. Cambridge: Polity Press.

Bauman, Z. (1992) *Intimations of Postmodernity*. London: Routledge.

Bauman, Z. (1997) *Postmodernity and its Discontents*. New York: New York University Press.

Bayley, S. (1986) *Coke: Designing a World Brand*. London: Conran Foundation.

Beck, U. (1992) *Risk Society: Towards a New Modernity*. London: Sage.

Bell, D. (1976) *The Cultural Contradictions of Capitalism*. New York: Basic Books.

French, P. (1997) 'Cannes', *The Observer*, 11 May.

Harvey, D. (1989) *The Condition of Postmodernity: An Enquiry into the Origins of Cultural Change*. Oxford: Blackwell.

Katz, D. (1994) *Just Do It: The Nike Spirit in the Corporate World*. Holbrook, MA: Adams Publishing.

Kottak, C.P. (1978) 'Rituals at McDonald's', *Natural History*, 87, 1: 75–82.

Kroker, A., Kroker, M. and Cook, D. (eds) (1989) *Panic Encyclopedia: The Definitive Guide to the Postmodern Scene*. London: Macmillan.

Lash, S. and Urry, J. (1994) *Economies of Signs and Space*. London: Sage.

Lash, S. Szerszynski, B. and Wynne, B. (eds) (1996) *Risk Environment and Modernity: Towards a New Ecology*. London: Sage.

Law, J. (1984) 'How much of society can the sociologist digest at one sitting? The "macro" and the "micro" revisited for the case of fast food', *Studies in Symbolic Interaction*, 5: 171–96.

MacClancy, J. (1992) *Consuming Culture*. London: Chapmans.

Marx, K. (1973) *Grundrisse*. Harmondsworth: Penguin.

Millar, S. (1997) 'Television shatters dinner chatter',*The Guardian*. 29 September.

Mills, C. Wright (1970) *The Sociological Imagination*. Harmondsworth: Penguin.

Pearman, H. (1993) 'The good burgers of NW3', *The Sunday Times, The Culture*, June 6.

Pendergrast, M. (1993) *For God, Country and Coca-Cola*. London: Weidenfeld.

Preston, P. (1997) 'Too many cooks spoil the pot noodle', *The Guardian*, 3 November.

Ritzer, G (1996) *The McDonaldization of Society: An Investigation into the Changing Character of Contemporary Social Life* (rev. edn). Thousand Oaks, CA: Pine Forge Press.

Ritzer, G. (1998) *The McDonaldization Thesis: Explorations and Extensions*. London: Sage.

Sayer, D. (1991) *Capitalism and Modernity: An Excursus on Marx and Weber*. London: Routledge.

Smart, B. (1994) 'Digesting the modern diet: gastro-porn, fast food and panic eating', in K. Tester (ed.), *The Flâneur*. London: Routledge.

Smart, B. (1999) *Facing Modernity: Ambivalence, Reflexivity and Morality*. London: Sage.

Smith, A.D. (1996) 'Mange tout de suite, waiter', *The Guardian*, 9 March.

Vidal, J. (1997) *McLibel: Burger Culture on Trial*. London: Macmillan.

Warde, A. (1997) *Consumption, Food and Taste: Culinary Antinomies and Commodity Culture*. London: Sage.

Weber, M. (1970) *From Max Weber: Essays in Sociology* (eds H.H. Gerth and C. Wright Mills). London: Routledge & Kegan Paul.

Weber, M. (1976) *The Protestant Ethic and the Spirit of Capitalism*. London: Allen & Unwin.

Webster, P. (1996) 'Left Bank balks at le Big Mac', *The Guardian*, June 22.

2   Golden Arches and Iron Cages:

McDonaldization and the Poverty of Cultural Pessimism at the End of the Twentieth Century

Christiane Bender and Gianfranco Poggi

Let it never be said again that sociology is an abstraction-mad discipline, incapable of capturing cognitively the lived reality of everyday experience! For lately George Ritzer has proven the contrary, by dealing with an everyday phenomenon, in evidence in nearly all major and many minor locales in Western countries and elsewhere, and for that very reason, paradoxically, not often subject to sustained observation – the fast-food restaurant. Since reading Ritzer's book, we have found ourselves watching our respective neighbourhood's McDonald's with keen interest; and we have occasionally allowed ourselves to still our hunger with an excellent Big Mac while feeling that we were practising the honourable professional method of participant observation in the field.

Most other customers seem to ignore what we have read in Ritzer's book, or at any rate consider it of no significance.[1] Yet since the first McDonald's opened in the USA in the 1950s, they have continued to sprout all over the place, in America and in all other parts of the planet, in what amounts to a colossal success story, as shown by continuously increasing turnover figures. We read in Ritzer's book that by 1993 there were already 14,000 McDonald's around the world, a third of these outside the USA, and that the Corporation's aggressive policy of expansion continues. Having conquered North America and Western Europe, the chain is now arousing in Eastern Europe, Asia and the Arab countries a growing taste for fast-food, catered to in a uniform manner through franchise arrangements.[2] Perhaps on this account, McDonald's, with its diversified offerings, its striking logo, its distinctive ambiance, has become the symbol of a self-standing universe, a world of its own, connected (especially for young people) with the stimulus and the promise of a participation in 'the American way of life'. McDonald's have become, for the young, a place to meet and to gather, among other reasons, because even they can afford it.

The greatest part of its customers, young and old, have no objection to what Ritzer conveys about McDonald's – the fact that what it offers is a machine-produced commodity, of relatively poor quality, and that not just its production (as in the times of Taylor and Ford) but also its consumption, are organized according to the assembly line model. What this entails (for Ritzer and for others) is the standardization, the functionalization and the control of the whole process, which render it predictable and calculable. Such forms of organization of human activity well deserve, in certain circumstances, to be considered inhuman.

If we adopt these positions of Ritzer's (whether or not they are grounded on Weber's own: we offer some remarks on this question below) on which he bases his own description of McDonaldization, we may declare some surprise that the chain's customers (which occasionally, as we have already said, include also the authors of this chapter) allow themselves to enter cheerfully and willingly (or so it seems) into a kind of 'iron cage', in which they become alienated from themselves. According to Ritzer this phenomenon acquires dramatic significance because its impact goes way beyond the question of fast food and the related environment, and affects strategies and forms of conduct relating to markets and consumption *in general*, in towns as well as in the country, marginalizing the local suppliers of products and services and colonizing and suppressing the sociocultural settings where they used to operate. In fact, matters are even more dramatic and threatening: such tendencies control the evolution of modern societies in general, as well as of those located in the third world.

'McDonaldization', then, comes to signify for Ritzer a set of menacing and probably inescapable tendencies toward de-humanization. Such tendencies are seen as part of an overriding trend toward the rationalization, modernization and globalization of social life at large, and as such they enjoy not only the special attention of sociologists, but the approval and legitimation bestowed by broader publics. Ritzer's description of the McDonaldization of birth and death imparts particular credibility to his own view of McDonaldization as a master trend toward impersonally configurated social organization. Furthermore, he seeks to establish the ubiquitousness of the McDonaldization and standardization of processes of commercialization affecting such further realms as child care, higher education or sexual conducts. The recourse to technology, in particular, is condemned by him as an expression of alienation, of the loss of personal relations.

One can easily see this argument's precedents in Neil Postman's (1992) thesis of the imperialism of the technopoly, or in previous exercises in the critique of modern culture such as Adorno's pessimistic interpretation of late capitalism as a 'total complex of blindness' or, in its more moderate version, 'the colonization of the life-world by the system' theorized by Habermas from a position half-way between Luhmann and Adorno. Ritzer's favourite source, however, is Max Weber, who at the beginning of our century made remarks oriented to 'cultural pessimism' in the context of his own view, which saw a particular form of rationalization as the central dynamic of modern societies. The advance of such a process within the central realms of work and occupation was accompanied, according to

Weber, by a decrease in freedom and in the meaningfulness of existence. But the critique of rationalization expressed a standpoint not derivable from the spirit of modernity itself – and again here Ritzer follows him.

As the twentieth century comes to a close, isn't it possible to develop new insights, to identify aspects of rationalization which contrast with the world-wide emergence of 'iron cages'? Is the only alternative to this phenomenon the recourse to utterly informal interpersonal relations? We do not think so. However, it is possible to think one's way out of the 'iron cage' only if one does not follow Ritzer in his one-dimensional character-ization of current conditions, if one recognizes instead their ambivalences and subjects to critique the categories of the critique of rationalization themselves. We will have to see, at some point, to what extent Weber's own thinking can assist in this task.

The Industrialization of the 'Service Society' (*Dienstleistungsgesellschaft*) and its Social Background

Ritzer describes a phenomenon the emergence of which presupposes that Western societies have been changing from industrial societies to post-industrial societies and especially to *service societies*.[3] Against the hopes of several theoreticians of the post-industrial society (Jean Fourastié, Alan Gartner/Frank Riessman and Daniel Bell among others) who had envisaged a society in the process of becoming more civilized and more humane, the change in question did not remove the basic features of the organization of industrial processes previously identified by Marx and Weber among others. The connection both of these had posited between the enterprise's orientation to profit and the effort to rationalize those processes had maintained its validity also outside the sector expressly identified as industrial (although it had never quite managed to establish its rule over all aspects of social life at large). However, there developed new needs, new consumer expectations were aroused and new markets were created. In so far as these were not provided for by industrial production of material goods, one could speak of a 'service society' (*Dienstleistungs-gesellschaft*) – a concept to which one could easily relate other charac-terizations of modern society, such as 'the knowledgeable society' or 'the information society' (see Stehr and Ericson, 1992). In any case, in so far as the required services were provided for by private suppliers, in the long run their provision was subjected to the principles of capitalist valorization.

In thus extending its territory, capitalism – in contrast both to Marx's expectations of its breakdown and to Daniel Bell's vision of a post-industrial society – confirmed its persistent ability to develop new material and ideal resources, to elaborate them, and to capitalize upon them.[4] While, on the one hand, everything is done in order to subdivide, standardize and control the labour process, also within the sphere of services performed for indi-viduals, it remains clear that capitalism depends enormously on creative ideas and operations. At the end of the twentieth century, one can summarily say the following: within modern societies (for all the differences they present) individuals are more and more involved in performing services, and such performances are increasingly consumed by individuals and by collective entities; this entails a continuous growth in activities that relate to persons (as against things), whether this growth takes place in public offices, in firms, in the context of commerce or of welfare work. However, this development has not fulfilled the positive expectation which many theoreticians of the post-industrial *service societies* had connected with this phenomenon – the expectation that the development would be characterized, in the long run, by particularly humane principles in the organization of work and consumption. Baumol (1967) and Gershuny (1983), in particular, have confronted the 'optimists of the service society' with different objections, whose pessimism was inspired by analyses of the trends concerning costs and of the tendency toward the growing reliance upon technology in the provision of services to individuals. And Ritzer articulates this disappointing realization.

However, if we are to understand correctly the relationship between industrial society and service society to which Ritzer's McDonaldization thesis refers (by using as paradigmatic the specific example of the commercialized consumption of foods), it is necessary to analyse some socio-cultural and socio-economic aspects of the phenomenon. And the analysis must refer in the first place to the differentiations established by industrial society between work and family, between labour time and leisure time, between the public and the private sphere.

At the heart of these differentiations lies a specific ordering of gender relations, which, on the one hand, institutionalized in economic, social and cultural terms the nuclear family (as a unit characterized by married love, parenthood and partnership) and, on the other, established industrial organizations as the site of paid labour. A significant aspect of this process was that the domains of work and occupation, and the public sphere, were to be occupied by men, while the realms of family and leisure and the private sphere were assigned to women, while both genders were committed to the nuclear family as an institutionalized form of existence.

While in the tradition shared by Marx and Weber sociologists paid particular attention to the conditions typical of the fully employed, breadwinning male, thematizing his deplorable alienation within the 'iron cage' of industrial society, for a long time one assumed that within the family social relations did not involve domination and were authentic. However, research was to reveal the compulsion involved in the fact that women were locked within the family domain, made solely responsible for assisting its members, for the provision of food, for housework, for raising the children and (where necessary) for the care of close relatives needing assistance. Among the components of this compulsion were the positive moral evaluation of these circumstances by conservative and Christian parties, their legal sanction by official codes, and the stubborn and successful opposition of workers' organizations controlled by men to alternative models which might reduce the inferiority of women. Women were therefore long excluded from the more secure and rewarding positions within productive organizations.

Because women remained largely excluded from the 'iron cage' of occupational organizations, the family was turned into their own iron cage, from which they could not escape (see Clegg, 1994: 50). However, both men and women could and had to conduct their own existence within and between two iron cages. But if one accepts this perspective, and views the family also as a form of social organization resting on domination, which imposes forms of conduct closely determined, variously controlled and sanctioned, and thus made calculable, it behoves one not to criticize the impersonal consumption of food at a McDonald's purely as an aspect of a colonized life-world without reflecting on the contrasting model, implicit in this critique, of a wife and mother who in the past willingly and lovingly cared for the material well-being of her dear associates. Sure, she may have done so; but did she have any choice?

Ritzer identifies an uncheckable dynamic of rationalization, which locks the actors it involves into the 'iron cage', leaving them no way out. However – here as in Neil Postman's (1992) thesis the determinants which control that dynamic, and whose outcomes are to be viewed as irrational since they diminish the human element, are left unclear. On this point, Weber had more to say. In his analysis of the growing rationality of mastery as a central component of the spirit of capitalism (see Schluchter, 1980), he did not seek to identify one single cause of this phenomenon, but he did emphasize the role played by ideas, images of the world, and concepts of ethics and morality centrally associated with Protestantism. The latter constituted for Weber an essential socio-cultural resource which, via actors' understandings of meaning, became a driving force behind capitalist rationalization.[5]

If we ask a parallel question concerning the driving socio-cultural determinants of the socio-economic structural change constituted by the service society, we are not able to give a satisfactory answer in this chapter. Yet, with reference to Ritzer's theory of McDonaldization, it seems possible to make some suggestions relevant to its focal object, the production and consumption of food, and to related changes occurring in the position of the family and role of women.

In the twentieth century a significant debate over the social position of women has taken place, without producing a solution. However, ideas implying the inferiority of women in general terms have lost legitimacy, and the notion of the equal entitlement of women has gained growing acceptance. This notion has influenced the changes occurring in the institutions of modern societies – the family to begin with, but also educational establishments, the state institutions dealing with welfare, as well as intermediate institutions operating between the state and the market, such as churches and foundations. Structural changes in the family, such as the de-institutionalization of specific, tradition-bound interaction forms concerning love relationships, biological or social parenthood, and companionship, as well as the diffusion of alternative patterns such as 'singlehood', communal residences or 'phased marriage', are not entirely due to changes in the role of women, but the latter have certainly played a very significant part.

However, the structural changes in the family, and the growing integration of women in productive organizations, have taken place largely without changes of the same magnitude in the role of the full-time employed male breadwinner in respect of participation in housework. We would argue that this is a key reason why tasks previously performed by the family have had to be increasingly performed through societal arrangements, whether market- or state-centred – the very phenomena which Ritzer emphasizes and dramatizes. We are thinking of such tasks as those concerning the upbringing of children (child minding, child care, pre-primary education); the nutrition of family members, which conventionally took place chiefly through the family meal; the management of leisure time; the assistance to close relatives needing care; and the conduct of body-based interactions relating to sexuality, eroticism and emotionality.

A look both at this set of themes and at Ritzer's book suggests that over the course of our century these tasks have been increasingly performed by means of services rendered by organizations active in the public domain: the state, private suppliers, and intermediate organizations (O'Connor, 1996). One can easily assume that changes in the quality of such services have been associated with their being rendered by 'public' organizations, rather than by the family. Yet to assume that this has always implied the much deplored 'loss of human warmth' would be to ignore the costs previously imposed on women by structures of patriarchal domination. One may catch a glimpse of those costs, as it happens, by perusing Guenther Roth's current studies of the Weber family history (Roth, 1995).

It is important to note that tasks which were previously performed in the context of the family undergo a new definition when they are performed or put on offer by public or private suppliers. They lose thereby that personal, intimate character which – at any rate in ideal terms – they possessed before. Cost considerations compel the organization to rationalize their performance, and as a consequence they come to constitute an impersonal, standardized provision. At the same time, the need for legitimacy and acceptance attending on their supply compels the organization to adopt professional standards in their performance, and to take into account the normative standards of the persons to whom they are directed, in so far as these are in a position to choose to a greater extent than family members who are not in such a position.[6]

In any case we are not willing simply to assume that, for example, the offerings of a fast-food chain are necessarily of lower quality than those of a private household. Whether that assumption applies depends on politics, and in particular on the extent to which the public sphere is aware of the potentially damaging impact on health of certain substances and certain processes involved in the preparation of food. (We need only mention the recent concern over 'mad cow disease', [BSE].) Obviously the preparation of food for family members – an unduly neglected research theme – depends very closely on what the household's resources are, beginning with the people involved, the time and knowledge available to them, and so on. It is true, as Ritzer remarks, that the individual customer of a fast-food restaurant cannot control what he or she is being served; but the restaurant is subject to public regulations concerning food. And at the other end from the fast-food restaurant, in one decorated with three stars by a food guide, sometimes it is only the astronomical figure the customer finds on the bill (and normally pays by credit card) which forbids her to make critical remarks on the quality of the ingredients. To do so would increase her suspicion that her own cost-and-benefit calculation is based, if not on irrational, at any rate on absurd assumptions. In certain cases (such as those of lobsters) it would make hardly any sense to turn certain delicacies into mass commodities, since this would endanger the survival of the species in question.

Yet we take very seriously Ritzer's critical aspersions, and would add to them some considerations relating to socio-economic changes in the structure of the service society, and again in particular to the family and the role of women. Empirical data suggest both that the increasing significance of the service sector of the economy (relative to the directly productive sector) is a world-wide phenomenon, *and* that the various modern societies show remarkable differences in the size and the internal configuration of that sector, especially as concerns services rendered to individuals.[7] In Germany, for instance, there seems to be considerable resistance to having various forms of activity pushed out of the domestic sphere and handed over to private or public suppliers; in particular, fast-food chains do not play a role in nutrition comparable to the one they play in the USA, where the recourse to fast-food for lunch seems to be roughly equal across social strata. Why? Because Germans are more knowledgeable and sensitive about what they eat, or because in Germany family relations are more harmonious than elsewhere? Hardly!

Comparative analysis, we suggest, indicates a cause in the fact that the rate of female participation in the labour force remains lower in Germany and that in the judgement of Germans (or rather of the leadership of the parties, the unions, the churches) the chief responsibilities of women continue to be centred on the household (Borchorst, 1996; Schmidt, 1993).

A look at developments in Germany confirms Gershuny's (1983) pessimistic prognosis: in private households the provision of capital- and technology-intensive consumer goods has increased in response to the demand for personal services. In the post-war period the family kitchen has been slowly transformed into a factory with its own set of domestic machines. Refrigerators, freezers, washers and dryers, microwaves, and electric ovens, impose even on the domestic environment of average-income families the observance of Taylorist and Fordist principles of the division of labour, the economy of time and the use of mass-produced commodities. In Germany the persistence of conservative value conceptions functions to limit the technical rationalization of housework by virtue of the fact that women remain committed (and self-committed) to domestic duties. For this reason the technicization of private households in post-war Germany took care first of the needs of men, while the modernization of the kitchen – following the American example – took place later and hesitantly.

This technical rationalization of households placed women in a difficult position. The maintenance of the standards of family provision depends more and more, for the funding of its requirements on the income earned through employment. Premodern forms of provision (for instance, maintaining a vegetable garden) have become too expensive in terms of time and money. At the same time, however, the already mentioned value conceptions represented by such opinion-making agencies as parties, unions and churches contribute to keeping women out of secure positions of employment which would provide them with the income flow necessary to equip the household. Given this difficult position, many women end up accepting wholesale the traditional role of the housewife – a choice which sets limits to a thoroughgoing McDonaldization and technologization of housework and particularly of the everyday workings of the kitchen. In no way does this situation become, thereby, more humane and less alienated.

In the current German discussion on employment policies, the models of occupation, such as part-time work, proposed for women would leave with them (and not with men) the responsibility for coupling together occupational and family work, condemning them to the consequent 'double burden' and to diminished opportunities for occupational success. It is on this account that strategies of McDonaldization oriented to the service sectors have a lower probability than elsewhere of asserting themselves. A set of conservative cultural images stands in their way, at considerable cost for women, who generally find themselves alone in performing housework and still struggle to get themselves accepted as members of paid occupations. Yet the expansion of the fast-food chains, which alone are able to command the best sites in the middle of towns, is unmistakable. In particular, those commercial temples of the *Erlebnisgesellschaft* (a recent German expression sometimes translated as 'fun society') exercise a strong attraction on young people, who no longer prefer to locate their leisure-time activities in the household and to whom impoverished local authorities cannot offer publicly funded recreational centres.

After reunification, Germans find themselves on unsteady ground, confronting, on the one hand, the Scylla of the public provision of services (represented in the public mind chiefly by the unfortunate example of state socialism as understood in the former GDR) and, on the other, the Charybdis of McDonaldized, private, commercialized suppliers, whose activities Ritzer justly criticizes. Critics inspired by conservative values, and who – in the tradition of Émile Durkheim – view modernization and individualization as societal processes which loosen up social bonds and erode feelings of belonging, demand that the family should remain responsible in the future for the provision of its members' needs.

Weber has shown that distinctive cultural visions have constituted at one point the immaterial determinants of capitalist rationalization; to an extent, they continue to orient structural change in an economy currently characterized by the growing significance of the service sector, with its own trend toward rationalization. Those who disapprove of both the two great models for the provision of services – the state socialist model and the market-centred model – unless they are willing to subscribe to the conventional confinement of women to the domestic sphere, with sole responsibility for many of the services required by individuals, must be ready to jettison the standard arrangement of the relations between the occupational sphere and that of the family. Much has already been done in this direction by the growing access of women to the former sphere; but this needs to be complemented by a growing involvement of men in the latter.

To sum up: the phenomenon of McDonaldization described by Ritzer represents an important viewpoint concerning the rationalization of work within the frameworks of the service society and of the private household. However, the societal causes of the rationalization tendencies Ritzer criticizes for their impact on person-related activities lie deeper than he himself sees. Among those causes we would place cultural conceptions of the division of labour between the genders. From this viewpoint, 'resisting McDonaldization' would require the development of novel ideas concerning the organization of domestic work. A consideration of those determinants, and in turn of their socio-cultural components, might blunt the critical edge of Ritzer's account; for the structural conditions under which personal services were rendered in the pre-McDonaldized world were not as humane as all that, if one takes notice of the toll of inferiority and subjection they imposed on women.

A Few Conceptual and Empirical Questions

Having thus clarified some of the determinants of the McDonaldization phenomenon, and some of its value implications, we shall make a few broader comments on the theoretical structure of Ritzer's argument and on its empirical basis. In conceptual terms, the argument presents some weaknesses that may deserve to be brought to the reader's attention; particularly, it does not sufficiently differentiate various social and cultural domains, and some of its concepts are inadequately defined. These theoretical failures induce some empirical difficulties: essentially, Ritzer overstates the significance of McDonaldization for contemporary society. These lines of criticism are expounded in the comments that follow.

(1) Ritzer puts forward McDonaldization as *the* master process of contemporary society. This view we find objectionable, on various grounds. It may be true that McDonaldization has a logic of its own, a relatively autonomous dynamic; it may be true that, once it has been applied to a unit operating within a given sphere it confers upon that unit competitive advantages which compel others, willy-nilly, to imitate it lest they 'go to the wall', as Weber would phrase it. But this should not make us forget that McDonaldization is a *policy*; it is a process set in motion by binding decisions. And the locus of those decisions is left relatively unexplored by Ritzer, whose analysis focuses on those affected by those decisions, and neglects those making them.

A symptom of this neglect, or perhaps a source of it, is (as we see the matter) Ritzer's inadequate rendering of Weber's views on bureaucracy. Ritzer forgets that Weber's theory of bureaucracy is conceptually located chiefly within his analysis of politics and domination. Also, he does not reflect on Weber's express argument that bureaucracy itself is not a system of domination, but an aspect (however significant, quantitatively and qualitatively) of a system of domination that is not, itself, entirely bureaucratic. Simply put: 'bureaucracy' characterizes a specific way of confronting the administrative phase and dimension of (political) domination.

A symptom of Ritzer's lack of attention to this point is that in his analysis the theme of the organization of productive and distributive activities is very closely (in our judgement, *too* closely) associated with the theme of control. In other terms, bureaucracy becomes a particular way of configuring the division of labour, not a particular way of shaping and exercising power. In fact, the power phenomenon itself plays a very minor role, if any, in Ritzer's book, where it is largely subsumed under the notion of control. There is some legitimate overlap between these two concepts, but on the whole 'control' points in another direction from 'power'.

If we regret this conceptual imbalance, it is not simply in order to be bloody-minded and stress the hold of the powerful on the powerless. 'Power' has a correlate concept in 'resistance' (at least as a potentiality, in one of Weber's definitions of power). This suggests the possibility of a dialectical relationship, wherein those subject to power can raise the price of their subjection, or attempt to balance it by imposing some dependency on those who exercise power.

We may give as an example a point Ritzer himself makes when he cites someone's comment on Vatican television: 'The big advantage to the Vatican of having its own television operation is that they can put their own spin on anything they produce. If you give them the cameras and give them access, they are in control' (Ritzer, 1996a: 119). We would say: up to a point, Ritzer does not sufficiently reflect on some implications of 'the Vatican . . . having its own television operation'. One implication is that it will have to accommodate itself, to some extent or other, to aspects of televisual technology *and culture* which are totally foreign to the Catholic tradition, and are going to impinge on it and distort it. Put otherwise, the church cannot 'get into the media' without, to some extent, the media 'getting into the church'.

(2) There is a whole dimension of contemporary social reality not reducible to McDonaldization but complementary to it, and located, so to speak, upward of it. This applies first and foremost to the economic system itself, which is strongly structured by power relations, and where McDonaldization seems to apply primarily to the lower levels in the resulting hierarchy. In particular, at the end of the twentieth century the global economy seems to be dominated chiefly by three overlapping components: financial businesses; business dealing with the production and distribution of knowledge and information and with the transformation of knowledge into technology; and businesses operating within the 'cultural industry', and thus addressing individuals' need for the formation and maintenance of personal identity and/or for entertainment. If this is so, then one should not overstate the societal significance of McDonaldization, which for the time being is not strongly present in these three kinds of businesses, although increasingly the distribution of their products at the local and the mass level is being McDonaldized. These and similar considerations suggest that, at the end of the millennium, the realms most affected by McDonaldization are *not* 'where the action is'.

We may briefly articulate this critique with reference to something we all know quite a bit about: the educational realm, and higher education in particular. Ritzer speaks knowledgeably and enlighteningly of the advances McDonaldization has made in that realm. However, his remarks do not throw sufficient light on other aspects of higher education which are complementary to those he analyses.

In particular, the deterioration of pre-university education (itself the regrettable result of wrong policy choices) *requires* that academic institutions, in the first years of their students' education, take charge of educational needs that can be effectively addressed through McDonaldized practices, such as computerized grading and the employment of graduate students as first-line teachers.

Furthermore, some demanding and creative educational processes are shifted to the context of graduate education, which has not been McDonaldized to the same extent: typically, smaller classes and seminars prevail over large classes, less qualified teachers are not involved, essays rather than exams and quizzes are the favourite mode of examination. This applies in spades to particularly significant, elite educational settings such as the great schools of business administration or of engineering, which still place great demands on both students and teachers, and involve the latter in practices, such as consultancies and the design and conduct of research projects, which are hardly McDonaldized.

Finally, Ritzer ignores the fact that, within the world-wide academic system, some economically significant aspects of the educational and research enterprise are more and more the exclusive domain of a small minority of universities, which recruit faculty and students from the world at large and compete for research funds allocated by the great international corporations. It is the other universities, those which political and economic decision-makers consider less significant for the great global game of knowledge creation and technological innovation, that continue to cater to local constituencies *and* that increasingly McDonaldize their operations.

(3) As we suggested earlier, the dynamics of contemporary society continue to show the peculiar strength of capitalism – the coupling of an irresistible tendency to standardize and uniformize most kinds of productive and distributive processes, with a spectacular capacity to produce innovation. The latter capacity, we suggest, is still cultivated and put to work chiefly within contexts relatively resistant to the former tendency. There is little awareness of this persistent 'layering' of socio-economic structures within Ritzer's vision of an all-encompassing McDonaldization trend. Yet that layering finds expression also at the local level, with microcontexts.

Let us give an example. Every theatre, no matter how small, has its own apparatus for arranging and handling the lights as required by the script and/or its interpretation by the director. This apparatus is operated by one or more skilled technicians, working to the director's specifications. However, over the last couple of decades or so, those operations have been taken over, in many instances, by a computer tape, which needs only to be activated at the beginning of the play and thereafter activates and moves the lights in a (more-or-less) fixed sequence – which may be the same not just from one performance to another but even from one theatre to another. There is much to be regretted in this form of McDonaldization – particularly the de-skilling of the personnel involved and the decreasing opportunity for creatively rearranging the lighting from performance to performance or from theatre to theatre. But one might also note that the new process involves the emergence of new and much more sophisticated skills involved not just in lighting but in programming the lighting; a new level of theatrical intelligence, located upstream of the local theatrical experience, and thanks to which at least one aspect of stage action is much less exposed to the vagaries of chance and of inadequate training.

(4) One may also suggest that Ritzer not only overestimates the significance of realms where McDonaldization is rampant, but neglects some significant aspects of those realms which do not fit his picture of them. Consider the question of food itself. One of us, who has visited the United States many times over several decades, has been struck from the 1980s on by the growing attention of Americans to that question, by their increasing concern with (to use a hackneyed expression) *the quality of the eating* (and drinking) *experience*, by the sheer amount of energy, sophistication, and imagination many Americans have learned to invest in that experience. Where, what, how one eats (and drinks) seems to have become, at any rate for Americans of a certain age and income level, a matter relevant to their self-definition, or at the very least to the image of themselves they try to construct and to project. But if this is so, then the tremendous success of

fast-foods is definitely *not* the whole story of food in America in the second half of the century: that story presents other aspects the disregard of which unbalances Ritzer's account. We are thinking of the increase in the variety of ingredients and of modes of preparing food associated with the middle classes' growing interest in eating.

So far we have chiefly criticized Ritzer for overstating the empirical significance of those phenomena on which his key concept throws light, by failing to explore complementary and counter-balancing phenomena. Turning now more expressly to conceptual matters, let us refer again to Ritzer's use of Weber's views. As we see the matter, Ritzer extends to the development of the service sector in contemporary economies some aspects of the theory of economic rationalization developed by Weber with reference to industrial capitalism. This worthwhile – and largely successful – attempt lends itself to a few critical comments.

To begin with, Weber himself emphasizes not only the irrational *consequences* of the rationalization process (as one might infer from Ritzer's use of Weberian arguments) but also its irrational *premises*. According to him, the Western choice for rationality is not itself rational – nor is the choice for a particular *kind* of rationality, that aiming at *mastery* over the world instead of *harmony* with or *adaptation* to it. Otherwise put: irrationality for Weber lies both *upstream* and *downstream* of the rationalization process.

Apart from this, Ritzer's application of Weber's theory of bureaucracy to McDonaldization appears to overstretch that theory. Basically, it's been a long time (relatively speaking) since *significant* economic units have typically been bureaucratically organized in Weberian terms. As Burns and Stalker (1994) argued long ago, those units have had to acknowledge the limitations the bureaucratic model meets in the fact of highly turbulent technological and competitive environments; they have had expressly to *de*-bureaucratize themselves. Overstating the point a bit, one might say that firms that are bureaucratic do not matter, while firms that matter are not bureaucratic. Perhaps already the strategy of divisionalization applied by Alfred Sloan to General Motors expressed this contrast; Ritzer mentions it, but does not acknowledge this implication.

One final comment on 'Ritzer on Weber on bureaucracy'. Weber himself had, we think, a more sophisticated sense of the ambivalence of the bureaucratic phenomenon than we recognize in Ritzer, for whom basically 'bureaucracy' is only a term of abuse. Perhaps because, as we have already suggested, he conceptualized that phenomenon chiefly within his political sociology, Weber was aware of the human advance the bureaucratic mode of administration represented not only in terms of the efficiency and calculability of public action, but also in its bearing upon such liberal values as the security of individual rights, the rule of law, and citizenship. Although of course it could be instituted and employed in a very different spirit, and in particular in the direction of totalitarianism, bureaucracy was for Weber a necessary though not a sufficient component of constitutional politics. Little if anything in Ritzer's multiple statements on bureaucracy, many of which refer explicitly or implicitly to Weber, conveys his own recognition of this aspect of the phenomenon.

As we have already noted, to validate his concept of McDonaldization, Ritzer directs our attention to the processes taking place in the service sector at the bottom level within the firms he discusses – at the point of delivery, as it were. This is of course a perfectly valid concern. But it is not complemented by a concern (which we consider equally legitimate) with the broader institutional environment wherein those processes take place. If Ritzer had asked himself some questions about the nature of the firms in question – 'What is the McDonald's Corporation like *as a whole?*' for example – he might have confronted phenomena of some theoretical relevance which cannot be easily subsumed under the 'bureaucracy' concept.

Nothing indicates Ritzer's lack of concern with this level of discourse as clearly as does the astonishingly summary manner in which he deals with the *franchise* phenomenon, which is mentioned but not discussed. (The expression 'franchise', incidentally, does not appear in the index.) How bureaucratic can a firm be where the key couplings between the units-on-the-ground and the corporate level are typically represented by franchise relationships? For that matter, in what sense *is* McDonald's one firm?

We would like to emphasize this question for three reasons. First, it is probably of considerable empirical significance: as complex a juridical phenomenon as a franchise arrangement is likely to vary in its nature from one national setting to another, simply because the respective legal systems are likely to vary, to a greater or lesser extent; however, Ritzer has simply nothing to tell us on this realm of variation.

Second, we feel that Ritzer displays a similar – and equally disconcerting – lack of interest in the makings and consequences of technical juridical arrangements – and their variations – in the companion book to *McDonaldization*, that is, *Expressing America* (Ritzer, 1995).

Finally, in our view, what amounts to Ritzer's wilful disregard for questions of law, and of sociology of law, instances a serious theoretical weakness in one of his broader arguments – the argument to the effect that McDonaldization entails the progressive replacement/displacement of (to use his own terms, for the time being) human by non-human technology. Franchising, and more generally legal arrangements, are institutional matters through and through; there simply is *nothing* intrinsically non-human about them – yet they are virtual to the whole realm Ritzer explores, and on that very account he can sustain that argument only by (basically) ignoring them, or by giving an unacceptable account of their nature.

A very good (although inadvertent – or, indeed, good *because* inadvertent) example of such an account is the following sentence relating to Taylor's scientific management: 'managers were to take a body of *human skills*, abilities and knowledge, and transform them into a set of *non-human rules*, regulations, and formulas' (Ritzer, 1996a: 25, original emphasis). One does not need to be a Wittgensteinian or a Winchian to wonder: what can be more human than rules?

Ritzer may not have sufficiently reflected on the results of recent – and less recent – work on organizations: for instance, on the distinction between material and social technology, a distinction whose relevance is suggested by historical reflection on the role played, respectively, in the military field by the invention of the musket and by the invention of the drill. Ritzer replaces such a distinction, as we have noted, with one between human and non-human technology. This distinction, apart from generating the problem we have just noted concerning legal arrangements, is worded in such a way as to suggest a strong normative bias. We have no objection to such a bias, as long as it is self-consciously adopted and declared, and as long as it has no misleading consequences.

We detect such a consequence, in particular, in the following sentence: 'most of the messages in the "virtual community" of cyberspace are impersonal; communication via the "net" is thus dehumanizing' (Ritzer, 1996a: 147). Our reaction on reading this was – hold it! The equation of 'impersonal' with 'dehumanizing' is categorically unacceptable. The ability to de-personalize relationships underlies such essential and distinctive human achievements as – among other things – the role phenomenon. That facile equation betrays a normative bias of Ritzer's which, respectable as it may be in moral terms, is analytically misleading.

One final suggestion. Ritzer occasionally acknowledges but does not sufficiently analyse the vital causal role played in the story he recounts by the massification of the relationships he discusses – by the sheer fact that these involve, and affect, increasingly large, and in the end huge, numbers of people. This is most obvious, we think, in the field of higher education. We find it difficult to imagine how else it could have been opened up to millions without streamlining and standardizing it to a large extent – and thus McDonaldizing it.

In sum, some phases of Ritzer's argument indicate a somewhat inadequate reflection on its conceptual and theoretical foundations, as well as a neglect of aspects of contemporary society which complement and to some extent balance out those thematized as McDonaldization.

The Critique of Alienation and its Political Aspects

We shall bring our contribution to a close with some general remarks concerning the relationship between critique and theory. The critique of dehumanization is connected with the critique of the division of labour and of alienation – a recurrent motif of sociological theory, common to Marx, Weber and Durkheim at one end, and Adorno, Habermas and Ritzer at the other.[8]

In Weber, we find aspects of a critique of dehumanization, especially in his pessimistic statements about the cultural condition of modern man.

Particularly in connection with the 'Protestant Ethic' thesis, Weber lamented the structural constraints which modern organizations impose upon professional work, leading the atomized protagonist of the latter to a painful loss of meaning and of connection with the world. But also in Weber this situation lends itself to a political solution: a constitutional nation state exercises its domination upon societal forces with legal means and imposes on society a specific ordering through bureaucratization. In the context of the nation-state Weber views bureaucracy as the ideal-type of control and order, to which such different social systems as science, the economy, the churches or private households must orient themselves. Bureaucracy ensures order and within such order guarantees functionality and effectiveness. Thus the system of political domination constitutes also a way to express and to realize the will of individuals who articulate their interests within various levels of politics. The nation-state as Weber knew it had at its disposal mechanisms (however constituted) for imposing constraints on the configuration of working relationships.

At the close of the twentieth century, modern and modernizing societies see their future shaped by the breakdown of political blocs, and by the opening of their local systems to communication, to exchange, and to the formation of networks on a global scale. At this point a critique of dehumanization and the division of labour which takes as its premise the vision of expressly unitary ways of working and living becomes anachronistic. It is, in any case, utopic, for not even in the past has there ever existed an autarkic society, without division of labour, without power and domination. Yet the concept is not surrendered because of the critical implications it still possesses, and indeed it seems to gain relevance in the face of globalization.

To conclude this chapter, we would like to stress the political dimension of the phenomena in question. In his *Work of Nations*, Robert B. Reich (1991) speaks of the differentiation between the national system of political domination and socio-economic change, which takes place at both the national and the global levels. He stresses the uncoupling which has taken place between financial markets, on the one hand, and national economies, on the other. As a result, the state is no longer able to control and make use of the valorization process, and on this account is less and less in a position to keep the welfare state in existence. If one compares it with Reich's depiction of a possible future for American society, Ritzer's McDonaldization thesis gains an extraordinary significance.

According to Reich, public investments fall farther and farther behind, and something like a secession takes place under the impact of such tendencies as the following. The occupational sphere encompasses three main groups of occupations: routine production services, client-focused services and services oriented to 'symbolic analysis'. The first two groups embrace the great majority of the employed, who, however, are trained by an educational system which imparts to them only lowly qualifications. In the future those who currently ride the trend toward the increasing significance of information and knowledge within national systems will also find themselves in one of these two groups; and here Reich mentions expressly lawyers, accountants and professors, in so far as they operate in a more and more routine fashion.

Over against these, a decreasing proportion of people, professionally involved in symbolic analysis – above all lawyers, top managers, investment bankers, brokers, traders – present a staggering productivity, and find at their disposal enormous resources of education and capital. Between the top-level symbolic analysts, who always seek new ways of defining and solving problems, and who command quality working positions of the highest significance, and the rest of the employed, who occupy by far the greatest number of work places, there develop colossal differences in economic security, cultural capital and capacity to exercise influence. Such differences are liable to remain relatively stable over the life course of individuals: the respective family conditions, educational experiences, memberships, experiences of sociability, material belongings, residential patterns, life standards, medical provisions, and arrangements for old age, vary systematically in predictable fashion. Taking schooling as an example: those meant to become symbolic analysts are trained to abstraction, to systems thinking, to experiment, and to work in teams. For the overwhelming majority of other pupils the school is like a factory school, which trains them in what Ritzer would call McDonaldized fashion, at low cost.

A dismaying implication of this picture is the drastic reduction of the role of politics and the state. Symbolic analysts take into account the state exclusively as a cost factor, because the components of this group do not depend on the services it renders. But the impoverished Leviathan no longer has much to give the rest of the population. The welfare state is no longer affordable.

Within this scenario, the countries of South-East Asia are slowly entering the twentieth-century stage, the century during which were built up the welfare states of the Western hemisphere, whereas now these very states threaten to fall back to the level of the nineteenth century. How can one resist this global process, which one can designate unwittingly as McDonaldization? Resistance can only come from nation-states which retain and/or regain the capacity to exercise political domination by means of international agreements and arrangements. The reformulation of national identities, according to Reich, must find expression in a renewed sense of political responsibility.

So our message is: *resisting McDonaldization requires in the first place that we do not lose and indeed that we reinforce the political power of the democratic state.* It is not inevitable that education, welfare, and culture, should follow the logic of economic processes associated with a completely McDonaldized world, one that would concern itself exclusively with minimizing related costs. The policy inspired by neo-classical economics seeks to reduce the state, even if this entails a neglect of the conditions under which the great majority of people live and work, and the loss of their ability to give political expression to their interests. Those who find this unacceptable should confront the big challenge posed by globalization: how to preserve and to enhance the people's democratic right to organize themselves, to formulate demands, to influence and shape public policy.

Notes

1 The references that follow are to Ritzer (1996a).

2 We may characterize franchising as follows. The term designates an agreement which a producer of (in this case food) articles makes with self-standing traders. These commit themselves to adopt a pre-conceived arrangement concerning the product and the related organization, and are assisted in doing this by the producer. For the latter, the investment costs are kept to a minimum, while there is an adaptation to the local markets. The other party, in turn, can rely on the fact that the products in question are known and accepted, and gains from becoming inserted into a global strategy.

3 We will not, at this point deal with the problems – not even the basic ones – concerning the concept itself of the post-industrial or service society. We refer the reader to the following writings: Bell (1973), Fourastié (1949), Gartner and Riessman (1974).

4 Below, we shall pay some attention to these innovation processes, contrasting them with the rationalization processes on which Ritzer fastens his attention.

5 Such different authors as Fourastié, Bell and Gartner/Riessman agree in perspectiving civilizing processes associated with post-industrial society, and affecting needs, value perspectives, forms of the organization of work and of consumption.

6 For the question of professionalization, see Ritzer and Walczak (1988) and Ritzer (1996b).

7 Differences appear, for instance, in respect of the proportion of the gainfully active population in a given country represented by those employed in the service sector: the most frequently discussed cases are those of the USA, Sweden and Germany. For example, services to consumers account for 42.4 per cent of the active population in Sweden, 38.8 per cent in the USA, and as little as 29.1 per cent in Germany. See the data from the OECD Labour Force Statistics given in Häussermann and Siebel (1995: 51ff).

8 Marx derived it from a particular rendering of Hegelian philosophy, which he transposed to the relationship between the human person and work in the context of the division of labour and of capitalistic wage labour. Hegel had thought that work and objectification, as inescapable liabilities of the formation of human self-consciousness, could only be superseded within the constitutional state, whose legal foundation lay in the freedom of the individual, but not within the relationships of the civil society (*bürgerliche Gesellschaft*), necessarily mediated through work. As against this, Marx characterized as alienation the expropriation of producers from the product of their work, wage labour, and the commodification of that work. Here the concepts of division of labour and of alienation apply both to the activity of work and to social relations. On the other hand, for Marx there is also a political dimension, which does not constitute ideological alienation (superstructure), but rather the future dictatorship of the proletariat as the beginning of the supersession of alienated work.

References

Baumol, W.S. (1967) 'Macroeconomics of unbalanced growth: the anatomy of urban crisis', *American Economic Review*, 57: 416–26.

Bell, D. (1973) *The Coming of Post-Industrial Society: A Venture in Social Forecasting*. New York: Basic Books.

Borchorst, A. (1996) 'Welfare state regimes, women's interests and the EC', in D. Sainsbury (ed.), *Gendering Welfare States*. London: Sage.

Burns, T. and Stalker, G.T. (1994) *The Management of Innovation* (3rd edn). Oxford: Oxford University Press.

Clegg, S. (1994) 'Max Weber and the contemporary sociology of organization', in L.S. Ray and M. Red (eds), *Organizing Modernity: New Weberian Perspectives on Work, Organization and Society*. New York: Routledge.

Esping-Anderson, G. (1990) *The Three Worlds of Welfare Capitalism*. Princeton, NJ: Princeton University Press.

Fourastié, A. (1949) *Le grand espoir du Xxe siècle*. Paris: Presses Universitaires de France.

Gartner, A. and Riessman, F. (1974) *The Service Society and the Consumer Vanguard*. New York: Harper & Row.

Gershuny, J.J. (1983) *Social Innovation and the Division of Labour*. Oxford: Oxford University Press.

Häussermann, H. and Siebel, W. (1995) *Dienstleistungsgesellschaften*. Frankfurt: Suhrkamp.

O'Connor, J. (1996) 'Trend report: from women in the welfare state to gendering welfare state regimes', *Current Sociology*, 44 (2).

Postman, N. (1992) *Technopoly: The Surrender of Culture to Technology*. New York: Alfred A. Knopf.

Reich, R.B. (1991) *The Work of Nations*. New York: Alfred A. Knopf.

Ritzer, G. (1995) *Expressing America: A Critique of the Global Credit Card Society*. Thousand Oaks, CA: Pine Forge Press.

Ritzer, G. (1996a) *The McDonaldization of Society: An Investigation into the Changing Character of Contemporary Social Life* (rev. edn). Thousand Oaks, CA: Pine Forge Press.

Ritzer, G. (1996b) 'Münch(ing) on McDonald(ization) of social theory', *Swiss Journal of Sociology*, 22 (2): 247–50.

Ritzer, G. and Walczak, D. (1988) 'Rationalization and the deprofessionalization of physicians', *Social Forces*, 67: 1–22.

Roth, G. (1995) 'Heidelberg–London–Manchester: Zu Max Webers deutsch–englischer Familiengeschichte', in H. Treiber and K. Sauerland (eds), *Heidelberg im Schnittpunkt intellektueller Kreise*. Opladen: Westdeutscher Verlag.

Schluchter, W. (1980) *Rationalismus der Weltbeherrschung: Studien zu Max Weber*. Frankfurt: Suhrkamp.

Schmidt, M. (1993) *Erwerbsbeteilung von Frauen und Männern im Industrieländervergleich*. Opladen: Leske & Budrich.

Stehr, N. and Ericson, R.V. (1992) *Culture and Power of Knowledge: Inquiries into Contemporary Societies*. Berlin and New York: de Gruyter.

3 Have You Had Your Theory Today?

John O'Neill

As he says: Ritzer has not written a book about McDonald's but about 'ization'. Leaving aside what is disingenuous in this denial, we may question the legitimacy of explaining the American social order as a gastric system, however familiar its locations. Everything suggests the reverse order of explanation. But this means we need an account of American society sufficient to explain its eating practices as activities congruent with its industrial and ideological arts. For this purpose, I would recommend a Parsons blender rather than Ritzer's single-cylinder Weberizer. Nothing is served by repairing Ritzer's theoretical apparatus. It is irredeemably part of the phenomenon it proliferates but does not explicate. The result is a text that, not having discovered McDonald's, has nothing to say about it beyond invoking its metastasis as a sufficient explanation for larger trends in the American social order. This is a strategy that immediately loses the hierarchical order of institutions, their stratification and domain-specific features. The same strategy also loses what is specific to sociological theory and its object choices. Was Marx able to study the factory but not the restaurant? Was Durkheim able to study religion as an elementary form of social life but not commensality? Did Weber's study of the spirit of capitalism lack 'evidence' until Ritzer could apply it to McDonaldization? Are we to understand that the critical task of sociology is to place health warnings on McDonald's doors but not to place union pickets to block them? Ritzer is certainly right that McDonald's is no postmodern funhouse anymore than it rides high as a post-Fordist organization. Far less is McDonald's an outpost of libidinal economy (O'Neill, 1993). Ritzer's view of things seems to be that McDonald's is an organizational dinosaur, largely unimprovable but viable until it is swept away in some greater cataclysm than postmodernism:

> No social institution lasts forever, and McDonald's is not immune from that dictum. While McDonaldization and McDonald's remain powerful forces in a postmodern world (if that is what we want to call today's society), there will come a time when they, too, will pass from the scene. McDonald's will remain powerful until the nature of society has changed so dramatically that McDonald's is no longer able to adapt to it. Even after it is gone, McDonald's will be remembered for the dramatic impact it had, both positive and negative, on the United States and much of the rest of the world. (Ritzer, 1993: 159)

Sic transit gloria McMundi. Meantime, attitude is what counts. How do you like your cage: velvetized, rubberized or ironized? Once again, character shapes theory. The comfortable (Type I) Weberian loves the impersonality of the cage and can't wait for it to become completely robotized. The busy (Type II) Weberian is resigned to McCage because after all one isn't in it all that long and it does have its conveniences. The ambivalent (Type III) Weberian, of whom Ritzer appears to be the prototype, combines McCriticism and icy resignation to the irreversibility of McDonaldization. How do Type III Weberians survive? Why don't they go mad or go to prison? They perform skunk works, that is, in the name of the personal and organizational need for creativity and innovation they find time/space niches that, although work-related (and profitable), make cage-life bearable, for example writing McTexts.

Where's the Beef?

Ritzer's burger is innocent of the history of the food industry and the political economy of the beef complex (Ross, 1980) that has so forcefully set the table at home and abroad:

> the etic preference for beef over pork in the United States is of rather recent origin. The designation of beef as a symbol of wealth, generosity, and virility did not generate the ecological, technological, demographic and political ascendancy of the beef industry; it was the ascendancy of the industry as a result of those processes that has bestowed upon beef its special symbolic pre-eminence. It is not the magic of arbitrary symbols that restricts the composition of hamburgers to beef and only beef (and beef fat), but the beef industry's political clout in Congress and the Department of Agriculture. (Harris and Ross, 1987: 61)

The US cattle complex derives from an extraordinary British colonization of the American West (cows and cowboys) and the Midwestern farmlands (corn and farmboys) joined by railroads, financial capital and government legislation:

> Today, a century after the British successfully combined the free grass of the plains with the surplus corn of the midwestern grain belt, 106 million acres of U.S. agricultural land is used to grow 220 million metric tons of grain for cattle and other livestock. In the United States, livestock, again mostly cattle, consume almost twice as much grain as is eaten by the entire population. Globally about 600 million tons of grain are fed to livestock, much of it to cattle.
> If a worldwide agricultural production were shifted from livestock feed to grains for direct human consumption, more than a billion people on the planet could be fed. (Rifkin, 1992: 98–9)

Beef is no more edible than pork, yet it has been promoted to burgerdom by large corporations whose geopolitical clout has permitted them to colonize Central America for 'burger pasture'. Latin American exports of beef (best beef reclassified as US cow-meat) to the US the fast-food industry acts to considerably dampen the impact of the US rate of inflation upon poorest families and individuals – a policy similar to that of Britain's importation of food from its colonies in the nineteenth century. The increased nutritional deprivation of the 'third world' is matched by the malnutrition in the 'first world', itself caused by over-feeding on 'industrial-grade beef'. The extent of pasture lands required for the cattle complex expands deforestation, flooding, soil erosion, peasant dislocation and under-employment, while landholdings become larger and offer even greater collateral in the credit markets than fuel the burger economy and its new elites.

A beefburger must contain beef fat because it is a US Department of Agriculture requirement that in turn underwrites the US cattle complex. The American burger is a compound of cheap grass-fed beef from abroad and US grain-fed beef. This grind is the essentially pliable material that moves through the (Taylorized) cattle yards to the fridges, frying pans, barbecues and fast-food outlets of burgerdom. It is upon this patty that family dining can be moved outside the home – or inside from outside: it is upon this patty that the transubstantiation of food to feed, of family to fun and of service to self-service can be enacted a billion times over. The twist of history is such that, having itself been colonized by the British trade for fatty beef, America now stands as the world's model for successful eating (however inefficient, however questionable the quality of its iconic food):

> The question of privilege and power, of expropriation and exploitation in the modern world, has worked itself down into the very calorie count of every human being on the planet. The disparities are troubling. Three-fourths or more of the diet of the average Asian is composed of grain. Asian adults consume between 300 and 400 pounds of grain a year. A middle-class American, by contrast, consumes over a ton of grain 2,000 pounds each year, 80 percent of it by way of eating cattle (and other livestock) that are grain fed. On a daily basis, the average Asian consumes about 56 grams of protein, only 8 grams of which is animal protein. The average American, in comparison, consumes 96 grams of protein a day, 66 grams of it derived from animals. (Rifkin, 1992: 163)

The great paradox of the world's under-development is that those who barely eat feed those who overeat. Worse still, they are encouraged to measure their own advancement in terms of moving up the very meat-processed protein chain that distorts the world's food agenda. Nowhere is this insanity more clearly expressed than in the world burgermetric produced by a Swiss bank to express standards of living in terms of the relative effort expended in acquiring a burger (Table 3.1).

Where's the Restaurant?

Hamburgers are beefburgers. They are not pork burgers – though they might have been. Nor are they veggie burgers, fish burgers or chicken

TABLE 3.1   *Work attack for a Big Mac*

City	1 kilogram of bread in minutes	1 Big Mac and fries in minutes
Amsterdam	9	31
Athens	9	33
Bogota	23	98
Bombay	27	131
Brussels	12	31
Buenos Aires	26	105
Cairo	–	–
Caracas	75	103
Chicago	18	18
Copenhagen	4	39
Dublin	12	29
Düsseldorf	12	22
Frankfurt	13	22
Geneva	10	21
Helsinki	27	40
Hong Kong	14	24
Houston	10	27
Jakarta	–	–
Johannesburg	7	35
Kuala Lumpur	40	57
Lagos	216	130
Lisbon	23	–
London	11	36
Los Angeles	15	20
Luxembourg	9	20
Madrid	10	54
Manila	86	165
Mexico City	37	235
Milan	17	33
Montreal	10	21
Nairobi	31	82
New York	22	26
Nicosia	8	40
Oslo	12	43
Panama	50	66
Paris	18	39
Rio de Janeiro	30	79
São Paulo	32	106
Seoul	18	30
Singapore	39	70
Stockholm	40	61
Sydney	12	18
Taipei	16	34
Tel Aviv	9	33
Tokyo	14	21
Toronto	10	20
Vienna	12	30
Zurich	9	20

Source: Union Bank of Switzerland (price of product is divided by the weighted net hourly earnings in 12 occupations); cited by Bennell, 4 December (1991)

burgers – though they may be. Beefburgers have been challenged regarding their size and even their beef content. What cannot be contested is the fat in beefburgers. This fat makes burgers stick together so that they can be pattied and processed to meet the precise McDonald mould:

> This basic machine-cut hamburger patty weighed 1.6 ounces, measured 3.875 inches in diameter, and contained no lungs, heart, cereal, or soybeans. In each pound of meat there were ten hamburgers, that were to contain no more than 19 percent fat. Everything was calculated down to the exact size of the bun (3.5 inches wide) and the amount of onions that went on it (one-fourth of an ounce). In addition, the bun had to have a higher-than-normal sugar content for faster browning. (Rifkin, 1992: 269)

This is the limit of the low-fat, lean burger whose challenge to the cholesterol lifestyle of the hurried American has largely failed. Anything added to the hamburger in the name of health, alternative lifestyles or multiculturalism threatens the essential nature of the beefburger. The rock on which 'McDonald's Family Restaurant' is founded is the speed and profitability of the burger's marriage to a few stringy potatoes whose essential charm is their skinnyness turned to cornucopia by restrictive packaging.

McDonald's binds it aesthetics to the productive order it imposes upon its workers and its customers. McAesthetic guarantees the iterability of its settings:

(a)   spatio-temporal *repetition* of local settings as global places;
(b)   the *corporeal suture* of sensory variation to McTaste;
(c)   the *mortification* and *infantilization* of the family meal: burger–fries–coke;
(d)   the *computerized suture* of worker and customer variation to McFordism;
(e)   the *foreclosure* of the political economy of burgerdom.

The principal relay in McFormat is the computerized cash register which links sales, inventory, product-mix, customer counts and worker productivity. This permits the projection of both hourly sales and part-time staffing needs. Computerization is what rescues the fast-food operation from restaurantization. Fast-food is factory-food . . . low-cost ingredients, minimum wages, fast turnover (service) and high profits through peak periods. Taylorized time and motion controls permeate material and labour inputs to the most exacting degree (Yanarella and Reid, 1996). Standardized food ingredients plus Taylorized labour and computerized management controls provide an extremely high profit ration for McCorporation. Despite the huge turnover in the McLabour force, the minimum wage, low skill and non-union status, the Corporation nevertheless insists upon portraying its labour relations in terms of a happy family of teens, moms and seniors looking for flexible hours and variety of tasks from baking biscuits to community work. Working at McDonald's allows one to be at home whenever one likes! In fact, because one can quit any time one likes, that is, any time one does not like the work system, managerial authority remains both strict and easy. This contradictory formula, however, is perfectly suited to McDonald's position as the largest corporate employer of youth. It offers work discipline, corporate identity and non-credential careers in its own management – an offer that is appealing to inner city minorities, however much it exceeds them.

While it is adamant about its status as a 'Family Restaurant' (Helmer, 1992), it is essential to McDonald's that it not surrender to the authority of the family body or to the familized eating pace of a restaurant. Thus there is little evidence that anyone prepares McFood. No one supervises its consumption. The absence of the mother body is assured in the first place, as is the absence of the father body in the second; and this double absence is triangulated by the child's decision to take the family to McDonald's at the outset because it is a 'restaurant' where a child can be sure to get a burger! Since McFeed is neither prepared nor served, the parental bodies are themselves reduced to defamilized and desexualized bodies with nothing to say that hasn't been said in its advertisements. Thus the defamilized child is the perfect inhabitant of McDonald's. Admission nevertheless requires that the child be seen but not heard. Children's birthday parties are welcome of course, since they serve to recruit clients. Thereafter, children are frozen. They must not become teenagers since this would reintroduce the body with unpredictable controls, the juvenile body that is noisy, dirty, sexual and laughing.

Teenagers work at McDonald's. But they do not linger or hang out there. Teenage culture belongs in the advertisements but not in the 'restaurants'. The absence of teenage or rock-age music in McDonald's is more noticeable than the absence of dirt, of conversation, and of the family. McDonald's is the bastion of child labour – even when the labour is performed by recycled elders. Kids work at McDonald's. They do not play there – although ideally all kids should play at going to McDonald's. Between the fantasy and the reality lies the world of labour at minimum wages. This is the young body that McDonald's cannot hide however much it may dress it up. It is, therefore, especially horrendous should any of its sites be contaminated by murder, homeless beggars, prostitutes and drug dealers who can work out of the unsurveyed area between the street and the service counter of the 'restaurant'. Here the urbanization of McDonald's brings it into uncanny contact with the economy from which it offers an escape that is increasingly precarious.

McCommunion

To receive McPatty, the body must be of a certain kind. It cannot be a body ready to risk mere indigestion or obesity. It must be an *atresic body*, one that is indifferent to its feed. McBody is a body of perfectly open passages like the junkie's body, a body-without-organs, served by over 90 billion burgers!

As I have argued elsewhere (O'Neill, 1985), *consumption is work*, it takes time and it competes with itself since choosing, hauling, maintaining and repairing the things we buy is so time-consuming that we are forced to save time on eating, drinking, sex, dressing, sleeping, exercising and relaxing. The result is that Americans have taught us to eat standing, walking, running and driving – and, above all, never to finish a meal in favour of the endless snack (McSnack is literally the 'square' meal it momentarily replaces). Thus the high-altar of the fast-food complex is the trash-can, the half-concealed garbage pail that offers us 'Thank you' or 'Service' as we struggle to fill it without spilling garbage over ourselves, or that functions as the table around which we eat, and in the belly of which previous deposits of garbage are held.

The counterpart of McDonald's cheap labour is the hurried consumer, whose total time in the restaurant can exceed five to 10 minutes only if s/he is prepared to eat burgers/fries that have turned cold and gone to mush. Thus the artful McDonald's consumer is pitted from the moment s/he leaves the counter against food that (never having been hot) is already beginning to turn cold and to decompose (nor can it be reheated). A decision must be made to swallow fast – facilitated by meat and potatoes that in any case need no biting or chewing, and by condiments that soften them up further – or else to garbage even before swallowing-and-garbaging! Because this alimentary behaviour is artful, it must be learned from infancy if it is to be achieved readily – even though it tends to repeat on the elder stomach, yielding McBelch, the last gasp of McBody in its surrender to McMouth. McFood is fast because only you can slow it down. In other words, since you serve yourself – only you are responsible for how and what you eat. This is because, once you have paid for McMeal, you are on your own. You serve the food; you seat yourself; you pace your meal; you clean up the remains. Fast-food not only recruits cheap labour on the production side, it relies on free labour donated as 'self-service' to complete its delivery and disposal:

McCommunion

1 Get in line
2 Look up to the menu
3 Order food & drink & extra condiments
4 Pay when order is registered
5 Serve yourself napkins, straws and implements (no cutlery)
6 Seat yourself
7 Eat and Drink
8 Clean away after yourself – Thank you
9 Exit
10 Steps (5–8) can be saved in Drive-Away and (5–6) in Drive-In, where the automobile *is* the restaurant.

Fast-food imposes upon its casual communicants a strict order of service. Intolerant of fuzziness, the fast-food line requires that its customers flow towards their goal with the same precision that its supply lines move their contents towards the counter. To achieve this, the customer must be oriented from the point of entry to the 'menu' above the pay counter. Choices are made on foot, while approaching a server who will register an order that must be paid for *before* it is eaten. (These two features already violate the restaurant code.) The next sequence involves turning to the 'service' area, counter (pail), where the customer condiments 'hir' meal. However, since this is a phase where there may occur inordinate expenditures of ketchup, mustard, onion and pickle in the personalization of the purchase, McDonald's (unlike other outlets) controls the dispensation of these items at point of ordering and payment. It thereby restricts the 'service' area to a dispensary of paper and plastic products in the service of dirt control. These features eliminate the restaurant functions of the waiter in the mediation/recommendation of elements in the meal and its complements, as well as in clearing the table. The next phase of the post-purchase period is involved with finding a seat or seats *after* the meal is served rather than before. Here customers' allegiance to fast-food is most in evidence. It requires that previous communicants have disgorged themselves from McDonald's in a continuous flow so that there is always a place for the next one because the furniture is bolted down and cannot be rearranged to correct seating imbalances. Once seated, the fast-food communicant proceeds to eat with 'hir' hands amidst the garbage that has been created by unwrapping the food – garbage that is carefully reserved in order to rewrap the remains for self-disposal, garbaging and exiting. By then, any illusion of having eaten in a restaurant has faded. Here the mortification of the fast-food communicant reaches its highest point, whereafter it fades into (in)digestion off the premises, as the customer moves back into the flow of traffic.

McDonaldization and Its Discontents

Americans are unsure whether America is built upon individuals or upon families. In practice, each covers for the other – and the same is true of individual and corporate relations. The American ideology phrases institutions as nothing but a set of individuals while promoting the individual as America's greatest institution (O'Neill, 1992). This encourages Americans to regard themselves as more alike than not, however unequal their corporate institutions render them. The ideological construction of the Average American services industry and democracy so that mass-produced commodities reproduce the American who consumes them. Cars, cokes and burgers are the ideal material carriers of the American ideology.

The corporate rendition of solidarity and individual personality, however, requires the familization of its transactions. It benefits from the lived

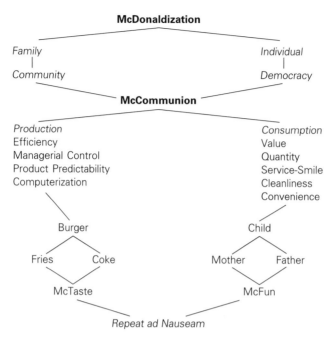

FIGURE 3.1   *Eating America*

contradictions of personality and family while promising a temporary relief from the family in servicing its pleasure and practicality. At McDonald's the family escapes from itself to celebrate a meal it has not cooked, a meal about which nothing need be said that has not already been said and that can be forgotten the minute it is over – give and take a little indigestion, unless one is quite young. At this point the organized informality of McDonald's is particularly important since it pre-empts criticism while nevertheless invoking it as suggestions for improved service. As in every confidence game, the onus is on the victim to change the game!

The institutionalized discontent of McDonaldization is only intelligible in terms of the discontents endemic to the American Dream. Americans are conscripted to the unseasonable pursuit of abundance. The impossibility of the dream is saved by the translation of quality into quantity and the identification of availability with desirability. The American pursuit of a deal has the added merit that it cheapens the cost of deception. Thus America is the only country in the world where the rich eat as badly as the poor, who in turn eat slightly worse than they might have but for McDonald's. Such is the democratization of taste (see Figure 3.1).

McDonald's is a prime site of family decay. It is fast food, not served and swallowed without the use of cutlery. The civilized distance that all human societies have set between themselves and nature (meat and potatoes) is erased (Lévi-Strauss, 1969). McSpace is entirely decathected by its users. They are not interested in the service-smile because they know that there is no civil distance between workers and customers at McDonald's. Behind it all is the anxiety induced by food with a short shelf-life and the lack of time to gather round it as family and community. McDonald's purveys a taste for the uncouth whose only virtue is that its crudity is classless. Classlessness also demands informality and fun. McDonald's is one of many sites where the production of tasteless trivialization and massification reproduces a social order that is structured by class domination to which reference is foreclosed (Bourdieu, 1984). Failure to recognize the material structure of cultural reproduction confounds the mythology of taste with the sociology of corporate order (see http://www.mcspotlight.org). Where everything is done for you, you do everything to yourself!

McDonald's Family Restaurant is neither a restaurant nor a family site. The family that no longer eats at home doesn't eat at McDonald's for the same reason. To the extent that the new household lacks anything more than the hurried time it takes to disperse itself to work, school and daycare, it lacks mealtimes. All eating occurs on the run – in a race that begins with speedy/high-energy breakfasts, continues with extended snacks and ends with a quick dinner more or less bought, eaten in or out. Because families are not very happy with these arrangements, McDonald's is happy to be happy for them. Hence the service-smile. Because American families lack the time to be families, they also lack the time to be members of communities. McDonald's is happy to declare itself a community agent. Because Americans are not sure how much change they can stand, McDonald's is happy to reassure Americans that nothing changes at McDonald's because it is timelessly devoted to the primordial values of food, folk and good clean fun. Because Americans have little time for their children, McDonald's happily offers them a haven, a treasure house of birthday memories across the generations.

It is essential to McDonald's Corporation that its success be read simply as a commercial effect of the American bonanza. Americans get rich by making America a market that is rich. America's wealth is not produced. It is desired. Wealth and poverty are effects of greater or lesser desire which is a matter of character but not of class. America is governed by socially structured anomie, that is, by the limitlessness of its desire. In such a society, all objects are constructed to meet the denial of scarcity. The result is that shoddy rules in the material order while mortification rules in the spiritual order. Americans are destined to disappointment rather than disaffection. McDonald's is the perfect venue for this daily experience. Here the customer is a self-serving sovereign whose taste dictates every movement within a menu designed to eject him or her and his or her family as fast as possible. What is this taste for McDonald's? However it looks, what is in it is fat and sugar (Mintz, 1986). What is at the end of the line is obesity – a less hidden injury of social class since it is expensive to battle or to buy off fat. Some do, some don't. Some celebrate obesity – Roseanne at least until recently; others ride the roller coaster – like Oprah. Either way, the American diet is moralized rather than politicized, leaving the food corporations free to batten on their profits from selling diet foods to counteract America's daily foods.

Have You Had Your Theory Today?

The trivialization of sociological theory with which we are concerned is probably best served through its complete speed-up. The commodification of sociology textbooks demands that they meet the double standard of homogeneity and diversity. They do so artfully. Theory is married to method in order that theory shall not stray. This leaves method free to wander through a smorgasbord of social problems, through subcultures of crime and sexual deviance:

> Dispersed texts of money, science, edifice, and figure are desirable today because they seem to have abandoned the infantile passions of polemic antithetical to the mien of the skeptical realist – Weber's culture hero. (Agger, 1989: 56)

Any topic can be framed by symbolic interactionism, functionalism, conflict theory and social constructionalism, according to student taste. By and large, theory is Weberized on the right and on the left. In this way, moral despair hides behind value-neutrality and social conflict is dispersed in social complexity. Sociology survives as one of the convivial arts of human interest and social concern (O'Neill, 1992). The Americanization of theory and methods occurs because there is no true alienation-effect (*Entfremdungseffekt*) in American pedagogy, any more than there is any socialism in American politics. American theory is never served apart from the meat and potatoes of evidence, facts, data. When American theory becomes German, as it does in Ritzer, it is like a hamburger that has migrated to become a beefburger: what it lacks in style it makes up in ubiquity. When American theory is sublime, as it is in Parsons, it is because the theorist's calling (*Beruf*) is answered unswervingly. When American theory is French, as it is in Goffman, it suffers exclusion by reason of its subtle irony. Because American theory has never been Catholic, it lacks cosmology and romance as much as it lacks Irish wakefulness and the divinity of Italian comedy.

Current American sociology is like corporate coffee. It is blenderized to suit your taste by buying it out locally to sell it back globally. System integration, consumerized and personalized, increasingly presents an ethical face. How would you like your coffee, or your theory, today? The question, of course, is weak, like the faint smile that accompanies it. Having integrated our choices for us, the ethical corporation is anxious to warn us about the dangers that lie beyond their concern for us. Ethical theorists are no different. In the struggle for McSouls, George is hard pressed by Regina:

O'NEILL'S DINER

If you must eat at McDonald's, bring someone to act as your maître d' . . . to keep a table for you and to provide plates, cutlery, glasses, cups and saucers for your meal. Introduce wine or beer since McDonald's accepts this practice abroad. Arrange for a friend to bring in a dessert trolley to expand your choice of sweets. Invite the employee of the month to sit over coffee and a liqueur while going through the family album. Hold a book launch – sign free copies of The McDonaldization of Society.

FIGURE 3.2   O'Neill's Diner

Schrambling's Warning
Remember that the strawberry crop is really as fleeting as fireflies, that sweet corn waits for no one; it's best when eaten within hours of leaving the stalk. (Schrambling, 1991: 185)

Ritzer's Warning
Habitual use of the McDonaldization systems are destructive to our physical and psychological well-being as well as to society as a whole. (Ritzer, 1993: 182)

George and Regina know, of course, that Americans have nowhere to go that they are not already 'at', so to speak. Hence all those lovely captive audiences for George's priestly advice:

- Avoid living in apartments or tract houses . . .
- Avoid daily routine as much as possible . . .
- Avoid hair-cutting chains . . .
- Avoid most finger foods . . .
- Avoid classes where tests are short answer and graded by computer . . .
- Go to your neighbourhood doctor . . .
- Frequent a local greasy spoon . . .
- Read *The New York Times* . . .
- Keep the channel selection PBS . . .
- If you are a regular at McDonald's, develop personal ties with the counter people . . . (Ritzer, 1993: 183–5)

What is at issue here are two styles of ethical discourse, one psychosomatized and the other socio-somatized, each claiming the legitimacy of ethico-rationality (O'Neill, 1995). Both engage the illusion of spiritual autonomy with a critical discourse that fails to challenge its own interest in the reproduction of the structural relationships between priestly or prophetic advice and its lay reception. But neither allows a glimpse of the carnivalesque incongruities invoked by every social order because they involve a folk wit that is professionally inappropriate (O'Neill, 1972).

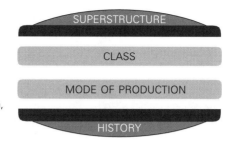

Toppings:
Ideology, commodity fetishism,
alienation, religion, state

FIGURE 3.3 *The Marx Burger*

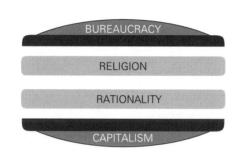

Toppings:
Vocation, asceticism,
disenchantment, charisma

FIGURE 3.4 *The Weber Burger*

Ritzer cannot entertain Weber's distinction between enthusiasm and routinization because his conception of social needs remains on the same level as his students' experience. Such sociology has nothing to offer its students beyond what they already know. But the price of its 'truth' is that McSociology cannot differentiate its own position in the field of popular knowledge, any more than it can identify the social location of those who teach and study McSociology rather than any other pseudo-pedagogy. Since Ritzer advocates student subversion of a variety of McPractices, why not try the game of building one's own theory-burger? (Figures 3.3–3.6).

As Weber showed, the struggle to monopolize legitimacy in the provision of lay world-views results in the translation of prophetic insight into the priestly paradigm of routine spirit. Thus Weber suffers Weberization (Ritzer, 1991). Like other classics, Weber's work is demonized – along with Marx and Durkheim – because it exceeds the level of interest in sociology that is redeemed in the McDonaldization of the social sciences. The question of the theoretical legitimacy of Ritzer's use of Weber's account of rationalization does not arise. This is because Ritzer's text answers prophetically to the need for McTheory at certain levels of undergraduate education. McText, of course, is not Ritzer's singular product (its critique, therefore involves nothing *ad hominem*). It is not to be analysed for its logical coherence but for its practical assembly of experiences recognizable by a population to which it is attuned. For a lay population interpretation is

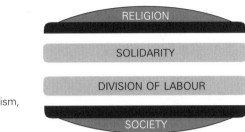

Toppings:
Integration, egoism, altruism,
sacrifice, anomie

FIGURE 3.5 *The Durkheim Burger*

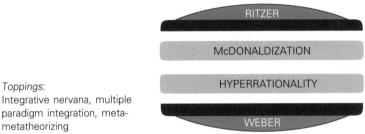

Toppings:
Integrative nervana, multiple
paradigm integration, meta-
metatheorizing

FIGURE 3.6 *The Ritzer Burger*

achieved through the extrapolation and proliferation of examples derived from 'one's own experience'. At most, the teacher will be asked by students whether they are expected to make a habit of such introspection. Students, after all, understand the violation of everyday life that results from pro-longed breaks with extroversion. They also understand that the professoriate dispenses those capital goods (grades) that are the reward for routinized repetition of the banalities of instruction. How this teacher/student pact operates to individuate undergraduates, while confirming their position in a class-divided society, is beyond the scope of McDonaldized instruction. In the meantime, McText will provide the breviary of a parochial sociology whose evangelical success injures the mind as much as fast-food injures the soul's body.

O'NEILL'S WARNING

ONLY YOU CAN STOP TEACHING/READING RITZER!

References

Agger, B. (1989) *Fast Capitalism: A Critical Theory of Significance*. Urbana, IL and Chicago: University of Illinois Press.

Bennell, B. (1991) 'World toils for a burger', *The Globe and Mail*, 4 December, 1991.

Bourdieu, P. (1984) *Distinction: A Social Critique of the Judgement of Taste*. Cambridge, MA: Harvard University Press.

Harris, M. and Ross, E.B. (1987) *Food and Evolution: Towards a Theory of Human Food Habits*. Philadelphia: Temple University Press.

Helmer, J. (1992) 'Love on a bun: how McDonald's won the Burger Wars', *Journal of Popular Culture*, 26 (2): 85–98.

Lévi-Strauss, C. (1969) *The Raw and the Cooked: Introduction to a Science of Mythology*, Vol. 1. New York: Harper & Row.

Mintz, S.W. (1986) 'American eating habits and food choices: a preliminary essay', *The Journal of Gastronomy*, 2 (3): 15–22.

O'Neill, J. (1972) *Sociology as a Skin Trade: Essays Towards a Reflexive Sociology*. London: Heinemann.

O'Neill, J. (1985) *Five Bodies: The Human Shape of Modern Society*. Ithaca, NY: Cornell University Press.

O'Neill, J. (1992) *Critical Conventions: Interpretation in the Literary Arts and Sciences*. Norman, OK: University of Oklahoma Press.

O'Neill, J. (1993) 'McTopia: eating time', in K. Kumar and S. Bann (eds), *Utopias and the Millennium*. London: Reaktion Books.

O'Neill, J. (1995) *The Poverty of Postmodernism*. London: Routledge.

Rifkin, J. (1992) *Beyond Beef: The Rise and Fall of the Cattle Culture*. New York: Penguin Books.

Ritzer, G. (1991) *Metatheorizing in Sociology*. Lexington, MA: Lexington Books.

Ritzer, G. (1993) *The McDonaldization of Society: An Investigation into the Changing Character of Contemporary Social Life*. Thousand Oaks, CA: Pine Forge Press.

Ross, E.B. (1980) 'Patterns of diet and forces of production: an economic and ecological history of the ascendancy of beef in the United States diet', in E.B. Ross (ed.), *Beyond the Myths of Culture: Essays in Cultural Materials*. New York: Academic Press.

Schrambling, R. (1991) 'The curse of culinary convenience', *The New York Times*, 17 October: 8.

Yanarella, R. and Reid, H.G. (1996) 'From "trained gorilla" to "humanware": repoliticizing the body–machine complex between Fordism and post-Fordism', in T.R. Schatzki and W. Netter (eds), *The Social and Political body*. New York: Guilford Press.

4 McDonaldization Enframed

Deena Weinstein and Michael A. Weinstein

With its gears, levers and large clock, the murky brick-walled factory, straight out of Charlie Chaplin's *Modern Times*, is forbidding. Freshly scrubbed children in their school uniforms close-march onto the assembly line in single file. 'We don't need no education. We don't need no thought control,' they sing earnestly and resolutely. The first batch processing renders them all alike; in snouted pig-face masks, they are seated at school desks on the moving assembly line. They still shout their doomed sing-song protest.

Further down the line, the children march along a narrow railed passageway that ends abruptly. One by one, they drop down into the next processing station, a large meat grinder, where they merge into a completely uniform product, ground meat. (McDonald's has no product placement in Pink Floyd's movie *The Wall*, where this scene appears, so we don't see the patty-shaping machine.)

Abruptly, the scene shifts back to another take on the same raw material, kids in their classroom; now they are in full-blown revolt, smashing, trashing and finally burning down the school.

Both the meat-grinding factory and the school rebellion are fantasies, one despairing, the other hopeful. They emerge from the active imagination of Pink, *The Wall*'s protagonist. Their immediate stimulus was the schoolmaster's discovery of the boy's poetry, which he proceeded to ridicule severely because it expressed feelings.

The ways in which society, here represented by the teacher, suppresses the individual's ability to communicate genuinely with others is the theme of all of Roger Waters's work. Waters, who wrote *The Wall*'s screenplay, was Pink Floyd's lyricist. The wall separates us from one another. Each brick in the wall is another social repression, like the schoolmaster's reaction to Pink's poetry. Pink can resist being challenged forth by society, but only at the cost of great pain, at best rendering him 'comfortably numb' and ultimately destroying his sanity.

Redescribing Ritzer

George Ritzer's essay on the McDonaldization of the world acknowledges several influences, including Karl Marx, turn-of-the-twentieth-century classical sociology (especially Max Weber's writings on bureaucracy and rationalization) and contemporary critical theory (particularly Jürgen Habermas), but it has most in common, in style and conception, with American popular sociology of the 1950s, most notably David Riesman's *The Lonely Crowd* and William Whyte's *Organization Man.*

Popular sociology is a peculiarly American discourse that mediates academic social theory to a mass educated audience by deploying abundant specific examples of contemporary social phenomena, metaphors, images and metonymies to illustrate theoretical propositions. The genre's advantage of rich description is usually counterbalanced by scanty clarification of general principles, leading to imprecision in the application of concepts and vagueness.

The McDonaldization of Society is no exception to the rule of the popular-sociology genre. The essay is based on metonymy, a figure of speech in which a particular feature of something is made to stand for that thing as a whole, for example using the 'White House' to stand for the American presidency. In Ritzer's essay, 'McDonaldization' is the guiding metonym, standing for a set of processes more or less united under the concept of 'rationalization'.

What is McDonaldization precisely? The problem with using a metonym to substitute for carefully defined concepts is that a particular instance of a process always contains more and less than can be subsumed under that process. In Ritzer's text, there is a chain of metonymy with McDonaldization as its base that moves through hamburger chains, to fast-food, to other similar services, to the process of rationalization in general. At each step in the chain there is a difference between that step and the one that preceded it. Would we be confident that we understood the social dimension of fast-food only by studying McDonald's? Will bringing everything back to the metonym of McDonald's bias and skew our interpretation of rationalization?

Sometimes it seems as though Ritzer is simply using McDonaldization as a synonym for rationalization, pouring all of the old theoretical cola into a glitzy new cup, just as he observes that McDonald's takes the old hamburger and packages it as entertainment. In such instances, McDonaldization adds nothing new to Weber's interpretation of rationalization; it is another word for the same thing, comprehending the factory system and conventional bureaucracies, as well as any succeeding developments along the same lines. In other cases, Ritzer seems to want McDonaldization to refer to specific recent developments in social organization that differ importantly from earlier forms and for which McDonald's serves as a paradigm or model. Unfortunately, he never brings those differences into conceptual clarity and, thus, his text suffers from vagueness.

We will briefly tighten up and fill some gaps in Ritzer's interpretation of McDonaldization as a preliminary to encircling it with a broader perspective that makes sense of some of its imprecisions and ambivalences.

The theory that backs up Ritzer's social criticism moves through three stages, which are co-present throughout the text. First, there is the notion of rationalization, taken from Weber and identified with 'Fordism', which is a metonym for the assembly-line factory system. Second, there is the notion of McDonaldization, with any specific extensions it might make to or differences that it might have from Fordism. Third, there is the notion of humanism, through which Ritzer criticizes rationalization–Fordism and McDonaldization.

Rationalization is the best theorized of Ritzer's main terms; he appropriates an extant term in sociological discourse and interprets it as it has been traditionally understood, without adding anything new to it. 'Rationalization' was one of the great contributions made at the turn of the twentieth century by Weber to understanding the emerging organizational society in the West. Ritzer has followed Weber, constructing an ideal-type of rationalization, including the four dimensions of efficiency, calculability, predictability and control. Getting desired results at the least cost, measuring means and results in terms of quantities, confident that the results will be the same across repeated actions, and the replacement of human judgement by automated processes and externally imposed rules are the constituents of a social organization for which Henry Ford's assembly-line system for making automobiles is the paradigm. Such a system is directed by elites of highly skilled and relatively autonomous managers presiding over a de-skilled workforce that is reduced to being an appendage of machines: welcome to the machine.

McDonaldization is the application of the partially automated factory system to the provision of services that involve interactions between service providers and individual human beings (clients and consumers). Whereas classical Fordism rationalized industrial processes, McDonaldization rationalizes social interactions.

The basis of McDonaldization is the imposition of a fixed formula on the provision of a service, such as food and dining. As much of the servicing as possible is done by automated technologies and the rest is governed by a rigid set of rules that are executed by a de-skilled workforce. Consumers and clients are controlled as much as possible by rules and human engineering, for example uncomfortable seats in fast-food restaurants to encourage brief stays. They are also made to participate in producing the service, for example by busing their trays.

Ritzer's concern with McDonaldization centres on its effects; Fordism in the service industries is dehumanizing. Here he takes up the longstanding critique of the alienation of factory labour and applies it to emerging and well-established trends in the service industries. Gracious dining, personal service, acquaintanceship with food providers and creativity of cooks are all conspicuous by their absence in fast-food restaurants. Individualized attention and professional autonomy are being progressively eliminated in such sensitive areas as medicine and education. All of this is happening under the banners of efficiency, safety and convenience, but those claims themselves, the purported benefits of rationalized services, might be a sham. As Ritzer points out, it is probably better not to lift the bun on a fast-food hamburger and contemplate it for what it is and what it is not.

Humanism is the most scantily interpreted of Ritzer's major concepts. He declares that he is not pleading nostalgia for a more commodious life of the past, but looks forward without much hope to a better future, yet his examples all refer to amenities and freedoms that are being taken away by McDonaldization rather than to visions of possibility.

More importantly, Ritzer leaves vagueness in his notion of humanism by failing to adjudicate between the claims of the society and of the individual in a desirable rational, rather than an undesirable rationalized, society. What does it mean to be human in the laudatory sense Ritzer uses the term? Does it mean having individual discretion? Does it mean closer and more multi-faceted human relations? Both?

There is no doubt that human beings on the whole are falling increasingly under the control of rationalized systems and processes of servicing, but it is not clear exactly what is being lost. Ritzer can only criticize McDonaldization by throwing its deprivals against it while having to admit that it seems to satisfy certain human interests, which are presumably inferior to the ones that he champions. He refuses to say that we are all being gulled by capitalist manipulation, yet we seem to come off in his discussion as at least partly witting and willing dupes in McDonaldization. Are we dupes of our own base desires? Are we dupes of organizational elites? What is the contemporary state of human nature that makes some things about us and our lives seem 'inhuman' to Ritzer and some not? Is humanism the most accurate way to interpret the effects of rationalization–Fordism–McDonaldization?

Encircling Ritzer with Heidegger

By basing his criticism of McDonaldization on values and, perhaps, human interests and needs, Ritzer's text takes on the cast of a polemic in a fight over values, with all the fruitlessness that such a conflict implies. He has not worked out a theoretical basis for claiming that his preferences for certain practices and ways of life from the past have any basis but his own taste; he does not present any argument for why his preferences are congruent with human nature and the things that he criticizes are inhuman. He readily admits that people seem to be able to get used to McDonaldization and even like it, particularly for (the perception of) its efficiency, predictability and convenience. Why are the values of the partisans of McDonaldization any less worthy than the ones that Ritzer upholds?

Ritzer also admits that McDonaldization is winning the cultural war; indeed, his impulse for writing his book was to make some small contribution to stemming the tide. We agree with Ritzer that probably nothing can be done to roll back McDonaldization and we will not criticize his strategy of small resistances to the process for betraying the cause of social change or for failing to mount a spirited defence of modern liberal or premodern values. Instead, we will provide another basis for his critique than the one grounded in human interests that he seems to pre-suppose; our ground avoids conflict over values and puts everyone in the same boat, elites as well as underlings. We do not expect much practical effect from our (re)framing of the McDonaldization process, but we hope to provide greater understanding of its stubbornness and seeming inevitability.

The discourse that we will use to frame Ritzer's McDonaldization is the philosopher Martin Heidegger's essay, 'The question concerning technology', published in 1954 (see Heidegger, 1977). For Heidegger, modern technology does not mean its normally accepted definition, tools or instruments that have been devised under the guidance of modern sciences, but a comprehensive way of existing, of which those tools are an aspect or index. According to Heidegger, we live by and for technology; it is our destiny. Therefore, he claims that whether someone is for or against technology, defined as scientifically based instruments and tools, they are within the horizon of technology defined as a way of being.

What is a way of being and, specifically, the technological way of being? For Heidegger, human beings are primarily defined as beings who reveal the world by being aware of it and by bringing things forth that are not yet revealed in it through their aware conduct. For example, premodern agri-culture throughout the world is a process of bringing forth crops by the peasant in close collaboration with natural forces. In premodern agricul-ture the earth is a partner in growing food; the peasant assists a process that is not under his or her control. An even better, perhaps the root example is pre-technological birthing, in which a midwife assists a process of bringing forth a new human being, but does not exert control over the timing of the event or many of its vicissitudes. The way of being and revealing encapsulated by the term 'bringing-forth' reveals the world as autonomous potentialities to be appreciated, revered and cultivated. Human beings are participants in that world who do not stand over and against it with their demands, but who find their place in it as participants in its processes.

Heidegger believed that in modern times the way of bringing forth had been supplanted by the technological way, which he called 'challenging-forth'. Rather than through cooperation with the world that reveals things by bringing them forth, things are now revealed by 'setting upon' them and mobilizing them in a 'standing reserve' so that they can be 'challenged forth' to perform pre-designed operations. Heidegger com-pares the pre-industrial peasant who tends the land, sows seed and harvests the crop (bringing-forth) to the miner who attacks the land in order to extract its energies and resources from it (challenging-forth), and then observes that industrial farming is patterned on the mining model, assaulting the land with chemicals and heavy machinery to make it yield designer foods, like the standard potato that McDonald's demands for its fries.

For Heidegger, we are 'enframed' by the condition of challenging-forth, in which all things are revealed as the energies that can be extracted from them. No longer are we collaborators in the world and with it. Instead, we believe that we can command the world, standing over and against it, and ruling it according to our whim and will. We have no idea that we are engaged in revealing things in a certain way, but are confident that we are satisfying our desires by contriving ever more effective means to use, manipulate and transform things in order to secure our ends. We believe that our instruments are extensions of ourselves and that they are or can be made to be under the control of our wills rather than being primarily elements in the way that we are allowing the world to be revealed.

Heidegger warned that the logic of challenging-forth would lead to making ourselves into a standing reserve of 'human resources'. Nearly 50 years after he wrote his essay on technology, it is abundantly clear that Heidegger was correct. From a Heideggerian viewpoint, all of what Ritzer ranges under the rubric of McDonaldization evidences the process of mobilizing human beings into a standing reserve and challenging them forth to expend their energies in pre-designed performances. Everyone is implicated in this way of being, elites as well as masses; it is the way, to use one of Heidegger's favourite phrases, that we 'proximally and for the most part', exist. All of our desires are played out within this 'enframing', the ways that we satisfy and even define our needs are defined within it. Technology is not a bunch of tools; it is our destiny and we understand ourselves within it, even though most of us are not even aware that we are enframed: we are the fish who are the last to discover water.

If we are enframed, acting out a drama of revealing the world and ourselves as standing reserve, then it no longer makes any sense to speak about humanism, the idea that our destiny is to serve our needs and desires through the world and, as it often turns out, at its expense. From Heidegger's viewpoint, we participate within a technological way of being, and humanism is one of the symptoms of the manner in which that way of being affects us. If we need evidence that the technological way of revealing the world is trans-human (not inhuman, since we remain human beings engaged in revealing things), we need only look at the general attitude toward the instruments of technological life, the sense that anything that can be done (for example, cloning human beings) will be done; whether tinged with fatalism or affirmed enthusiastically, that attitude is an acknowledgement of 'destiny'.

Ritzer's essay on McDonaldization is a gold mine of examples for illustrating how we are increasingly turning ourselves into standing reserves. There is no need to proliferate new examples, but only to reinterpret and supplement the ones that Ritzer has provided.

McDonald's, Ritzer's root metonym, is, in an obvious sense, part of a system of mobilizing standing reserves of foodstuffs to be processed for sale and consumption, and is implicated in industrial agriculture and animal husbandry. However, more important than that is how McDonald's mobilizes its customers as standing reserve. McDonald's 'sets upon' its potential customers through aggressive outreach, spending more than $300,000,000 per year in the USA alone to flood the media with advertising and contriving endless promotions (in the case of the 'Beanie Babies', many people came to get the toy and threw away their burgers) to create a reserve of potential customers who can then be challenged forth to be processed by its food-service system. Just as the burgers and fries are processed according to formula, the employees are programmed to enact certain pre-designed motions and to recite scripts, and managers are trained at Hamburger University, so the customers are 'serviced' within a programme of human engineering that steers them through pre-designed steps.

Through its aggressive marketing, from advertising through promotions to the packaging of its products as entertainment and even religion (the Golden Arches as a symbol of consumer heaven where Ronald McDonald reigns as demi-god), McDonald's mobilizes a standing reserve of consumers through seduction. As Jean Baudrillard (1990) has noted, people are seduced just because there is nothing satisfying at the end of the process; the poor excuse for a burger that McDonald's offers is sought just because it offers nothing exciting or memorable: it is an excuse for eating that makes no demands; all of the demands come in being processed. McDonald's is a way of revealing the people who become implicated in its system as what they have been designed to be: elements of a reserve of customers who are challenged forth to be serviced properly for a price.

Other sectors of contemporary life that are discussed by Ritzer illustrate the mobilization of human standing reserves even more forcefully than McDonald's does. Technological medicine, for example, sets up standing reserves of organ donors who are challenged forth to yield their body parts for harvesting when they die. Cloning creates similar reserves, as does the more familiar practice of storing sperm and eggs. Nursing home patients are drugged and are made a reserve to be challenged forth for programmed procedures.

The educational system mobilizes a standing reserve of workers–consumers–citizens to be challenged forth by other social organizations. Moves for national educational norms and universal standardized testing are geared to challenging-forth human resources to compete in the global economy. Various disciplinary measures, such as behaviour-control drugs, uniforms and drug testing, are meant to create a docile reserve.

Do people want to be McDonaldized? From the Heideggerian viewpoint, that question does not matter. We are not being McDonaldized against our wishes or because we wish it; whatever motives support the process, and they range from a desire for a quick, predictable and inexpensive meal, to a fascination with seduction and a will to submit to the logic of 'enframing', we are engaged in a way of revealing the world and ourselves that is indifferent to those motives.

The Perfection of McDonaldization

Although the origins of a way are, as Heidegger observes, shrouded in mystery, it is possible to show the cultural and social conditions that arise within its horizon and the motivations that support it.

The cultural conditions associated with the technological way of revealing centre on what early twentieth-century German sociologist Georg Simmel (1971) called 'the hypertrophy of objective culture'. Human beings, in Simmel's view, create systems of things (tools, rules, products and symbols) to serve their needs and desires. The sum of those systems is objective culture.

In the industrial age, systems of objective culture, like the fast-food industry, higher education and organized medicine, become highly specialized, inventing their own particular procedures and techniques for achieving their narrow aims. At a certain point in the process, systems developed their own logics, 'rationalizing' their own operations so that they were efficient and neglecting their overall impact on individual human beings and communities. Over-development of objective culture ends, according to Simmel, by tyrannizing people through making them serve the functions and goals of systems rather than their own interests.

For example, the 'right to die' and 'assisted suicide' movements are in great part responses to a medical system that, through technologies, prolongs the lives of individuals beyond the point at which some of those individuals can bear the pain and torture of their diseases and sometimes of the treatments that are supposed to help them; ruthlessly pursuing the aim of prolonging a narrowly defined biological life challenges forth a standing reserve of the potentially ill to submit, when they fall seriously ill, to mechanical and chemical torture so that some of their life functions remain operative for a while longer.

Similarly, the dysfunctions that Ritzer notes in McDonald's food service come from the obsession with efficiency, calculability, predictability and control in providing fast-food for a profit. As long as McDonald's makes a profit that is satisfactory to its large shareholders, it will have no concern about what it does to its customers; for example, whether its meals are healthy and its service is actually convenient.

The primary social factors that drive the specialization and over-development of objective culture are capitalism and democracy. In capitalism, the economic system in which demand is served for a monetary profit and goods and services are provided according to the demander's purchasing power, producers are constrained to use all the legal means at their disposal to meet effective demand more efficiently than their competitors, fostering the innovation of specialized systems adapted to particular demands.

Democracy, in the social sense of careers open to talents rather than allotted by birth, frees masses of individuals to enter the standing reserve of the labour market, where they are challenged forth into differentiated systems of production and service. Their wages give them purchasing power and they are served as consumers by systems created by profit-making organizations like McDonald's, completing the social enframing.

When all of the specialized activities have been rationalized, demand is no longer independent of the ways and means by which it is served; whether or not we like automobiles, for example, we have become dependent on them to satisfy our demand for mobility, which is, in turn, rooted in other demands, like the demand for employment so that we can subsist with the degree of autonomy that having our own purchasing power permits.

When systems that challenge forth are the only games in town, people are mobilized into standing reserves and are challenged forth regardless of their wish or will; people have to eat.

Cultural and social factors do not tell us why people are content with or at least accepting of the low standard of the products they consume and the environments in which they consume them; why their demand for food can be satisfied by a lame patty of meat, which does not bear visual inspection, that has been inserted in a tasteless bun, and eaten in a cheap plastic environment on uncomfortable seats. Ritzer gives part of the answer when he cites the appearance of efficiency (fast-food), calculability (cheap food), and predictability (always the same food). All of these values can be gathered under the seduction of the undemanding. It makes sense that people who are challenged forth into technology to do its bidding at work will wish to be challenged forth again to be served in a way that superficially seems to demand very little of them in effort, monetary expense and taste.

Beyond such easily intelligible motives are more complex ones like the wish to be controlled (no decisions are necessary) and, specifically, the wish to be controlled by technology. As objective culture draws people into its systems and uses them in ways that they do not affirm or are not good for them, and that they cannot avoid, they begin to worship it as a jealous god that intimidates, awes and fascinates them. They feel themselves oppressed by objective culture, yet they appeal to it for salvation. They are humiliated by technology, they feel abject before it, and they desperately collaborate with it, because they are radically dependent on it. The chess-playing computer humiliates the grand master. What does it do to the novice? We feel that our machines are superior to ourselves and, therefore, we worship them, even though many of us sense that objective culture is failing us.

In the 1996 revised edition of *The McDonaldization of Society*, Ritzer added a section on the Nazi death camps and a chapter on the McDonaldization of birth and death, because he felt that the original text had not attended sufficiently to the 'dark side' of McDonaldization. Indeed, what would be the point of Ritzer's book if McDonaldization did not have a dark side? It would simply mark a criticism of low-brow consumption.

Although Ritzer does not define what he means by 'dark side', we can follow Heidegger and still be very close to Ritzer by defining it as life in the shadow of death.

Rationalized death camps, wherever they appear, embody the Fordization of the destruction of life, Fordized genocide. In a lecture that Heidegger gave that was the basis of 'The Question Concerning Technology', he compared the death camps to mechanized agriculture, citing both as examples of challenging-forth. Rationalized death camps are a limit point of modern industrial society, because they show that technology, understood as systems of mechanized tools, is indifferent to moral purpose: technology holds nothing sacred but effectiveness.

The McDonaldization of birth and death might be better called the bio-medicalization of life, covering the entire life-process, in which no phase of that process is exempt from therapeutic/medical intervention. Unlike the death camps, the bio-medicalization of life holds itself out as a great benefit to human beings, but its ultimate effect is to reveal the human being as lacking, as needing envelopment by technologies to sustain it in its being as an organism, and to make it fit to participate in systems of objective culture that place stressful demands on it.

When bio-medicalization enframes life, even choosing to die outside the medical complex of life-sustaining machines and chemicals is McDonald-ized. Hospice care regularizes terminal illness, challenging dying organisms forth to die a 'natural' death with 'dignity'. There is a rationalized system for everything.

If human beings must be placed under continuous care to keep a tech-nological society going, why not engineer replacements for them that would be better adapted to its demands and better able to enjoy the satisfactions that it offers? The logic of challenging-forth to serve a system leads to challenging-forth human beings to engineer forms of life, artificial organisms and robots, that will serve the system and be served by it better than human beings. Feeling humiliated by technology and awed by it, human beings are gaining a will to be replaced that is compatible with the autonomous logic of a system of objective culture: bio-engineering (build better organisms). Genetic engineering, cloning, artificial intelligence and robotics converge on the project of altering and superseding human life for the sake of revealing being through challenging-forth. We can view con-temporary life on the dark side as a holding action until our replacements come on line; our practical function is to keep things going while some of us invent the androids and, otherwise, the world is a hospice where we, as members of a terminally ill species, wait for the androids as we watch TV and eat McDonald's,

In a post-human McDonald's, robots would prepare the food, and organisms that were especially engineered to enjoy it and to be content to follow all the procedures of being serviced would consume the food. Their entire purpose for existing would be to delight in the McDonald's experience and they would know nothing beyond that.

McDonaldized Rock: MTV

Despite Baudrillard's ravings, we have not yet been fully implanted in an endless recurring loop of engineered production and consumption. Baudrillard believes that we are already at the pinnacle of simulating ourselves; he is Hegel to Heidegger's Marx. Yet only androids could be so perfect. Until they arrive, we amuse ourselves in the hospice.

Roger Waters is wiser than Baudrillard; we have not yet been reduced to homogenized chopped meat, though the tendencies in that direction are clear and seemingly overpowering. Even youth, with its imperfectly socialized energy, is being ground down, including that metonymy for and expression of youthful energy, rock music. When some of his fans would ask, 'Which one's Pink?', believing that Pink Floyd is the name of a band member, not a tribute to two old blues singers (Humphreys, 1997), Waters would cringe; he knew that he had challenged forth people who would docilely march into the grinder, who would be seduced by the undemanding and who had no wish for genuine relationships or for poetry.

The enframing of rock music, its conversion into seduction rather than expression, has been most fully achieved by music videos and their promotion by MTV. The music video enframes rock music by contextualizing it in a series of visuals that are usually contrived by experts outside the band. The music and its performance do not take place in the wider world, where they might have unexpected effects, but are interpreted within a closed, imaginary visual field, the TV screen; music videos put rock music into an imaginary world.

For both artist and audience, MTV is a deprivation of personal imagination in favour of an engineered collective imagination. Music video is a sorcerer's apprentice; it began as a vehicle for promoting bands and has become the arbiter of the meanings of the music that they make.

MTV's interpretation of songs and performances is not ideological, imposing a new meaning that effaces some original meaning, but deconstructive, eviscerating meaning through strategies of quick intercuts that destroy narrative flow and create visual contexts that are either irrelevant to the songs or subversive of them. MTV neither reinforces nor opposes music, but neutralizes it by dispersing its meaning, making it underdemanding. Music videos leave the viewer with impressions and feelings, not with focused experiences. Like a Big Mac, an MTV video is sizzle without substance.

MTV challenges forth artists and audiences to perform and appreciate music within its frame.

What is that frame? For pan-capitalism, everything is a commodity to be bought and sold. When Fordist productionism is completed by McDonaldized consumption, the consumer becomes a factor of production and the producer becomes an element of consumption; everything is promoted to make sales.

With MTV, pan-capitalism becomes hyper-capitalism. Originally an advertisement for a band, when the music video becomes the interpretative frame for rock music it remains an advertisement: unlike postmodern art, which uses the content of advertising to subvert it, MTV is an ad that is incidentally meant to be consumed as an art-entertainment object; it sells albums, concert tickets and T-shirts for the band and its recording company, and it sells an audience to advertisers.

MTV is endless promotion, moving from ads to videos seamlessly and offering the same undemanding seduction in both. It calls forth a mass youth audience that always already wanted its fragmented images that evoke blunted emotions.

During July 1997, a McDonald's advertisement ran on MTV. The advertisement, in heavy MTV rotation, shows a burger, dripping with catsup atop a Greek marble column intercut with images from the Disney cartoon-flick *Hercules*. The burger is the band part of the video, and Hercules is the fantasy part, the sizzle, the image, with which the product is associated. In one of its many intercut scenes, a teenage burger-flipper stands next to a less-than-life-sized Hercules cardboard cutout and flexes his muscles in a self-aware lame imitation. Here is an advertisement, made as an entertaining video, that sells a burger, that sells a movie, or is it the reverse?

The requirements of the pan-capitalist merchandising of rock music enframe both artist and audience.

MTV videos challenge forth the band and the nexus in which it is embedded. Onstage (live), performers reproduce note for note, the video's soundtrack, their recorded songs. Their costume and set design, and when they play larger venues, their giant above-stage videos and their on-stage props, recur to the imagery of their TV video. They write, or have written for them, new songs that vary only slightly from their previous heavily rotated video. Finally, their record producer directs and shapes their sonic inclinations in the same fashion as a video director shapes scenes.

Superficially, MTV videos challenge forth the audience as consumer: buy the CD, buy and wear the T-shirt (pay for the privilege of being a walking sandwich board advertising the band), and buy the concert ticket. At a deeper level, videos challenge forth attitudes and activity. Even first-time concert-goers know and perform the proper moves (the moshing, body surfing, Dead-twitching, headbanging, and so on) with the appropriate facial expressions, body piercings and nail polish, as if they were from central casting. Videos also challenge forth the audience's response to the song, standardizing emotions.

Rock music has been McDonaldized. What it took to be its rebellious energy has been channelled into technological entertainment systems eliciting standardized behaviour and attitudes available to anyone.

Rock & Roll McDonald's

At 'The Original Rock & Roll McDonald's' in Chicago (there is another one in Finland), the music becomes a small part of a merchandising strategy. Located in the trendy River North district, across the street from the Hard Rock Café, Rock & Roll McDonald's is a cross between a hamburger stand and a themed restaurant.

The white brick walls of the pink-roofed building are festooned with pop-culture icons from bygone years, including two dancing teenagers, Ralph Kramden and Ed Norton of The Honeymooners, and Betty Boop. Inside, encased in glass, are life-sized white sculpted figures of the Beatles, walking in single file down a corridor, as though they were zombies marching to play a concert for the undead. Next to the neon-lit service counter, staffed by teenagers from the nearby Cabrini Green housing project, is 'Peggy Sue's Boutique', selling a T-shirt advertising the restaurant, a blow-up of the Elvis Presley postage stamp, and a Ronald McDonald doll. Rock, movie, TV and automotive nostalgia catches the eye at every turn, as 1950s pop music, often in the form of contemporary remakes, fills in the sonic dimension of the total environment.

The video/advertisement comes to life at Rock & Roll McDonald's; producers and consumers are players in the fragmented scene.

Everyone but the power elite comes to Rock & Roll McDonald's – members of all ethnic groups, people of all ages and sexual orientations, derelicts, the underclass, cornfed white-bred middle-class suburban Midwestern families, construction workers, cabbies, secretaries and art gallery types, most of them blasé and seemingly unaware of the roles they are playing: McDonaldized democracy.

References

Baudrillard, J. (1990) *Seduction*. New York: St Martin's Press.

Heidegger, M. (1977) 'The question concerning technology', in D. Krell (ed.), *Basic Writings*. New York: Harper & Row.

Humphreys, P. (1997) *Pink Floyd: An Illustrated History*. London: Chameleon.

Reisman, D., Glazer, N. and Denny, R. (1961) *The Lonely Crowd*. New Haven, CT: Yale University Press.

Ritzer, G. (1996) *The McDonaldization of Society: An Investigation into the Changing Character of Contemporary Social Life* (rev. edn). Thousand Oaks, CA: Pine Forge Press.

Simmel, G. (1971) 'The metropolis and mental life', in D. Levine (ed.), *Georg Simmel: On Individuality and Social Forms*. Chicago: University of Chicago Press.

Whyte, Jr, W.H. (1957) *The Organization Man*. Garden City: Doubleday.

5   Rich Food:
McDonald's and Modern Life

Joanne Finkelstein

*the degree of slowness is directly proportional to the intensity of memory;
the degree of speed is directly proportional to the intensity of forgetting.*

(Kundera, 1996: 39)

The process of becoming modern has to a large extent been synonymous with the systematic ordering of knowledge. Modernity has come to be associated with the achievements of scientific rationality and a sense of control exerted against confusion, contestation and ambiguity. From such a perspective, a better world is achieved through technical virtuosity. Technology has supposedly been the best means for freeing us from tricks of nature, the effects of chance and metaphysical circumstance. Much modern social thought has privileged the technical, making it a metaphor of a utopian society. The image of society as a machine, in which all the components function to produce the best possible world, endorses the view that society can be a rational creation, shaped by human will.

At the same time, it is obvious that the twentieth century has been a period of disorder and excess. There have been two world wars and almost continuous parochial battles. There has been a massive population explosion, as well as migration and genocide. It is an era in which knowledge and ideas have been democratized and commodities have been mass-produced. The antinomies of the modern are so easy to recount that it makes the early optimism of the era seem naive. The legacy of the Enlightenment beliefs in the inexorable progress of Western society have faltered on the catastrophes of this century – the Gulags, Hiroshima, Nazism – including the insidious cyclical rupturing of economic stability caused by the underestimated volatility of the capitalist system.

It is in this context of debate that Ritzer (1993) has positioned his study of modern Western society. He has accepted the view that we live in a technologically sophisticated and systems-oriented world in which there is an ideological commitment to an instrumentally rational, technological future. He recognizes such an ideology in the practices of much everyday behaviour; it is evident, for example, in the rationalities and efficiencies advocated by the multinational corporation McDonald's and other enterprises which emulate its principles. Such practices sustain a zealotry for order; they obscure what Adorno called underground history and Foucault the dark side of human history. At the same time, Ritzer recognizes that there are frequent eruptions of disorder which challenge the belief in a technically perfectable society, and it is these instances which he nominates as evidencing some resistance to McDonaldization (1993: 160–88).

While Ritzer's focus on the McDonald's fast-food chain as a means to critique modernity is engaging in so far as it recognizes the importance of banal formations (such as those associated with food) in an analysis of modern society, his reliance upon it as an effective metaphor for most of the ills of modernity cannot be convincingly sustained. In the following chapter, I want to support Ritzer in his focus on food as an important code through which to read modernity, but I do not want to endorse his view that the McDonaldization of society is a sufficient analysis of the modern experience.

Food Practices and Modern Life

Food is a form of entertainment. Restaurant reviews in magazines and newspapers, travel accounts which include details of local foods and wines, and cooking programmes on television all illustrate the popularity of food as a consumer practice. Food is more than body fuel, as Lévi-Strauss has stated, 'in any particular society, cooking is a language through which that society unconsciously reveals its structure' (1978: 495). The preparation, distribution and consumption of food functions to define and sustain gender, age, religious and ethnic relations; the sociability around food reinforces cultural proprieties. In short, the food repertoire is a synedoche of a society, as most anthropologists and commentators have long acknowledged (Brillat-Savarin, 1970; Douglas, 1972; Elias, 1978; Goody, 1982; Lévi-Strauss, 1978). Ritzer tacitly concurs with the view and supports it with his case study of the McDonald's fast-food phenomenon, which, he demonstrates, has entered the history of food practices as a site where, amongst other achievements, new (and he would argue anti-human) habits of eating and new (anti-)social appetites have been formulated.

The manners governing diet and eating redefine food as quite remote from the base and simple process of fuelling the body and maintaining human survival. In every culture, in every historical period, food is thickly surrounded by symbolic cultural meaning – bread and wine become flesh and blood in the Christian sacrament. Food is always something else; it is deeply associative. Proust begins 4,000 pages of *Remembrance of Things Past* with the memory of madeleines. Even the modern restaurant as a purveyor of food functions to mystify it with elaborate social rituals which have more to do with fashions in tastes than bodily nutrition.

From a sociological perspective, the customs of everyday life are seen as normative and ideological proclamations of regnant views on human nature and the social order. As such, everyday practices are summaries of broader cultural configurations which simultaneously reiterate an idealized, imaginary status quo. With the integration of public events with private sensibilities, Ritzer's analysis of modern society resonates with the assumption, similarly advanced by Norbert Elias (1978: 201) in his history of manners, that the structures of society generate specific interior and individualistic responses. The significance of this for a habituated event like eating is that the self-conscious and regulated performance required of the individual is not a trivial aspect of circumstance but must be seen as inseparable from the imaginary universe the individual inhabits, and from which various kinds of pleasures and social pursuits derive their shape and substance.

In his analysis of McDonaldization, Ritzer includes the influences of the late twentieth century's unique culture and entertainment industries with their capacity to interpellate the individual and promulgate styles of behaviour and fashions in conduct. He is concerned to show that these everyday habits complement corporatist interests and that there has been a submergence of humanist ideals, such as individual autonomy and expressiveness, into the machinery of the highly rationalized entertainment and service industries. Ritzer argues that the normative now includes modes of conduct and patterns of discourse which privilege structural and corporate interests in an unprecedented way. The traditional humanist values of individuality, reflexivity and inventiveness are being eroded by the homogeneity promulgated by the processes of McDonaldization.

Ritzer's concerns are part of the critical commentary on late modernity which has developed throughout this century. Umberto Eco (1986) has argued that individual autonomy is constantly challenged by the ascendency of the popular and the fashionability of cultural practices. In that dimension of social life known as hyperreality, the absence of critique and the difficulty of separating publicized views of an event from individualistic responses means that fashions and fads become naturalized. A popular practice such as eating at a restaurant can be easily overlaid with advertising hyperbole and prescriptive representations. As a cultural practice it provides individuals with ideologically imbued habits of public performance which Eco and Ritzer, among others, identify as a challenge to the Enlightenment value of an autonomous subject. The homogenization of the public domain, or, to use Ritzer's term, the McDonaldization of society, reiterates the structuralist problem of somehow ensuring the stasis and determinancy of social structures without suppressing the innovation and agency of individual action. Ritzer regards this dynamic as currently being out of balance in so far as it privileges those popular social practices which reinforce the ethos of instrumental rationality.

Constructing Tastes

In the twentieth century, the culture industries with their consumerist ethic have generated a new layer of social knowledge which can obscure the polysemy of social life and gloss over the contestatory processes of dissemblance. The ready availability of prescriptive social guises means that the necessity to devise effective social roles is displaced from the individual onto culture producers who are capable of offering repertoires of discourse and emotion; they can, in short, commodify human sensibilities. Stephen Papson gives a vivid example in his analysis of the greeting card industry, where, he argues, 'everyday life has been invaded by a discourse which originates outside of it, and that our most intimate relationships have been constituted into an alien form' (1986: 99). The mannerisms and practices used habitually in the everyday world are less likely to originate from the reasoned exchanges of engaged individuals and are more likely to be ritualized performances offered by giant corporations and assimilated by individuals through mass promotion. Papson's analysis of the greeting card exemplifies how an ostensibly innocent object, filled with sentiment and used as a gesture of concern to mark personal and social events, has been reconstituted into a largely unacknowledged form of repression:

> to speak to one another through the greeting card is to speak through the greeting card industry. It is to use their language; a language produced and refined in corporate bureaucracies. It is the language of spectacle, the exaggeration of essence. As such, it objectifies, rationalizes, and fictionalizes relationships. Buried in the insignificance and innocence of the greeting card is the corporate invasion of everyday existence. (1986: 100)

Ritzer (1993: xv) suggests that much the same can be said of the modern restaurant, and it is his complaint that in this era of simulation where social events are cast in hyperbolic terms that images threaten to obscure or replace real events, that the humanization of society is being threatened. However, that conclusion is difficult to sustain, especially so in relation to the restaurant, because from its modern beginnings the restaurant has been associated with experiments in new sensory pleasures such as the performative pleasures of being seen in public and being entertained. When César Ritz opened the opulent dining room at London's Savoy Hotel in 1889, it was with the understanding that his bourgeois patrons were most interested in the theatricality of the restaurant, that is, the opportunities it offered to disport oneself, to play act, to occupy an extravagant and opulent setting as if it were one's own (Latham, 1972). From the stage of the restaurant, one could look about and scrutinize others as objects in a spectacle. In other social settings such behaviour would be unacceptable, but in the restaurant this intermingling of exhibitionism and voyeurism has been a source of ongoing pleasure. That the restaurant affords such social pleasures along with the delivery of foodstuffs is the point which makes Ritzer's focus on the instrumental rationality of the restaurant too narrow.

Food as a Social Code

During its history the restaurant has enticed the social classes to imitate one another, it has been the arena in which class divisions have been safely breached, and where diverse human exchanges such as business deals, seductions, and family quarrels, have taken place. It is where displays of social pretension, guile and the dictates of fashion have all been in evidence. In the restaurant, one is not only consuming food, one is consuming social positions and experiences. One can variously pretend to be rich, urbane, powerful, radically chic and even anti-social. The restaurant is a site so rich in social possibilities that it encourages practices which transcend its own formal structures.

Brillat-Savarin famously stated in the early nineteenth century. 'Tell me what you eat and I shall tell you what you are' (1970: xxxiii). Now a truism, this idea, when applied to contemporary practices, underscores the value of thinking about food as a code of modernity. The same point is made by Norbert Elias: 'conduct while eating cannot be isolated. It is a segment – a very characteristic one – of the totality of socially instilled forms of conduct' (1978: 68). While our relationship to food is a credential of humanness, and what we eat represents both social status and membership of a group, the changing social function of food also highlights other cultural formations such as the globalization of food production, delivery and the associated economic empires that are generated.

The increased popularity of eating out in Westernized societies has contributed to the economic significance of the food industries as well as having consequences for domestic life. It is estimated that by the close of the twentieth century, more meals will be consumed outside the home than in (Hodgson, 1982; Sargent, 1985). Ritzer uses food as a social code and this underlies his anxiety that in its commodified form, as a highly regulated, rationalized system, it is emblematic of a generalized decline in quality in everyday life (1993: 96, 141). Ritzer's anxiety is shared to some extent by other social theorists, including Gianni Vattimo (1992: 8–9), who states we are on the brink of losing 'our sense of reality' as technologization, or, to use Ritzer's term, McDonaldization, continues. However, Vattimo, unlike Ritzer, reads this situation as also having the potential to produce a plethora of different, local rationalities which, in the final analysis, may create a new emancipatory or 'transparent society':

> By a perverse kind of internal logic, the world of objects measured and manipulated by techno-science (the world of the *real*, according to metaphysics) has become the world of merchandise and images, the phantasmagoria of the mass media. . . . But what exactly might this loss of reality, this genuine erosion of the principle of reality, mean for emancipation and liberation? Emancipation, here,

consists in disorientation, which is at the same time also the liberation of differences, of local elements . . . (1992: 8–9)

The social rituals around food, irrespective of their location in an elegant restaurant or a fast-food outlet, are more elaborate than the structures which frame them. The repertoire of behaviours which become associated with food are thus conducive to the development of novel social practices. Barthes (1982) has eloquently demonstrated this in his analysis of the Asian restaurant as a vehicle for crossing cultural divides. Europeans find Asian cuisine appealing because it allows them to experience the exoticism of the 'Orient' without actual contact with the culture. The Asian restaurant is popular because of the Occidental's imaginary fear of contamination. Eating the Orient through its 'foreign' but Westernized foods can be a flight from the everyday as well as the purchase of entertainment that is safe, sanitized and contained. The Asian restaurant, like the fast-food outlet, paradoxically amplifies the postmodern ethical confusion of contemporary life by allowing the pursuit of the new, exciting and interesting to be followed in a thoroughly mediated way. These circumscribed experiences contain the challenge of the exotic and naturalize the coerciveness of the new while simultaneously allowing the individual to feel socially adventuresome. In short, the practices circulating around food have the capacity to both reinforce and rupture conventions. Yet Ritzer focuses more on the formal structures of a restaurant, making them seem, particularly in the instance of the McDonald's outlet, much more coercive and limiting than they need be.

Ritzer describes how individuals are herded through the restaurant with little opportunity to diverge from a set pattern. Such a regimen, he argues, produces pseudo-interactions (1993: 85, 134) and a world without surprises (1993: 85, 96). In contrast, other scholars of food rituals, such as Douglas (1972: 61–81) and Elias (1978), do not find them always restrictive, and recognize that a great deal takes place despite the regulatory patterns which surround a meal. For Elias, in particular, this provides the circumstances necessary for the origination of new forms of social conduct. When codes are violated and opposed, when conventions cannot contain the eruptions of conflict and misadventure, then new modes of sociality are invented. The diverse interests surrounding a meal such as the ethical training of the young, the negotiation of obligations in the gift exchange between a provider and receiver, the satisfaction of bodily appetites, the offering of hospitality, the enjoyment of play and physical intimacy, all provide sites for innovations in social practices. So when we choose to eat in the public domain, even when we do so at the popular fast-food outlet, there are still pleasures in the practice which are highly personal, that are capable of expressing our own particularities, as well as advancing, to use Elias's term, the civilizing process.

However, it is still the case that all restaurants – whether they are spectacular tourist attractions, elegant bistros or franchised outlets – are in the business of creating atmosphere and in this way influencing, even controlling, the conduct of their patrons. This is part of the theatricality of eating out and it begins before one enters the door, with the advertising and social meanings that precede the event. These prescriptions, however, do not always succeed in containing the event; the sharing of food is a generative and volatile social moment, capable of re-enacting the social repertoire but also igniting new social experiments. It is this latter point which Ritzer seems to overlook too readily, even though he recognizes, at odd moments, the capacity for McDonald's to be recruited to other interests (see 1993: 109).

The Pursuit of Pleasure

It is axiomatic that in the late modern period Western individuals have come to expect to experience pleasure on a daily basis. The entertainment and recreation industries of the twentieth century are implicated in the manufacture of such feelings, and the restaurant, as part of those industries, is also in the business of cultivating values, constructing appetites and marketing desires. The entertainment industries promote certain practices as embodiments of subjectivity with the ultimate aim of substituting idiosyncratic pleasures with those capable of being commodified. The statistics demonstrating the popularity of these practices seem to prove their success. Ritzer uses them and the global network of McDonald's, with its collective claim to having sold over 96 billion hamburgers, as evidence of the influence mass entertainments exert on individual behaviour and taste. Even though the presence of McDonald's on the world's major continents is an instance of remarkable economic and cultural penetration, it is not a sufficient basis to make the next claim, as Ritzer does, that the ubiquity of these mass entertainments heralds the end of the autonomous subject.

Part of the global success of McDonald's, KFC, Pizza Hut and other chain restaurants has been their emphasis on social pleasures rather than culinary ones. Their advertising concentrates on atmosphere, service and the uniform standard of the experience. The McDonald's Golden Arches have themselves become eloquent cultural icons which not only physically locate the outlet but iconically summarize the McDonald's promise – to provide a sense of security and inclusiveness, and to be included in the McDonald's family. None the less, it is consonant with Ritzer's argument that the ritualization of food presentation and consumption, which makes it into a symbolic and meaningful event, has been significantly altered by the popularity of the fast-food outlet. The ritual exchanges taking place around fast-foods have produced novel social practices which, on the face of it, seem antithetical to Enlightenment ideals. It does not take long to eat a hamburger and french fries, drink a coke and wolf a pastry. Ritzer tells us that most McDonald's diners are out of the restaurant (and the restaurant personnel ensure this is so) in well under 20 minutes (1993: 109).

However, these trends are not the full story. Other constructions of the meaning of the fast-food outlet exist which gloss Ritzer's position – they do not necessarily oppose it – and in so doing provide further ways of interpreting the McDonald's experience. For instance, the McDonald's Golden Arches have been parodically coded into iconic lips and buttocks, thereby sexualizing in unanticipated ways the well-publicized invitation to join the McDonald's family. The food products, too, address other, more submerged interests. Ritzer's description of the food presentation at McDonald's gives an example of how the modern mythology privileging affluence and abundance is imbricated in the junk food experience. The french fries, for example, are arranged to appear as if they were bulging from the container, and the beef patty is always larger than the bun, making it appear as if the hamburger were too big to be contained. Such tricks on the eye have been noted elsewhere by Umberto Eco as part of popular American culture. Eco describes this in his travels into hyperreality (1986: 8) as a bargain mentality endemic to late capitalism. It is a pervasive cultural value expressed through mass advertising which always promises 'more' in the sense of a bonus, something extra. As Eco describes:

> The announcer doesn't say, for example, 'The program will continue' but rather that there is 'More to come.' In America you don't say, 'Give me another coffee'; you ask for 'More coffee'; you don't say that cigarette A is longer than cigarette B, but that there's 'more' of it, more than you're used to having, more than you might want, leaving a surplus to throw away – that's prosperity. (1986: 8)

The restaurant is a ubiquitous example of the new pleasures associated with abundance, prosperity and wastage. As Eco goes on to describe:

> It is hard to eat those dishes that many classy American restaurants, all darkness and wood paneling, dotted with soft red lights and invaded by nonstop music, offer the customer as evidence of his own situation of 'affluence': steaks four inches thick with lobster (and baked potato, and sour cream and melted butter, and grilled tomato and horseradish sauce) so that the customer will have 'more and more', and can wish nothing further. (1986: 23)

Modern Sensibilities

Are these examples of consumers being persuaded by advertising and mass culture evidence enough to conclude, as Ritzer does, that the ideals of Western humanism are at risk? Even if we accept the theoretical pro-position that the constitution of subjectivity is inextricably linked with social structures, is the prevalence of McDonaldization as described by Ritzer sufficient evidence of the contemporary failure of the autonomous self? Ritzer's assumptions about Western subjectivity and individuality can be theoretically pedigreed, thereby strengthening his position. For example, the early twentieth-century American social philosopher Charles Horton

Cooley and the contemporary continental philosopher Agnes Heller each express similar positions. When Cooley (1902: 36) stated that 'a separate individual is an abstraction unknown to experience, and so likewise is society when regarded as something apart from individuals', he was arguing that neither society nor the individual can be fully separated from one another. What is privately and emotionally valued by individuals is simultaneously an aspect of the everyday realm of public activities. More recently, Agnes Heller (1982: 20) has pointed out that the individual's consciousness of the general, of how s/he thinks society works, can be seen in the particular, in how s/he conducts the affairs of the everyday. Like Cooley, Heller shows that the individual's sense of the totality of reality, of understanding how society works, is implicitly expressed through the ordinary routines of the everyday. On this basis, eating at McDonald's can be taken as an illustration of how characteristics of historical and economic structures enter human imagination and play a significant role in the manufacture of those nuances of behaviour which are conventionally described as private, personal and idiosyncratic. But even having assented to this mutuality, it is not the same as assuming, as Ritzer does, that social rituals and human subjectivity are fully homologous.

Certainly, the popularity of fast-foods has implications beyond the monetary and dietary. It influences the social practices of engagement which accompany the quick consumption of a canned drink, a hamburger or a frozen dinner. Furthermore, it seems reasonable to assume that the increased appetite for fast-foods has shifted attention away from the more traditional rituals surrounding food-sharing – those which value culinary knowledge and table talk. However, to take the next step, as Ritzer does, and claim that the McDonald's experience negatively inflects human interaction is a slippage which is difficult to endorse.

Kundera (1996) tells us in his meditation on time and memory that a slow meal can be memorable, a fast one forgettable. As fast and convenience foods are one of the most rapidly expanding segments of the consumer market, Ritzer finds it appropriate to ask whether our preference for fast, forgettable meals is indicative of a more serious moral crisis such as that also alluded to by Kundera. Ritzer is concerned with the social consequences which follow from the increasing circulation of cultural practices which appear to embody dehumanizing aspects of the modernist project. However, in his analysis, where he places great significance on the social valuation of speed and efficiency, calculability and predictability, he is distracted from recognizing other social innovations which resist the tendency toward dehumanization.

Although fast-foods seem relatively new, they are not. The cities of medieval Europe provided fast-foods hundreds of years before KFC, Pizza Hut and McDonald's, and without the deleterious effects Ritzer describes. The progenitor of the fast-food outlet can arguably be traced to the seventeenth-century British coffeehouse, which played an important part in redefining the social character of the public domain. These coffeehouses were venues for more than the dispensing of coffee, tea and tobacco. They also traded in news about shipping, cargo arrivals, public events and government proceedings. They became sites of journalistic discourse and political intrigue. They were places where individual men of different social classes could freely mingle and cross class barriers. Coffeehouses were the site where particular interpersonal practices and cultural manners associated with the modern era were formulated. Coffeehouses acted as a social stage where novel styles of conversational exchange took place. Here, men (women were not commonly present) learned to talk across class and occupation. They learned the manners of conversation with the stranger; they constructed new rules for conducting oneself under the surveillance of an anonymous public gaze (Sennett, 1976). Such opportunities have been important in the history of manners and social life, and, to some extent, the modern restaurant still provides this. The suburban café, street-corner food outlet and some franchise restaurants still function in this capacity as sites for social cross-over. Although Ritzer points out that the social exchanges in a McDonald's are so highly structured that they prevent spontaneous ruptures (1993: 85, 134), none the less, the propensity to remake these sites to meet local interests (such as a gay beat, a teenage street haven; see Ritzer, 1993: 109), means that the new forms of sociality are not always prevented or constrained.[1] In this sense, the casual restaurant retains some commonalities with its coffeehouse progenitor in so far as it is a site where innovations in sociality can take place.

Conclusion

The fast-food industries, like the entertainment industries, are highly technologized and efficient. And like other successful flow industries such as cigarettes and alcohol, they are highly rationalized factory systems following the same principles of continuity, uniformity and standardization. The success of these industries to create markets, manufacture tastes and appetites, and control consumer spending, provokes Ritzer's concern that their social impact is too pervasive. McDonald's is an ambiguous product of modernity. It is both a debased application of technical virtuosity and a successful application of Taylorist principles. As an economic structure it has realized the logic of industrialism, making a product efficiently and profitably, while at the social level, it lends credence to Weber's prediction of a modern existence in an iron cage.

Ritzer has made a persuasive case that industrialism, Taylorism and McDonaldization are sources of diminished human happiness in the latter half of the twentieth century. The renovations of the workplace which have made it safer and more efficient have simultaneously disturbed and dehumanized the individual's relationship to meaningful work. These same alienating forces have entered the everyday world, making vacations, shopping expeditions and entertainments also equally unrewarding (Ritzer,

1993: 121–44). The advent of fast-foods has adversely influenced the topography of society: at the street level, suburbs are more homogeneous with their food alleys, billboard and neon advertising and franchised minimarts. Fast-foods, too, have altered urban eating habits. Grazing, or all-day snacking, means individuals eat constantly, and often highly processed foods without much nutritional value. The physical appearance of foodstuffs has altered: snack and fast-foods in contrast to fresh foods are highly packaged, creating more surface space for the printing of advertising hyperbole. The industrialization of food may have the benefit of releasing women from the shopping and preparation of formal and longer-lasting meals, but it also eliminates a traditional ritual through which individuals have frequently been schooled in social skills. From Ritzer's perspective, this decline in popularity of the long, family meal is a lost opportunity for imparting social capital to the young.

With these and other reasons, Ritzer can make a strong case. The popularity and success of McDonald's means that it is deeply inserted into the practices of everyday life (Ritzer, 1993: 8). This is not confined to the West, but is now almost universal. The ubiquity of McDonald's across diverse national and cultural contexts emulates other transnational products such as Coca-Cola and Marlboro cigarettes. Like them, McDonald's has become a feature of a universalizing cultural landscape. McDonald's has the added distinction of entering the vernacular as a joke (Ritzer, 1993: 4). Its name is constantly parodied – soft or pseudo-news headlines are called News McNuggets, ecological disasters related to corporate greed are instances of McDamage, and social homogenization is described as McBlah. This capacity for self-irony, even if it has a history of litigation (McLibel cases), underscores the cultural impact of this industrial giant (*Age*, 1996). The name, logo, product and idea of McDonald's seems all-pervasive.

At some level, though, the popularity and lampooning of McDonald's makes Ritzer's analysis counter-intuitive. He suggests that despite the popularity and levity, the McDonald's experience is an unhappy and dehumanizing one (1993: 9). To support this claim, Ritzer must assume that most consumers of mass entertainment fail to recognize the misalignment of the actual with the hyperbolic. It seems to Ritzer that it is harder now than ever before to discern the disjunction between the promise and the realization. He accounts for this widespread failure of recognition by describing how the routines of the bureaucratized, rationalized and industrialized society have schooled us in passivity and deadened our critical faculties. From this position, it becomes clearer that Ritzer's commentary on the McDonaldization of society is also a lament on modernity and industrialism.

Ritzer has presumably employed McDonald's as his prime example not only because of its economic success and ubiquity, but because it has also become synonymous with the mythology of Western culture and the global spread of Americanicity (1993: 4, 5). The cultural penetration and economic success of McDonald's has challenged local diversities. In order to construct universal desires for mass products there has had to be a McDonaldization of tastes. In part, this has been advanced by the universalization of an array of products, logos and images. Jeans, for instance, are no-longer non-specific dungarees but are Levis or Giordano, T-shirts are DKNY or Mossimo, hamburgers are Big Macs, drinks are Pepsis. These vibrant, penetrating images influence everyday speech and the manner in which goods are valued and identified. At the same time, this universalizing dimension of social knowledge has produced a discourse in brand name commodities that straddles national and language barriers and cuts across cultural differences.

Ritzer's work on McDonaldization indicates some of the dangers that this universalizing discourse presents to modern, urban life. The declaratory mantras – 'Coke Is It', 'Coca-Cola Forever', 'It's McTime', 'Great Time', 'Great Taste McDonald's', 'Take it to the Max', 'Just Do It' – may be recognizable on a global level but they are also utterly meaningless. An unintended benefit of this discourse, from which Ritzer could derive some comfort, is the heightening of our understanding that we live in a semiotic universe. The ubiquity of messages such as *Have a nice day* has now been satirized enough to teach us to recognize and resist the fatuous and empty social exchange. Thus it is possible to see in these self-parodies the possibility of resistance, but Ritzer is too focused on the emphasis given to efficiency, predictability, calculability and control to see it. Similarly, he is reluctant to see how the history and anthropology of food rituals provide myriad examples where resistance to the engineering of tastes and social values takes place. Ironically, Ritzer's primary example of fast-foods has a long history of social innovation yet Ritzer has overlooked this in order to emphasize how the industrialization of food, through McDonaldization, functions most effectively to globalize and homogenize cultural practices. Ritzer's privileging of technology, as if it cauterized human will and judgement, activates a bleak Orwellian future, which is an unconvincing conclusion, especially so given that the primary example of food ritual-ization has been such a rich historical source of much human innovation.

Note

1 In most urban areas, convenience stores and fast-food outlets have been colonized by the least valued members of society – the aged homeless, estranged teenagers, drug addicts, night-lifers and low-life inner-city inverts. These outlets, which are open all hours, provide a warm shelter in winter, and a cool one in summer. They are places where street people and the socially isolated can find sanctuary, and they provide office space for transactions they do not ideologically support such as illegal dealings of various kinds. In the cinema, they are popular back-drops for scenes of urban violence. Even the image of the benign clown, Ronald McDonald, has been recuperated into a frightening figure of violence and mayhem in mainstream horror movies.

References

Age, The paper (1996) 'Big Mc fries an opponent', 25 August.

Barthes, R. (1982) *Empire of Signs*. New York: Farrar, Straus & Giroux.

Brillat-Savarin, J.A. (1970) *The Physiology of Taste: Meditations on Transcendental Gastronomy*, trans. H. Knapik. New York: Liveright. (1825)

Cooley, C.H. (1902) *Human Relations and the Social Order*. Chicago: University of Chicago Press.

Douglas, M. (1972) 'Deciphering a meal', *Daedalus*, 101 (1): 61–81.

Eco, U. (1986) *Faith in Fakes*. London: Secker & Warburg.

Elias, N. (1978) *The Civilizing Process*. New York: Urizen.

Goody, J. (1982) *Cooking, Cuisine and Class*. Cambridge: Cambridge University Press.

Heller, A. (1982) *A Theory of History*. London: Routledge & Kegan Paul.

Hodgson, M. (1982) 'Ambiance of eating: what is its role?' *The New York Times*, 3 February.

Kundera, M. (1996) *Slowness*. New York: HarperCollins.

Latham, J. (1972) *The Pleasure of Your Company: A History of Manners and Meals*. London: Adam & Charles Black.

Lévi-Strauss, C. (1978) *The Origin of Table Manners*. New York: Harper & Row.

Papson, S. (1986) 'From symbolic exchange to bureaucratic discourse: the Hallmark greeting card', *Theory, Culture & Society*, 3 (2): 99–111.

Ritzer, G. (1993) *The McDonaldization of Society: An Investigation into the Changing Character of Contemporary Social Life*. Thousand Oaks, CA: Pine Forge Press.

Sargent, S. (1985) *The Foodmakers*. Ringwood, VIC: Penguin.

Sennett, R. (1976) *The Fall of Public Man*. Cambridge: Cambridge University Press.

Vattimo, G. (1992) *The Transparent Society*. Oxford: Polity.

6 McCitizens:

Risk, Coolness and Irony in Contemporary
Politics

Bryan S. Turner

This chapter compares and contrasts two visions of modern society by
Ulrich Beck and George Ritzer, both of whom are profoundly influenced
by Max Weber's theory of rationalization. Beck and Ritzer are both concerned with the impact of scientific rationality on social organization, but
they come to ostensively different conclusions, despite the common intellectual origins of their perspective on modernity. Furthermore, I consider
McDonaldization as a form of coolness in social relations which provides a
model for modern citizenship, or at least global McCitizenship, and explore
irony as a mode of social interaction in McDonaldized societies. The
chapter concludes that Richard Rorty's postmodern defence of ironic
lifestyles is an ethic (in the Weberian sense) which is highly compatible
with McDonaldization. My mode of analysis is itself, of course, ironic.

The Sociology of Risk and Regulation

In this chapter I examine the standardization of political involvement as a
form of McDonaldization and analyse the relationships between markets
and citizenship. Whereas markets are associated with instability and
scarcity, citizenship provides a basis for solidarity in modern societies
where the religious order has been weakened as a consequence of secularization. Markets do not necessarily respond to the instabilities and vagaries
of life; markets are essentially concerned with the distribution of resources
between competitive social groups and individual actors. It is for this
reason that capitalism as a whole is often regarded as a highly unstable and
precarious social system. In classical sociology the analysis of capitalism
can in fact be examined along two rather contrasted dimensions, namely
between market risks and rational regulation. Karl Marx, for example, saw
capitalism as a highly unstable social system, not only subject to the
endless booms and slumps of the marketplace, but also prone to revolutionary transformation as a consequence of the endless struggle between
social classes. In fact Marx treated capitalism as an orgy of social change,

subject to constant revolutions of production, the uninterrupted disturbance of all social relationships, and in economic terms prone to endless uncertainty and agitation. Indeed Marx argued that 'all that is solid melts into air, all that is holy is profaned, and men at last are forced to face with sober senses the real conditions of their lives and their relations with their fellow men'. Marx's account of capitalist instability in 'The Communist Manifesto' (Marx and Engels, 1968) in 1848 is the classic statement of the experience of modernity, particularly the sense of personal insecurity and cultural demolition associated with urbanization and secularity (Berman, 1982).

A very different picture of capitalism emerged in the writings of Max Weber, particularly in *The Protestant Ethic and the Spirit of Capitalism* (Weber, 1930). For Weber, the principal experience of capitalist modernity was a process of rationalization in which the principles of ascetic discipline and scientific regulation were imposed upon the everyday world through a process of increasing bureaucratic constraint and state regulation. Weber was particularly impressed by the loss of individuality following from the ineluctable effects of bureaucratization and rationalization. Whereas Marx viewed capitalism in terms of a series of metaphors of organic change and turbulence, Weber pictured capitalism as an iron cage in which everything is subject to exact calculation. Capitalist economic relations required a predictable and secure administrative and political environment in which to operate. Legal regulations had to be dependable and clear, and thus alongside the rationalization of means of production, there was a clear growth in administrative and legal rationality. The consequences of this administrative iron cage were for the individuals significant because

> the capitalist economy of the present day is an immense cosmos into which the individual is born, and which presents itself to him, at least as an individual, as an unalterable order of things in which he must live. It forces the individual, insofar as he's involved in the system of market relations, to conform to capitalist rules of action. (Weber, 1930: 54)

There was a brief period in Weber's life when, through the influence of the von Richthofen sisters, he became interested in the communitarian sexual experiments of Otto Gross at Ascona, which he saw as a counter-cultural alternative to the negative consequences of an ascetic lifestyle. In the end, Weber rejected 'Freudianism' because he saw no alternative to the strict regulation of the individual which was imposed by the rationalized life conditions of the capitalist economy, but he remained ambiguous about the consequences of rationalization for the spiritual life of individuals.

In Marx and Weber, we have two contrasted views of capitalism, one emphasizing the importance of risk and change, and the other focused on the significance of regulation, rationalization and routine. These two pictures of capitalism have in fact continued to influence the metaphors by which social theorists have conceptualized capitalist relations. It is interesting that the radical thinkers of the Frankfurt School followed Weber in their description of advanced capitalism as an administered society in which critical thinking had been contained by the administrative regime imposed by instrumental rationalism. In a similar fashion, with his emphasis on discipline, restraint and control, Michel Foucault has created an image of advanced capitalism as a huge panopticon within which the individual is fully exposed to the gaze of centralized surveillance. Following the penology of Bentham, Foucault has imagined contemporary society as a vast carceral organization which is minutely controlled. The disciplinary order of Western society has moved from the scaffold to the detailed administration of a rational system organized by panopticism (Foucault, 1977). These images of discipline and order have been influential in sociology, despite the fact that we have in the last decade experienced a major deregulation of society as a consequence of a new emphasis on markets and administrative devolution. Despite the uncertainties of the macro-economic environment, many sociologists have persisted with the image of society as an iron cage, as the administered society or as the panopticon.

In contemporary sociological theory in recent years these contrasted images of order and disorder have been perfectly illustrated by two competing perspectives on risk and regulation which are presented in two influential books, namely Ulrich Beck's *Risk Society* (1992), which was originally published in Germany in 1986, and George Ritzer's *The McDonaldization of Society* (Ritzer, 1993). These two publications perfectly encapsulate the contradictions between risk and regulation as perspectives on modern social relations, and an examination of these two studies provides a useful context within which to think about the problems of citizenship in the late twentieth century.

Risk Society and Individualization Theory

For Beck, risk is an inevitable and necessary outcome of the very process of modernization, which has given a centrality to science in everyday relationships. Risk society is in fact the radicalization of modernity itself, leading to a new stage of reflective modernization. If primary modernization involves the rationalization of tradition, reflective modernization means 'the rationalization of rationalization' (Beck, 1992: 183). Risk has, however, changed significantly over time. In traditional societies, risk was individual, palpable, localized and hierarchical. Individuals were obviously concerned to control risk through various patterns of individual security and insurance. In an advanced industrial civilization, risk is now collective, invisible, ubiquitous, democratic and uninsurable. With the growth of reflective modernization, risk becomes systemic and involves the distribution of 'bads'; conventional economics by contrast is concerned with the distribution of goods through market exchange. For Beck, the most useful illustration of this modernization of risk is the growth of environmental pollution and hazard. Environmental pollution is democratic, because it influences all social groups regardless of their class of origin and these risks are collective and invisible, because they influence all aspects of modern life, but they are not necessarily observable or palpable. These risks create a new type of community in which solidarity is based upon insecurity and anxiety rather than confidence and mutual dependency. Our anxiety about the environment brings us into new sets of social relations which are structured around these individual patterns of anxiety.

Risk society requires a new type of politics and brings new forms of experts into the public arena and into public debate. A society based upon analysis of risk places a particular importance on intellectuals and experts in the conduct of rational debate in the public sphere. In claiming that environmental hazard and disaster have produced a new form of risk, Beck may not be arguing a particularly original thesis but simply expressing the political concerns of various aspects of the green movement in Germany. However, Beck's argument may be more important if we realize that he is claiming that the risks of contemporary society are in fact the unintended but inevitable outcomes of the process of modernization itself, and in particular they are the product of the scientific organization of society and culture. The consequences include a major politicization of science and scientific debate, because science and scientific bureaucracies attempt to obscure or deny the fundamental character of environmental and scientific risks by developing the apparently neutral notion of 'acceptable' levels of risk. It is the application of instrumental rationalism in the form of modern science to the production of social wealth and the management of the environment which is itself the core of the risk society, because the unintended consequences of this rationality are to destabilize human societies, or at least to open them up to the overwhelming threat of global hazard. Public relations is a fundamental feature of risk society, because it represents an attempt to bring about a stable political environment through the creation of rational communications management strategies. As risks multiply in the political environment of major corporations, risk management through public relations institutions becomes a basic tool of crisis management (L'Etang and Pieczka, 1996).

Beck illustrates his argument through a number of examples, but his commentary on medical science is central to his general thesis (1992: 205–14). Medical practice is protected from public scrutiny by the development of the clinic, and this clinical institution provides an organizational roof where medical research training and practice can be securely interrelated. It is within this professional context that medicine operates in what Beck calls an arena of sub-politics, that is, medicine can bypass the formal political institutions (partisan parliaments) to develop its own professional power base. Medicine within the experimental laboratory operates beyond the regulation of law and the state. Furthermore given the speed of medical innovation and invention, the general public is typically presented with the results of the problems of medical innovation long after they are relatively well established within the experimental setting. Beck refers to this 'as a policy of fait accompli' (1992: 210). The negative consequences of these developments include thalidomide babies, 'mad cow disease' (BSE) and Creutzfeldt–Jakob disease (CJD).

To this analysis of science and modernization, Beck adds the notion of reflexivity. In Beck's work, reflexivity is associated with the process of detraditionalization whereby individuals and social groups become more self-critically aware of their own social circumstances. The notion of reflexivity includes the idea of self-reflexive rational scrutiny and self-reflexive critical inspection. Reflexivity involves a constant critical discussion of the circumstances of modernity at both the personal and institutional level. To some extent, Beck's position follows that of Weber in placing rationalization at the centre of the modernization process, which involves the application of critical scientific knowledge to everyday social reality. Again in an argument which relates to Weber's notion of personality, risk society is also associated with a new form of individualism in which the self becomes an endless process of self-evaluation and reflection. It is, however, somewhat misleading to place the burden of this notion of reflexivity at the individual or subjective level. Beck's concept of modern risk is based upon the notion that modernization brings with it a multiplication of the difficulties, problems and contradictions which engulf modern institutions, and as a result social institutions become reflexive in the sense that the complexity of the problems which they face compels them to enter into a process of collective or institutional self-evaluation and relegitimization. Modernization involves the multiplication of the contradictions within which institutions are forced to operate. These processes of problematization and contradiction are analysed by Beck as a process of detraditionalization. He argues that 'the process of individualization is conceptualized theoretically as the product of reflexivity, in which the process of modernization as protected by the welfare state detraditionalizes the ways of living built into industrial society' (Beck 1992: 153).

There are a number of important criticisms which can be lodged against Beck's argument. Interestingly enough, Beck fails to provide a systematic or precise definition of risk. He often defines it by reference to a specific example such as Chernobyl or by reference to processes such as the medicalization of modern life. Alternatively he defines it by contrast to some other related process or case such as the contrast between 'risk' and 'threat' (Beck, 1995: 25; Japp, 1996). The failure to provide a systematic definition of risk is not necessarily a profound weakness in his argument, but he must attempt to distinguish more clearly between risk and environmental threats, technological risk, environmental hazard, and the unpredictable outcomes of the process of modernization and social change. His failure to present a systematic definition is related to the fact that he wants to make a clear distinction between traditional societies, where risk is palpable, individual and localized, modern society, where the radicalization of modernity is incomplete, and risk society, where the radical impetus of science and technology is fully realized. That is, he wants to present a model of history as a process through a number of stages from traditional society, to industrial society and finally to risk society, which is characterized by reflexive modernization. His reluctance to present a clear definition of risk is therefore not perceived because he offers an implicit definition of risk through the analysis of a particular historical process. However, the failure to provide a definition of risk is curious in combination with the fact that Beck fails to analyse the intellectual background to modern theories of risk in economic theory and anthropology.

We also need to ask whether this perspective is an adequate historical paradigm, that is, whether it presents an adequate account of risk. It is possible to think of some risks in traditional society which look strikingly modern and which have the characteristics which Beck associates with risk in the conditions of reflexive modernization. For example, the history of epidemics would illustrate many of the points presented by Beck with respect to modern risks. The epidemics of syphilis and bubonic plague in early modern society also produced risks which were impersonal and democratic in the sense that they had devastating consequences for populations at large. Peasants and aristocracy died in considerable numbers as a result of the bubonic plague. The bacterial diseases of the middle ages and the ancient world were also carried by parasites which were distributed globally as a result of the expansion of world trade. These viruses could not be detected by simple observation and they were individual or localized but global in their consequences. The idea of trans-oceanic disease exchanges between 1500 and 1700 is a fundamental idea of the historical epidemiology of human civilizations in contemporary demography. In medieval society these devastating epidemics also had a profound impact on how traditional people thought about life, death and God. In short, these diseases brought about a reflexivity which was fundamental to the ideological development of these societies. For example, there was a profound fascination with death which was expressed through new religious and artistic developments such as the *danse macabre*. With the spread of colonialism, it is also evident that many aboriginal native peoples in North America, South America and Australia were devastated or destroyed by the environmental and political catastrophes which were brought about by the globalization of imperial relationships.

One might say, in defence of Beck's attempt to differentiate between traditional and modern risk, that in traditional societies risks were somewhat random rather than systematic. Risk, for Beck, is a *systemic* feature of modernization not an unanticipated and random outcome of social change. Nevertheless these historical doubts about Beck's account lead me to suggest that we need to distinguish between two types of risk, and that Beck's failure to provide a definition lies at the root of his somewhat undifferentiated approach to the nature of risks. I shall call techno-environmental risks 'type one risks'. In fact most of Beck's illustrations are to do with ecological politics. They involve industrial pollution of the environment, industrial hazards and technological disasters. Beck feels that sociology has a special duty to address green issues because in Germany these issues are seen by the general population to be fundamental to modern politics. His recent work (Beck, 1995) is indeed primarily about the relationship between ecological crisis, political debate and the role of sociology as a critical discipline.

We need to distinguish these type one risks, which are basically about hazard, from type two risks, which we can describe as 'socio-cultural risks'. Of course, Beck wants to extend the idea of hazard more broadly to the analysis of social-cultural economic risks. However, he attempts to analyse political risk and cultural risk within the same paradigm or framework as type one (environmental) risks. Now the concept of social risk (such as uncertainty) has been fundamental to economic theory since the foundations of capitalism, with the development of international trade risks and investment risks. The notion of risk, uncertainty and danger has also been extensively explored by anthropologists in their work on taboo, pollution and magic (Douglas, 1966). The anthropological study of magic suggests that magical practices and beliefs are present in social circumstances where risk and uncertainty are maximized and the outcomes of social action are not clearly understood by social actors. Magical practices in response to risk decline as social circumstances become more predictable and understandable. One minor criticism of Beck is that his theory has neglected, for example, the work of Mary Douglas and the history of economic theory in relation to risk and uncertainty.

Beck in fact covers the idea of social risk (type two risks) in his work on so-called 'individualization theory' (Beck, 1994). Individualization theory was concerned to defend six basic ideas or theses about the nature of reflexive modernization, risk society and detraditionalization. First, the argument was that class, culture and consciousness in capitalist society had been both detraditionalized and individualized, producing a society which is described as capitalism without classes, but with a continuity of individualized forms of social inequality and their related problems. Thus inequality has become individualized and is no longer collective. A second and related argument was that the labour market had become flexible, fragmented and uncertain. Notions of class community and political struggle could no longer adequately address a society in which large sections of youth population might never experience work. Thus individualization theory is part of a broader argument which suggests that class analysis in its strong form is obsolete and redundant (Lee and Turner, 1996). His third thesis was that there has been a significant decline in status and class characteristics, which again have become increasingly individualized, and that new forms of poverty through the feminization of poverty have significantly changed the traditional nature of status and class positions. Fourth, with the decline of these traditional structures the individual becomes the basic unit of the social in the life-world (Beck, 1994). In short, in reflexive modernity, the self becomes a project. His fifth thesis is that individualization and standardization are ironically and paradoxically merely two sides of the same coin. There has been a profound detradition-alization of individuals, who become dependent as a result on social arrangements that provide regulation and control of the life-world. The result is that there is the emergence of new and special forms of social control which address the individualization of social issues and social problems. Finally we should understand individualization as a contra-dictory process of 'societalization'.

Beck's approach to the individualization theory debate has stimulated important research on the fragmentation and diversity of the life course from youth to old age. The German debate is interesting because it proposes a new notion of individuality and the end of the individual. Beck's idea is that the instabilities of the marketplace, the fragmentation of employment and the growth of significant unemployment have all con-tributed to transformation and erosion of traditional family practices and institutions, because the traditional life course or life career can no longer be sustained. There is no longer a set pattern to the life career, and domestic and personal arrangements are segmented, fragmented and diversified. It is no longer possible to assume or to expect a single career for the duration of the life course and professional people within the middle classes may in fact constantly re-educate themselves throughout their life careers in order to take up multiple positions in the labour market. At the same time large sections of society will be unable to find any employment during their life course and will be permanently excluded from the conventional or respected positions in the social structure.

Social changes in sexual practices, marriage arrangements and household patterns involve a radical change of the nuclear family, which was the dominant form in the industrial revolution. This change is manifest in the diversity of household arrangements in modern society, including childless marriages, family communes, unmarried men adopting children and a general pattern of delayed parenthood. Changes in labour markets, flexibilization and casualization of employment, and the erosion of com-pulsory and official retirement have resulted in the disappearance of a fixed and predictable life course. The relation between generations is totally transformed by these life changes and by the diversification of the life course. There is therefore a profound pluralization of the life course which is equivalent to the notion of social risk. As a result, there has been a democratization of previously exclusive lifestyles and opportunities (Beck, 1995).

In assessing Beck's analysis of individualization, we should note critically that he has failed completely to refer to the work of Peter L. Berger and Thomas Luckmann, who in *The Social Construction of Reality* (1967) anticipated much of Beck's argument by noting the importance of the pluralization of the life-world in modern societies, the attendant existential anxiety of individuals, and finally the importance of a sacred canopy to counter the risk and uncertainty of such fragmentation of the life-world. While Berger and Luckmann concentrated extensively on the notion of pluralization, and its relationship to culture, Beck has in fact very little to say about culture in his analysis of risk society. His views on cultural democratization in the levelling of lifestyle opportunities run counter to many of the arguments presented, for example, by Pierre Bourdieu in his work on distinction (1984). Bourdieu's work suggests that lifestyles have not become individuated and diversified but rather that they correspond closely to the structure of inequality in modern societies. In summary, in Beck's sociology individualization theory is a substitute for a genuine theory of social risk, because he is primarily concerned to discuss ecological risks under the label of risk society (which I have referred to as type one risks). Beck has failed to provide a systematic definition of risk which would differentiate between the idea of environmental hazard, on the one hand, and social uncertainty, on the other. While Chernobyl and Bhopal are perfect examples of risk society in terms of type one risks, we could argue that the pluralization of the life-world and the individualization of social structures and experiences are good illustrations of type two or socio-cultural risks. In short, not all risks involve technological or environmental questions, but clearly type two risks are indeed very closely associated with the whole process of modernization.

We can regard Beck's sociology of risk as a sociological response to the deregulation of contemporary society which has followed from the liberalization of international finance markets, a new emphasis on accountability from the perspective of economic rationalism and a growth in the consumerization of society. Alongside the growth of social risk, however, there are other processes of standardization and rationalizaton such as the computerization of office work and the de-skilling of the working class.

McDonaldization and Rationalization

An alternative theory of modern society, based on Weber's rationalization thesis, is presented in George Ritzer's analysis of the McDonaldization of society (Ritzer, 1993). For Ritzer, Weber's rationalization thesis that society is standardized and normalized by the processes of scientific reasoning and their application to all spheres of life provides a valid interpretation of the general culture and structure of modern society. McDonaldization is defined by Ritzer (1993: 9–10) in terms of four dimensions: efficiency, calculability, predictability and control (through the substitution of non-human for human technology). These dimensions in fact constitute what Weber intended by the notion of 'formal rationality'.

As an operational definition, McDonaldization produces a society in which there are no surprises, that is, there are no type two risks, or at least these risks are contained by processes of quality control to ensure standard outcomes. The fast-food industry is a prime example of the application of Taylorism and Fordism to modern society and the everyday world. The fast-food industry produces food which is cheap, reliable, standardized and global in a social environment (the fast-food restaurant setting) which is wholly predictable. The Big M (Golden Arches) around the world confirms the belief that one is about to enter a well-known, predictable, riskless eating experience. McDonaldization involves a focus on detail in order to produce a simple and predictable eating context where all forms of uncertainty (surprises) have been eliminated by bureaucratization. Of course the principles of McDonaldization have been extended to many areas of social life. There is a process of McDonaldization in the medical arena where McDoctor involves a drive-in simple and cheap form of medication. There is also McNews whereby information is simplified into digestible chunks which can be consumed by an audience without effort and again without surprise. In principle the process of McDonaldization can be applied to any area of social existence because the underlying principle of McDonaldization is in fact rational bureaucratization. In his recent work on banking, Ritzer (1995: 134) argues that the credit card rationalized (that is, McDonaldized) the consumer loan business.

What, however, is the relationship between the theory of risk society and the McDonaldization of society? On the surface, these two processes of increasing risk and uncertainty, on the one and, and increasing rationalization and McDonaldization, on the other, appear to be entirely contradictory. They appear to indicate entirely different processes in modern society, pointing towards radically alternative futures. In response to the thesis of McDonaldization, one could argue that McDonaldization represents an early stage of modernization prior to the development of risk society with its ethic of self-reflexivity. Specifically, McDonaldization corresponds to Fordism and Taylorism in the period of industrial society, but it does not correspond to reflexive modernization which attempts to cope with increasing cultural diversity, social differentiation, political fragmentation and a more unpredictable economic environment. The process of individualization would require a more flexible and pluralistic food industry to correspond to a stage of capitalism involving reflexive modernization. If this were the case, one would expect that McDonaldization as a set of organizational principles would decline as more reflexive and flexible patterns associated with risk society began to dominate.

An alternative scenario would be that the principles of risk society and McDonaldization would exist simultaneously, not as a premodern stage of rationalization, but at different levels. One might argue that deregulation and uncertainty have been more prevalent at the global and macro level, whereas at the local and micro level processes of discipline, administration and bureaucratization (that is, McDonaldization) have been more common. Risk society in this case is primarily an account of deregulation of the macro economy (type one risks) and its negative cultural consequences (type two risks). The best illustration of these processes have been in finance markets resulting in spectacular economic uncertainty and unpredictability. Macro deregulation has resulted in global uncertainty about economic futures where governments are unable either to predict or to control the external environment of the national economy. By contrast, McDonaldization would refer to micro rationalization of social or economically productive units. For example, while banking units operate in a highly uncertain financial environment, individual banks are highly rational, highly organized and very predictable. In fact one could imagine the McDonaldization of banking occurring in a context of macro risk and uncertainty. With external tellers, banks already have some elements of McDonaldization, involving the concept of the drive-in bank providing a minimal set of functions to a mass audience where services are relatively undifferentiated. In this case risk and McDonaldization would be simultaneous social processes where one would expect uncertainty at the macro level. Ritzer's *Expressing America* (1995) can be read as an account of this standardization of banking services (to provide cheap, efficient and reliable services to customers) in a context of global economic risk. Globalized uncertainties require, at a different level, increasing patterns and mechanisms of control, regulation and surveillance (Turner, 1997: xviii).

Of course one objection to this argument would be that McDonaldization creates an impression of certainty and safety which in reality is not present. McDonald's eating outlets are safe in the limited sense that one is unlikely to get serious food poisoning as a client of McDonald's, but a McDonald's diet, as a lifestyle, would expose one to the possible risks, in the long term, of stomach cancer, type two diabetes and obesity. A diet based almost exclusively on McDonald's products would expose one to the risk of a low-fibre diet with high cholesterol intake, which from a nutritional point of view is not a form of safe eating. These would be significant type one risks, with the added possibility of type two risks (of cultural pollution). Here again risk and rationalization would be closely interconnected, occurring simultaneously and representing two facets of modern society (Vidal, 1997).

We have already seen that Beck derives social and cultural risks (type two risks) from changes in the economy, particularly changes in the labour force and labour market. Casualization and flexibility in employment practices are part of the economic scenario of late modernity, because they offer the employer a more sensitive strategy for coping with rapid changes in the nature of demand for commodities. Employers do not want to be committed in the long term to an inflexible labour force, and casualization offers them opportunities for responding rapidly to changing political and economic circumstances. However, the consequences of casualization, particularly for young people, are negative, because they do not provide for a stable employment career path and they imply instability in lifestyles and life courses. One can argue that extensive McDonaldization also implies a process of de-skilling. In fact the debate over the nature of employment in late capitalism is yet another illustration of the contrasting paradigms of individualization in Beck's sociology and McDonaldization in Ritzer's version of Weber's theory of bureaucratization. Whereas the de-skilling thesis (Braverman, 1974) was associated with Fordism, the theory of flexible specialization (Piore and Sabel, 1984) is associated with post-Fordist labour processes. A Fordist labour market corresponds to a mass production system, whereas flexible specialization is focused on niche markets where production processes are highly differentiated. Labour flexibility is required by a post-Fordist economy in order to allow employers to respond to the systemic uncertainty of an advanced industrial system. The implications of a risk society environment for youth unemployment is therefore pessimistic in the sense that there will be an extensive casualization of blue-collar manual and white-collar employment. The growth of flexible specialization would suggest that Beck's account of the labour market is a more valid analysis and description of current labour market developments, but one can also expect a fairly extensive McDonaldization of the service sector involving a process of de-skilling.

Defining Cultural Risk

In connecting McDonaldization with modern citizenship, I am more concerned with the complex issue of cultural relations and cultural citizenship than with more traditional debates concerning welfare, employment and social citizenship. We need to explore the implications of both Beck and Ritzer's arguments for cultural practices. As we have seen, Beck's theory is more concerned with type one risks, that is, with environmental and technological risks, rather than with social or type two risks. Indeed his argument is that 'the ecological issue focuses at heart on a systematic legalized violation of fundamental civil rights – the citizen's right to life and freedom from bodily harm' (Beck, 1994: 8). The questions posed by Beck and Ritzer are: is modern culture going through a process of standardization (McDonaldization) as a result of cultural democracy, or is contemporary culture, following Beck's argument, becoming more diverse, uncertain, fragmented and consequently more reflexive?

Here again the contrast between Beck and Ritzer is parallel to the debate between modernity and postmodernity. Ritzer's account suggests a process of modernization as standardization where culture becomes a mass culture in a modernist environment, whereas Beck's analysis resembles postmodernism in suggesting a more diversified, complex and reflexive culture where expert opinion becomes highly problematic. Once more, these two processes appear to be working, simultaneously and also at different levels. From the point of view of critical theory, 'the culture industry' has certainly brought about a standardization and McDonaldization of culture where, in order to meet the needs of a mass market, cultural distinction and diversity have been simplified and broken down into acceptable consumer commodities. There has in these terms indeed been an erosion of cultural standards through the process of McDonaldization as a form of inauthentication of culture. The Weberian critique of modern culture implicit in Ritzer's argument would thereby be highly compatible with the writings of, for example, Theodor W. Adorno.

The real issue behind Beck's analysis is whether the theory of risk society can indeed be transferred to the socio-cultural arena, that is, whether type two risks actually exist and whether the language of risk and uncertainty can be used to analyse culture. In the notion of social risk, one would have to include the idea of cultural pollution, commodification of folk society, tourist prostitution in third world societies, and pornography. Of course, these risks have always existed, but the changing nature of risk in late modernity suggests that Internet communication systems would extend social risk to a global level so that modern electronic communication systems which are indeed reflexive would be the main conduit for globalized pornography. Global networks of child pornography would be a useful illustration of the idea of type two risks, because pornography would become globally available as a result of the positive benefits of international communication systems which both facilitate democratization and expose social groups to the threat of cultural contamination. The global Internet also threatens traditional cultures through the individualization of cultural products for a global audience.

Finally, one important difference between Beck and Ritzer can be considered in the context of political action. Whereas Weberian sociology has often been analysed as a pessimistic apolitical form of sociology where the fact–value distinction is often used as an excuse to avoid political involvements, the whole logic of Beck's position is to bring sociologists into political debate and political action, particularly over the issue of ecological disaster and environmental pollution (Lash et al., 1996). Ritzer's sociology does not necessarily lend itself to a protest movement against McDonaldization, because his principal objective is to describe and understand an interesting facet of contemporary bureaucratization. In terms of citizenship studies, Beck's position is designed to facilitate political analysis, political debate and political action on the basis of a better understanding of the environmental context of modern societies. If we apply Beck's argument to type two risks, then of course the implication of his analysis is that contemporary citizenship requires a strong educational programme because one of the bases of contemporary democracy is the existence of an educated and discerning citizenry. While Ritzer's position is less overtly political, I want to suggest in the second section of my chapter that his approach to McDonaldization might present us with a fruitful and important perspective on the requirements of citizenship (as a form of cultural lifestyle) in globalized social systems.

Cool Citizenship and Ironic Commitment

I want therefore to suggest a more interesting reading of Ritzer by an examination of eating styles in McDonald's as a metaphor for political commitments in a global and multicultural environment. There is obviously an important difference between eating and its social role in modern societies by contrast with traditional societies. In presenting this difference between a continuum that ranges from the orgy to a McDonald's snack, I draw upon Pasi Falk's *The Consuming Body* (1994). Falk's aim is to connect the emergence of the reflexive self with the growth of consumerism, because the modern self is produced through the notion of unlimited consumption. The consuming self with its insatiable desires is elaborated through and by the consumer industry. Changing patterns of food consumption are an important part of this evolving self. In traditional societies, the self was closely bound into the rituals of social solidarity, associated with festival. The ritual meal of sacrifice in the Abrahamic religions was the basis of the bond between God and humans, and between people. Eating together was a fundamental basis of social order in which the exchange of gifts (especially food) took place. In Christianity, the bread and wine are exchanged as symbols of the sacred gift of body and blood.

If we treat McDonaldization as a secularization of religious patterns of friendship and familiarity associated with sacred meals (Kottak, 1978), then the McDonald's snack represents a privatized and individualistic pattern of consumption which does not aim to build bonds of belonging. Brand loyalty does not lead to the creation of societies. McDonaldization involves a limited menu, precise measurements of food, the standardization of taste and the elimination of surprises; it stands at the opposite end of a continuum from ritualized orgy.

I wish to argue that, borrowing somewhat the terminology of Marshall McLuhan (1964), we can compare and contrast these traditional and religious patterns of eating with the modern fast-food restaurant in terms of two dichotomies: thick/thin solidarity, and hot/cool commitments. Traditional religious festivals generate a thick solidarity, characterized by its intensity, duration and complexity; ritualized meals take place within and produce patterns of social solidarity such as brotherhoods, tribes and communities. The social solidarity of eating in McDonald's is superficial, transient and simple. McDonaldization produces global identities and images (the Big M), but these create thin communities. At the same time, the commitments of tribal festivals are hot; they involve hysteria, effervescence, mystical trances and spiritual possession.

Eating in McDonald's requires the participants to be cool. Customers form short queues and assemble quickly to give their orders, they retire to their tables in well-regulated movements, and they sit quietly eating their standardized and predictable meals. There are no expectations that the meal will receive an applause. The regulated patterns and general silence are punctuated only by the occasional children's birthday parties where party uniforms are issued to small groups of children. These social forms are thin and cool. In terms of conventional sociology, participation in McDonald's outlets has many of the features described by Erving Goffman (1959) in his analysis of 'role distance', where social actors learn techniques of subjective neutrality. University professors out with their children for Saturday lunch at McDonald's learn to show to others that they are not really there. These patterns of coolness of commitment and thin solidarity offer a model of social interaction which perfectly conforms to the emerging patterns of global citizenship.

We can briefly trace the development of Western citizenship through four broad historical stages (Turner and Hamilton, 1994). In medieval society, the status of citizen in the city-state was more or less equivalent to denizen. It involved minimal privileges of immunity and a limited range of obligations. Although there was considerable pride in civility within the city walls, there was little notion of city identity and membership (cool commitments and identity). There was, however, a density of social involvement within the narrow confines of the city (in the guilds, for example) which resulted in thick membership. Modern citizenship as we know it really started with the nation-state, which through doctrines of nationalism in the nineteenth century encouraged hot nationalist commitment in order to create a homogeneous community as the base of the state. The nation-state attempted to overcome internal divisions within civil society (religion, ethnicity and regional membership) to forge patterns of thick solidarity. These patterns of involvement were threatened by class divisions, but under welfare capitalism the welfare state functioned to reduce class divisions and to enhance commitment to the state. Finally, with the growth of a world economy and the globalization of cultures, the increase in migration, trade and tourism creates a more diverse culture, and multiple political loyalties. For example, there is an increase in dual citizenship. With globalization, the traditional forms of hot loyalty and thick solidarity become irrelevant to modern citizenship forms, indeed hot loyalties of a national or local variety can often become dangerous in a world system which needs tolerance as a functional basis of political interaction. The ethnic conflicts of Eastern Europe, Russia and Northern Ireland can be understood in terms of the negative consequences of hot nationalist loyalties in societies which require cooler modes of identification and thinner forms of solidarity. Global citizenship, organized around high levels of labour migration, might form a cultural pattern which is parallel to McDonald's – political loyalties should be formed on the assumption of high mobility in which citizens would enjoy the privileges of a drive-in democracy, which in turn had cool assumptions about the level of political commitment.

These assumptions also fit the account of liberalism provided in Richard Rorty's view of 'private irony and liberal hope' (1989). An ironist is a person who believes that their 'final vocabulary' is always open to criticism and revision. Ironists are nominalists and historicist, and as a result they do not believe there is a natural order to which language approximates. An ironist is sceptical about the legitimacy of 'grand narratives' and hence there is a similarity between J-F. Lyotard's version of postmodernism (1984) and Rorty's language theory. In political terms, Rorty's philosophy is also minimalistic – liberals support 'bourgeois freedoms' as a basic level for social consensus, not because liberalism is true, but simply because it offers opportunities for self-creation and personal liberties. Ironic liberals do not commit themselves to a grand vision of history and social reform. Their basic assumption is that the worst thing we can do to another person is to inflict pain by an act of intentional cruelty. In short, ironists are cool about their commitment to political systems, they do not feel that thick solidarity is necessarily helpful in the realization of personal freedoms, and their detachment from traditional ideologies (especially nationalism) has an elective affinity with the concept of a drive-in McDemocracy.

Conclusion

The response to McDonaldization among intellectuals has been typically hostile and critical, because it is associated with standardization and mediocrity. The fast-food industry undermines or at least threatens folk cuisine, regional variations in food production, home cooking and traditional forms of hospitality. It is also thought to have a negative impact on the natural environment by supporting beef production against less damaging food products such as soya beans. McDonaldization has also penetrated other social and cultural spheres to create similar patterns of standardized consumption: McUniversity, McNews and McMedicine.

Ritzer is also criticized because his work is seen to be not only a description of McDonaldization but a subtle defence of the processes of Fordist rationalization. Ritzer's deployment of Weber's sociology of rationalization offers no recipe for resisting McDonaldization, because the objective is to understand rationalization rather than to counteract the rationalist ethic and its practices.

In this chapter, I have suggested an ironic response to both McDonaldization and its critics. The typical sociological response to urban anomie, economic alienation and cultural rationalization has been nostalgia – the search for community, authenticity and coherence. Postmodernism challenges such responses by showing that the contemporary world is necessarily diverse, fragmented and complex. As an alternative to nostalgia, it offers parody. The quest for community has been particularly powerful in the imagination of political philosophers where the legacy of a small Greek democracy continues to haunt the debate about democratic participation. Now Greek democracy, like Protestant sects, requires hot commitments and thick solidarities; modern democracy, as we know, presupposes large nation-states, mass audiences, ethnic pluralism, mass migrations and globalized systems of communication. Hot democratic identities are probably dangerous in such an environment, where, to continue with this metaphor, nationalist fervour can fan the coals of ethnic hatred and difference. Bosnia, Cambodia and Algeria are contemporary examples of the quest for thick homogeneity and hot loyalty in societies which are in fact subject to forces of global diversification. If we were to seek out a metaphor for modern citizenship, we may be better to look neither to Athens nor Jerusalem – in the political philosophy of Leo Strauss (1959) – but to McDonald's for our political models of association. Modern societies probably need cool cosmopolitans with ironic vocabularies if they are to avoid the conflagration of nationalistic versions of political authenticity and membership.

References

Beck, U. (1992) *Risk Society: Towards a New Modernity*. London: Sage.

Beck, U. (1994) 'The reinvention of politics: Towards a theory of reflexive modernization' in U. Beck, A. Giddens and S. Lash (eds), *Reflexive Modernization: Politics, Tradition and Aesthetics in the Modern Social Order*. Cambridge: Polity Press.

Beck, U. (1995) *Ecological Politics in an Age of Risk*. Cambridge: Polity Press.

Berger, P.L. and Luckmann, T. (1967) *The Social Construction of Reality*. New York: Doubleday.

Berman, M. (1982) *All That is Solid Melts into Air*. New York: Simon & Schuster.

Bourdieu, P. (1984) *Distinction: A Social Critique of the Judgement of Taste*. London: Routledge & Kegan Paul.

Braverman, H. (1974) *Labor and Monopoly Capitalism: The Degradation of Work in the Twentieth Century*. New York: Monthly Review Press.

Douglas, M. (1966) *Purity and Danger: An Analysis of Concepts of Pollution and Taboo*. London: Routledge & Kegan Paul.

Falk, P. (1994) *The Consuming Body*. London: Sage.

Foucault, M. (1977) *Discipline and Punish: The Birth of the Prison*. London: Tavistock.

Goffman, E. (1959) *The Presentation of Self in Everyday Life*. Garden City, NY: Doubleday Anchor.

Japp, K.P. (1996) *Soziologische Risikotheorie: Funktionale Differenzierung, Politisierung und Reflexion*. Weinheim and Munich: Juventa.

Kottak, C.P. (1978) 'Rituals at McDonald's', *Natural History*, 878 (1): 75–82.

Lash, S., Szerszynski, B. and Wynne, B. (eds) (1996) *Risk, Environment and Modernity: Towards a New Ecology*. London: Sage.

Lee, D. and Turner, B.S. (eds) (1996) *Conflicts about Class: Debating Inequality in Late Industrialism*. London and New York: Longman.

L'Etang, J. and Pieczka, M. (1996) *Critical Perspectives in Public Relations*. London: International Thomson Business Press.

Lyotard, J-F. (1984) *The Postmodern Condition: A Report on Knowledge*. Manchester: University of Manchester Press.

Marx, K. and Engels, F. (1968) 'The Communist Manifesto', in *Selected Works*. London: Lawrence & Wishart.

McLuhan, M. (1964) *Understanding Media: The Extensions of Man*. Toronto: McGraw Hill.

Piore, M. and Sabel, C.F. (1984) *The Second Industrial Divide*. New York: Basic Books.

Ritzer, G. (1993) *The McDonaldization of Society: An Investigation into the Changing Character of Contemporary Social Life*. Thousand Oaks, CA: Pine Forge Press.

Ritzer, G. (1995) *Expressing America: A Critique of the Global Credit Card Society*. Thousand Oaks, CA: Pine Forge Press.

Rorty, R. (1989) *Contingency, Irony and Solidarity*. Cambridge: Cambridge University Press.

Strauss, L. (1959) *What is Political Philosophy?* Glencoe, IL: Free Press.

Turner, B.S. (1997) 'From governmentality to risk: some reflections on Foucault's contribution to medical sociology', in A. Petersen and R. Bunton (eds), *Foucault, Health and Medicine*. London: Routledge.

Turner, B.S. and Hamilton, P. (eds) (1994) *Citizenship: Critical Concepts* (2 vols). London: Routledge.

Weber, M. (1930) *The Protestant Ethic and the Spirit of Capitalism*. London: Allen & Unwin.

Vidal, J. (1997) *McLibel: Burger Culture on Trial*. London: Macmillan.

7 Theme Parks and McDonaldization

Alan Bryman

Although Ritzer (1993) had little to say about the inroads McDonaldization was making into theme parks, it is clear from a few references to them in his book that he regarded them as fully implicated in its inexorable advance. More recently, he has written specifically on McDonaldization in relation to tourism, coining in the process the notion of 'McDisneyization', and from this discussion it is clear that he regards them as exemplifications of its characteristics (Ritzer, 1998). In the following discussion, I examine the suggestion that theme parks, and Disney ones in particular, exemplify McDonaldization, thereby allowing me to amplify my discussion elsewhere of the 'McDisney' theme park (Bryman, 1995).

The links between McDonaldization and Weber's theory of rationalization have been amply demonstrated by Ritzer, but it is ironic that he should observe that Weber associated rationality with a decline in charisma (Ritzer, 1996), for Walt Disney possessed most of the features that we would anticipate from a Weberian reading of charismatic leadership. Elsewhere I have suggested that there are three main criteria that distinguish charismatic from non-charismatic leaders (Bryman, 1992): they possess a radical *vision*; they are viewed by their followers as *exceptional*; and they enjoy the unflinching *dedication* of those who follow them. Walt possessed these characteristics in spite of being a notoriously difficult person to work for and with (Bryman, 1995: 14–18). His radical vision is evident in the fact that he both changed forever our idea of what an amusement park should be like and created the very idea of a theme park. As a result, while not exactly copies of Disney theme parks, many of those that have followed on from Disneyland, which opened in 1955, have adopted many of its templates. Even though Knott's Berry Farm in Southern California is an amusement park that predates Disneyland and advertises itself as 'America's first theme park', it has gradually themed itself with separate 'lands' (Ghost Town, Fiesta Village, Roaring 20's, and so on). Similarly, in spite of Gallic horror at the globalizing impact of Euro Disneyland, French theme parks like Parc Asterix have adopted a similar approach.

Like most charismatic leaders, Walt realized the importance of self-publicity in the social construction of charisma. One of the ways he did this was by repeating key events or moments in his personal life and development so that these junctures were recycled from biography to biography.

As a result, books and articles written about him display a similarity that is a direct result of the biographical template that Walt had created, in spite of often quite divergent views about the man himself. One such key recurring motif in the biographies was his distaste for traditional American amusement parks when he took his daughters to visit them. Coney Island was symptomatic of the tawdriness to which such parks had succumbed. The blueprint that became Disneyland had a very long gestation during which it underwent many transformations in character and intent. In the end, Walt's vision was for a park which adults would want to visit as much as children and which therefore would be required to exhibit characteristics, such as vestiges of nostalgia, cleanliness, good quality and safety, that would appeal personally to adults and yet be suitable destinations for their children. The theming would allow a celebration of America – its past, its present, its culture, its achievements and its future – through a heady mix of utopian planning, self-referential allusions to the movies, and a transparent motif of progress. The successful implementation of Walt's vision can be gauged from the results – adults outnumber children by a ratio of 4:1 (Findlay, 1992), a simple fact that Buckingham (1997) has ignored in his misleading depiction of Disney theme parks as 'children's media culture'.

However, the key issue in the present discussion is whether the theme park is a McDonaldized institution. To examine this issue, each of the main facets of McDonaldization will be analysed in relation to theme parks. Increasingly, Ritzer's writings on McDonaldization suggest that he sees 'the irrationality of rationality' as a dimension of the process rather than as an adjunct (for example, Ritzer, 1996), and this approach will be followed here.

Efficiency

The most obvious evidence of the efficiency of theme parks is the fact that they are able to deal with very large numbers of people (Ritzer, 1998). From the moment you drive to Disney World and many other theme parks you know that you are in the hands of a highly rationalized machine. Huge numbers of cars descend on the parks at any point in time, so that the potential for utter chaos in the parking lots is considerable, with drivers and pedestrians as they exit their cars weaving across each other. Instead, Disney employees ('cast members') channel each car on arrival into a specific organized slot in a strict rota, and by the time everyone gets out, cars are being parked quite a few slots down the aisle where you have been instructed to park. Consequently, you are less likely to be mown down by subsequent drivers eager to get into the park. 'Guests' are then asked to make a note of where their cars are parked since the lots are huge and they could easily walk for hours looking for their vehicles. Each area of a Disney parking lot has been designated a theme-park relevant name (Pluto,

Harvest, and so on) and each line of cars in that area has a number. You are then asked to wait for a tram that will take you to the theme park. Such a high level of efficiency is necessary to deal with the traffic associated with the modern theme park, which was created to capitalize upon the growth in automobile ownership, in contrast to many earlier amusement parks, which were designated to be accessible to public transport (Adams, 1991).

With their cars parked, the guests must gain entry to the theme park. Virtually all theme parks have gone over to the pass/ticket which allows unlimited access to all the site's rides, shows and many other amusements. For many years, Disneyland had a fairly nominal entry charge and guests then had to purchase further tickets for each ride. This was not an efficient system because it required cast members to take money, hand out change and check tickets at each attraction. Moreover, it created the impression that a visit to the park was expensive, since the guest was continuously having to hand money over for the attractions. This concerned Disney staff, because to the extent guests had this impression, they were less likely to spend their money on food, drinks and merchandise, which are hugely profitable (Bright, 1987). Passes were introduced around 1982. There was an interim period when guests bought stubs of tickets which were graded and allowed variable access to different attractions (that is, a small number of tickets allowed access to the more popular attractions). These also required checking by Disney cast members and were dispensed with in favour of the general pass. Many visitors to Disney World in Orlando purchase multi-park passes which allow unlimited access to the parks (Magic Kingdom, EPCOT Center, Disney-MGM Studios and the minor parks) over four or five days. These passes work out cheaper than purchasing single tickets, but are efficient from the point of view of the company because fewer sales staff are required. In 1996 in Orlando, two of the area's other major theme parks – Sea World and Universal Studios, along with Wet 'n' Wild, a water theme park – came together to supply multi-park tickets, while Sea World in Orlando and Busch Gardens in Tampa (both owned by Anheuser-Busch Company) also sell multi-park tickets.

While in the park, efficiency reveals itself in a number of ways. Most eating establishments are decidedly McDonaldized in the almost literal sense of being organized along the lines of a McDonald's restaurant. In recent years, Disney parks have been going slightly in the opposite direction of providing some upmarket eating opportunities in waiter/waitress restaurants, most notably in the World Showcase restaurants in EPCOT Center where each 'country' has its own 'ethnic' restaurant(s), though here, too, McDonaldized establishments exist. Mexico and China, for example, have both types of restaurant serving ethnic food, though they are much more extensively themed than the McDonaldized Taco Bell-style eateries or ethnic restaurants in the outside world!

Efficiency is further revealed in the tendency for many theme parks to restrict the opportunity for guests to gawk at exhibits for extended periods of time, the objective seeming to be to get them on their way as quickly as possible. Thus, in the Future World exhibits in EPCOT Center, Haunted Mansion, Jungle Cruise or Pirates of the Caribbean in Magic Kingdom, the Great Movie Ride in Disney-MGM Studios, the Kong ride in Universal Studios, and many others, guests are instructed to enter moving cars that allow the item to be seen (an audio-animatronic tableau of the development of the motor car, a ghostly scene, an audio-animatronic John Wayne, or a growling Kong) but for only for a few moments. This feature, which is a function of the 'conveyor-belt' control exercised over guests (see below), means that large numbers can be processed without any build-ups of onlookers.

Many other indicators of efficiency could be cited. For example, many theme parks have quite large theatres for shows (particularly evident at Sea World parks). These allow large numbers of guests to be entertained at relatively low cost, compared to the expense of developing new rides that cost millions of dollars and may have a fairly brief life if they are superseded by other parks or go out of fashion. Moreover, a large number of people can be taken away from attractions that require extensive queuing, and without theatre shows lines would become intolerable (though many would suggest that they are anyway). Efficiency also reveals itself in such things as specially developed quick-drying paint which allows the Disney theme parks to be spruced up overnight and so never develop the tarnished appearance that so offended Walt when he visited amusement parks. Moreover, the underground utilities (electricity, water, food distribution, waste removal, cast member changing rooms) are highly efficient and much lauded mechanisms that permit the smooth running of the whole operation without interfering with the allure of the theming. In these and so many other ways, Disney and many of the other theme parks are monuments to efficiency.

Control

The Disney theme parks exemplify the dimension of control extremely well. Control operates in connection with both guests and cast members, and it is to the former that we will turn first. As the examination of the car parking facilities suggests, efficiency is achieved through direct control over parking strategies and subsequent movement away from one's vehicle. Once in the park, there is a system of pathways that considerably restricts the movement of guests between attractions. In the Magic Kingdom, one reason for this restriction is to retain the integrity of the theming of the different lands – to reduce the disorientation caused by sharp disjunctions as one moves from one land to another. But much of it is to ensure the efficient handling of a large number of guests and to maximize their opportunity to spend money. A writer for the business magazine *Fortune* has suggested:

While trying to hit just the high points, guests are forced to see almost all the park. Easily distracted by features that may not have seemed worth seeing at first, they stay longer. And around each big magnet, as well as on the paths that link them, guests find food and merchandise outlets eager to help them endure the wait for the thrill ride or the meandering journey between rides. (Uttal, 1977: 177–8)

These comments were made in relation to the design of Six Flags parks, but they apply equally well to other major theme parks. Food and merchandise outlets, which for theme parks are sources of a very large percentage of their profits, are liberally provided and situated cleverly along the pathways that guests are forced to travel. Moreover, as guests exit many attractions, particularly the major ones, they are decanted immediately into stores selling merchandise appropriate to the particular attraction. Thus, as you exit the Back to the Future simulator ride in Universal Studios, you enter a large store selling a large range of relevant merchandise (de Loreans, clocks, T-shirts, Einstein dolls, and so on). Most people do not purchase items there and then, particularly if it is early in the day, since they have all read the guidebooks that recommend that you defer your shopping no matter how shrill the pleas of your younger co-visitors. However, most do look and perhaps go back later in the day for that 'essential' de Lorean.

Shearing and Stenning have gone somewhat further in that they suggest that control over guests at Disney World is inscribed in the very fabric of the park: 'virtually every pool, fountain and flower garden serves as both an aesthetic object and to direct visitors away from, or towards, particular locations' (1984: 344). Moreover, what appears to be a family- or group-friendly policy of allowing groups of people to enjoy attractions in each other's close company (you are always being asked 'How many in your party?' as you near the end of the time spent waiting in line) is in fact a clever control device: it ensures that possibly unruly children will not be separated from their parents' gaze and so the potential for disruption is reduced. The lines themselves are interesting control devices in their own right. They bend and twist in such a way that their true length is never fully apparent. At times, you seem to get close to the attraction itself but then find yourself being taken away again as the line bends away or as you are taken into another room. The effect is to keep your interest going and to reduce the ennui that would be associated with queuing for the lengths of time that are frequently, if not invariably, necessary.

Control is further underscored by Disney cast members, who are typically dressed in such a way as to conceal their true function, namely as guards. They are there to deal with such rule infractions as queue jumping, anti-social behaviour, walking barefoot, eating or drinking in line, consuming food not bought in the park, or seeking to walk where one should not. Somewhat more openly, Disney cast members are continuously directing movements in preparation for attractions. For example, for popular shows or films in theatres like *Captain EO* or *Honey I Shrunk the Audience*, cast members are always instructing guests to 'move *aaaaaaall* the way down the row', assuring them that the view is no better in the middle than at the sides. Of course, some are not convinced and sit wherever they feel the American Constitution entitles them to sit, but the Disney cast members have an ace up their sleeves – they give permission to anyone coming after the delinquent guests to trample all over them. It also appears that the costumed cartoon characters are now equipped with mini-cameras to reduce the excessive exuberance of some guests when encountering them – apparently, Snow White's breasts have been a particularly popular target (Letts, 1996). The use of such surveillance devices may increase after reports that children have been attacking costumed characters in Disneyland Paris (Burchill, 1998).

However, it is not just Disney guests' physical movement that is controlled but also their gaze. As numerous commentators have observed, the messages that the company seeks to project are overwhelmingly positive. There is, in other words, a uniquely 'Disney gaze'. In its depiction of science and technology and of the future, the reigning message is one of progress, and more particularly of the capacity of scientific progress to continue to deliver a constant stream of consumer goods for our enjoyment. The downside of scientific and technological advance – pollution, deforestation, depletion of scarce resources, and so on – is concealed from view or reserved for upbeat treatments in specific locations like The Land in EPCOT Center. Portrayals of the future simply promise more of the same only better. The clear message is that we will by then have realized the errors of our past ways, so that a problem-free world of munificence (that is, lots of consumer goods) will be at our disposal. When the family is depicted, it is invariably a white, middle-class, heterosexual nuclear family of two adults and two children (usually boy and girl). In this way, it is a particular form of the family that is presented. In its rendering of the past or of the present, Disney occludes poverty, wars, racism, discrimination against ethnic minorities or women, except in very brief optimistic renderings. Similarly, while Sea World parks rail against the horrors perpetrated upon sea mammals (drift nets, accidents involving speedboats and the like), it is extremely silent about its own captive holding of whales, dolphins and manatees.

Control extends to Disney cast members as well. Ride operators submit to technical control, in that the arrival and departure of the method of conveyance (flume, car, ghost buggy, spaceship) into which riders are deposited are tightly controlled by a computer. Of course, this represents both a further dimension of control over guests and an instance of 'the replacement of human with nonhuman technology' which Ritzer (1993: 101) views as a notably modern aspect of control through McDonaldization. The most extreme form of this feature in the Disney parks is of course the audio-animatronic figures that appear in both shows and rides. While these figures are often in animal form (intrepid riders on the Jungle Cruise could hardly be expected to be confronted with real crocodiles, for example), they often substitute for actors. With rides like Pirates of the Caribbean, in which there are a large number of audio-animatronic figures, it is not feasible to use humans since they would be required to repeat words and actions every 15 or so seconds. However, there are many instances, such as Hall of Presidents, Great Moments with Mr Lincoln, Carousel of Progress and the American Adventure, where live actors could easily be used. Audio-animatronic figures are far easier to control and are likely to be viewed as more reliable than actors, an issue that shades into the matter of predictability (see below).

Second, the employee is likely to be forced to submit to both bureaucratic and supervisory control. The former reveals itself in a panoply of rules and regulations enshrined in manuals regarding dress and appearance, language, demeanour, appropriate responses to questions, and so on. Conformance with these rules is under the scrutiny of supervisors, who, according to the sociologist John Van Maanen who worked as a Disneyland ride operator, 'catch [employees] out when they slip over or brazenly violate set procedures or park policies' (1991: 68). Guests act as supervisors as well in that the folklore about the ever-smiling, helpful, clean-cut Disney cast member is well known, so that flagrant deviations from the image are likely to be reported (Van Maanen, 1991). Finally, cultural control is a pervasive aspect of control over employees. This control is an extension of Walt's early recognition that the Disneyland experience would be far more enjoyable if he arranged for the training of employees at all levels so that they enhanced the guest's experience. Nowadays, new recruits are put through one of the Disney universities where they learn about Walt, the company's heritage, the Disney way of doing things, and so on.

Predictability

The immense popularity of Disney theme parks and of other parks in the same mould is in large part due to their predictability. You simply *know* what you are going to get before you depart on your vacation. You *know* that you will encounter a safe, litter-free, traffic-free, immaculately landscaped fantasy world. You *know* that Disney staff will be helpful and seek to enhance your vacation. You *know* all this for a number of reasons: all the guide books tell you, the publicity materials tell you, your friends and family will have told you, it is part of Western folklore, and since a massive proportion of guests are (multiple) returnees, the chances are you will *know* first-hand anyway. Nowadays, Disney provides prospective guests with planned itineraries which enhance the predictability of the experience (and their ability to exert control over you). It is this very predictability that makes Disney-style theme parks attractive to many parents. They *know* that their children will love it and be safe and that the chances are that they will love it too, since they are always being told that adults love the parks too.

The tight control of guests and employees is one of the main vehicles for the enhancement of predictability. Control is meant to reduce the variability in guests' experiences of the theme park and in employees' behaviour, which are related of course. The widespread device of placing people in moving seats has the effect of ensuring that guests see exactly the same things and for the same length of time. Even the unpredictable is made predictable as far as possible. For example, in the event of a guest having an accident, there is a set of established procedures for making the person comfortable, minimizing damage to other people's enjoyment and to the company, and responding to suggestions that the company was at fault (for example, offering free tickets, meals).

Because of its emphasis on predictability, Disney has tended to shy away from attractions involving live animals. As some early attractions in Disneyland indicated, the unpredictability of animals made them unsuitable, either because they were sometimes the cause of accidents or because their 'performance' was difficult to guarantee. It is somewhat surprising, therefore, that the company opened Disney's Animal Kingdom in Disney World in 1998. Although the park has the familiar combination of thrill rides, simulators, exhibits and audio-animatronics, live animals also take part. As one journalist observed before the park opened: 'Given Disney's obsession with safety, it's unlikely that you'll be chased across the Savannah by a pack of salivating hyenas' (Hatchwell, 1997: 12). In any case, theme parks in which animals are integral to the theming – like Busch Gardens in Florida and the Sea World parks – do not have a realistic choice about whether to include live animals. In these parks, animals can be viewed in 'natural' environments, but one takes the risk that the animals will be asleep or out of sight, or in the case of sea mammals that the main encounter with them will be in shows. Disney's response to such potential problems in its Animal Kingdom is to make the unpredictable animals as predictable as possible. While the park simulates the Serengeti, there are a number of devices to ensure that the animals do not behave too much as if they were in the wild: while on 'safari' guests are well insulated from them; the different breeds are subtly separated by concealed moats so that they do not eat each other; a great deal of time has been spent conditioning the animals as to where they can roam (including electric fences); feeding stations are positioned on the safari trail to keep them in sight of cameras; and certain areas are air conditioned so that animals will be attracted to them and so be in sight even in the middle of the day in the Florida heat (Churchill, 1998; Corliss, 1998; Tomkins, 1998).

Calculability

I have slightly changed the order in which Ritzer typically presents his dimensions of McDonaldization, because while there is ample evidence to suggest that theme parks conform well to the three aspects already discussed, I am less certain about this fourth one (Bryman, 1995). Ritzer writes that calculability 'involves an emphasis on things that can be calculated, counted, quantified' and 'a tendency to use quantity as a measure of quality' (1993: 62). Theme parks did not figure in any of the illustrations of this dimension. More recently, as signs of McDisneyization he points to: 'The set prices for a daily or weekly pass, as well as the abundant signs indicating how long a wait one can expect at a given attraction' (Ritzer, 1998: 135). Ritzer has also pointed to the fact that the guest seems to be offered a *lot* of different attractions for what seems to be *little* money.[1]

Such allusions to calculability may be fair but they seem a far cry from such indicators of quantity over quality as Big Mac, Whopper and Biggie. It is true that Disney and other theme parks make quantitative references in their publicity material to such things as the number of attractions or of parks in the case of Disney World, the size of the area covered by a park, value for money passes, and sometimes the number of visitors (Disney sometimes celebrates landmarks, such as the millionth visitor and anniversaries). One area where calculability definitely surfaces among theme parks that specialize in ratcheting up the 'scare factor' is in relation to rollercoasters. Thus, a press release for the Superman coaster in Six Flags Magic Mountain just outside Los Angeles claims it is 'the tallest, fastest, most technologically advanced thrill ride ever built' (quoted in Whittell, 1997). In its publicity materials, Busch Gardens in Tampa describes the new Montu ride in 'Egypt' as 'the world's tallest and longest inverted steel rollercoaster, named after a hawk-headed human-bodied Egyptian sun god'. It also refers to being home to over 350 species of animal. Another flier refers to Montu's 3.85 G Force and to the over 60 mph attained on Kumba (another rollercoaster). However, it may be misleading to treat such references solely as indicators of calculability. There is a long tradition of using quantitative markers to enhance the prospective fear factor and so entice visitors (Cartmell, 1977), although this trend undoubtedly appears to have intensified in recent years (for example, Nuki and Steiner, 1996; Whitworth, 1997). Typically, it is the non-Disney parks that build up the quantitative indicators of scaring people. Disney has tended to prefer somewhat tamer fare. Indeed, Walt had never wanted Disneyland to include a rollercoaster since he aimed to differentiate his park unambiguously from the traditional amusement parks that he so despised. In later years, such attractions were added, albeit in heavily themed form (Big Thunder Mountain Railroad, Space Mountain, and so on), in order to attract the teenage market.

The difficulty is one of deciding whether such quantitative allusions are genuinely to the detriment of quality. From the outset, Walt emphasized the importance of ensuring that the quality of the guest's experience was paramount. This was why he cultivated and promoted many of the features of the Disney and other parks that we take for granted nowadays. Such features include visible indicators of quality such as cleanliness, neatness and the friendliness and helpfulness of the staff. However, the emphasis on quality also includes elements that are either invisible or less strikingly visible, such as the expensive decision to channel utilities (power cables, waste disposal) underground, to shut off the outside world from view, and to limit encroachment of different themed areas upon each other. These elements are integral to Disney theme parks and to many of those that have followed Disneyland's lead and are there to enhance the quality of the guest's experience. However, it is also the case that the parks reveal calculability in the sense that precise timing and quantities are required for the rides to process guests and for the restaurants to serve meals. This aspect of the parks is symbolized in the story of Walt's anger when he was taken on a Jungle Cruise ride and found it to be two minutes shorter than should have been the case (Schickel, 1986: 344).

However, in its publicity materials, Disney tends to make reference to 'dreams', 'fantasy' and 'magic' instead of quantitative intimations. A lengthy publicity item ('holiday planner') for Disney World that was available in British Disney Store outlets around the beginning of 1997 is fairly typical. The cover refers to the resort being 'the place where your wildest dreams come true'. The next page describes it as 'a wonderland of fun, where fantasies become reality and where reality is fantastic. So let the magic begin.' The next page follows up with:

> It all adds up to a 'different' world with a special kind of holiday magic, unlike anywhere else, and there's always something new and exciting on the horizon. . . . *Follow that dream and come to the anniversary party of the year.* (original emphasis)

And later on the same page: 'Don't forget though, this is just the beginning of the dream. Wait till you get there, you won't believe your eyes.' There is also a reference to 'the fantastic variety and sheer size' of the resort, but this kind of intimation of quantity seems relatively subordinate to the emphasis on quality. Even though the non-Disney parks tend to be more disposed to refer to quantitative dimensions of their attractions, there is typically still an emphasis on the quality of the guest's experience. At the very least, quantity does not appear to be 'to the detriment of quality' (Ritzer, 1993: 82).

The Irrationality of Rationality

There is little doubt that to the extent that theme parks are McDonaldized in the foregoing respects (calculability aside), they have created their own irrationalities. The most obvious feature of this is that the sheer efficiency of theme parks, and Disney ones in particular, in attracting and processing large numbers of people leads to what seem to be interminable lines, especially at the more popular attractions. Waits for such attractions at busy times of the year can run to over two hours. Thus McDonaldized efficiency frequently leads to *in*efficiency for the park visitor. At Universal Studios in Orlando, the amount of time spent waiting for popular attractions like Back to the Future is notorious. This may be why one of its most recent attractions, Terminator 3-D, was developed in such a way that it is able to absorb two very large numbers of people at any one time: one audience watching the show, the other in a pre-entertainment area which leads into the show itself.

Passes for Disney World seem expensive but good value, since the multipark passes provide access to a large number of attractions. But Bob Garfield (1991), a writer for *Advertising Age*, demonstrated that the notion of good value is difficult to sustain. His family of four purchased a five-day pass and stayed in Disney accommodation and ate at Disney restaurants. They spent just under 114 hours on Disney property but only six hours and 47 minutes was spent either on rides or at shows, in very large part because of queues. This worked out at $261 'per fun hour'. Such a calculation strongly suggests that if a purely instrumental stance is taken, a Disney World holiday is a very expensive proposition. The efficiency that is a feature of McDonaldization works, but it works for the company not for the guest.

Then there is the wider impact of these efficient tourist destinations on the local ecology and economy. When Assistant Editor of *National Geographic*, Joseph Judge, visited the Orlando area in the early 1970s,[2] he was confronted by several negative views in spite of the obvious growth in jobs that Disney World was beginning to bring to Central Florida. The chair of the Board of Commissioners of Orange County told Judge:

> Unless he is a land speculator, owns a bank, or sells insurance . . . the average tax payer . . . has not only had zero profit from this tremendous growth – he is paying for it. And I don't mean in our new bumper-to-bumper style of driving, increase in crime, and all that. I mean in cash, for new roads, additional law enforcement, and the rest. (Judge, 1973: 596)

Judge was also met with consternation from conservationists about both declining water quality and the depletion of water supplies. While such views are disputed, they continue to be voiced (for example, Fiore, 1990). Indeed, the opposition to Disney's America, a theme park that was to have been built in Virginia, was partly to do with historians' opposition to Disney versions of history being played out in close proximity to land and monuments with special meaning to Americans, but also with fears about the ravages that would be wrought on the local environment and the quality of life of its inhabitants (Synnott, 1995: 45–6).

Resistance to McDonaldization

To many, the foregoing account represents an acutely depressing picture that recalls Weber's famous epithet of the iron cage. But can the appeals of

McDonaldized tourism be resisted? One response is the simple one: don't go.[3] However, it is very unlikely that in so doing people will really be resisting McDonaldization or McDisneyization. As Ritzer (1998) argues, just about every nook and cranny of tourism has become or is in the process of becoming McDonaldized. Such a view recalls MacCannell's (1976) depiction of tourists as people who are in search of the authentic tourist experience but who are constantly thwarted in their quest by a tourism industry that nudges them away from the back regions of tourist destinations towards the front regions that have in fact been fabricated for touristic consumption. MacCannell refers to this as 'staged inauthenticity', a process whereby not only has the version of reality with which tourists are confronted been designed more or less exclusively for their consumption, but also they know this to be the case. Many feel frustrated by the barriers that prevent them from penetrating these front regions. Moreover, many traditional tourist haunts, like museums and heritage centres, are taking on the characteristics of theme parks (Walsh, 1992). While 'terror tourism' (visiting danger spots throughout the globe) may seem like a niche that is an unlikely area for McDonaldization, an Italian company organized packages to the Croatian and Bosnian front lines (Byrne, 1997). While this is a far cry from the Magic Kingdom, the point is that the notion that a decision not to visit theme parks enhances one's opportunity of encountering destinations that have not been McDonaldized is at the very least questionable.

One way of resisting Disney's attempts to control your movements in the parks is to acquaint yourself with the recommendations for avoiding queues, alternative routes, and so on, that can be found in the 'Unofficial Guides' (for example, Sehlinger, 1994). These guides approach the Disney theme parks in the manner of a military operation and are full of advice about how to get ahead of both the crowds and the company. The problem with this solution as a form of resistance is that many of your fellow guide-toting tourists will have read them too and will be following the same strategy as you. You end up with 'an irrationality of *ir*rationality'.

Another strategy is to limit your expenditure in the parks as far as possible to keep down your cost per fun hour. This means keeping control of your purchase of food and merchandise as far as possible and not staying in Disney accommodation. The latter tends to be more expensive than the numerous hotels in their environs. A factor in Garfield's (1991) spiralling expenditure would have been the fact that he stayed at a Disney hotel. In Disney World, Disney has radically increased the number and range of accommodations that it offers in the last 10 years. Euro Disneyland was similarly well endowed with Disney hotels when it opened in 1991. Of course, Disney knows that its hotels tend to be more expensive, so it offers special advantages to those staying in them. In Disney World, hotel guests are able to secure early entry to the parks so that they can beat the crowds to the more popular attractions and they can make early bookings for the popular sit-down restaurants (particularly the ethnic

EPCOT ones) and have unlimited use of Disney's transportation system. Also, they are able to purchase special 'duration of stay' passes offering unlimited admission. Although the vast majority of visitors still stay at non-Disney accommodations, it is clear that Disney has responded to this mode of resistance by cranking up the advantages of staying in the Resort.

Conclusion

There can be little doubt that Ritzer's characterization of McDonaldization fits theme parks well. As in my earlier examination (Bryman, 1995), I am still not convinced that calculability fits the Disney theme parks closely, though a stronger case can be made that it applies to many of the non-Disney ones. But in suggesting that they are McDonaldized institutions, we must guard against implying that this is all they are or that their wider significance resides exclusively in this facet. It is striking that some writers have seen Disney theme parks as emblematic of the postmodern sensibility (for example, Baudrillard, 1983; Eco, 1986), whereas Ritzer (1993) depicts McDonald's restaurants as prototypically modernist. Although the postmodern impulse at Disney theme parks is open to dispute (Bryman, 1995), the very fact that such a possibility is considered suggests that for many writers there must be something more to them than depicting them as McDonaldized implies. Or to take another illustration: whether by design or accident, Disney hit upon the advantages of selling merchandise within a themed environment. Today, many restaurants and forms of retailing are 'Disneyized' in the particular sense of clothing consumption in themed contexts and thereby reducing (not to say eliminating) the distinction between consumption and fantasy. The effect is to soften the commercial nature of the transaction. Moreover, while the Disneyization of consumption is probably not as extensive or as significant a process in terms of the organization of commodity consumption as is McDonaldization, it suggests that we do not exhaust the range of interpretative possibilities of theme parks when we describe them as McDonaldized, and that we do not capture their broader importance in doing so (Bryman, 1999).

Notes

I wish to thank Alan Beardsworth, Robin Allan and Barry Smart for their helpful advice on this chapter.

1 This comment was made by George Ritzer in a handwritten letter dated 15 July 1996. The emphases are his. I had previously written to him and in response he had kindly complimented my book *Disney and His Worlds* (Bryman, 1995), but had some quibbles about my application of calculability to the Disney theme parks. I asked him to elaborate on this point, since I had just agreed to write this chapter.

2 What is extraordinary about this date is that the Magic Kingdom only opened in 1971 and the expansion since then has been vast.

3 This is not a solution that I would want for myself, however!

References

Adams, J.A. (1991) *The American Amusement Park Industry*. Boston: G.K. Hall.
Baudrillard, J. (1983) *Simulations*. New York: Semiotext(e).
Bright, R. (1987) *Disneyland: Inside Story*. New York: Harry N. Abrams.
Bryman, A. (1992) *Charisma and Leadership in Organizations*. London: Sage.
Bryman, A. (1995) *Disney and His Worlds*. London: Routledge.
Bryman, A. (1999) 'The Disneyization of society', *Sociological Review*, 47.
Buckingham, D. (1997) 'Dissin' Disney: critical perspectives on children's media culture', *Media, Culture and Society*, 19: 285–93.
Burchill, J. (1998) 'Taking the Mickey', *The Guardian* (Travel section), 10 October.
Byrne, C. (1997) 'Terror tourists queue for trips to war zones', *The Sunday Times*, 16 March.
Cartmell, R. (1977) 'Rollercoaster: king of the park', *Smithsonian*, 8 (August): 44–9.
Churchill, D. (1998) 'Beware, it's a jungle out there', *The Times* (weekend section), 28 March.
Corliss, R. (1998) 'Beauty and the beasts', *Time*, 13 July: 64–8.
Eco, U. (1986) *Travels in Hyperreality*. London: Pan.
Findlay, J.M. (1992) *Magic Lands: Western Cityscapes and American Culture after 1940*. Berkeley, CA: University of California Press.
Fiore, F. (1990) 'Disney's Florida critics warn of a greedy monster', *The Los Angeles Times*, 20 February.
Garfield, B. (1991) 'How I spent (and spent and spent) my Disney vacation', *Washington Post*, 7 July.
Hatchwell, E. (1997) 'Taking the Mickey in Orlando', *The Independent* (Long Weekend section) 12 April.
Judge, J. (1973) 'Florida's booming – and beleaguered – heartland', *National Geographic*, 144: 585–621.
Letts, S. (1996) 'Snow White gets mini-camera to keep bodice pure', *The Times*, 7 October.
MacCannell, D. (1976) *The Tourist: A New Theory of the Leisure Class*. New York: Schocken.
Nuki, P. and Steiner, R. (1996) 'Ultimate "free-fall" rollercoaster promises to go down a treat', *The Sunday Times*, 25 August.
Ritzer, G. (1993) *The McDonaldization of Society*. Newbury Park, CA: Pine Forge Press.
Ritzer, G. (1996) 'The McDonaldization thesis: is expansion inevitable?', *International Sociology*, 11: 291–308.
Ritzer, G. (1998) *The McDonaldization Thesis: Explorations and Extensions*, London: Sage.
Schickel, R. (1986) *The Disney Version*. London: Pavilion.
Sehlinger, B. (1994) *The Unofficial Guide to Walt Disney World*. New York: Prentice Hall.
Shearing, C.D. and Stenning, P.C. (1984) 'From the panopticon to Disney World: the development of discipline', in A.N. Doob and E.L. Greenspan (eds), *Perspectives in Criminal Law*. Aurora, Ont: Criminal Law Books.
Synnott, M.G. (1995) 'Disney's America: whose patrimony, whose profits, whose past?', *The Public Historian*, 17: 43–59.
Tomkins, R. (1998) 'Fair game for a gentle savaging', *Financial Times*, 25 April.
Uttal, B. (1977) 'The ride is getting scarier for "theme park" owners', *Fortune* (December): 167–84.
Van Maanen, J. (1991) 'The smile factory: work at Disneyland', in P.J. Frost, L.F. Moore, M.L. Louis, C.C. Lundberg and J. Martin (eds), *Reframing Organizational Culture*. Newbury Park, CA: Sage.

Walsh, K. (1992) *The Representation of the Past: Museums and Heritage in the Postmodern World*. London: Routledge.

Whittell, G. (1997) 'Hi-tec Superman ride takes off at 100 mph', *The Times*, 27 March.

Whitworth, D. (1997) '£15m rollercoaster goes to new lengths in the funfair wars', *The Times*, 2 January.

8   The McDonaldization of Sport and Leisure

David Jary

One great team supporting another . . .

(Strapline advertising McDonald's sponsorship of the English soccer
team Ipswich Town's 'Football in the Community' scheme)

There is a rising awareness of the 'infiltration' of capital into areas of life
which until now were sheltered from it by tradition.

(Habermas, 1979: 76)

It is the opening ceremony of the Atlanta Olympic Games. There comes
into view the Olympic flame, the central symbol of the cultural continuity
between the original games in ancient Greece and the modern games. But
on closer inspection the flame is burning brightly within a large McFries
box, thus confirming one key element of Ritzer's 'McDonaldization of
society' thesis, namely that:

Since its proliferation in the late 1950s, McDonald's (to say nothing of the
myriad other agents of rationalization) has invested enormous amounts of money
and effort in convincing us of its value and importance. Indeed, it now proclaims
itself as a part of our rich tradition rather than, as many people believe, a threat
to many of those traditions. (Ritzer, 1993: 149)

As Ritzer puts it:

There is a lot of emotional baggage wrapped up in McDonald's, which it has
built on and exploited to create a large number of highly devoted customers.
Their commitment to McDonald's is more emotional than it is rational, despite
the fact that McDonald's built its position on rational principles. (1993: 149)

Advertising and sponsorship of sport and leisure and the linkage of
corporate reputation and products by this means with cultural icons and
contemporary cultural values – at which other prominent leisure-oriented
corporations Coca-Cola and Pepsi-Cola as well as McDonald's are prime
exponents – is, however, but one, *secondary*, element of the wider process
of McDonaldization proposed by Ritzer.

For Ritzer, McDonaldization is a process in 'which the principles of the fast-food restaurant are coming to dominate more and more sectors of American society as well as the rest of the world' (1993: 1). The principles and processes of the 'Weberian' rationalization and bureaucratization and commercialization identified by Ritzer as *primary* in the phenomenon of McDonaldization are: efficiency, calculability, standardization and predictability, and technological control. Their increasing application in the realm of sport and leisure is a central part of Ritzer's thesis. What I will suggest – and this will also provide the basis of a revised view of McDonaldization (or its replacement) – is that the *secondary* element may be more important in the transformation of sport and leisure, arising from a wider fusion of sports and leisure corporations, especially TV and sportswear corporations.

The Rationalization and McDonaldization of Sport and Leisure

As Ritzer sees it, the contemporary bureaucratization and 'rationalization' of recreational activities is a particularly 'good example of what Weber feared':

> Recreation can be thought of as an effort to escape the rationalization of our daily lives. The nonrationalized world of recreation is an escape route from the rationalized world in which we all live. The only problem with this is that over the years the escape routes have been rationalized and have come to embody the same principles as bureaucracies and fast-food restaurants. Recreation has become yet another domain of rationalization, not an escape from it. (Ritzer, 1993: 23)

For Ritzer, McDonald's itself, but also Disney World, package tours, theme parks, and the like, can all be seen as 'conveyancing machines', resulting in efficiently produced, predictable, controlled leisure environments. Like McDonald's:

> The package tour is as oriented to predictability as it is to efficiency. That is, a person who signs up for a package tour is looking for a trip that offers no surprises. What this often translates into is an effort to have minimal contact with the people, culture, and institutions of the countries being visited. This creates a paradox: People go to considerable expense and effort to go to foreign countries where they hope to have as little contact as possible with native culture. (An American amusement park, Busch Gardens, offers European attractions, such as a German-style beer hall, without having its clientele leave the predictable confines of the United States and the even more predictable surroundings of the modern amusement park.) The tour group is likely to be made up of like-minded fellow Americans, and the vast majority of one's time is spent with those (highly predictable) people. Further predictability is ensured by the fact that people on such tours often travel with family members and friends. Travel is

undertaken, wherever possible, on American carriers. Local transports offer the amenities expected by the American tourist (perhaps even air conditioning, stereo, bathroom). Tour guides are either Americans, people who have spent time in America and with Americans, or at least natives fluent in English and knowledgeable about the needs and interests of Americans. Restaurants visited on the tour are either American (for example, one of the American fast-food chains) or those that in structure and menu cater to the American palate. Hotels are also likely to be either American chains, such as Sheraton and Hilton, or European hotels that have structured themselves to suit American tastes. (On the opening of the Istanbul Hilton, Conrad Hilton said, 'Each of our hotels . . . is a "little America".') Each day has a firm, often quite tight schedule, so that there is little time available for spontaneous and unpredictable activities. Tourists can take comfort from knowing the day's schedule before the day's outing begins and perhaps even before the trip commences. They can know exactly what they are going to do on a daily, even hourly, basis. (Ritzer, 1993: 90)

According to Ritzer, many pre-existing forms of sport and leisure are also being transformed by the spread of McDonaldization. Significant instances include sports domes and all-weather plastic pitches, and rule changes in games designed to speed up the action, not least for TV – for example, in basketball, the introduction of the rule in which the attacking team must shoot within 24 seconds.

Locating Ritzer's Critique of McDonaldization

Ritzer's original book is avowedly a 'critique' of – or at least a corrective to – alternative perspectives on contemporary society such as 'post-industrialism', 'post-Fordism' and 'post-modernism' (1993: 152). While he accepts that society is undoubtedly post-industrial in some respects, Ritzer insists that the spread of McDonaldization indicates that aspects of 'industrial society' are likely to be with us for some time to come (1993: 153). In contrast with, for example, Daniel Bell's (1973) thesis of a 'post-industrial society', 'low-status blue-collar and service occupations show no signs of disappearing, and, in fact, the latter group has been expanding and is central to a McDonaldized society' (1993: 153; see also Ritzer, 1996a). Ritzer accepts that an association exists between 'McDonald's and *some* elements proposed as characteristic of post-modernism' (for example, 'time-space compression'), but he also argues 'that there has been *no* clear historical break with Fordism' (1993: 155). As does David Harvey in *The Condition of Postmodernity* (1989), Ritzer emphasizes continuities between modernity and postmodernity, endorsing Harvey's major conclusion that while 'there has certainly been a sea change in the surface appearance of capitalism . . . the underlying logic of capitalist accumulation and its crisis tendencies remain the same' (1993: 157).

Elsewhere in this volume my colleague John O'Neill suggests that Ritzer's book should be seen as merely a 'McCritique', dismissing the

McDonaldization of Society as an easily digested and bowdlerized repackaging of Weber largely for student consumption, a veritable 'McText'. There is some fairness in this but it would be wrong to be quite so dismissive. Even if partly in ways he did not intend, Ritzer's book *is* provocative and a stimulus to debate.

Not only do leisure activities' interests and associated 'lifestyle' values have especially high saliency for many individuals, they have increasingly become the basis for the creation and management of markets for new leisure products. The proliferation of branded 'junk foods' and 'designer' leisure clothes and equipment (from Adidas to Nike) and the standardization of sport and leisure forms more generally – for example, tie-breaks in tennis, Packer's reforms in cricket, or 'golden goals' in soccer, along with the TV-formatted (cf. Whannel, 1992) and hyped sports presentations such as *The Big Match, Fight of the Century* – are part of a rapidly intensifying 'signing' and commodification (and revalorization) of sport and leisure that is global in its focus. The issues raised by Ritzer – including his twin emphases on rationalized leisure and an emotionalized attachment to brand – are significant issues, but they require far more grounding to take account of a burgeoning literature on sport and leisure – including media and cultural studies – largely ignored by him.

Despite some subtlety of presentation (for example, recognition of the 'democratic' and egalitarian and 'populist' elements in McDonaldization) and an emphasis on the possibilities of resistance, there's a good deal that is simply hit and miss about both Ritzer's thesis and his illustrations of it. Although by profession a social *theorist*, he must be adjudged a relatively unsystematic one, and a polemicist and a popularizer – at times almost a latter-day Vance Packard[1] – who prefers never to jettison a colourful potential illustration of his thesis even if on careful reflection its force is likely to prove less than convincing, not least to his critics.

Alternatives to the Simple Thesis of McDonaldization

McDonaldization does appear to be *one* aspect of an intensifying rationalizing and globalizing process that is strongly in train. However, this process is far more complex than Ritzer begins to address. (This is so even if one takes into account his recent postscript to his thesis, 'The McDonaldization thesis: is expansion inevitable?' (1996b), where he does attempt to get to grips with some of the issues that arise.)

There need be no quarrel with the notion that much about contemporary society remains Fordist, rather than post-Fordist or postmodern, and 'that much about McDonald's exemplifies this'. But Ritzer does *not* do *full* justice to either the modernist or the 'postmodern' elements of McDonaldization as a process and the links between the two.

With regard to the 'modernist' elements of the thesis, the increasing vertical and horizontal integration of leisure corporations is largely ignored by Ritzer, as is the increasing tendency for sports organizations in particular to become indirectly controlled or monopolized by media organizations and/or major advertisers – a wider and more significant trend perhaps than McDonaldization alone, even if in part associated with it.

With regard to the 'postmodern' elements, the creativity – and the complex 'uses' and 'readings', and the potential resistance – of consumers, although recognized, is much under-played by Ritzer, who at times greatly over-states the compliancy of consumers.

With regard to both 'modernist' and 'postmodernist' elements, McDonaldization (and 'Americanization') must be seen as only *one* form of modernizing–postmodernizing globalization. This needs to be weighed far more carefully in the balance against the complex interaction of the local and global and the flux and polysemy of meaning (as discussed by theorists such as Robertson or Giddens), the continuous appearance of new leisure forms (evident especially, for example, in the phenomenon of 'world music' or in the realms of 'cyberspace'), many of these 'semiotically' highly complex (cf. Hebdige, 1979; Willis, 1978, 1990).

In appraising both Ritzer's thesis and possible alternatives and resistances to the McDonaldization of sport and leisure, this chapter will utilize the work of theorists of cultural consumption, sport and leisure (including Elias and Dunning, Guttmann, Hebdige, Whannel and McGuigan) and draw upon general theorists (including Foucault, Barthes, Bourdieu and Baudrillard, as well as Robertson and Giddens) whose work is largely ignored by Ritzer.

Stages and Issues in the McDonaldization of Sport and Leisure

Figure 8.1 presents schematically what I take to be the main steps or stages in Ritzer's thesis (steps 1–3), and what I want to present, in addition (steps 4–6), as both a critique and an enhancement/replacement of the simple McDonaldization thesis. As well as this, I will argue that once steps 1–6 are identified as an expanded thesis, these also need to be located more fully in the context of what in Ritzer's account of the McDonaldization thesis remains an unexamined 'prehistory' of modern sport and leisure forms. Once this 'pre-history' is inserted into the account, a very different picture from simple 'McDonaldization' is confirmed, which will also enable us to better identify both 'alternatives' and 'resistances' to McDonaldization.

Steps 1 and 2 in Figure 8.1 together represent the fundamental 'innovative' steps as seen by Ritzer leading to the establishment of McDonald's as the pre-eminent, exemplary fast-food restaurant, and a model for other leisure organizations. Essentially what step 1 involves is the application of Taylorist labour process techniques to the 'restaurant' and the application of much more rationalizing technology besides.

As John O'Neill (in this volume) emphasizes, at the heart of the process stands the computerized cash register which links sales, inventory, product-

0. 'Pre-history'. Rationalizing, 'civilizing' and 'sportization' process *prior to* McDonaldization (Bourdieu, 1978; Elias and Dunning, 1986), including control of bodies, of carnivalesque, of public places, etc., and the introduction of commercialized leisure

1. Rationalization of 'restaurant' production (and consumption) process:

   (i)   Efficiency
   (ii) Calculability
   (iii) Standardization and predictability
   (iv) Technological control

2. Signing/emotional linkages of product with cultural traditions (e.g. 'family' restaurant), product enhancement by 'sign' enhancement – first stage in 'hypersignification' and 'iconization' of the product (e.g. iterated local settings as 'global places')

3. Wider rationalization/commodification/marketization/ spectacularization/McDonaldization of sport and leisure: e.g. Hollywood, Disneyland, theme parks, mass tourism, professional sport and sport franchises, etc.

4. Amplifying circuits of signification/iconization: McDonald's ↔ sports stars/sports teams/sports events

5. Further circuits of sign amplification, commodification/ valorization: 'prolympism' (Donnelly, 1996):

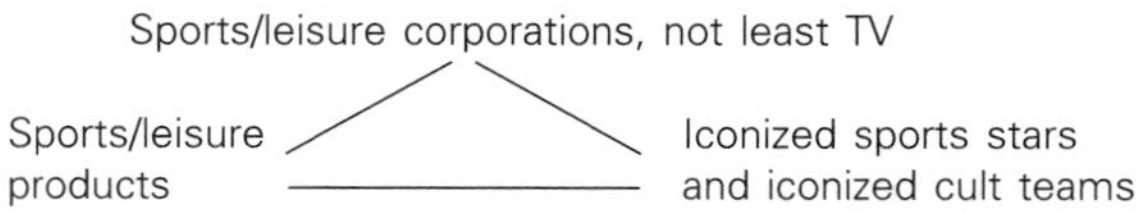

   Sports/leisure corporations, not least TV

   Sports/leisure products ——— Iconized sports stars and iconized cult teams

6. Sponsorship as 'marriage' of leisure corporations and 'sport' (Taylor, 1997) – especially sport and TV – and further transformations of sports forms (Whannel, 1992), associated with further standardization/predictability and technological control of the sports product (e.g. control of the framing, timing and flow of sports events, pay-as-you-view, digital broadcasting).

FIGURE 8.1   *Stages and issues in the McDonaldization of sport and leisure*

mix, customer counts and worker productivity. And, of course, the consumer is also caught up in the Taylorist–Fordist process, in that he or she must stand in line to receive a meal from a standardized menu, must carry this food to the table, and then also clear away the left-over debris from the meal.

One problem for this part of Ritzer's account is not in its basics, but rather why McDonald's is presented as *the* exemplar rather than Taylorism itself? Presumably for Ritzer it becomes exemplary because it appears to be the step that carries Taylorism beyond the workplace, and also involves the consumer – *especially* the consumer 'at leisure' – in Taylorist practices. But, even here, one might ask whether McDonald's was not simply one of several leisure corporations pushing down a broadly similar road. None the less, the account of McDonald's and McDonaldization *is* significant with respect to step 1, even – especially – if McDonald's is simply part of a more general trend. The proliferation of fast-food and franchises in the USA and globally, especially along with the extension of the principles of fast-food to other forms of retail selling and to services more generally (the later step 3 in Figure 8.1), does underline the basic significance of the step 1 phenomenon identified by Ritzer.

Turning next to the significance of step 2, we can regard this in our expanded account of McDonaldization as an extended *initial* stage in the manufacture and ultimately 'hypersignification' of product identity undertaken by McDonaldization (cf. Goldman and Papson, 1994). Once again it is possible to argue that other corporations – for example, Coca-Cola, involved in the Olympic Games since 1928 – were perhaps ahead of the game (see also Williams, 1980). As with step 1, so with step 2, however, whether or not McDonald's was first or the main exemplar, and whatever reservations there may be about Ritzer's account in detail, there is no doubt that McDonald's does constitute an important exemplar of a significant trend that Ritzer is right to emphasize. The marketing of McDonald's as a 'family restaurant', implausible initially as this may have been, none the less, becomes a highly valorized 'reality' as the result of the hypermarketing and hypersignification of McDonald's as a site of 'family fun', for birthday celebrations and such.

Given step 1 and step 2, step 3 – the third element in Ritzer's account – then becomes an especially important additional trend: the extension of McDonaldization-type methods to other types of organization. In sport and leisure in particular it is not difficult to find numerous examples that fit the bill, including a number already mentioned. As suggested, what is missing in Ritzer's account, however, is any grasp of historical or ethnographic detail or any subtlety of theoretical analysis – especially economic or semiotic analysis – in relation to the complexity of what is going on in relation to sports and leisure organizations and where all this might lead. These absent elements are covered by steps 4–6, as well as by my brief sociological 'prehistory' of sport and leisure forms, to which we now turn.

The Historical 'Civilizing' and 'Sportization' Processes in Industrial Societies: A Brief 'Prehistory' of the McDonaldization of Sport and Leisure

In Ritzer's account modern sport and leisure forms arise as if from thin air. An insertion of the absent 'prehistory' into Ritzer's account is important in its own right and is also essential as a basis for the further steps I see as required to revise this account.

Elias and Dunning (1986) and Dunning and Sheard (1979) (see also Dunning and Rojek, 1992; Rojek, 1985) provide a prominent general account of the transformation of leisure and what they see as a historical 'sportization' process – the transformation of informal English 'pastimes' into organized sports – which they view as the outcome of a wider 'civilizing process' associated with modern state formation. Indeed the entire 'social construction' of 'leisure' as a social category can be seen as shaped in this context. The very term 'leisure' – original root 'licence' – takes on its modern form in part in contrast to the new rational 'disciplines' of work, but also leisure is itself increasingly subject to the disciplines of 'rational' control – to 'licence' in the sense of being 'permitted'. Control of both the content of leisure and leisure spaces, 'the frost on Merrie England' associated with Puritanism, conceptions of 'rational recreation', and so on, were part of this process of transformation of sport and leisure forms. (Alongside the work of Elias and Dunning, see also Hargreaves's (1986) comprehensive account and Bourdieu's (1978) brief but incisive analytical discussion of rational *predictability*, *calculability* and *control* within sport and the role of 'habitus' and 'distinction' in influencing the supply and demand for sport.)

In sport specifically, the 'invention' of new 'rule-governed', socially controlled sports in the nineteenth century is central. Rule specification, and also quantification in sport – competing against the clock, by distance or against 'self-targets' – are part of a process of Protestant rationalization of previous folk games, a process in which the purging of the 'real' violence associated with folk games is steadily replaced by mimetic sport and 'civilized' leisure forms (cf. Guttmann, 1978). Although the conception of 'civilizing process' is not unproblematic (Jary and Horne, 1994), the basic account of the formation and transformation of 'leisure' and sportization processes provided by theorists such as Elias and Dunning or Bourdieu is one that can be seen as essential to contextualize Ritzer's 'thin' description of the context from which McDonald's springs. Analysis of the entire development of leisure forms – especially sports forms – cries out for the construction of nuanced Foucaultesque 'genealogies' of the 'disciplining' of bodies intrinsic to both the civilizing and sportization processes (cf. Andrews, 1993; Hargreaves, 1986, 1987). Analysis of the cultural positionings and the labellings of the body have acquired a major significance in our understanding of sport and leisure, as Hargreaves demonstrates in his discussion of the significance of the icons of 'youth', 'health', 'beauty' and 'personal freedom' in relation to modern sports. Also important are those more detailed historical studies (for example, Bailey, 1979; Gruneau, 1983) which paint a 'neo-Gramscian' picture in which sport and leisure history can be understood neither as imposed from above nor as generated from below, but rather as continually contested terrain in which particular sports and leisure forms wax and wane with the shifting outcome of this contest. But there is little awareness of any of this possible depth and complexity of analysis in Ritzer's account, which generally skates over the surface.

'One Great Team Supporting Another': Aspects of the Rise of TV-Dominated Sports and Leisure Corporate Culture

If a historical analysis of the rationalization of sport and leisure is required to fully contextualize the significance of steps 1–3 in Ritzer's account of McDonaldization (Figure 8.1), then further developments of the promotion and 'iconization' of McDonald's and sport and leisure as 'signs' (steps 4–6) represent important additional steps in the processes associated with McDonaldization which also remain under-analysed by Ritzer.

In the twentieth century sport has become foremost among the most potent of global 'idioms'. Without the necessity of a common language, sport can cross national boundaries, its appeal can be classless, it can unite generations, and it is increasingly overcoming barriers of gender. Certain sports, notably association football, might be seen as even having acquired a 'world historical' or 'evolutionary universal' status (see Edgell and Jary, 1973; cf. Williams, 1994). In these circumstances, sports 'names' – both sports stars and sports clubs – have become 'household names' and also potent means of identification and connecting with 'others'.

Not surprising, then, that McDonald's, along with other major corporate players such as Pepsi and Coca-Cola, have sought to interconnect their brand names, the other household names of modern times, with the increasingly 'iconic' imagery of the 'great names' of sports teams and sporting heroes (steps 4 and 5 in Figure 8.1). By means of extensive PR – its sponsorship of sports events as well as its 'associations' with sports stars and sports teams in its advertising (cf. Izod, 1996) – McDonald's as a non-sporting corporation has positioned itself so that it feeds on the potency of sport as a source of near magical signs.

Thus it is that

> as we buy, wear and eat logos we become henchman and admen of the corporations, defining ourselves with respect to the social standing of the various corporations. Some would say this is a form of tribalism, that in sporting corporate logos we ritualize and humanize them, we redefine the cultural capital of the corporation in human terms. . . . (Willis, 1993: 132–3)

The spectacular rise of the sports goods corporation Nike provides an especially significant recent example of the phenomenon. From its formation in the 1960s Nike has grown into a world-famous sports goods label by exploiting its links initially with the baseball star Michael Jordan. As John Williams asks: 'Does the clothing promote Jordan, or does Jordan promote the clothing?' (1994: 393). The answer is clear. If Jordan helps to create Nike, Nike amplifies Jordan, who can count appearances on Warner Brothers cartoon epics with Bugs Bunny as confirmation of his escalation along with Nike to the status of contemporary cultural icon: one a sports superstar, the other a hypersignified product line. A spiralling of mutual aggrandisement of both the Nike sneaker and the Jordan 'persona' as icons is the outcome. As Andrews has remarked, from one perspective, 'people have become manipulated by the hedonistic iconography of consumer culture . . . directed at the body' (1993: 15). From another perspective, however, the reward for Nike consumers is that they can bathe vicariously in the glamour and the glory of Nike and Jordan as a designer label and a role model – even if the 'world' they inhabit exists, in part at least, as merely a 'hyperreality' in Baudrillard's sense. More recently the black English footballer Ian Wright has been employed by Nike to similar effect. By such means, Nike has been successful in challenging and overtaking the German corporation Adidas, prior exploiters of the sports goods–sports star relation. As Cole and Hribar have commented:

> Nike did not become Nike because of the immediate supply of or sudden demand for fitness clubs, equipment, and apparel, but Nike became Nike through a complicated network of economic, cultural and psychic relations. (1995: 335)

Borrowing from Durgnat, we can suggest that 'the social history' of such a corporation 'can be written in terms of its stars' (1967: 137).

The escalating circuits of signs and sign amplification that take place under these circumstances is outlined as step 5. In addition, however, a number of changes are also occurring in which leisure corporations like Nike have become utterly crucial in the general trajectory of the development of sport. As Williams observes, 'a neat distinction between the sports event and the promotion' no longer holds (1994: 393). Among these expanding leisure corporations are also the sports teams themselves. Sports team franchises where the primary function was profit-making appeared early in the USA but were far less common elsewhere. In the UK it is only relatively recently that sports goods franchising, in association with major advertising and TV, has begun to lead to the transformation of professional sports teams from non-profit-making clubs or companies to highly rapacious, stock market-quoted corporations. In recent years, especially with the advent of satellite TV, this process has gathered increased momentum.

Television is particularly important (see also Cashmore, 1996) because, in the first instance, it gives access to large audiences for advertising and promotion. It is especially important for the tobacco industry, whose advertising elsewhere is subject to major restrictions. The development of Nike as a major transnational sports goods company would have been simply unthinkable without TV. The signing prior to the 1998 World Cup by Nike of a contract with the Brazilian national soccer team has ensured a continued world-wide visibility for Nike products, begun in the 1994 World Cup, that has taken the company way beyond its original relatively parochial base in US basketball.[2]

Both the two most recent – highly commercialized – Olympic Games (1992 and 1996) and the 1994 and 1998 World Cups are rightly viewed by many commentators as establishing a new high-water mark in the articulation of sport, media and leisure corporations (see Sugden and Tomlinson, 1998; Whannel and Tomlinson, 1984; Williams, 1994).

As Rogan Taylor (1997) has noted, the term 'sponsorship' has as its root the word 'spouse'. What this latest stage, in which sponsorship has been crucial to the development of sport, can be seen as constituting is a 'marriage' of leisure corporations and sport (Taylor, 1997) – especially between sports and TV – and a further escalation in the transformation of sports forms (Whannel, 1992; see step 6 in Figure 8.1). This latest stage is associated with further standardization, technological control and predictability of the sports product (for example, control of the framing, timing and flow of sports events, pay-as-you-view, and digital broadcasting).

In the UK, BSkyB, owned by the global communications giant Rupert Murdoch, has played a crucial role in the process underway. A relentless oligopolistic absorption of rival corporations has enabled it to achieve a significant dominance in TV coverage of major sports events. It is significant that coverage of the new English Premier League football, because of the potency of its iconography, was chosen as the 'key cultural product' in establishing BSkyB as a dominant European satellite channel with wider global aspirations (Williams, 1994).

With the alliance between BSkyB and football in place, the way has become clear for a further escalation of the commodification and the iconification of the sports product. Traditional bases of the sports chosen for colonization had to be circumscribed, perhaps even jettisoned, and new affluent audiences enticed. Exceptions exist to this general tendency, such as the successful community-owned American football team Bay Green Packers in North America, but these are increasingly rare. For example, Nottingham Forest, for long one of the few UK soccer teams not to have the status of a limited company, have recently succumbed to the dominant trend. Competitive pressures make it difficult to resist.

Some of the most spectacular recent capitulations have been in English Rugby Union and Rugby League. The transformation wrought in English Rugby League has been particularly striking. Rugby League, the northern winter and quintessential working-class game, also largely a male preserve, was in the space of a few months transmuted into a family summer game, with the traditional names of clubs transformed into newly invented Americanized totemic forms – 'Bradford Bulls', 'Leeds Rhinos', and so on – with newly reformed teams located in Paris and London to ensure a cosmopolitan image for a previously thoroughly provincial genre. At the same time the sport has also been made ready for new North–South inter-hemispheric league and cup competitions, with the aim of heightening its appeal to an extended global audience while also increasing TV and advertising coverage.

English Rugby Union previously stood out as a bastion of amateurism – even if compromised in practice by undercover payments to players. The speed of the collapse of its highly conservative previous order is a further indication of the power of the forces now at work.

Similar remarks can be made about the reorganization of both Australian and Japanese sport. In Australia the term 'corporate sport' has been coined by McKay and Miller (1991).

> The once hegemonic amateur ideology has become increasingly marginal and residual as all professional (men's) sports have been reorganized on the basis of management science with executive directors and specialists in advertising, marketing and public relations. (McKay and Miller, 1991: 87)

In Japan a new professional soccer league, the J-League, has been formed. Expressly conceived to help cope with the down-turn in the Japanese economy, and to switch consumer demand to leisure and to promote regional development, the launch of the new league was associated with extensive recourse to PR and sports goods promotion (see Horne and Jary, 1994). The Japanese example underlines what Williams remarks on more generally as increasingly true of modern sport:

> The colonization of sport by the broadcasting marketing, and advertising net-works means, clearly, that there is no longer a neat distinction between the sports event and the promotion. (1994: 393)

Evaluating the McDonaldization Thesis

What all of this already confirms is the existence of a rationalizing process of much greater complexity than Ritzer recognizes. The account provided of the primary and secondary steps in Ritzer's thesis – steps 1 to 3 – can be regarded as basically satisfactory, even if it over-states the importance of McDonald's in the general process. But aspects of this account and the absence of any elaboration of steps 4 to 6 must be seen as crucially deficient, among other things:

- in failing to provide an adequate political economy of the processes of McDonaldization, for example the relative silence on the relationship of McDonaldization to agribusiness (see O'Neill in this volume) and, in relation to sport and leisure in particular, no consideration of the activities of sports goods corporations in third world labour markets;

- in lacking sufficient consideration of the subtle and shifting semiotics of PR and advertising and consumers' reception and interpretation of these, for example it can be suggested that the advertising of Nike or Coke with their blending of soccer and youthstyle – 'Just do It' – has made far more effective use of 'globalized' imagery than McDonald's (cf. Goldman and Papson, 1994);

- in failing to indicate in any (ethnographic) detail how consumers 'actively' use and interpret their involvement with McDonald's – the fact that there is likely to be far more going on than Ritzer assumes, for example he provides no detailed ethnography of 'family use' (cf. Parker, 1997);

- in failing to examine how far the transformations of sport and leisure should *in fact* be seen as *largely* 'Fordist' and part of the continuing cultural logic of late capitalism or viewed instead as a much more ramified mix of 'modern' and 'postmodern' phenomena as portrayed by numerous other theorists;[3]

- and finally, in failing to in any way relate to the questions widely posed – not least in cultural studies – by a neo-Gramscian model of cultural 'hegemony' and 'resistance'.[4] What Ritzer has to say about resistance to McDonaldization is in fact surprisingly tame and can be seen as consisting of a largely under-theorized mix of elitist nostalgia (cf. Parker, 1997) and defeatist acceptance of the near inexorability of McDonaldization, which is related to his acceptance of McDonaldization as a 'modern' rather than a 'postmodern' phenomenon.

Resisting McDonaldization: Ritzer's View

Resistance to McDonaldization, of course, has a potential double meaning: resistance to the phenomenon of McDonaldization *and* resistance to Ritzer's account. Since Ritzer's account of McDonaldization has such obvious weaknesses, our discussion of 'resistance' to it will include both.

As noted, what Ritzer appears to do is to equivocate between inexorability and resistance, and because of this equivocation, the analysis of neither is taken very far. Ritzer seeks both to recognize and to encourage resistance to a 'McDonaldizing world'. For example, he applauds the remarks of a French socialist politician in acknowledging both 'the link between Disney and McDonald's as well as their common negative effects', while declaring that 'Euro Disney will "bombard France with uprooted creations that are to culture what fast food is to gastronomy"' (Ritzer, 1993: 12). However, in his 1993 volume, apart from this he mainly suggests that we should individually simply refuse to consume McDonaldized leisure products.

In his later postscript (Ritzer, 1996b) he does belatedly – but still inadequately – seek to address the general issues in a wider way. Noting that the McDonaldization thesis holds to a position of *globalization* at odds with the more two-way view of theorists like Featherstone or Robertson, he merely seeks to defend his previous position. Four reasons are offered in defence of such an account of McDonaldization as a process and as *explanation* of its global effectiveness: that it (a) 'makes money'; (b) 'reflects consumer preference for American culture'; (c) 'fits well with dual career families'; (d) 'benefits from the death of socialism'. While this list is something of a rag-bag, it has some cogency, as evidenced by the success of McDonald's and Pizza Hut in the former USSR. I was present in Moscow when McDonald's arrived and witnessed the extent of this support! But such evidence as this is hardly systematic or in-depth. Even if we were to add here what the historian Cross (1993) sees as the significance of a 'work-and-spend' culture and the decline of primary groups as favouring developments such as McDonald's, Ritzer's case for any overwhelming inexorability for McDonaldization remains thin.

Resisting McDonaldization: Wider Conceptions

In her media research, Ien Ang (1993: 417) reported a respondent who said: 'When I say I like watching *Dallas*, I often get odd reactions . . . but I also like eating at McDonald's and like poetry a lot!' It has to be accepted that from the viewpoint of sports fans and leisure consumers more generally the developments associated with McDonaldization are not necessarily 'all bad'. Leave aside the issue of 'healthy eating', and McDonald's does provide a cheap, clean, family-friendly service. Though some sports fans 'resist' the tendencies set in train by 'corporate sport', others undoubtedly welcome such changes (TV sport, for example, is in some respects now better presented, though of course it costs the consumer much more). Obviously since consumers must be considered active 'readers' and 'interpreters' of leisure forms, we *must* take consumer demand seriously. Equally, however, we must not accept any simple notion of 'consumer sovereignty' as the whole story, or fall into the trap of recent 'populist' readings in media studies (such as Fiske's [1987]) which sometimes seem to suspend critique and evaluation (see McGuigan, 1992, for an extended discussion).

It is highly relevant *vis-à-vis* the McDonaldization thesis that in media and cultural studies and in accounts of globalization there is ample evidence of 'active' interpretations that point to resistances of a more systematic kind than Ritzer identifies. In his most recent accounts of McDonaldization, Ritzer does now acknowledge a degree of 'resilience of local culture'. Furthermore, it is now clear to all, including Ritzer, that too much has sometimes been made of the spread of cultural commodities such as Coca-Cola or McDonald's burgers. Concepts such as 'Americanization' and McDonaldization must also all be found wanting *if* it is implied by these that they describe forces which are overwhelming and essentially one-way (cf. Donnelly, 1996). It is evident that the global processes of rationalization neither create a Weberian 'iron cage' nor lead to the total manipulation/seduction of the innocent/passive consumer of the kind previously suggested by critical theorists or, at one point, by Baudrillard (1988).

Even in those areas where the tendency has often appeared mostly one-way – for example, the dominance of Hollywood – there exist many exceptions. In other areas – not least popular music – the tendency is for subcultural *bricolage*, for 'creolized' and cosmopolitan outcomes, rather than Americanization or McDonaldization. Even in relation to advertising, recent commentators note how 'a sign's exchange value can be diminished':

> Advertising strategies such as hyperreal encoding, reflexivity and the use of hypersignifiers have been motivated by intertwined crises in the political economy value of the sign value. Advertisers not only confront disaffected, alienated viewers armed to foil ads with their remote control zappers, they also face the problem of differentiating their commodity signs from the clutter of formulaic advertising. (Goldman and Papson, 1994: 24)

In sport, specifically, Peter Donnelly's conclusion is that as regards globalization the situation that exists is 'two-way but with imbalances'. On the one hand, international sport is

> more Americanized than music, film or television in that corporate sport itself, and its mediated forms, has become even more of a forum for the sale and promotion of products, and ideas. . . . In corporate/Americanized sport, the game has become somewhat less important than its capacity to be a vehicle presenting particular messages to a particular select and often massive audience, but the game itself also expresses ideas about competition, excellence, corporate efficiency, and what it is necessary to do to win – ideas that have their origins in the United States but have now come to characterize global capitalism. (Donnelly, 1996: 246)

Donnelly (1996: 246) refers to the new global sports monoculture as 'prolympism', reflecting its origins in 'the merger of professional sport and corporate Olympic sport'. On the other hand, despite the existence of prolympism and the rise of corporations like Nike, Donnelly concludes that accounts of global tendencies are not best served by conceptions such as 'cultural imperialism' – among which he includes 'McDonaldization'. As Williams also points out, national-centred views and presentations of sport remain vibrant. Houlihan (1994) and Harvey et al. (1996) are among a number of commentators who distinguish several different dimensions and forms of globalization in relation to sport and leisure: economic, political, cultural and psychic, and so on – particularly emphasizing that 'sportization' is not a *unitary* process. There exist many examples of counter-tendencies to and contestation of, dominant commercial and globalizing tendencies (see Jary et al., 1991, on the oppositional stance of many football 'fanzines'). The relation of sports to 'new social movements', and the relative success of the anti-racist and feminist movements in sport can also be mentioned. Finally, sport's 'important, saving grace is that the joys of performance and the excitement of unpredictable drama still have the ability to transcend the commodification of sport' (Williams, 1994: 394).

Conclusion

At its simplest, McDonaldization is occurring but the counter-tendencies are equally obvious. As one none too sympathetic commentator on *The McDonaldization of Society* has suggested, 'Places like McDonald's are proliferating, but so are extremely congenial cafés and sandwich bars' (Gilling, 1996).

What has been suggested in this review of Ritzer's treatment of sport and leisure in his 'McDonaldization of society' thesis is that he raises important issues but simply fails to sufficiently ground his concerns in the now extensive research literature on sport and leisure. I have sought to indicate how this thesis can be given a more substantial grounding by identifying a number of 'stages' in the development of the social processes associated with McDonaldization. However, in doing this I have also identified significant limitations of the thesis. In the first place, I would claim to have identified crucial issues left unexamined or under-examined by Ritzer which undermine his treatment of 'resistance' to McDonaldization. In the second place, my discussion might also be seen as raising the issue of whether in the final analysis 'McDonaldization' provides a suitable formulation of many of the complex developments in sport and leisure that can be observed.

Notes

Thanks to Erwin Bengry – postgraduate research student at Staffordshire University researching on Nike – for assistance in locating sources and material for this chapter and for his perceptive observations on modern cultural phenomena, which have alerted me to some issues. Thanks also to Ellis Cashmore, Daniel Jary, John O'Neill, Martin Parker, Alan Sillitoe and Barry Smart for generously sharing their thoughts on McDonaldization and helping to sharpen up a number of points in the chapter.

1 Vance Packard wrote a number of best-selling books on advertising and consumer issues seen as pseudo-psychological and pseudo-sociological by many academic commentators. These books raised public consciousness about consumer issues, but, paradoxically, also helped to raise the profile of advertising agencies! Attention to McDonaldization may have similar paradoxical effects.

2 As an illustration of this, Nike are reported to have intervened to try to prevent the transfer of the Brazilian superstar Ronaldo from Barcelona fearing loss

of TV exposure. It is also significant – even if it has not been substantiated – that it has been rumoured that the decision to play Ronaldo in the final, despite his suffering a 'convulsion' on the morning of the game, resulted from pressure from Nike, reluctant to see their star resource absent from this most prominent of all sources of media attention.

3 Ritzer stresses the 'continuities' of 'modernization' and 'postmodernity', but it has to be recognized that the issues raised by 'postmodernity' are much more multi-faceted, involve more difficult dilemmas, and are far more open-ended than Ritzer allows. While there are some commentators (for example, McKay and Miller, 1991) who, like Ritzer or Harvey, argue that the political economy and social arrange-ments of modern sports and leisure can be seen as primarily 'post-Fordist', there are many others who to varying degrees see contemporary global society in markedly more complex 'postmodern' terms – including Featherstone (1990,1991), Giddens (1990, 1991), Lash (1990), Lash and Urry (1994) and Robertson (1990).

4 See McGuigan (1992) for an especially valuable account of 'submission' or 'resistance' to 'popular' cultural forms. What McGuigan, following both Bauman and Giddens, recommends as a way of avoiding simply having to accept either elitist or market determinations of sport and leisure is a 'Utopianism' – 'Utopian realism' in Giddens's terms – which can help us explore 'future options' guided by a consideration of competing general models of modernity, 'postmodernity' and globalization. Such an approach provides a fuller basis than provided by Ritzer for identification of possible 'resistance' to seemingly dominant trends. In such a mode, for instance, Sugden and Tomlinson (1998), in their examination of FIFA, provide a thoroughgoing exploration of both the complexity and the scope for, and limits to, resistance to commercial global tendencies.

References

Andrews. D. (1993) 'Desperately seeking Michel: Foucault's genealogy, the body, and critical sports sociology', *Sociology of Sport Journal*, 10: 148–67.

Ang, I. (1993) '*Dallas* and the ideology of mass culture', in S. During (ed.), *The Cultural Studies Reader*. London: Routledge, pp. 403–20.

Bailey, P. (1979) *Leisure and Class in Victorian England*. London: Routledge & Kegan Paul.

Baudrillard, J. (1988) *Jean Baudrillard: Selected Writings* (ed. M. Poster). Cambridge: Polity Press.

Bell, D. (1973) *The Coming of Post-Industrial Society: A Venture in Social Forecasting*. New York: Basic Books.

Bourdieu, P. (1978) 'How can one be a sports fan?' *Social Science Information*, 17 (6).

Cashmore, E. (1996) *Making Sense of Sport*. (2nd edn). London: Routledge.

Cole, C. and Hribar, A. (1995) 'Celebrity feminism: Nike style, post-fordism, tran-scendence, and consumer power', *Sociology of Sport Journal*, 12: 347–69.

Cross, G. (1993) *The Making of Consumer Culture*. London: Routledge.

Donnelly, P. (1996) 'The local and the global: globalization in the sociology of sport', *Journal of Sport and Social Issues*, 23: 239–57.

Dunning, E. and Rojek, C. (eds) (1992) *Sport and Leisure in the Civilizing Process*. London: Macmillan.

Dunning, E. and Sheard, K. (1979) *Barbarians, Gentlemen and Players*. London: Martin Robertson.

Durgnat, R. (1967) *Films and Feelings*. London: Faber & Faber.

Edgell, S. and Jary, D. (1973) 'Football – a sociological eulogy', in S. Parker and C. Smith, (eds), *Leisure in Britain*. Harmondsworth: Allen Lane.

Elias, N. and Dunning, E. (1986) *The Quest for Excitement*. Oxford: Blackwell.

Featherstone, M. (1990) *Global Culture*. London: Sage.

Featherstone, M. (ed.) (1991) *Consumer Culture and Post-Modernism*. London: Sage.

Fiske, J. (1987) *Television Culture*. London: Methuen.

Giddens, A. (1990) *The Consequences of Modernity*. Cambridge: Polity Press.

Giddens, A. (1991) *Modernity and Self-Identity*. Cambridge: Polity Press.

Gilling, A. (1996) 'Where there's Mc there's brass', *The Higher*, 18 August.

Goldman, R. and Papson, S. (1994) 'Advertising in the age of hypersignification', *Theory, Culture & Society*, 11 (1): 23–53.

Gruneau, R. (1983) *Class, Sport and Social Development*. Amherst, MA: University of Massachusetts Press.

Guttmann, A. (1978) *From Ritual to Record: The Nature of Modern Sports*. New York: Cambridge University Press.

Habermas, J. (1979) *Communication and the Evolution of Society*. London: Heinemann.

Hargreaves, J. (1986) *Sport, Power and Culture*. Cambridge: Polity Press.

Hargreaves, J. (1987) 'The body, sport and power relations', in J. Horne, D. Jary and A. Tomlinson (eds), *Sport, Leisure and Social Relations*. London: Routledge.

Harvey, D. (1989) *The Condition of Postmodernity: An Inquiry into the Origins of Social Change*. Oxford: Blackwell.

Harvey, J., Rail, G. and Thibault, L. (1996) 'Globalization and sport: sketching a theoretical model for empirical analyses', *Journal of Sport and Social Issues*, 23: 258–77.

Hebdige, D. (1979) *Subculture: The Meaning of Style*. London: Methuen.

Horne, J. and Jary, D. (1994) 'Japan and the World Cup: Asia's first World Cup hosts?' in A. Tomlinson and J. Sugden (eds), *Hosts and Champions: Soccer Culture, National Identities and the USA World Cup*. Aldershot: Arena Books.

Houlihan, B. (1994) 'Homogenization, Americanization and creolization of sport: varieties of globalization', *Sociology of Sport Journal*, 11: 356–75.

Izod, J. (1996) 'Televised sport and the sacrificial hero', *Sport and Social Issues*, 22: 173–93.

Jary, D. and Horne, J. (1994) 'The figurational sociology of sport and leisure revisited', in I. Henry (ed.), *Leisure: Modernity, Postmodernity and Lifestyle*. Brighton: Leisure Studies Association.

Jary, D., Horne, J. and Bucke, T. (1991) 'Football fanzines and football culture: a case of successful cultural contestation', *Sociological Review*, 39: 581–98.

Lash, S. (1990) *Sociology of Postmodernism*. London: Routledge.

Lash, S. and Urry, J. (1987) *The End of Organized Capitalism*. Cambridge: Polity Press.

Lash, S. and Urry, J. (1994) *Economies of Signs and Space*. London: Sage.

McGuigan, J. (1992) *Cultural Populism*. London: Routledge.

McKay, J. and Miller, T. (1991) 'From old boys to new men and women of the corporation: the Americanization and commodification of Australian sport', *Sociology of Sport Journal*, 8: 86–94.

Parker, M. (1997) 'Nostalgia and mass culture: McDonaldization and cultural elitism', in M. Alfino, J. Caputo and R. Wynyard (eds), *McDonaldization Revisited: Essays on the Commodification of Culture*. Westport, CT: Greenwood.

Ritzer, G. (1993) *The McDonaldization of Society: An Investigation into the Changing Character of Contemporary Social Life*. London: Pine Forge Press.

Ritzer, G. (1996a) *The McDonaldization of Society: An Investigation into the Changing Character of Contemporary Social Life* (rev. edn). London: Pine Forge Press.

Ritzer, G. (1996b) 'The McDonaldization thesis: is expansion inevitable?', *International Sociology*, 11: 291–308.

Robertson, R. (1990) 'Mapping the global condition', in M. Featherstone (ed.), *Global Culture*. London: Sage.

Rojek, C. (1985) *Capitalism and Leisure Theory*. London: Tavistock.

Sugden, J. and Tomlinson, A. (1998) *FIFA and the Contest for the World Cup – Who Rules the People's Game?* Cambridge: Polity Press.

Taylor, R. (1997) 'The death of football', BBC Radio 5 Series, April.

Whannel, G. (1992) *Fields in Vision: Television in Sport and Cultural Transformation*. London: Routledge.

Whannel, G. and Tomlinson, A. (1984) *Five Ring Circus: Money, Power and Politics at the Olympics*. London: Pluto Press.

Williams, J. (1994) 'The local and the global in English soccer and the rise of satellite television', *Sociology of Sport Journal*, 11: 376–97.

Williams, R. (1980) 'Advertising: the magic system', in S. During (ed.), *The Cultural Studies Reader*. London: Routledge. pp. 320–36.

Willis, P. (1978) *Learning to Labour*. Farnborough: Saxon House.

Willis, P. (1990) *Common Culture*. Milton Keynes: Open University Press.

Willis, S. (1993) 'Disney World: public use/private space', *South Atlantic Quarterly*, 92: 119–37.

9   McDonaldized Culture:

The End of Communication?

Richard Münch

With the development of a world-wide culture in the process of global-ization, the critique of contemporary culture links the triumph of the culture of entertainment with the end of authentic culture. This prognosis, however, tells us only half of the truth. What we can observe is a simul-taneous growth in the culture of entertainment and authentic culture, whose mutual linkage takes the place of the antagonism of classic middle-class orthodoxy and the avant-garde. Instead of clearly identifiable, successive styles in revolutionary breakthroughs, we see the increasingly faster change in the cycles of popular culture. Global and local culture are mutually linked to each other in a comprehensive cultural market. Urban middle-class culture disintegrates and makes room for a global network of amusement centres.

The Globalization of Cultural Production and Cultural Consumption

'Globalization' has become the most used term in the public discussion of the nineties. Hardly a commentary in the press, radio or television can manage without the use of this term. With frequent use, the semantic content of the term expands. It is supposed to include and explain everything, whereby the term increasingly loses selectivity and is devalued as a means of com-munication. Let's begin then with an ascertainment of the semantic content of the term with regard to our problem, the transformation of culture (Featherstone, 1995; Friedman, 1994; Giddens, 1990: 71–156; Robertson, 1992).

Globalization here means the fact that cultural products are less and less attached to a specific place of production, presentation and appropriation; rather, they are able to be offered in increasingly shorter amounts of time, even simultaneously, to the whole world. All the innovations of the tech-nology of communication lead to more and more people everywhere in the world being able to be reached by cultural production (Flichy, 1995). Anyone who has complete access to and makes full use of the capacities of the Internet can come into contact with anyone in the whole world

(Shields, 1996). On the one hand, that means one and the same cultural product can be passed on to every person in the world. An increasingly greater number of cultural products are liberated from their local ties and via the information superhighway find entrance to an increasingly more open world. On the other hand, it means that every single person has an increasingly greater number of cultural products available.

The sources of inspiration pour into the production of culture. The production of culture can, in principle, come into contact with everyone and be inspired by them. Novelty in literature, painting, music, theatre or musicals emanates from crossing borders, meeting with strangers, foreigners, and from unexpected experiences. Vast distances, which previously separated people from each other, are overcome by the global network, and thus the mutual exchange of ideas with people all over the world becomes possible. Those who were previously separated and lived a life of their own can now enter into association and create something new. The easing of the exchange of information by means of increasingly more efficient communication technology enables spatial, technical and temporal boundaries to be crossed: boundaries between cultural areas, cultural specialties and historical epochs. Hybrid forms of art, which are fed by various cultures, specialties and epochs, spread throughout the world and, moreover, are brought to the public on a multi-media basis (McLuhan, 1994: 231; McLuhan and Fiore, 1967: 63; Stevenson, 1995: 123–4).

Competition is intensified by the above-described globalization of the production and presentation of culture. Between artists and the public there is no previous standard, as for example, that which was established by the court of a prince or a king in the courtly culture (Elias, 1983), or that which was supported in middle-class culture by communities of the educated middle-class public – by theatre clubs, music clubs or reading societies (Dann, 1981; Hermann, 1982; Münch, 1991: 228-57).

In advanced modernity at the end of the twentieth century, the reading societies, theatre clubs and music clubs have long since lost their influence; the development of literature, theatre, music and art has been subjected more to the law of supply and demand of the expanding cultural market. At the same time, increasingly broader sections of the population – as a consequence of the expansion of education – are involved in the passing on of cultural productions. Movies are a medium that for the first time reaches the entire population. The powers of commercialism and the democratization of culture are united in this medium. A cultural industry arises that aims at the maximization of profit and the satisfaction of the preferences of the masses. Elitist high culture faces an increasingly all-encompassing mass culture.

Triumph of the Culture of Entertainment; End of Authentic Culture?

The characterization of this development as the disintegration of culture sees classic middle-class culture displaced by the culture of entertainment and takes classic middle-class culture as the measuring stick against which the culture of entertainment appears to be superficial. The cause for this was already seen by Horkheimer and Adorno in the commercialization of culture by the cultural industry. Culture becomes a commodity which is subject to the constraint of producing profit (Horkheimer and Adorno, 1972; Jameson, 1991; McAllister, 1996). Profit takes the place of aesthetic quality as the selection criterion for the development and dispersal of culture. The competition for consumers demands increasingly higher investments, which can then only make a profit if a cultural product can be sold more broadly and to different strata of the population. *Jurassic Park* is considered as the most successful example thus far of this cultural enhancement of capital setting a new trend in intensive global marketing (Palm, 1994). The high sums of capital that were invested in this project had to be turned over into a lucrative venture, and unique world-wide marketing brought that about. The product was brought on the market with great advertising expense everywhere in the world at the same time. Besides the movie as one kind of product, a previously unsurpassed number of special products, from toys to T-shirts, were driven deeply into all sectors of society, so that for a while the whole world seemed to be made up almost entirely of dinosaurs (Scriba, 1993). The many individual parts of the product chain allowed advertising to run independently because every individual product served as an advertisement for all of the accompanying products.

These wide and media-transgressing sales of cultural products to all sectors of society are forced, by virtue of the great amounts of capital invested, to earn a large profit. For this purpose, their production and dispersal have to be carried out professionally to a great extent and become an organized business down to the smallest detail (Wernick, 1991). Efficiency, calculability, predictability and control of the process of producing, presenting and distributing culture are of increasing importance (Ritzer, 1993: 9–11). The industrial production of culture directed toward sales to all sectors of the population is therefore unavoidable, independent of whether it comes from a private, capitalist business or from a governmental one, and especially when the private, capitalist and governmental businesses compete with each other in the same market for consumers. The globalization of cultural events creates such a unified market for all cultural products. Consequently, no production of culture can pull itself away from the constraints of the market. These can only be overcome by two strategies: to grow with the big competitors or to specialize in the special interests of a small segment of the market, which can again open up a new market world-wide for a product when successful.

If the invested capital is supposed to achieve the broadest sales possible and include various cultural specialties, then the standardization of culture is an inevitable consequence. One and the same product is offered everywhere in the world in the same form and is converted into a multitude of accompanying products. The book that comes out as a movie or the movie that comes out as a book belong to this strategy of multiplying market successes (Hoffmann, 1994). The media concerns, therefore, search for specific combinations to be able to deliver one and the same product to all specialty markets. Specialists like Andrew Lloyd Webber market their musical productions uniformly throughout the world. The original is played everywhere, that is, the same musical performed in the same way everywhere. There is no room for deviation. The public can accordingly count on the same professionally assured quality, the product itself can bring in the largest possible profit on the world-wide market (Gockel-Böhner, 1994). It is the same strategy introduced by McDonald's for serving the whole world with the same fast-food product. In this sense we can speak of the McDonaldization of culture (Ritzer, 1993).

The standardization of the global culture, resulting from the logic of selling cultural products to the broadest and most varied sectors of the public, is added to again through the standardizing effect of the repetition and imitation of successful products in successive production by the same manufacturers, equal-ranking competitors and lower-ranking cultural producers. The most successful cultural productions set the standard for all further cultural productions. The content of the imitation is less important, though, than the imitation of the technical perfection of the cultural products. Behind the many and diverse cultural events on the global market hide a small number of similar recipes for success. That doesn't mean that there is no place here for innovation. Due to sales to broad sectors of the population and to the quick imitation of successful products, a quick saturation of the market sets in, which can only be overcome by product cycles becoming increasingly shorter and the constant innovation of products. Cultural producers searching for success have to have prepared for the next generation of products before the current product has finished running. The global cultural market is, therefore, simultaneously characterized by a high degree of standardization and a high rate of innovation. Successful productions produce a tendency to imitate the form of the product, thus a standardization, but are replaced in increasingly shorter waves of new production successes with the same standardization effect. The replacement of a product line involves as a rule, no new revolutionary breakthrough, but rather the continuation of a product through the use of technological advances and adaptation to the fluctuations of the spirit of the time. Progress takes place first of all in the sense of technical perfection. That means cultural development is subject to the interplay of technical rationalization and the dynamic of the cycles of pop culture.

The sequence of fashion cycles is determined by the logic of innovation and satiation. Novelty appeals to the public's curiosity and need to be different, which are quickly satiated by the massive run to the new product and which have to be challenged again by something new (Coupland, 1991). The shorter these cycles become, the less a new cycle of pop culture can actually offer something new. Rather, old ideas are time and again packaged in a new way. Novelty reduces itself over the long run to the use of new technological possibilities. Beyond technological armament, culture seems to be spinning in a circle of fashion cycles without genuine innovations. At any rate, the cycles of popular culture move faster than the actual cultural innovations, which produce the picture of a cultural standstill with incredible movement (Virilio, 1992). We appear to be on the treadmill of pop culture cycles, moving ourselves ahead, without experiencing anything new. Innovations become blown up to mass phenomena and are again quickly robbed of their news value in an inflationary process (Münch, 1995: 93–101).

The standardization of entertainment culture is not only broken by the innovations of technical rationalization and by fashion cycles, but also by the logic of the diversification and pluralization of products. If a producer wants to serve a bigger market than before, the diversification of his or her palette of products offers a possibility to achieve success. A product is adapted to the expectations of the consumers of the different markets through variation, or it is augmented by other related products up to the point at which, with existing know-how, rationalization can maximize profits. In this way, the wide variety of authentic cultures are turned into a professionally produced diversity of commodities to serve a multitude of consumption preferences. McDonald's itself has diversified its standardized products and, in doing so, is complemented by a whole array of fast-food chains which offer different ethnic cuisines in a highly standardized form. The fast-food centres of the shopping malls present a whole world of cultural diversity within the confines of a small circle. As this professionally produced diversity in a standardized form spreads all over the world and marks out perception of the world, it becomes the real thing for us pushing the authentic origins of its presentations far into the background so that they no longer have any meaning for us. We are captured by the iron cage of a McDonaldized world and are cut off from any ties to the authentic world in which we would be able to take part in producing and reproducing a life that we could consider a good one (Ritzer, 1993: 147–59).

Along with the markets, the infrastructure of the means of transportation and communication also grows, and as a result so does the possibility for a growing number of suppliers to bring their products to the market. With the help of this infrastructure, new suppliers can open up new markets. Through the corresponding use of marketing, entirely new markets can also be created. In this respect, the global cultural market offers not only standardized mass products, but also a multitude of specialization for special interests. For the individual cultural consumer, the selection swells in the course of the globalization of the cultural market because every cultural product in the world tends to be accessible to him/her, be it through a trip to the appropriate place, through the global travel activities of the cultural producers, or through retrieval on the Internet or in the department store of interactive television. Next to the abundant selection of the department store exist an immense number of individual cultural programmes. Today's modern culture consumer is not only confronted with the standardized diversity of cultural fast-food chains and the diversity of Disneyland, but also has access to a greater number of more authentic cultural presentations. He/she can travel from Frankfurt to Mexico to see the relics of the Mayas, listen to Mexican street musicians or attend a performance of Mexico City's state ballet, but he/she can also attend an exhibition on Maya culture, listen to Mexican street musicians and enjoy the performance of a Mexican state ballet in Frankfurt.

From the Antagonism between Revolution and Restoration to the Sequence of Fashion Cycles.

It would be wrong to regard the expansion of commercial culture as nothing else but cultural decay. We generally lean toward this opinion because the sheer growth of entertainment culture draws our attention to it and distracts our gaze from non-commercial culture, and because the mechanisms of cultural reproduction have changed. The unity of the artist and the public in classic middle-class culture with standardized measures of quality has been broken apart. Bohemian society as the spearhead of an avant-garde culture looking for innovation also no longer exists. It lost its lustre long ago and has been replaced by a much less emphatically pronounced existence of a multitude of alternative subcultures, which serve as a reservoir for the talent search of the entertainment culture. Instead of the antagonism between bohemian society and the middle class, there is an interplay of experimental culture and entertainment culture that is profitable for both sides. In this sense, the manner of cultural reproduction has changed. Peaceful cooperation and mutual inspiration of experimental and entertainment culture shapes cultural reproduction, not the sequence of revolution and restoration.

Classic middle-class culture developed in the eighteenth century through emancipation from courtly culture and differentiation from simple folk culture. In Germany this meant the establishment of High German in literature against the dominance of the French language in courtly culture and against the splintering of folk culture into innumerable dialects. Classic middle-class culture achieved a dominant position. In the nineteenth century, however, it came up against the avant-garde culture of bohemian society. The contrast between these two cultures turned the development of middle-class culture into a sequence of revolution and restoration.

Commercial entertainment culture has taken the place of classic middle-class culture in the twentieth century. Entertainment culture now occupies the centre ground of society, while classic middle-class culture is in a peripheral position together with avant-garde culture and folk culture. Classic middle-class culture and avant-garde culture, as well as regional folk culture, have not disappeared; rather they themselves have gained in magnitude. They have, however, moved from the core of society to the periphery and play the secondary role of a reservoir of innovation for global entertainment culture.

Classic middle-class culture has lost the power to define what is beautiful. Avant-garde culture has been subdued by the approval of a broad playing field on which one can indulge oneself. The avant-garde can do anything, nothing commits a breach of the prevailing norms of good taste anymore. Therefore, it can no longer produce anything that is surprising. Rather, it provides for the unremitting siphoning off of usable commercial goods. Everything that tries to be 'avant-gardish' therefore, either remains trivial or is greedily absorbed by the entertainment industry and as a result becomes superficial. The antagonism between revolution and restoration is replaced by the ever quicker sequence of fashion cycles. As Baudrillard (1993) said, we are leading a life after the 'orgy'. Every freedom has been exploited, everything has already been tried out. Nothing can provoke us, nothing can claim to be new.

After the End of 'Middle-Class Culture': The New Cultural Diversity

The growing diversity of culture associated with the process of globalization is a different one from the diversity of relatively closed cultures which exist next to each other in a less intensely interconnected world and which reproduce themselves mainly independently and only a little by disputes with outsiders. In the case of minimal interconnection, local, regional and national cultures are still clearly differentiated, their uniqueness immediately stands out to the observer. The increasing number of external relationships and the accompanying economic and cultural exchanges that result blur the boundaries. More and more, one can find in one place that which can be found in another until all places are alike, because they offer that which is offered everywhere. Every year the pedestrian zones look more alike, regardless of the city in which one is at the moment, although the selection of goods and cultural events becomes more extensive (Greiner, 1996; Winter, 1996). When the same colourful diversity of Benettons, H&Ms and GAPs accost us everywhere, the world seems more monotonous to us, although each individual town has become more diversified. This arises, though, from the perspective of the cosmopolitan, who can no longer find anything in his/her restless search for something new because everything already exists everywhere. The local world becomes more diversified for the local population, however, because the whole world tends to be present in one place.

For both, the locals and the mobile, the individual town certainly loses its original character, even if old traditions remain intact or are again revived because this now constitutes a spot of colour in the colourful bouquet of locally presented global diversity. Local traditions also lose the actual character of a tradition because they represent one event alongside many others. They are not kept up out of a sense of continuity, but because traditions as means of self-identification have come to be employed for the purpose of differentiation from others with the hope of opening up a market niche for domestic consumers and future consumers from all over the world. In a *Heimatabend*, the traditional German social evening, a municipality sells itself to its guests with the help of the more or less successful commercial adaptation of local traditions.

Presented to us locally, the complete diversity of the world now stands ready for selection and therefore inevitably represents a selection of commodities from which we can choose. Local culture itself, however, is forced into the same market and can only continue to exist if it asserts itself in the competitive struggle and sees itself as a ware to be sold. Global culture comes to us as a ware and we have to take local culture to market in order to keep it alive. Traditions reproduce themselves in the wake of their market success. As a result, the nature of culture and its reproduction change. This has less to do with meaning and the production of meaning contexts than it does with profit and utility and the relationship between cost and services. This exchange between global and local cultures is part of the so-called 'glocalization' of modern life (Featherstone, 1995: 86–125; Friedman, 1994: 102–16; Robertson, 1992: 173–4).

Owing to the extent to which we professionally organize the local representation of global diversity, historically evolved municipal structures are no longer improved only by colourful window displays on the outside, but are replaced by artificially created entertainment centres (Brinkemper, et al., 1994; Rowe, 1995). Municipalities which previously had an independent existence with their interconnections outwards are then downgraded to the status of the consumer colony of the closest amusement park. A good example of such a structural change can be observed in the CentrO project in Oberhausen (CentrO, 1996). There, an international group of investors created a multi-functional amusement park which aimed to represent internationally the colourful diversity of the world. In the ring road-like shopping mall, the cuisines of the world can be appreciated in fast-food form; as if in time-lapse photography, the consumer traverses the whole world in the smallest space for a short visit to an Irish pub and on to a Chinese restaurant: very efficient, thoroughly calculated, completely predictable and strictly controlled so that no bad surprises can occur. McDonaldization of urban life at its highest. 'Fun, fun, fun' as the meaning of urban life (Ritzer, 1993: 126–9). According to the calculations of the group of investors, the new amusement centre is located in a two-hour catchment area of 30 million people, whose home towns are demoted to the status of residential satellites of the new centre. The centre has access to no less than 12 connections to five expressways within a distance of 2.5 km. Streetcars bring visitors to the inter-city train station every five minutes. Within 30 minutes one international and two national airports can be reached. With these interconnections to the outside world, visitors to the centre can change in seconds from the local ring road to the global traffic circle and continue their pleasure-trip in another amusement centre or they can revolve around the world for a while in outer orbit from amusement centre to amusement centre. Everything is offered here, in external as well as internal orbit: local colour, folk culture, and that which appeals to the tastes of the classic middle class, the avant-garde and to those looking for an alternative. Even cabaret, which critically attacks the whole show, is a must. There is no lack of anything, except for one thing: exclusivity. When everything is inclusive, it can logically no longer be exclusive.

Towns lose their right to exist by themselves. They owe their existence to the global world of wares' openness to colourful diversity and to the fastest possible connection to the orbital system of transportation. The more a town can pack global diversity into itself and the quicker it is to reach and be left again, all the more chances it has to be able to survive in the global competitive struggle for the time spent by residents and visitors. 'The most important location is no longer the downtown area in which everything happens. The most important locations are the expressway road, the airport, the train station' (Greiner, 1996). The development of a globally interconnected system of amusement centres pushes cities and municipalities, which had previously provided the backdrop for cultural development, into the role of the centres' dormitory communities, and can only exist because of their connection to the system of centres. While some old metropolises, because of their internal varied content, can continue to survive in this system as a junction next to the newly emerged amusement centres, most cities and municipalities, which had previously evolved through the cultural development that they stimulated, now see their cultures disintegrate as the great centres draw to themselves the activities of people, snatching them away.

'In' and 'Out': Cultural Dynamic without Understanding

If cultural business changes into a pure market event whose cultural products emerge and diffuse solely according to the law of adaptation to supply and demand, societal life loses its context. An understanding not only of what is 'nice' or 'not nice', but also what is 'good' and 'not good', 'true' and 'false', is then no longer possible. An understanding solely on the basis of individual exchange processes in the current society is only conceivable, though, with the prerequisite that everything that people want as their own possessions can be produced and used without a negative effect on a third party. This prerequisite, however, does not exist. We can see already that the consumption of a multitude of individual goods does not occur without a negative effect on a third party. Even if we, more than before, were one day to turn culture into a multitude of individual goods via the Internet and interactive television culture (Flichy, 1995), this 'progress' would not release us from the dilemma that individual cultural goods also have negative effects on a third party. As long as we live in a community with others, have to explain ourselves to them and the shaping of our lives depends on their thoughts and behaviour, the ideas that they have about what is a beautiful, good and morally correct life cannot be unimportant to us. We are indirectly affected by their cultural consumption. If culture, however, is nothing more than a gigantic selection of wares, then the paths to an understanding with others are blocked.

With the advancement of the global cultural market, culture as a medium of mutual understanding disappears. What the nation-state had previously provided regarding mutual understanding becomes a stronghold of traditionalistic and particularistic counter-movements. A world society, which is more than the global cultural market and which disposes of institutions of understanding, is up to now, if at all, only initially recognizable as a silhouette upon the slow opening of the national cultural institutions and the development of a global network.

Without this complementary institutional development, culture is swallowed up by the dynamics of the market. It disintegrates into a multitude of subcultures between which no understanding is possible. Opinions of good taste become arbitrary and cannot, therefore, regulate communication beyond a small circle of people. As cultural production has expanded, cultural communication has broken down. Everything is possible, nothing is binding anymore. Labelling this condition as postmodern creates a new epoch for what in reality is nothing other than cultural anomie (Featherstone, 1991: 122–8), a condition under which everyone tends to come into conflict with everyone else (Hobbes, 1966), since we cannot live together without mutual obligations.

Without definite opinions about good taste that achieve validity in the general population, substitute currencies take the helm of cultural communication. Such a more frequently used substitute currency is the differentiation between 'in' and 'out'. It follows more the ups and downs of fashion cycles and is directed more by the law of the opening up of markets and market satiation than by the production of cultural understanding. What is 'in' is made into various trends by the interplay of market movements and their stylization by market observers. The more the market is satiated and consumption wanes, the more consumers have to be put on a new track by the cultural producers, who introduce the 'out' of the old trend and the 'in' of a new one. Culture moves ahead on the level of the least possible understanding. It thus allows for the increase of sales of cultural products; however, an understanding that goes beyond that and has an effect in other functional areas of societal behaviour is not achieved by this increase of cultural consumption. Society is handed over to the inherent dynamic of the powers of the market. We lose the ability to have an understanding about how we generally want to live. The global market dynamic enhances our ability for private choice extremely, but it devours the last scrap of our common self-determination, in the sense of deciding together on how to live on the basis of mutual understanding.

Conclusion

The present cultural transition gives us an increasingly closer linkage between global culture and regional culture, screen culture and written culture, mass culture and authentic culture. Both sides grow simultaneously, interpenetrate each other and through increasing competition are subject to an ever-faster change in the cycles of popular culture. Culture loses its status as a means of understanding and instead becomes a comprehensive animation machine. The increase in its short-term experiental value is accompanied by a steady reduction in its long-term value regarding understanding and self-ascertainment. Culture no longer passes on a way of thinking; rather it becomes the service station of an expanding spectrum of needs, which can be produced for the purpose of assuring the sales of cultural products through extensive marketing. Creativity does not get lost; rather it is constantly used more inclusively and quickly by a growing cultural industry. As a result of this, the moments of creative authenticity become shorter and shorter, are therefore exhausted faster, and correspondingly the faster they have to be replaced by something new. We are caught up in the circle of the ever-faster sequence of 'in' and 'out', which reduces our ability to define what good taste is on the global cultural market.

Cultural communication occurs less and less on the basis of an understanding about what is beautiful, true and good, and more and more solely as the consumption of cultural products in a global cultural market. As a result, all common standards of life vanish. Since, however, individual cultural goods are not able to be consumed without external negative effects on others, we are moving towards a world of increasing conflict in which a common basis of understanding about a proper life no longer exists. This is an irrational effect of a rationalization process which turns the whole world into a market ready for professional organization. What we gain in the multiplication of opportunities for private choice is lost in the chances for public choice in a public sphere. The McDonaldized world serves the private autonomy of the consumer but works against the public autonomy of the citizen. The good life is not just the sum of many individual choices, particularly in a world where each individual act is interdependent with a countless number of other individual acts anywhere in the world. This means that the chances for the realization of our plans for a good life are strongly dependent on each other so that there is a growing need for their coordination. Therefore the 'good life' calls very much for common deliberation in a public sphere. It cannot be left to the production machinery of a global fun industry in a completely McDonaldized world (Ritzer, 1993: 12–13, 121–46).

Translation by Susan C. Madiedo

References

Baudrillard, J. (1993) *The Transparency of Evil*. London: Verso.
Brinkemper, P.V., von Dadelsen, B. and Seng, T. (1994), *World Media Park: Globale Kulturvermarktung heute*. Berlin: Aufbau Taschenbuch Verlag.
CentrO (1996) *CentrO: Neue Mitte Oberhausen*. Promotional brochure. Spring.
Coupland, D. (1991) *Generation X: Tales for an Accelerated Culture*. New York: St Martin's Press.
Dann, O. (1981) *Lesegesellschaften und bürgerliche Emanzipation*. Munich: Beck.
Elias, N. (1983) *The Court Society*. Oxford: Blackwell.
Featherstone, M. (1991) *Consumer Culture and Postmodernism*. London: Sage.
Featherstone, M. (1995) *Undoing Culture: Globalization, Postmodernism and Identity*. London: Sage.
Flichy, P. (1995) *The Dynamics of Modern Communication: The Shaping and Impact of New Communication Technologies*. London: Sage.
Friedman, J. (1994) *Cultural Identity and Global Process*. London: Sage.
Giddens, A. (1990) *The Consequences of Modernity*. Cambridge: Polity Press.
Gockel-Böhner, C. (1994) 'Das wirklich nützliche *Phantom der Oper*: Andrew Lloyd Webbers weltweite Musicalvermarktung', in P.V. Brinkemper, B. von Dadelsen and T. Seng (eds), *World Media Park: Globale Kulturvermarktung heute*. Berlin: Aufbau Taschenbuch Verlag.
Greiner, U. (1996) 'Total vergnügt: Stadtkultur und Unterhaltungsindustrie im Widerstreit', *Die Zeit*. 5 April.
Hermann, U. (1982) *Die Bildung des Bürgers: Die Formierung der bürgerlichen Gesellschaft und die Gebildeten im 19. Jahrhundert*. Weinheim: Beltz.
Hobbes, T. (1966) 'Leviathan', in W. Molesworth (ed.), *Collected English Works of Thomas Hobbes. Vol. 3*. Aalen: Scientia.
Hoffmann, H. (1994) 'Der Buch-Film-Hit: Das neue Verhältnis von Literatur und Film', in P.V. Brinkemper, B. von Dadelsen and T. Seng (eds), *World Media Park: Globale Kulturvermarktung heute*. Berlin: Aufbau Taschenbuch Verlag.
Horkheimer, M. and Adorno, T.W. (1972) *Dialectic of Enlightenment*. New York: Herder & Herder.
Jameson, F. (1991) *Postmodernism, or, the Cultural Logic of Late Capitalism*. Durham, NC: Duke University Press.
McAllister, M. (1996) *The Commercialization of American Culture*. London: Sage.
McLuhan, M. (1994) *Understanding Media: The Extensions of Man*. London: Routledge.
McLuhan, M. and Fiore, Q. (1967) *The Medium is the Message*. Harmondsworth: Penguin.
Münch, R. (1991) *Dialektik der Kommunikationsgesellschaft*. Frankfurt-on-Main: Suhrkamp.
Münch, R. (1995) *Dynamik der Kommunikationsgesellschaft*. Frankfurt-on-Main: Suhrkamp.
Palm, G. (1994) 'Raptors in pursuit. *Jurassic Parc*: Aufbruch zum Hypermedium', in P.V. Brinkemper, B. von Dadelsen and T. Seng (eds), *World Media Park: Globale Kulturvermarktung heute*. Berlin: Aufbau Taschenbuch Verlag.
Ritzer, G. (1993) *The McDonaldization of Society: An Investigation into the Changing Character of Contemporary Social Life*. Newbury Park, CA: Pine Forge Press.
Robertson, R. (1992) *Globalization: Social Theory and Global Culture*. London: Sage.
Rowe, D. (1995) *Popular Cultures: Rockmusic, Sport and the Politics of Pleasure*. London: Sage.
Scriba, J. (1993) 'Dinomanie', *Focus*, no. 24, 14 June.

Shields, R. (ed.) (1996) *Cultures of Internet*. London: Sage.
Stevenson, N. (1995) *Understanding Media Cultures: Social Theory and Mass Communication*. London: Sage.
Virilio, P. (1992) *Rasender Stillstand*. Munich: Hanser.
Wernick, A. (1991) *Promotional Culture: Advertising, Ideology and Symbolic Expression*. London: Sage.
Winter, M. (1996) 'In Koblenz oder anderswo', *Süddeutsche Zeitung*, 16 February.

10 Art Centres:

Southern Folk Art and the Splintering of a Hegemonic Market

Gary Alan Fine

Some slogans haunt the sociological imagination; they are *bon mots* of the scholarly class. In a pithy form, they seize upon a complex truth, holding it up for readers to pay attention. They capture a fundamental concern of which social scientists, given their habitus, feel certain. George Ritzer's (1996) profound image of the 'McDonaldization of society' is one such example. Part of the power of Ritzer's resonant phrase is that it embodies the scorn that many in the academy feel toward mass feeding. Academics re-present (or believe they represent) a 'highbrow' mentality effectively depicted nearly a half-century ago by essayist Russell Lynes (1954) in his essay *The Taste-makers* on highbrows, middlebrows and lowbrows. We are predisposed to treat the provision of culture to mass audiences as being *in itself* something of which to be wary. The absence of the differentiation of taste cultures threatens our status as tastemakers. Many elites are prone to accept the outlines of what Herbert Gans (1974) labelled 'the mass culture critique' (cf. Rosenberg and White, 1957). Underlying this view is the claim of a negative correlation between popularity and quality, as well as the confident, if arrogant, assumption that the speaker is able to judge quality definitively.

For Herbert Gans, a vigorous critic of this approach, the mass culture critique is composed of four fundamental themes: that the process of creation of mass culture harms high culture; that mass culture drives out high culture; that mass culture harms individuals; and that ultimately mass culture saps the strength of society, leading to totalitarianism. In an age in which 'cultural grazing' among all genres is more the rule than the exception, these claims are problematic. Yet more than a few cultural critics have an often inchoate feeling that provision of culture (and culinary products surely qualify, even if hamburgers and fries do not always seem very cultural) should not be homogenized and modified to be acceptable to the lowest common denominator. Diversity in culture as well as in politics is ennobling. Cultural products should be seen not simply as products, displayed within a marketplace, but as personal creations.

The degree to which products and services are locally or regionally segmented is highly variable. Market segmentation is not absolute but relative, depending on the economic structures and characteristics of the audience. For instance, the selling of fried chicken, burritos and hamburgers has become oligopolistic, with a relatively small number of large corporations dominating the market, with increasingly little local variation. Contrast these foods to *moo shu* pork, *pad thai* or crawfish *étoufée*. These delicacies have not been effectively franchised, as yet. This does not mean, of course, that ethnic or regional foodways haven't spread across the country, but only that these culinary domains have proven to be relatively resistant to franchising and national control. Most Chinese, Thai and Cajun restaurants are locally owned and operated. This resistance to corporate homogenization is a matter of degree; small establishments do exist and there is a motivation among some restaurateurs to modify their cuisine to make it acceptable to a larger proportion of potential diners (Shun and Fine, 1995).

Art and McDonaldization

In this analysis I focus on another corner of the cultural realm: the art world. To what extent is there evidence of a McDonaldization of contemporary art? By this I mean to what extent, if at all, are art markets becoming increasingly homogenized, with art works being produced more like commodities, rather than as personal inspirations? To what extent are these cultural objects being fabricated under the guidance of others, who, attuned to the market, direct the production in light of consumer demand? In other words, to what extent are works produced in accordance with the goals of efficiency, predictability, calculability and control: values that have been regarded as inimical to the creation of aesthetic objects?

Art market consumers, being cultural elites, would seem to be ideologically opposed to the development of mass culture. But to what extent is this opposition to the routinization of styles and content merely a comforting delusion among those who wish to believe that they are discerning, while simultaneously demonstrating a considerable need to conform to established tastes? Any cursory history of contemporary art demonstrates that art worlds are highly fragmented, and, at least on some dimensions, they seem to be becoming more so. I suggest that this is a function of the demise of the hegemony of modernism since the 1960s (Gablik, 1984), coupled with an increasing segmentation and specialization of art audiences. In making this argument I focus primarily on the development and growth of one domain of the art world, now typically labelled 'self-taught art'. Twenty-five years ago there were no US galleries that focused exclusively on this art genre, although some galleries, such as Gallerie St Étienne in New York and the Janet Fleisher Gallery in Philadelphia, had displayed the work of self-taught artists, such as Anna Robertson 'Grandma' Moses, William Edmonson or Horace Pippin since the 1940s and 1950s. However, these galleries also showed other styles, such as, in the case of the Gallerie St Étienne, German expressionists. Today the number of galleries that specialize in 'folk art' has grown exponentially. A 1993 research volume (*Twentieth Century American Folk, Self Taught, and Outsider Art* by librarian Betty-Carol Sellen) lists 137 galleries and dealers with self-taught art as one of their specialties. While not all of these have self-taught art as their singular focus, the evidence reveals the growth of this particular market segment. A 1997 list, as judged by the number of new galleries and increased number of advertisements in magazines directed to the folk art community, would indicate an increased number of galleries selling self-taught art. As the number of books and articles published on self-taught art increases, this segment of the art world gains increased prominence, and develops a critical infrastructure. The establishment of the Museum of American Folk Art in the early 1960s, and this museum's greater focus on contemporary folk art in the 1970s and 1980s, is part of this growing prominence. So, too, is the decision of the High Museum of Art in 1994 to appoint a curator of folk art, the first major general art museum in the USA to do so. The earlier establishment of the Folk Art Society of America in 1986 had similarly provided collectors with an organization in which to share their interests and enthusiasms.

Several dimensions exist through which we can explore the extent to which there has been a McDonaldization of the art world. First, to what degree are art galleries part of a *hegemonic distribution system* – directly linked to each other through tight network ties? Is the art world directly or indirectly a hegemonic world in terms of ownership of the means of distribution – either through direct control or through franchising? Second, to what extent is the art world characterized by the *mass production of products*? Is uniformity a primary goal of the production of art works, or is each object expected to be a unique expression of a producer? Third, are the range of products available to consumers functionally similar, that is, designed to appeal to a *mass audience*? Whatever the nature of the control of the distribution, is the art market reticulated so as to comprise numerous specialized markets, with different products – with distinctive content and price to appeal to different sets of collectors – or is there a single market that is being appealed to? The final dimension concerns the existence of a *production community*. Is this occupation ('artist') comprised primarily of individuals who are similar and interchangeable? While all occupations are internally segmented to some degree (Bucher, 1962; Fine, 1996) with individuals serving different markets within the umbrella of the occupational label, what is the extent of these internal occupational divisions in light of the abilities and ideologies of the community of producers? Does a single production community exist?

Hegemonic Distribution System

It is readily apparent that the art world has been segmented, and that galleries are known for specializing in certain periods of art, in certain styles, or for selling work in a particular price range. Galleries are not interchangeable, and, in the words of economists, art works are not fungible goods. The question is whether the art world as a whole can be said to be characterized, in any respect, by McDonaldization. In one obvious – and important – sense, unlike the example of McDonald's itself, there are not large numbers of franchised galleries. Several galleries have locations in a few US cities, such as PaceWildenstein in New York and Los Angeles or Phyllis Kind Gallery in New York and Chicago. Often such multiple locations are a function of the lifestyles of the gallery directors, such as the America Oh Yes! galleries in Hilton Head and Washington or the Anton Haardt gallery in Montgomery and New Orleans. However, these are exceptions. Few art galleries maintain outlets in multiple locations. Art galleries typically have not been subject to economies of scale, perhaps because they depend to such a great extent upon personal relations between gallery directors and a handful of prosperous customers – relations that cannot be duplicated through a national brand name. The selling, however focused on particular material goods it might seem to be, is ultimately based on friendship and on social pressures. Franchising art galleries, especially at the high end, but also generally throughout the market, has not occurred. Whether the local orientation of service is inevitable is an open question. While there are reasons to doubt the possibility of franchising and national expansion of retail outlets (particularly at the high end of the market), it is well to remember that not too long ago real estate firms or hospital corporations were localized in particular cities. Further, many galleries, while they are small businesses that are situated in particular cities (frequently New York), have a national clientele.

The size and income of most galleries and dealers who specialize in folk art are small, even by art world standards – few, for example, are members of the prestigious Art Dealers' Association of America (only three of the 137 listed in the Sellen volume are members of the 147-member ADAA). These are small businesses, typically under-capitalized, and, if the owners are not supported by other means of earning a living (framing, writing or consulting), are hand-to-mouth affairs, continued because of the satisfactions and status associated with the business. That the owners do this as a matter of love means that the businesses are not as fragile as they might otherwise be; however, few gallery owners have the resources to think of expanding, and many galleries, even those of major dealers, are run out of private homes, such as Bonnie Grossman's Ames Gallery in Berkeley or Robert Reeves Art and Antiques in Atlanta. These gallery owners live over the store, or, more precisely, in the store. Franchising is not thought of as a viable option.

Mass Production

Fine art has been treated and understood as a unique good, not subject to duplication. Creativity is linked to the production of the original, singular and personal. However, this is applicable only to a point. The legitimacy of printmaking reminds us that under certain circumstances multiples have been considered a viable part of the art market. Even excluding the exact duplicates that print, sculptural and photographic technology can provide, the artist is expected to be relying upon a distinctive style – a style that should change slowly and deliberately. An artist should have a recognizable *oeuvre*. Just as music audiences crave the 'old favourites' of singers, bands, orchestras and opera companies, the same process operates for visual artists. One wishes to purchase a Jasper Johns or a Georgia O'Keefe that, while unique in some measure, must look recognizably like the other works of that artist. A signature, while important, does not obviate the need for a recognizable canvas. Most artists are pressured directly or implicitly to continue to produce work within the same stylistic and thematic choices that have previously characterized their work. While some artists do change their styles markedly in the course of their career, these changes typically must not come too often or be too radical. When stylistic changes occur, artists are expected to explain what decisions (or aesthetic theory) produced these alternations. Once an artist has been labelled according to critical or public typifications of his or her work, change becomes problematic. While artists are expected to 'change' or 'grow', that is, *not* to produce in precisely the same way, any changes must be limited in time and in scope.

Self-taught artists pose particular problems in this regard. Since these artists are not trained as to what proper range of variation of one's style constitutes 'artistic growth', one may find that a self-taught artist's style changes either too much or too little. The works produced by Mose Tolliver, a Montgomery, Alabama, self-taught artist, have remained remarkably consistent over the past two decades. Tolliver paints the same subjects again and again, and this has served him well as the demand for some of his subjects continues to be strong. Dealers can request that he paint them 10 birds, knowing that each will be recognizably a Mose Tolliver work. Although there have been changes in his paintings over the last two decades, the similarities of the works are more prominent than the differences, at least in the eyes of many critics. Further, Tolliver permits his children to paint 'his' works, which he then dutifully signs with his recognizable signature. When these family members market their own works, painted in a very similar style, under their own names, the prices that they receive are far less than half of what their father receives for the works that he signs. In effect, Tolliver has established an art factory, not unknown in the history of art (Corot and Rubens come to mind), but it is a project that challenges the image of individual and isolated genius.

Other self-taught artists may alter their style or production in a radical fashion during their artistic 'career' – dramatically changing the nature of their artistic reputation. Collectors can date precisely when the Rev. Howard Finster's work changed, and markedly decreased in value. During September 1989 Finster began using coloured markers on his works, instead of paint, thereby changing the aesthetic character of his work. This corresponded to a speeding up of production, which led to the creation or fabrication of 'cut-outs' that had far less value on the art market, but retained considerable popular appeal. Perhaps this change in audience and reputation mattered less for Finster, since his objective to get his pieces into as many hands as possible was a function of his religious missionary work. In light of this goal, cheaper, more efficiently produced art works had value over works of art that were more distinctive and more time-consuming to create. Often there is a push towards efficiency and sameness, particularly for those who have not fully embraced the ideology of elite art markets, which affects the valuation of the 'art' work. In a sense this process suggests a degree of McDonaldization of art markets, as pieces are produced in a rapid sequence that meet audience expectations. To the degree that folk artists see themselves as creating reproducible and similar objects for a market, they are open to embracing a style that exemplifies a homogenization of production.

Mass Audience

One indication of whether a market is characterized by McDonaldization is the degree to which its audience is segmented. Is there a single market for art works, or do different markets exist that are largely non-intersecting? Posed this way, the question almost answers itself.

Consider the dynamics of collecting. As David Halle (1993) has noted in his book *Inside Culture*, most individuals choose to place objects on their walls and tables throughout their residence that they consider to have aesthetic or emotional appeal and that say something about their taste and social identity. This desire for decoration applies in upper-, middle-, and working-class homes. Of course homes are not interchangeable, and size is not the only feature that differentiates houses. Collectors can reasonably be divided by social class and taste cultures (Gans, 1974). In addition, artistic audiences also tend to be segmented by the form of the objects they collect (sculpture, photography, textiles, ceramics), genre (landscape, portrait, abstract) and by what we might loosely label 'style' (expressionism, pop, hyperrealism, self-taught). That these divisions cover so much ground suggests that even these categories are insufficient to segment an audience fully. Collectors have their own agendas and tastes that guide them in the selection and placement of aesthetic objects in their homes and places of business.

When we change focus from collecting – a highly personal and often idiosyncratic culling of objects from an enormous pool of potential arte-facts – to all cultural consumption, we discover that artistic preferences are less segmented in the sense that individuals with considerable levels of cultural capital attend a range of cultural domains. As Peterson and Kern (1996) have pointed out, the range of cultural preferences of elites is quite large, indicating that the traditional division between high culture and popular culture is not valid. Elite audiences enjoy jazz, blues, symphonies, impressionism, abstract expressionism and self-taught art. Still, the mere fact of diversity does not presume a homogenization of taste, but suggests instead what we might label *artistic grazing* – a recognition of the reality that cultural elites find it self-enhancing to sample from a variety of genres and styles. The best, the highest form of every artistic realm is potentially worthy of appreciation by cultural connoisseurs.

The existence of a distinct and publicly recognized field of collecting that we can label as Southern contemporary self-taught art reveals the diversity of the collecting market. Further, the existence of such a collecting domain validates the importance of multiculturalism and artistic diversity. In addition, this young collecting field has found a market niche in that the prices for even high-quality works are sufficiently reasonable that highly educated but moderately paid collectors can participate – precisely those individuals who might be seen as most open to an art world with diversity as a hallmark. With the dramatic price inflation that characterized the art market of the 1980s, purchasing significant art works became difficult for many educated professionals. Works of reasonable quality selling in the five-figure range proved beyond the reach of many young collectors, but other, newly formed markets emerged to satisfy the collecting urge. During the 1980s it was easily possible to purchase significant works of Southern contemporary self-taught art for three-figure prices, and high-quality pieces ('museum quality') for four figures. As the infrastructure of galleries began to expand, a legitimate folk art market became possible. A sufficiently large number of collectors believed in the desirability of multicultural expression and could afford the prices asked; some gallery owners found that they could make a living catering to this market. A combination of ideological support for multiculturalism and economics proved to be irresistible in overcoming claims that the art works produced were ugly or strange objects that anyone could have created, given a similar lack of formal training. The fact that there developed a group of collectors with their own magazines, galleries, museums, art fairs, books and the like, suggests a fragmentation of the art market. Over the course of two decades, a distinctive new, recognizable art market segment has been created, one which is now discussed in magazines such as *Artforum* or *Art in America*.

Production Community

One of the characteristics of McDonaldization is the claim that those who produce similar products will be fundamentally similar in their social characteristics. That is, in our example, that, as a group, artists will be recognizably alike. While members of an occupation do have similarities, occupations are inclined to be internally segmented (Bucher and Strauss, 1961). This is demonstrably true of art as portraitists and environmental artists have distinctive goals and separate audiences. Although we may typify or stereotype artists in various ways, their diversity is profound. When one looks beyond the realm of trained artists and examines self-taught artists, even greater social and cultural diversity is apparent. Some observers have argued that it is precisely the outsider status of self-taught artists that gives their work its power (Cardinal, 1972; Maizels, 1996). These artists – impoverished, homeless, illiterate or mentally ill – stand in stark contrast to those trained artists who are rich in cultural capital. In an important sense it is precisely the reality that contemporary folk artists are not professionally trained that makes their products desirable for collectors. It is the shattering of the occupational boundary, and the ratification of that boundary breaking, that is central to contemporary folk art. Part of this process is evident in the central role that *biography* (and stories about biography) plays in the legitimation of artists' work. Dealers recognize this, and, as part of their selling strategies, exploit the outsider characteristics of the artists whose work they are hawking.

While some collectors and some dealers (and even some artists) claim to hope that there will be a time when there will be no division between this type of art and Art 'with a capital A', the fact that this genre is recognizable and that it has its own infrastructure suggests that this day lies far in the future. The three most common labels for this type of art are 'folk art', 'outsider art' and 'self-taught art'. Consider each of these in turn: each implicitly celebrates the difference between these art workers and other, more institutionally legitimate arts workers.

The term 'folk art' addresses issues of community boundaries. In some regards all groups can be considered 'folk groups', in the sense that every group has a sense of tradition, provided, that is, members recognize themselves as a community. However, in practice the label 'folk' refers to a group that lacks the cultural capital of elite groups – it is a group that is set apart from the mainstream of society – set apart from a capitalist-industrial manufacturing present, the 'culture industry', and from the present world of McDonald's and other corporately directed franchises. The term 'outsider artist' even more explicitly differentiates insiders from outsiders. The concept of an outsider presupposes the existence – and the recognition – of 'insiders' in relation to whom they are to be contrasted. There is particularly intense controversy within the critical community about this term as some perceive that it marginalizes the artists, separating them from society at large, even if the label is not meant to have pejorative implications. The label 'self-taught' similarly is used to differentiate 'folk' artists from others who are 'institutionally trained'. For many it is unclear as to what constitutes self-taught artists, as all artists require some information that leads them to produce certain products in particular ways, adopting some techniques and avoiding others. In addition, there are some accepted, professional artists who are recognized to be self-taught, for example Joseph Cornell. Further, all artists, whatever their relationship to the work world, are in some measure 'self-taught', indeed this is precisely where their creativity lies.

The reality that certain artists are recognized by collectors and dealers as forming a collectable group, no matter how imperfectly constituted around the margins the group might be, underlines the diversity of production communities in the art world. While McDonaldization suggests that personnel will be functionally interchangeable, the world of self-taught art presents evidence that this process is not occurring across the art world as a whole.

While the art world can be seen in some ways as exemplifying the process of McDonaldization in its economic changes, the bulk of the evidence suggests that the themes of McDonaldization are of limited relevance in an understanding of the world of art. While there are aspects of the art world where McDonaldization is evident, in general art depends for its power and its value on the ability of appreciative audiences to differentiate between classes of works. Not only are the products distinctive, but participating in this world allows consumers to situate themselves as distinctive. Art is a product that, like other forms of expressive culture (for example, clothing, furnishings), permits the holder to make a statement about self, personal identity and relationship with a larger community.

Still, we should be wary of pushing this hypothesis of social differentiation too far; expressive products serve both to set boundaries among groups of consumers and also to connect them to recognizable social groups. In practice one does not attempt to classify meaningless or fully idiosyncratic art objects, but rather art objects that are to be recognized as being linked to particular communities. In a sense, art works, like clothing, bear a label. In the case of art this label is generally the signature of the artist, and in most art worlds a signed art work will be regarded as more valuable than the same work unsigned. The signature is part of the 'value-added' quality of the piece. It is frequently the case in folk art, and throughout the art world, that art works will be referred to with the reference that this is an 'X' – X being the creator's name (a Rembrandt, a Monet, a Finster). Referring to the work by the name of the artist is explanatory – both because works by that artist have something in common ('style') and because of the fact that an object that is touched by a famous hand gains value from that connection.

In addition, an art work connects with a social group in another sense. The art work (style, genre and content) provides a message about the cultural capital of the owner, and others that one sees oneself as linked to. As noted above, collecting a certain body of work makes a statement that one is a member of that community. This is dramatically evident with regard to Southern contemporary folk art. By displaying a style of art work that many outside the community consider child-like, primitive or unaesthetic, the collector makes a claim to expertise. These are works that need defence when their evaluators reside outside of the relevant community. Within the boundaries of that aesthetic community they have their own accepted and taken-for-granted justification, and provide a social identity and an interactional field for the collector.

Thus, the collector does not operate in isolation; rather art is linked to group affiliation. To collect art is to adhere to a group and implicitly to endorse the social meanings that underlie that group. This role of group identity allows for a more subtle analysis of McDonaldization, focusing on the degree to which art communities can expand and be routinized.

The Forces of McDonaldization and the Production of Art

One of the most influential approaches to the sociology of art during the past two decades is the claim that the creation of art is a production process that is fundamentally similar to the production of any product. This goes by the label of the 'production of culture' approach (Peterson, 1979). If art is like any commodity, to what extent are the processes that Ritzer presents as characteristic of modern production applicable to art?

Ritzer's description of McDonaldization constitutes more than a claim that there are few choices and options in society. Such a claim is, even within the world of fast-food, generally misguided. McDonaldization is, for Ritzer, an instance of contemporary rationalization in the provisioning of commodities, involving four basic processes: efficiency, calculability, predictability and control.

Obviously in any production market, these are not all or nothing phenomena. All production is characterized by greater or lesser amounts of efficiency, calculability, predictability and control. Given that the art market is structured by the marketing of products from individual entrepreneurs, over whom distributors have relatively little direct control (although in many cases considerable influence), the effects of these processes vary considerably from producer to producer.

Efficiency

Efficiency in the Ritzer model is linked to temporal organization, and is concerned with how rapidly objects can be produced. When examining the realm of artistic products that are for sale in the market, an observer quickly recognizes that the *amount* of time different objects took to produce varies considerably. Nowhere is this more true than in the world of folk art. Some artists (notably the famous Rev. Howard Finster) essentially have established an assembly line for the production of art. Many of Finster's recent works are wooden cut-outs of famous figures (Elvis, George Washington, Jesus, Hank Williams). The wood is cut out and the background is painted by Finster family members, and then Howard Finster adds the writing and the details with a marker (some suspect that he does not always do that). Such a division of labour permits many more objects to be created than would be the case otherwise. (It is well to remember, as the 'production of culture' school emphasizes, that all art is a form of collective action (Becker, 1974), and such a division of labour is not discrediting *per se*.) In contrast, other folk artists obsess over their detailed creations, and in terms of an 'hourly wage' may receive far less than the official minimum wage.

In general, folk artists tend to produce works that appear very similar to each other. For those artists to which this applies, an ethic of efficiency is at work. The touch of individuality does not adhere to each piece, but rather to the body of the artist's work.

Calculability

Of the components that constitute the process of McDonaldization, the one with the least clear relevance to artistic production, to folk art in particular, is calculability. Many folk artists lack the entrepreneur's ability to calculate profit, and, indeed, some of these artists lack numeracy. Most, though not all, folk artists are not adept at record keeping, and many do not keep track of their own artistic output or their economic transactions with dealers or collectors. Yet in one sense some artists almost make a fetish of calculability. It is not uncommon for artists to number their creations – just as McDonald's kept track of the number of burgers that the firm had sold and widely advertised this number. Perhaps the very fact that for many years McDonald's trumpeted the number of burgers it sold may have inspired certain folk artists. This inspiration holds even though counting the number of unique works produced is analytically distinct from the numbering of 'identical' burgers. The Rev. Howard Finster, perhaps America's best-known folk artist, inscribes on each work of art the sequential number of the work (he has produced some 40,000 'art works' since 1976). As with McDonald's, the 'objective' extent of one's success is calculable through a quantitative indicator of productivity. However, despite this ritualistic use of numbers, business practices and decisions on the pricing of art works tends to be less calculated. For many folk artists a sense of what 'the market will bear' is inexact at best. While the works themselves as objects can be assigned a numerical place, this calculability often does not apply to one's financial situation, a circumstance that leads some observers to fret that these artists are particularly liable to be taken advantage of or cheated by those with greater financial savvy.

Predictability

As Ritzer notes, predictability is central to most industrial organizations. If one purchases two of the 'same' product, one expects them to be functionally interchangeable. Of course, production processes are never so exact that products are absolutely identical – all works are, because of machine variability and human imperfections, like snowflakes. However, this inevitable variability is expected to stay within tight limits. As the Holiday Inn hotel chain used to advertise, 'The Best Surprise Is No Surprise'.

While this slogan applies to manufactured goods and service providers, in the world of art predictability is typically seen as undesirable. The ideology of uniqueness is an important feature of the art market. While artists should maintain a style, they are expected to vary their content, and over time to alter their style in perceptible ways to indicate 'growth' or 'maturity'. An absence of any variability is the equivalent of giving up the title of artist, becoming a 'mere' fabricator. It is the unpredictability of what the artist's mind will produce that gives art its charter as *creative*.

Control

The final process that Ritzer specifies as characterizing McDonaldization is that of control. In order to maintain efficiency, calculability and predictability, control is necessary over the process of labour. Such a model works adequately for industrial production, but is largely inapplicable for individual creation, for those production circumstances in which artists serve as entrepreneurs within a market.

The ultimate form of control is the replacement of humans with non-human labour. With machines doing the work, some of the unpredictability and inefficiency of human actors is eliminated. However, for the production of creative work, the human touch is essential. Further, it is often the case that the temporal freedom of the artist, along with freedom from oversight, permits the creation of art works.

While the control that is exercised over the folk artist is not a 'proximal control', these individuals, like all entrepreneurs, may be controlled in practice by the market and the representatives of the market in the form of dealers and collectors. If an artist is committed to maximizing his or her returns from art works, information about the nature of the market will be critical in shaping the content of the works. However, this control rarely affects the immediate choices of the artist: the cycle of influence operates indirectly over a longer time-frame, as certain 'freely chosen' decisions help coordinate the artist with those on his or her production boundaries (Hirsch, 1972). In sum, the folk art world is far from the ideal of direct managerial control as characterized in more regularized fast-food restaurants and other production and service establishments.

McDonaldization and Southern Contemporary Folk Art

Few can doubt that the dynamics that George Ritzer has described so effectively have come to characterize a significant segment of American life and much of the industrial West. However, it is important to recognize that McDonaldization does not apply equally throughout all of society. McDonaldization occurs in degrees, and more significantly within particular markets some aspects of the process operate to a greater extent than others. McDonaldization as an ideal-type does not operate across the board. As I have suggested in this chapter, this ideal-type of McDonaldization does not adequately explain the dynamics of the art market.

A romantic view characterizes many art worlds; this vision demands that the production of art be 'authentic'. Authenticity at its core involves a rejection of the idea of rationality. While much, if not all, production is determinedly instrumental, the expressivity of art work challenges the assumptions of instrumental value. The assumption behind expressive production is that products are not predictable, but derive from creative power. The very features that Ritzer suggests characterize McDonaldization – efficiency, calculability, predictability and control – are opposed to the ideology and practice of art. Even though, as I have suggested, some of these features may in practice characterize some forms of artistic production, the dominant public assumption is that they do not do so.

The dynamics of the world of Southern contemporary folk art pose special challenges to the construct of McDonaldization. First by virtue of being a *regional* domain – and predominantly a regional market – it contrasts radically with the idea of the national (and/or global) homogenizing process implicit in the McDonaldization thesis. Further, by searching for producers outside of the mainstream art world – constituting an aesthetic multiculturalism that art critics, a notably 'politically correct' group, demand – these customers (collectors) and middlemen (dealers and gallery owners) expand the possibilities and range of art works. This art market can, in a sense, be said to incorporate producers who by virtue of their cultural capital do not properly 'belong' by training alone, thereby expanding aesthetic choices. Ultimately the interest in Southern contemporary folk art diminishes the possibility of a hegemonic art world, creating in its place a diverse and highly reticulated market.

Anyone who has spent time poring through the pages of contemporary art magazines is likely to leave with the impression that no clearly definable central tendency exists in contemporary art. Diversity is the watchword. In a community in which being 'avant-garde' is status enhancing (so much so that it is now relatively rare to hear of some artist being labelled as avant-garde, as all or most are so regarded), one is known by how distinctively different one's works are from those produced by others. In this sense, art is not to be considered fungible or interchangeable. Each producer must have his or her own style, which is supposed to correspond to a unique aesthetic vision. Art would seem, therefore, to be a worst case for McDonaldization as a theoretical construct, even if we can see some elements of Ritzer's model in the creation of work by artists whose economic imperatives are similar to those of producers of other commodities.

This analysis of the organization of the art world returns us to the general question: to what extent is it appropriate to refer to a process of McDonaldization being broadly present in Western society and, if that is the case, to what extent is that presence likely to continue? While production is increasingly highly organized and automatized, we have also witnessed a design revolution in many market segments. The expressive character of products is increasingly being seen as desirable by consumers. Corporations, while maintaining their interest in efficiency, calculability, predictability and control, have begun to provide products that *appear* to be unique, creative and personal. Where possible, and consistent with organizational demands, customers will be given a surfeit of choices (for instance, Burger King's slogan 'Have It Your Way'), even if these choices are limited in scope. Often producers are described by their corporate overseers as having some measure of personal autonomy (and will be described as 'professionals'). Organizations walk a fine line between corporate demands that are grounded in the principles associated with McDonaldization, and public ideals, often based on images of personalized, non-routine service and production.

The paradox is that Ritzer's McDonaldization hypothesis is simultaneously relevant and yet limited – applicable in part to a wide range of markets and venues, but applicable as a whole to very few. Pressure exists to rationalize production, while simultaneously there is a desire to have autonomy both in one's work and in one's consumption choices. Production communities must devise ways to address their needs for profit, while maintaining consumer loyalty. A short-term strategy of profit maximization may conflict with a longer-term strategy: what may be effective for internal bookkeeping may have negative effects upon worker morale and consumer patronage.

Art worlds with their idiosyncratic and individually created products are unlikely to provide the model for industrial production. However, the diversity found in art worlds can be a model for a world in which consumers are willing to pay for unique products. Some wish to retreat to the days in which small-scale, idiosyncratic, expressive production was dominant. However, this choice will produce substantial economic changes, including fewer consumer purchases, lower wages, smaller production units and a more limited division of labour. Such a change is unlikely to occur to any substantial degree. Yet the fact that this option remains open reminds us of the possibility of resisting McDonaldization should we be willing to assume the costs. Ultimately McDonaldization is only a brand name for a style of production that consumers can choose to reject, should they wish to do so.

References

Becker, H.S. (1974) 'Art as collective action', *American Sociological Review*, 39: 767–76.
Bucher, R. (1962) 'Pathology: a study of social movements within a profession', *Social Problems*, 10: 40–51.
Bucher, R. and Strauss, A. (1961) 'Professions in process', *American Journal of Sociology*, 66: 325–34.
Cardinal, R. (1972) *Outsider Art*. New York: Praeger.
Fine, G.A. (1996) 'Justifying work: occupational rhetoric as resources in restaurant kitchens', *Administrative Science Quarterly*, 41: 90–115.

Gablik, S. (1984) *Has Modernism Failed?* New York: Thames & Hudson.

Gans, H. (1974) *Popular Culture and High Culture.* New York: Basic Books.

Halle, D. (1993) *Inside Culture.* Chicago: University of Chicago Press.

Hirsch, P. (1972) 'Processing fads and fashions: an organization set analysis of cultural industry systems', *American Journal of Sociology*, 77: 639–59.

Lynes, R. (1954) *The Tastemakers.* New York: Harper & Brothers.

Maizels, J. (1996) *Raw Creation: Outsider Art and Beyond.* London: Phaidon.

Peterson, R.A. (1979) 'Revitalizing the culture concept', *Annual Review of Sociology*, 5: 137–66.

Peterson, R.A. and Kern, R.M. (1996) 'Changing highbrow taste: from snob to omnivore', *American Sociological Review*, 61: 900–7.

Ritzer, G. (1996) *The McDonaldization of Society: An Investigation into the Changing Character of Contemporary Social Life* (rev. edn). Thousand Oaks, CA: Pine Forge Press.

Rosenberg, B. and White, D. (1957) *Mass Culture: The Popular Arts in America.* Glencoe, IL: Free Press.

Sellen, B.-C. (1993) *Twentieth Century American Folk, Self Taught, and Outsider Art.* New York: Neal-Schuman.

Shun, L. and Fine, G.A. (1995) 'The presentation of ethnic authenticity: Chinese food as a social accomplishment', *Sociological Quarterly*, 36: 601–19.

11   Dennis Hopper, McDonald's and Nike

Norman K. Denzin

I want to read Ritzer's 'McDonaldization of society' thesis ironically and literally. Ironically, Ritzer finds perverse pleasures in pointing out how contemporary society has become McDonaldized. But his prescriptions (Ritzer, 1993: 182–5) for resisting the iron cage of McDonald's[1] read like a Ralph Nader manifesto for middle-class consumer protest. I want to take his protests to a deeper, more critical level. This will require an extension of his central theme. He literally reads the postmodern landscape through the lens of McDonald's. I want to extend this McDonaldization of society thesis to the Nike Corporation, its 'swoosh' logo, and its 'Just Do It', 'Be Like Mike', 'Air Jordan' advertising slogans. I will compare McDonald's to Nike. These two multinational corporations have taken the late-modern societies to landscapes and places scarcely imagined by Weber. How they have done this is my topic.

McDonald's makes hamburgers. Nike makes sports shoes. But McDonald's, as its founder Ray Kroc stated, is not 'in the hamburger business; we're in show business' (Kroc, quoted in Love, 1995: 303). Likewise, Nike is not in the shoe business; it takes ordinary bodies and transforms them into sporting spectacles, another version of McDonald's show business.

An individual who is willing to 'Just Do It' can have one of Nike's finely tuned bodies. Elaborate advertisement campaigns with performance-oriented messages for men and emotional, celebrity feminist messages for women create physically fit persons who wear Nike shoes and other sporting gear. Thus does Nike use the cultural logics of McDonaldization. In these ways Weber's iron cage is moved more deeply into the postmodern condition.

Nike has confronted a seeming dilemma in Weber's model of bureaucratic rationality, which is Ritzer's concept of McDonaldization. This is a dilemma that Ritzer recognizes; that is, how to fit the impersonal iron cage to the production of non-rational, emotional experience. But Nike has gone beyond Weber, and perhaps beyond Ritzer. Borrowing from McDonald's, Nike has fitted Weber's model, with its emphasis on efficiency, quantification, predictability and non-human technology, to the gendered, racialized human body.

Weber's classic model, as Ritzer notes (1993: 18–19), applied the theory of formal rationality to the paradigm case of the bureaucracy. Weber's insight was to show how systems of irrationality, including unpredictability, poor work quality, worker alienation, and robot-like production lines, would become central features of the modern bureaucratic system (Ritzer, 1993: 25). Workers were destined to be trapped in the iron cage of rationality.

Ritzer (1993: 19) moves Weber's model to a new paradigm case, McDonald's. Using the fast-food restaurant as his case in point, he suggests that we all bear witness to the McDonaldization of contemporary society, from Toys "Я" Us, to Jiffy Lube, H&R Block, Nutri System, Wal-Mart, to Dial-a-porn (1993: 8), Club Med, tourism and the annual family vacation (1993: 23), where families stay in chain hotels, eat at McDonald's, and take guided tours through Disneyland.

Yet Ritzer provides few concrete details on how the non-rational, the emotional and the personal have become rationalized. Nor does he deal with race (and gender) and the racial order implied by the McDonaldization of American society. The case of Nike shows us how this has been accomplished.

I examine the above arguments through a close reading of a series of Nike advertisements which were aired in the USA in 1993 and 1994. In those years Nike released four television commercials featuring Dennis Hopper in what soon came to be called the 'Crazed Ref' advertisements.[2] In each advertisement the viewer is presented with a jittery, nervous-looking, fast-talking, unshaven Dennis Hopper, wearing a black NFL referee hat, and a brownish-coloured trench coat. In the background lurks the Nike swoosh logo.

The Hopper advertisements allow Nike to deploy one of Ritzer's recommendations (1993: 188). We must, he argues, resist Weber's iron cage. Ritzer exhorts the reader, 'faced with Max Weber's iron cage imagery of a future dominated by the polar night of icy darkness and hardness, the least the reader can do is to follow the words of the poet Dylan Thomas, "do not go gentle into that good night . . . Rage, rage against the dying of the light."'. Wild-eyed Dennis Hopper seems to take Dylan Thomas's words seriously, for he rages against the light, and in his rage he carries Nike's message concerning a new football shoe, and the violent exploits of African American NFL players. Through parody and humour Nike applies the McDonaldization system to the gendered and racialized sporting body. My analysis centres on the consequences of these advertisements for life in contemporary American society. A complex five-part thesis organizes my discussion.

Nike, McDonald's and the Racial Order

First, a majority of Americans know and understand the US racial order through the media representations of the black, ethnic other. Increasingly, this other is a properly disciplined black male football, baseball or basketball player whose exploits are captured in a sports commercial and a televised sporting event. Indeed, race in America is based on a complex politics of cultural difference that is played out in the national media. Media personalities such as Spike Lee, Michael Jordan, Arsenio Hall, Oprah Winfrey and Bill Cosby 'focus, organize, and translate blackness into commodifiable representations and desires that [can] be packaged and marketed across the landscape of American popular culture' (Gray, 1995: 68).

In some cases seemingly separate cultural domains are joined. Consider Michael Jordan's Nike commercials with Spike Lee's Mars Blackmon (from Lee's film, *She's Gotta Have It*). Place these texts in tandem with Jordan's McDonald's commercials with Larry Bird, the former NBA all-star from the Boston Celtics, (Andrews, 1995: 21). Jordan's Nike and McDonald's commercials helped cement his public identity as a down-to-earth ordinary person. Importantly, this down-to-earth superstar held traditional family values; values basic to McDonald's media image. Race was ignored in these commercials.

Second, those who control the media control a society's discourses about itself. The racial discourses that circulate in the media reify and essentialize racial and gender differences. This discourse creates a series of cultural oppositions, pitting the black, ethnic other against a mainstream, white American. This discourse privileges full assimilation into the multicultural American racial order as the proper end point for all minority group members.[3]

Third, the American racial order is principally a sporting order. Nike controls a significant number of the racial representations that define this order.[4] An analysis of the Nike commercials should reveal the underlying logic of this mass-mediated racial system (see Andrews, 1995; Cole and Andrews, 1996; Cole and Hribar, 1995; Cole and Orlie, 1996). I ask, 'How did *Blue Velvet* go NFL?'

Fourth, this system of commercial discourse embodies three cultural logics. The first is the logic of late modern capitalism as it is connected to commodity consumption (Smythe, 1994). The second is the logic of emotional experience, which is central to commodity consumption. The third is the logic of reverse cultural racism. This logic refers to the so-called colour blindness of white racism (Feagin and Vera, 1995). It describes those media practices that turn blackness into a marketing category that is superficially free of racial stereotypes (see Gray, 1995: 9). The first logic values anything that makes a profit for the producer of a commodity. The second logic personalizes the norms of efficiency, quantification and predictability. At the same time it turns non-human technology (exercise machines) into an extension of human agency. The third logic erases race and replaces it with sporting conceptions of character, manliness, competition, good times, fun and racial assimilation. All three logics use the technologies of sport (Cole and Orlie, 1996) to discipline and maintain this assimilationist version of the American racial order.

Fifth, accordingly, I read the Hopper series for what it says about sports, celebrities, the media, advertising, Nike, McDonald's and the black male athlete in American culture today.[5] A reverse discrimination operates in the Hopper advertisements: a crazed, degenerate Hopper is contrasted to the violent black male. I begin with the advertisements (the NFL signs of Nike), focusing on the cultural and advertising logics that organize them, noting as well, the controversies that surrounded the series (Garfield, 1993; Magiera, 1994; Magiera and Jensen, 1993). I then examine the concepts of celebrity, sanity, insanity, race and violence that operate in these narratives. I conclude with observations on how the advertising media, McDonald's and Nike succeed in removing blackness from the American sporting arena, even as we witness the 'African Americanization' of American popular culture (Gray, 1995: 97).

Dennis Hopper and Nike on NFL Location

Scene One: An unshaven Dennis Hopper wearing a black NFL referee hat, and a brownish-coloured trench coat rushes into a locker room. Looking left and right, he stops in front of a locker, reaches up, and pulls down a large football shoe. Holding it carefully, as if it were a sacred object, he speaks directly to the viewing audience. 'I'm holding Bruce Smith's shoe.' (Frontal shot of Bruce Smith in uniform, then a shot of Hopper smelling the shoe, then a shot of Smith tackling a quarterback). A Hopper voice-over, 'Do you know what Bruce Smith does in these shoes?' (Shot of Smith tackling a quarterback.) Hopper, full face to audience, 'Bad things, bad things, things I can't just possibly talk about.' [Shot of Smith, eyes turned towards Hopper.] 'Do you know what Bruce would do [shot of Bruce] if he found me messing with his shoes?' [Hopper twitches his neck as he speaks, and his eyes roll to the right.] 'Bad things man.' The Nike Swoosh logo fills the screen.

Scene Two: Hopper, dressed as above, walks away from a sports mer-chandising counter in the Pontiac (Michigan) Silverdome. He verbally accosts a fan 'You don't even want to know about Barry Sanders man. He does things on the field that just make your eyes go crazy! I mean, one time, I saw him running right through people like a cannonball loose inside a pinball machine. [A Sanders highlight is seen.] . . . Bing, bing, bing, bing, bingbing Bing! bing! YAHHH! And then Barry did this [Hopper spins, and we see another Sanders highlight]. Sometimes I . . . I . . . I . . . still see it in my sleep. And I don't . . . I don't sleep that much.'

Scene Three: A harried Hopper enters a broadcasting booth, high above the playing field below. To the audience, 'Oh yeah, sure, the regular season, it was pretty intense out there – but this is the play-offs [shot of defensive line rushing a quarterback], this is where all the marbles get smashed into little bits. Oh, ho, horseshoes and handgrenades, man, horseshoes and handgrenades [gesturing with emphasis, in the viewer's face]. Ask the players. Ask the players about the play-offs. They know. But you people don't. You people think that its a game. Marbles [gesturing with his thumb, as if shooting a marble] is a game.'

Scene Four: Hopper (with shades of *Mission Impossible*) steps out from behind the corner of a cement wall in a parking garage at the Tampa Bay football stadium. With his left hand he holds up an 8 × 10 black and white photograph of a man's face. With his right hand he holds up a small tape recorder, which he clicks on. Hopper's voice speaks, 'This man plays for the Tampa Bay Buccaneers. His name is Hardy Nickerson [shot of Nickerson], but he often goes by the name of Dragon. He is very dangerous and often angry.' Hopper hears a sound off-screen; turning, he speaks to the audience. 'Act casual.' He eats the photo. The Nike swoosh logo fills the screen.

Reading the Stories

These four scenes, which can be read in any order, provide variations on the same crazed, schizophrenic character Dennis Hopper has been playing for the last 30 years. These variations include versions of Hopper's Frank Booth (*Blue Velvet*), a partial reclaiming of his *Apocalypse Now* character, a burned-out photojournalist (Magiera, 1994), and shades of other actors and their twitching characters: DeNiro's Rupert Pupkin (*The King of Comedy*), Hoffman's Ratso Rizzo (*Midnight Cowboy*).[6] Hopper skilfully invokes a blend of the paranoid schizophrenic, and the social misfit, with the deranged NFL fan.

In *scene one* Hopper displays a foot fetish, an unhealthy attachment to the shoe of one of the most acclaimed defensive players in the NFL. The viewer is asked to imagine Smith doing to Hopper what he does to NFL quarterbacks, 'Bad things, bad things.' But Hopper is not an NFL quarterback, and the viewer is unwilling to accord him this imposter identity. In his furtive, secretive behaviour Hopper is regarded as a sick, deviant, not healthy, someone in danger, perhaps even dangerous to himself. He is pathetic, surely not a person the viewer would admire.

But as I watch Smith watching Hopper I identify, if only for a moment, with this little man and his desire to be near greatness. And in that gaze, I separate myself from Hopper. I as viewer am aligned with Smith. I imagine myself as a regular, ordinary fan, a person who appreciates the problems players like Smith have to put up with, freaks like Hopper.

This advertisement is quite complex. It asks the white male viewer to assume the subject position of Smith, an African American male. (Only in this way can the viewer be aligned with Smith's position.) Yet in adopting Smith's imagined reactions to Hopper holding his shoe, the white male suppresses race. He becomes, then, just another man watching another man holding one of his shoes. The foot fetish imputed to Hopper is a psychological disorder. It displaces the implicit racism in the advertisement. That is, the commercial gives a white man the power and the authority to hold, caress and smell a black man's shoe. Racism, if it is present (for the viewer), now becomes a matter of personal not institutional pathology.

Scene two carries this fan involvement with the NFL and its stars to another level. Now Hopper accosts an innocent fan, a white male. He then turns to the innocent viewer, giving the viewer a glimpse of his problems, including not being able to sleep, and perhaps being driven crazy by the moves of Barry Sanders. Hopper is doing to the viewer what Smith might do to him, 'bad things'. And the viewer suspects that this fan was crazy before he watched Barry Sanders. Caught up in Hopper's tiny little story about Sanders, the viewer wonders about the fan who got away and didn't have to hear this story. The viewer also worries about this pathetic little man who tries to stop normal fans and tell them things like this.

Sanders's moves on the football field map the interior structures of Hopper's brain, which is likened to the insides of a pinball machine. 'I saw him running right through people like a cannonball loose inside a pinball machine.' Sanders makes Hopper's eyes go crazy! Bing, bing, bing, bing, bingbing Bing! bing! YAHHH!' But this is more than Hopper can stand. Sanders makes him lose sleep. Sanders drives him crazy. When the African American male enters the brain of the white male fan trouble is produced, insanity. Thus does this advertisement expose its own implicit racist logic.

Scene three increases the intensity that Hopper has brought to the series.[7] He rushes into the broadcast booth, telling viewers that the NFL's second football season is not a game of marbles. Sure, the regular season was intense, but this is a new season. It is horseshoes and handgrenades, explosions and violence on the field, regular season intensity taken to another level. In fact Hopper's intensity mirrors the intensity he finds in the second season. Fans must prepare for a whole new game. Only intense fans such as Hopper and the NFL players understand this new season. Thus the advertisement aligns Hopper with the players who are entering the play-offs. The oppositions between Hopper and the NFL players, established in the previous advertisements, are erased in this sequence. We are led by Hopper and the NFL players, the Pied Pipers of the new season, into the play-offs.

This next level, the new form of the game, is exaggerated in *scene four* when Hopper acts out what appears to be a part from *Mission Impossible*. The meeting in the garage suggests something subversive and dangerous (Deep Throat in *All the President's Men*). Hopper is on a mission, to locate, identify and perhaps disarm Hardy (aka the Dragon) Nickerson, who is on the loose. The Dragon is near. Because of this assignment Hopper's life is in danger. Hearing a threatening noise in the distance, Hopper, like a spy, eats the photo while telling the viewer to act casual.

Of course this assignment is yet another version of the one played in the earlier advertisements. Being an NFL fan is dangerous work. But this advertisement is crucial. It once again names an NFL player. This solves a problem addressed in the previous advertisements, namely Nike's failure as a major advertiser to showcase NFL talent (Magiera and Jensen, 1993). In naming specific players Nike, through Hopper, overcomes what was perceived to be an insurmountable problem, 'How to sell the personalities of helmeted football stars . . . [how] to reverse the long-held marketing belief that NFL players, seemingly violent and unlikable and unrecognizable without a name on a jersey, are ineffective as product pitchmen' (Magiera and Jensen, 1993).

In naming players, Hopper solves the problem of marketing the personality of the star who cannot be identified without a label. Hopper does the identifying. By stressing the violence experienced (and created) by the player, Hopper makes these violent men likeable. They risk their lives for our pleasure. And in so doing they are exposed to an even greater violence, the insanity of crazed fans like Dennis.

So two violent cultural places are identified, two places where organized, controlled and contained violence in this culture occur. In the public places, the playing (killing?) fields of the NFL, weekly male-centred spectacles of horseshoes and handgrenades are staged for a mass television audience. In the backstage, private regions of the NFL, in its locker rooms and garages, lurk the likes of Dennis Hopper's 'Crazed Ref', shady males of dubious masculine character. This man is no stranger to danger, marbles, horseshoes, handgrenades or things that are pretty intense. Indeed, being a fan requires doing dangerous things. The intensity of Hopper's Crazed Ref defines the series, leading many viewers to define him as crazy. But of course that is one of the major points of the series. Hopper's intensity is but an extreme version of the socially sanctioned intensity of the NFL. This intensity erases the presence of race in the NFL. Three of the named players whose virtues Hopper extols are African Americans.

Responses to the Advertisements

Not surprisingly, these advertisements aroused considerable controversy within popular culture, the advertising press and the NFL itself (Bird, 1993; Garfield, 1993). The controversy centred on two issues: Hopper's demeanour, and the ethics of advertising. Garfield (1993) described Hopper in these words.

> This character is the ultimate rabid pro football fan, only worse. He buses from city to city disheveled and overwrought, barking at strangers and blurting out non sequiturs with trashing gesticulations and facial tics . . . in other words, a charming blend of cinema's most memorable paranoid schizophrenics and misfits.

Garfield asks if this is an 'appropriate characterization for a national TV commercial?' Of course his answer is no, 'Hopper's deranged ref is misplaced in the role of selling athletic shoes.'

Garfield then makes a distinction between cinema (movie-acting) and advertising:

> an advertiser's relationship with the audience . . . is not the same as a film-maker's. Mental illness, even the broadest most over-the-top rendering of it, is certainly the province of cinema and certainly not the province of sneaker commercials. Thousands of people will be deeply offended.

The National Stigma Association, an advocacy group for the mentally ill, echoed Garfield's complaints (Magiera, 1994), also arguing that the advertisements 'trivialize mental disorders by using stereotypes' (Bird, 1993).

However, there was little consensus on this point. Few shared the negative views of Garfield and the National Stigma Association. *Advertising Age* (1994a) published nine letters responding to Garfield's article. Three of the letters were from women, one of whom worked for an advertising agency. Five of the six male letter writers also worked for advertising agencies. No letter was critical of the Hopper series. Here are samples:

Male, executive vice-president for Golfweek: What's Bob Garfield's problem? Dennis Hopper's Nike Ads are terrific . . . They are obviously meant (and they are) to be funny . . . Light up!

Male, junior account executive: The fans of the NFL are not mentally ill and paranoid schizophrenics. They are fans, which actually stands for fanatics, like Mr. Hopper. The True fan is a fanatic of the game.

Female: Why can't mental illness be the province of sneaker commercials, as Garfield stated? Think about it. How many football fanatics do you know tend to get out of control when describing, even trying to re-enact, an exciting play? I would hate to think of some of the closest people in my life as 'paranoid schizophrenics' unsuitable for society.

Male, senior writer: These spots [are] designed to appeal . . . to a target market of . . . Generation Xers – and other people who may actually wear them for football – looking for products with an attitude . . . and this group is even smart enough to enjoy a good TV spot even if we've never seen 'Blue Velvet'.

Female: The Nike Hopper ads work. They're fresh, funny and right on target. And they definitely do not leave me with the impression that Hopper's character is mentally ill.

Turning the word fan into fanatic, these letter writers normalized and then praised Hopper's antics. Hopper (quoted in Magiera, 1994) seemed to agree, 'It's obviously a comedy. . . . Nobody's making fun of crazy people' (Magiera, 1994).

The NFL was less certain, but remained quiet, although one marketing official for the league remarked, 'The new ads suck' (Magiera and Jensen, 1993), and another charged privately that 'Hopper upstages the players who appear in the spot' (Magiera and Jensen, 1993). Still, the league, Nike and the advertising agency downplayed any controversy.

Other advertising agencies were more vocal, calling the series 'Cool', 'totally outrageous', 'inspired' (Magiera and Jensen, 1993), and indicative of Nike's general position in the field: 'Nike has always been on the edge, and this time they picked somebody over the edge. But I always appreciate anyone trying to push out the borders' (Magiera and Jensen, 1993). Some advertising officials questioned the use of Hopper, who has low name recognition and likeability ratings, suggesting that Wieden and Kennedy (the advertising agency) and Nike 'could have gotten someone's brother-in-law and got the same effect. Mr Hopper is overpowered by the sneaker' (Bird, 1993).

Carol Moog, an advertising consultant, extends this analysis of Hopper. She reads Hopper not as mentally ill, but as a drugged-out street person:

> It is inappropriate for a guy like him to be running around the locker room. . . . I question seriously whether these ads are effective for Nike. If what they wanted was the ultimate sports nut, they haven't done it. There are too many uncontrolled interpretations of his behavior. . . . This ad wastes and squanders consumer responses. And it is not focused enough to be humorous. (Loro, 1994)

Advertising Age (1994b) disagreed: 'While this campaign probably won't sell more Nike shoes, it's reassuring to know that in this time of political correctness, one client out there is ready to have fun by supporting its agency's fartherest-out creative work.' And Hopper's performance is praised; it is 'somehow satisfying to know that . . . Hopper has finally emerged as an advertising hero' (*Advertising Age*, 1994b). So political correctness is undone. So much for the mentally ill.

Dan Wieden and his agency associates were of course delighted by all of this controversy. It meant that their advertisement and the product were getting free public attention. Wieden equivocates on the political correctness topic:

> The job of commercials is to wake people up and make them think differently and entertain them in the process. The role isn't to be politically correct. It's to be provocative . . . The responsibility of the advertiser is to develop a relationship with the audience, and a complex one. Mr Hopper's performance is sometimes funny, and sometimes complex. (Bird, 1993)

Garfield held firm:

> It isn't a question of political correctness. Advertisers have a special obligation to observe the golden rule. No one asks to see a TV commercial. . . . Advertising has to take special care not to be offensive or exploitative because it is completely unsolicited. (Bird, 1993)

The Racial and Cultural Logics of the Nike Advertisements

The Hopper advertisements were a success. Fans loved the series. It brought named NFL players in front of the football public. It showed how a white male could be fanatical about the exploits of an African American. It advertised the new Nike football shoe. It brought considerable attention to Hopper, the NFL, Nike, and Wieden and Kennedy.

The controversy that swirled around the advertisements served to clarify the cultural logic of commodity fetishism in this sporting culture. This logic is both simple and complex. Persons define themselves through the objects they possess, or identify with. By possessing Bruce Smith's shoes, Hopper merges with Smith. But in making Smith a fetish, an object of personal desire, Hopper loses his own sense of personal identity. He becomes wild and maniacal, crazed, nearly out of control, the fanatic, fetishistic fan. This is the form of commodity fetishism that Nike exploits in the Hopper series.

This fan is blind to race. The NFL helps here. Because its helmets and uniforms hide the skin colour of the player, race is secondary to a man's competitive abilities. And of course the properly disciplined player is assimilated into the multicultural racial order that defines the NFL. That order privileges cultural diversity, family, mobility, wealth, personal style, even God. The NFL is also privileged as a near-sacred cultural site, marked by prayer and the National Anthem. In the Hopper advertisements the NFL becomes a metaphor for life. Worshipping the shoes of NFL players, Hopper reaffirms the sacredness of this metaphor. The NFL is life itself. And this life is multicultural. It has a place for everyone and it is blind to race.

The Nike–Hopper advertisements are classic productions. They do what all good advertisements are supposed to do, that is, draw attention to themselves in a way that promotes audience awareness of the advertisement as a text. Few who saw the series forget Hopper's performance. Clearly exposure to the Hopper series increased brand familiarity – the Nike Swoosh logo and the new shoe. The advertisements communicated brand attributes, in this case the ability of the shoe to withstand considerable punishment. The series elaborated an image and personality (crazy Hopper) for the brand, the new Nike shoe and for the NFL. They linked the brand to a broad reference group, other fanatical, Hopper-like NFL fans (for a discussion of these features of an advertisement, see Batra et al., 1996: ix, 48).

Dan Wieden understands this model, which personalizes a product through celebrity endorsement while emphasizing what the product can do for the ordinary consumer. For Wieden, the goal of an advertisement is to make 'honest contact with the consumer . . . to create the personality that allows people to bond' (1996: 386). This is an ethical task, involving more than

> the movement of goods and services . . . this is a big stage . . . and . . . it is important to be reasonable . . . being provocative is more important than being pleasant . . . [but] a lot of big ad firms are struggling now precisely because they've ignored the ethical component of advertising. They've relied on manipulation and cunning. . . . Although, at one level, all we're really doing is selling sneakers, there's something about athletic shoes and clothes that can inspire . . . altruism. There's an honest-to-goodness belief that we are selling something that will help people. (1996: 386)

Of course, as noted above, Wieden modifies this position somewhat when discussing the Hopper series. To repeat: 'The job of commercials . . . isn't to be politically correct. It's to be provocative' (Wieden, quoted in Bird, 1993).

Phil Knight (quoted in Lipsyle, 1996) elaborates. While Nike likes controversy, and attention, it fills a need. 'After the controlling bodies, like the NBA and the NCAA, make their exorbitant TV deals, the networks then have to lay off the cost by getting commercials. The need for advertising money then gives power to the shoe companies.'[8] But more is going on here. Lipsyle (1996) comments on Knight's arguments, noting that the need for advertising money gives great power to the shoe companies, who have product contracts with star athletes.

The Nike advertisements, with their emphasis on sports and fitness activities, put the consumer centre-stage, stressing performance-oriented messages for men, and emotional fitness messages for women (Knight, quoted in Batra et al., 1996: 379). Knight continues,

> Our advertising tries to link consumers to the Nike brand through the emotions of sports and fitness. We show competition, determination, achievement, fun, and even the spiritual rewards of participating in these activities. . . . People at Nike believe in the power of emotion because we feel it ourselves. . . . Sport is at the heart of American culture, so a lot of emotion already exists around it. (Batra et al., 1996: 382).

Nike is a champion brand builder. Its advertising slogans ('Just Do it', 'Be Like Mike', 'Bo Knows', 'There is No Finish Line', 'Air Jordan') are legendary (Batra et al., 1996: 375), and have moved directly into American popular culture, turning that culture into an arena where the consumer becomes a sporting commodity.

Consumer as Sporting Commodity

Following Smythe (1994: 285), I understand the major intentions of the mass media advertising complex to be four-fold: to create audiences who (1) become consumers of the products advertised in the media; while (2) engaging in consumption practices that conform to the norms of possessive individualism endorsed by the capitalist political system; and (3) adhering to a public opinion that is supportive of the strategic policies of the state. At this level, the information and advertising technologies of late capitalism function to create audiences who use the income from their own labour to buy the products that their labour produces (Smythe, 1994: 285).

The primary commodity that the information, advertising technologies produce is not information, messages, images, meaning or education. The commodity 'form of mass-produced, advertiser-supported communications [under monopoly capitalism] . . . is audiences' (Smythe, 1994: 268). The fourth goal of the media is now clear: to do everything it can to make consumers as audience members think they are not commodities. Nike does this well.

A dual commodity form structures the media work of the communication industries: the consumer as a commodity form must be joined with a cultural object which is a media and cultural artefact (see Price, 1993: 133). This cultural object is a social text, and a commodity (see Price, 1993: 133). Herein lies the importance of the stories advertisers such as Nike tell in their commercials. Hopper's fanatic fan stories connect viewers as commodities to the NFL, and the new Nike shoe. This leads viewers-as-commodities to purchase NFL games for entertainment. Little Nike spectacles, these fans watch their football games wearing Nike apparel, their black swoosh hats on backwards, new Nike cross trainers on their feet, Michael Jordan-lookalike sunglasses perched on their foreheads, Miller Lites clutched in their right hands.

Consumers as commodities, and media artefacts cannot be separated from the larger institutional spheres and cultural codes that organize everyday life (Price, 1993: 133; see also Fiske, 1989; Schudson, 1984: 210). Nike attempts to anchor its viewer in America's sporting culture, in a culture that values competition, determination, achievement, healthy bodies, fun, the positive emotions of fitness. So the Nike Hopper advertisements connect the consumer to the product (NFL, new shoe) in informational, image, personalized and lifestyle formats (see Price, 1993: 131). The advertisements manipulate Couch's (1995) evocative symbols, creating a need (Hopper's intense fan identification), a desire for the need to be met (being like Hopper), and offers a product (Nike/NFL) which will meet that need. The format of the Hopper advertisements shows the person how to use (and not use) the object (foot fetishes), and how to associate its use with valued, emotional cultural experiences (being intense).

In order for a Hopper advertisement to work, a specific audience for the product must be created, hence Generation X and its special needs. Of course Generation X is an audience market category created by the media and the advertising industry. This market segment as a commodity must be interactionally and emotionally connected to particular products and their consumption. The NFL product, the game on TV, must have an audience. The advertisement then enters the audience's world through the event, in this case an NFL football game. But that media event must be connected to an audience-based event, people getting together to watch the game of the week. In so doing they encounter Crazy Hopper and his Mad Ref series, a series that has now become an event in its own right.

Generation X males and their parents are programmed to be sports-minded, to be NFL-literate. Thus Nike has a ready-made audience for its product. Emotional needs specific to this market category are then created (for example, gearing up for the second NFL season). These audience members are targeted for media campaigns focused on new cultural commodities – Hopper, the new NFL season and the new Nike shoe. Thus does the institution of advertising use the information technologies of the culture to create new commodified versions of the sporting consumer.

Gendered consumers bring different cultural meanings (dominant, negotiated, subversive) to these sporting commodities and the social texts that define them (see Fiske, 1989; Press, 1991: 173–8; Price, 1993: 166; Seaman, 1992). These meanings and the cultural practices associated with them are complexly embedded in culturally defined gender and class-based codes. Not surprisingly, the Nike–Hopper advertisements evoked similar meanings from males and females. Phil Knight has gone out of his way to create a consensual, gendered sporting culture where males and females can interact on a common, shared terrain. At the same time Nike has succeeded in anchoring cultural practices specific to the NFL (and other professional sports) to particular interactional sites – the family television room, the sports bar. These sites can be read as places where viewer-mediated cultural texts interact with one another – a viewing of the Bruce Smith–Hopper commercial, while watching half-time highlights of Bruce Smith playing in a real football game. In these cultural sites viewers as commodities come together. As in the Nike–Beatle Revolution commercial, viewers symbolically produce situated forms of resistance to this dominant Nike cultural order. Consumers engage in cultural resistance, while consuming the commodity they are resisting.

Emotional Bonds

The professional athlete is the key to Nike's success. Knight understands this:

> To create a lasting emotional tie with consumers, we use athletes repeatedly throughout their careers and present them as whole people. So that consumers feel that they know them. It's not just Charles Barkley [the NBA star] saying buy Nike shoes, it's seeing who Charles Barkley is. . . . We win their hearts as well as their feet. (quoted in Lipsyle, 1996: 382)[9]

The Hopper series seemingly follows, while flaunting, the above logic. Brand familiarity (the sign of Nike) is presumed. Hopper's name lends a personality to the product; his crazed fan conduct is immediately connected to the presence of an NFL player-star (Bruce Smith, Barry Sanders, Harvey Nickerson). The negative features of Hopper's personality are compared to the positive virtues of the NFL star, including their speed, power, force, grace, and even the violence they create and experience. Thus Hopper is bonded to the NFL player through the Nike (and NFL) products: the shoe, and the experiences produced by the person who wears (or holds) it.

But Hopper is neither fit, nor powerful, nor graceful. However, he demonstrates other Nike values. He is competitive, willing to go to almost any length to hold Smith's shoe. He is persistent and determined, perhaps even spiritual in his quest to be near an NFL star.

Celebrities

So this series creates a cultural space for the crazed celebrity-wannabe identity. The Hopper-lookalike who holds Bruce Smith's shoe. This space nullifies race. It does so by articulating a cultural logic that values the sporting body. A central cultural logic of Nike involves the ordinary person who is transformed into a healthy self who just does it. However, as indicated above, Knight and Nike have engaged in a form of gendered market and product segmentation. There are two sporting bodies: one male, the other female. These two bodies were originally connected to two separate sporting cultures: organized athletes for males, and the fitness movement for women.

By the late 1980s, as Knight (in Lipsyle, 1996) observes, Nike had unified these two cultures – the fit body now competed with itself. The fit male and female body were thus joined in a postfeminist celebrity-based sporting culture. Second-generation feminism was displaced by a commodity, or celebrity feminism (Cole and Hribar, 1995), which emphasized the new traditional woman who valued her healthy body, her family and her sexuality.[10] A new set of traditional cultural values were set forth: fitness, being natural, having an authentic body, good health, family, intimacy and personal freedom. Thus was the men's movement folded into the postfeminist project. The healthy male, like his female counterpart, values his body and takes care of it.

But a problem lingered for Nike, namely how to market the product of its chief clients, the NFL and the NBA. Michael Jordan could market Air Jordans, but who would market Barry Sanders, Bruce Smith and the NFL? This is the need addressed by Nike's version of celebrity product endorsement: Dennis Hopper and *Blue Velvet* selling the NFL. The crazed fan who over-identifies with a sporting celebrity.

This crazed fan performs three functions for Nike. First, always a male, he keeps the competitive, male sporting culture alive. Second, he racially sanitizes this culture, elevating celebrity status above racial identity. Third, in the Hopper form, he mocks the healthy body attached to celebrity feminism. In so doing he increases the value of that body and its identity.

Hopper is the antithesis of this self, his raged, crazed self, his deteriorating body, unshaven face, trembling hands speak to a self in awe of the Nike body and self. Hopper's fears, then, are mine, yours, those of the person who symbolically desires this self, but for psychic (mad) and physical reasons (uncoordinated, weak) is unable to enter this space. By troubling this identity, marring it with his insanity, Hopper sanctifies its ritual importance for celebrity fandom.

In transgressing its own sign, Nike erases the boundaries between its star athletes, and us (Hopper). The sign of Nike, the Swoosh, like McDonald's Golden Arches, emerges as one which is gentle, loving, uncompromising in its acceptance of cultural difference. This is forcefully presented even now in the recent postfeminist commercials (Cole and Hribar, 1995). Little women, if they just do sports (and are permitted to do sports), will not get pregnant as teens, will not live with violent lovers and husbands when they grow up, or have low self-esteem in high school. But when she does have a family, she can drive them in the family sports vehicle to the Golden Arches for dinner.

By creating a space for Hopper, who is now a sign for all that Nike would ordinarily not stand for, Nike, like McDonald's with Michael Jordan, validates its transnational public identity as a corporation which has a place for everyone. But more deeply, Nike has now transcended its own identity, for to be against Nike (and McDonald's) would be to be against all that is good and strong in a world-wide democratic, capitalist system.[11]

McDonald's Goes Green

The leaders of McDonald's understand this system very well. Throughout the 1980s McDonald's identified itself with two public issues: the environment and nutrition. The foam packaging that had traditionally held the Big Mac became a symbol of environmental waste, and McDonald's was identified as the major offender in this arena (Love, 1995: 455). In August 1990, in a dramatic move intended to sway public opinion, McDonald's launched its Environmental Defense Fund (EDF), emphasizing a solid waste reduction action plan, including recycling and composting (Love, 1995: 455). McDonald's was soon recognized as the national (and international) green company, ranked number one by US consumers in 1991 as the most environmentally conscious US corporation.

As the green story unfolded, McDonald's launched a second promotional campaign. It was organized around the concept called 'McDonald's Consumer Care Culture'. Not only would the Corporation begin to offer salad bars, but customers could custom-build their own meals, and vegetable oil would now be used for all deep-fry products (Love, 1995: 459). This concept of consumer care, connected to good eating, was carried by McDonald's International to Moscow, China and Eastern Europe. Love summarizes this international strategy: 'The McDonald's calling card – the second most recognized brand name in the world – is an impressive credential. . . . Governments we call on are one hundred percent supportive because they understand that we're selling a system and not a trademark' (1995: 463). To be against McDonald's is to be against capitalism, good food and a green environment.

Celebrity-Hood

The Nike–Hopper texts (and the controversies surrounding them) thus demonstrate the intersections of the public and the private in the third-space of celebrity-hood in American popular culture today. This third-space (Slowikowski and Kohn, 1994) is the site where new public identities are negotiated. These identities link the person to certain celebrities in popular culture, connecting back, at the same time, to the private sphere where the person becomes the celebrity, or displays an attachment to some form of celebrity-hood, perhaps owning a version of the shoes Bruce Smith wears.

Hopper of course mocks this version of the fan who seeks the recognition, and notoriety, of the celebrity. But Hopper's intensity, defined as a caricature, honours that which it mocks: the intensely involved fan. The true fan, as the male, junior account executive quoted above understands, is a fanatic of the game. Who doesn't get out of control when describing, even trying to re-enact, an exciting play? The Nike shoe thus becomes an identity marker linking Hopper to the NFL, and its masculine heroes.

At one level the issue is the game and its players, not the shoe. Hopper's little stories are about what these players do to one another (and fans) during the game. At this level, the celebrity space is the space created by the fan, in interaction with other fans, during the game itself. The fan is inserted into a performance space, those moves and plays made by Sanders and Smith. Caught up in that action, the fan becomes a fanatic in attempting to describe what has just been witnessed and experienced. Hopper models that behaviour.

Thus do the Hopper stories define a performance and sports-based aesthetic. This aesthetic enacts the core values that Nike attaches to male (and family) sporting culture in America. The key value in this culture, from the fan's point of view, is intense, unashamed, pleasurable involvement in the sporting experience itself. Hopper shows me how to throw myself into an experience: the NFL game, the NFL men and their moments, the moments and their men (see Goffman, 1967: 269–70). Following Hopper's lead, I can become Barry Sanders. In bringing the viewer to these NFL places, the places where the action is (Goffman, 1967: 269), Hopper and Nike increase the likelihood that chances will be taken. In these chance-taking actions, sporting character is built and displayed. Goffman would locate 'these naked spasms of the self . . . at the end of the world' noting that 'there at the end is action and character' (1967: 270).

Nike locates some significant proportion of these actions in the living room, all the while reminding its viewers that there is another world of action. This is the world of natural action which is located in the real outdoors, or in those real indoor places where the natural, authentic, masculine (hard, firm, tanned and manly) and feminine (hard, firm, tanned and beautiful) body tests itself against itself (see Cole and Hribar, 1995; Scott, 1993: 145, 154).

So this celebrity space that Hopper enters is multiple, an uncharted borderland, an unmarked, liminal space where embodied identities are fluid and multiple (Slowikowski and Kohn, 1994). Here sporting culture is turned into a fan performance, and like Bakhtin's (1968) carnival, many of the understandings that structure everyday life are challenged. Contemporary cultural discourses are turned into a spectacle, suspended, mimicked, parodied, celebrated, erased, contested, overturned, and mocked (Slowikowski and Kohn, 1994). Hopper takes on the actions of a Sanders, or acts like a spy. And this is an embodied space. The celebrity's body and its performances becomes the site of the trickster's performance. Hopper doing Sanders, horseshoes and handgrenades. This is the place where the fan's performance self is created, displayed and tested.

In these advertisements the fan is caught in a middle space. This is the dangerous zone of celebrity-hood, the insane fan pursuing recognition in American popular male culture. This space is marked by Hopper's insanity. Hence his is an unstable space whose only stability is anchored in the power of the Nike sign and the power of the male figure who wears the shoe. The fan must navigate these spaces, guided only by the underlying calm, swooshing, soothing sign of Nike.

Race and Celebrity-Hood

The celebrity spaces occupied by African American media and sports personalities, from Spike Lee and Oprah Winfrey to Michael Jordan, contribute, as argued above, to the growing 'African Americanization of American popular culture' (Gray, 1995: 97). Race and its proper containment has been a dominant cultural theme since the Ronald Reagan presidency, when the conservatives launched full-scale attacks on gays, lesbians, feminists and women of colour. Gray reminds us that 'Black popular culture was squarely at the forefront of [this] national political debate about morality, permissiveness, teenage sexuality, affirmative action, single parenthood, and multiculturalism' (1995: 60).

These discourses about blackness and morality were structured and 'staged' by the mass media, especially television (Gray, 1995: 6). Since the mid-1980s Nike and McDonald's have been the key players in the stagings of American male blackness and its containment within the spaces of professional sports, childhood (Ronald McDonald's) and middle-class family life. These stagings by Nike and McDonald's have been structured by four narrative devices: colour-blindness, nostalgia, normalization and blackness as spectacle (see Gray, 1995: 165–6).

The African American in Nike's and McDonald's celebrity space is colour blind. Being a celebrity in this version of corporate white culture means being some version of the 'house negro' (West, 1993: 97). A reciprocal colour-blindness is at work. Nike has no interest in the African American's blackness, and Dennis Hopper is too intense to even notice it. This means that Nike's and McDonald's house negro has been fully assimilated into a pluralistic, multicultural, media world. Indeed Nike trains its athletes to put Nike in all its whiteness on a pedestal.[12] Whiteness means conformity to white middle-class values, the values of McDonald's and Nike. This means that controversial (and criminal) black athletes (Mike Tyson, O.J. Simpson, Lawrence Phillips) have no home at Nike, no meal at McDonald's (see Lipsyle, 1996).

Michael Jordan Eats at McDonald's

A Big Mac with fries can, of course, be eaten anywhere; it's a basketball playground meal. In advertisement after advertisement Michael Jordan eats a Big Mac and fries while shooting baskets with other black NBA celebrities. Thus does McDonald's bring race to the dinner table. But at the same time race is folded into two other commercial strategies: Ronald McDonald's Children Charities (RMCC) and McDonald's employment programmes, McJobs and McMasters. McJobs and McMasters are aimed, in part, at minority workers and entrepreneurs. Today McDonald's is America's 'primary entry-level job trainer . . . a role previously filled by the armed forces' (Love, 1995: 468). As a major employer of minority youth, McDonald's widely publicizes its literacy, drop-out prevention and substance abuse programmes (Love, 1995, p. 469).

McDonald's has attempted to become publicly synonymous with minority employment and education, children and their welfare (Ronald McDonald). In times of crisis, McDonald's is always there with a helping hand. People, it seems, have come to depend on this, especially children. Love quotes a Red Cross worker who after the LA earthquakes stated: 'Children are disoriented after a major crisis, and seeing McDonald's helps them begin to feel that things are getting back to normal' (Love, 1995: 469).

Love expands on the significance of this commitment. After the LA riots of April 1992:

> McDonald's was barely affected by the looting, arson and vandalism that caused an estimated \$2 billion in damage to other businesses in the area . . . when the smoke cleared after mobs burned through South Central Los Angeles, hundreds of businesses, many of them black owned, had been destroyed. Yet not a single McDonald's restaurant had been torched. (1995: 469)

Love claims that this was vindication of McDonald's 'enlightened social politics begun more than three decades ago' (1995: 469).[13] Heaping praise on the organization, he then suggests that McDonald's 'stands out not only as one of the more socially responsible companies in America, but also as one of the nation's truly effective social engineers' (1995: 469–70). This is unregulated capitalism in the service of democracy and civil society. Nike is not immune to these arguments.

Serving White Society

Nike, like McDonald's, constantly recodes black performances within a nostalgic, normalizing and spectacular narrative frame. Spectacular frames repress blackness by calling attention to the outstanding performances of particular athletes: Hopper imitating Barry Sanders; Michael Jordan and Larry Bird shooting baskets together. Blackness as spectacle (Simpson trial) focuses on performance events (the second NFL season) where blackness 'operates as an empty signifier available for mobilization and use' (Gray, 1995: 171) by fans, the media and by advertisers. The nostalgic frame lingers on the past, while celebrating a star's accomplishments and name – Barry Sanders, Hardy Nickerson, Bruce Smith. The name, attached to an accomplishment, removes race from the situation.

Normalizing frames use exceptional blackness as it does service for whites – Sanders scoring a touchdown for his white owner; Whoopie Goldberg coming to Ray Liotta's assistance in the film *Corrina, Corrina*. Each of these strategies (nostalgia, normalization, spectacle) involve colour-blindness while making and remaking the signs of African American sporting blackness. Their use folds blackness into the existing repressive systems of gender and class, while celebrating the celebrity status of African American performers.

And in its multiple treatments of blackness, Nike, McDonald's, television and the advertising media operate as internal 'Orientalizing' agencies for the larger American culture. That is, Nike and McDonald's television is an institutional apparatus which describes, teaches and authorizes a particular view of the American racial order. As the site of our collective (and repressed) unconscious, Nike television is the place where the new American racial order will be first imagined, then created and then played out. Miami, Detroit, Los Angeles, and Chicago may burn, but the NFL second season will be played. There will be a super bowl, although there may be black-outs in the above-named cities. And the Golden Arches will still be standing.

Conclusions

Race, gender, and the media do not figure prominently in the Weber–Ritzer iron cage model of contemporary society. My reading of the Hopper–Nike series (and the Jordan–McDonald's advertisements) brings race, gender and family into sharper focus. This analysis suggests that nothing escapes the cultural logics of Weber's iron cage. The Hopper–Nike–NFL advertisements, like the Jordan–McDonald's advertisements, market a somewhat newer version of the American racial order. Unfortunately, for many Americans there is no empirical, racial world beyond the worlds of the 'small screen' (Gray, 1995: 8), the racial worlds that Nike and McDonald's control. This new racial order brought a psychotic white man up against a black superstar. Race, always on the surface, was displaced in the Hopper series by Hopper's mad performances.

The NFL racial order complemented the racial order previously established in the Nike–NBA advertisements (Cole and Andrews, 1996); both orders suppressed race. The Air Jordan, Michael Jordan, Spike Lee/Mars Blackmon, Larry Bird, Charles Barkley, David Robinson, Grant Hill,

Penny Hardaway series advertisements ignored the blackness of the NBA star, while using the same star as a pitchman for Nike products.

In the NBA racial order embedded in the Nike advertisements, properly disciplined, gifted, muscular, graceful, artful black male bodies fly through space, and interact with one another on the playing fields of corporate America. These black sporting bodies are hard, and firm and well trained. Violence always lurks just below the surface, as when the player slam dunks a basketball in a shower of shattering glass. This racial order is presented and contained within tiny little stories, tales about competitions between Michael, Larry and Charles.

Known for their flashy advertisements and sports celebrities, the signs of Nike and McDonald's are quite complex. Nike and its advertisements remain central to the creation and maintenance of a conservative racial order in post-Reagan American popular culture (Andrews, 1995). Nike defines and mediates this racial, sporting culture (Denzin, 1996). Paradoxically, the key to this culture is the ongoing production of a set of social relations that bring white and black males into contact with one another.

Maybe white men can't jump (Denzin, 1995), but Nike and McDonald's lead them to think they can. Often this leads white men to those playing fields where black men show them otherwise. In its superficial, racist treatment of race in America, Nike images a symbolic, white racial order, a racial order where race no longer matters. But race does matter. Nike and McDonald's may have their televised ways with race in America, of course this is the sporting way. But someday the African American sporting way will undo this sanitized, Nike myth. When that happens the field negroes will start to configure new places for Dennis Hopper and his mad performances. Who knows, maybe Dennis will serve up a Big Mac for Michael Jordan and his friends.

Notes

I thank David Andrews for his assistance in securing copies of the Hopper materials, James Haefner for comments on the advertisement series, Karin Admiraal and Jack Bratich for library research, and Barry Smart for his comments on earlier versions of this manuscript.

1 He recommends not eating finger foods, but dining in greasy spoons, not living in tract houses, and watching as little television as possible.

2 There were five advertisements in the original 1993–4 series. The advertisements contained real-life footage of Troy Aikman, Barry Sanders, Bruce Smith, Hardy Nickerson and a collage of players from teams competing for the NFL playoffs. (Subsequent versions of the advertisement would present Hopper with Sterling Sharpe, Michael Irvin, and Junior Seau.) In 1995 Hopper reclaimed his mad fan part 'reciting a lyrical paean to "the ballet of" football while standing before a Nike "swoosh" logo as enormous as the American flag behind George C. Scott during his famous scene in the film "Patton"' (Elliot, 1995). The commercials were produced by the Wieden and Kennedy Agency of Portland.

3 Gray (1995) argues that media discourse about African Americans is contained within one of three models: the frameworks of assimilation, pluralism or multi-culturalism. Under the assimilation model, race is a matter of prejudice and personal psychology. Pluralism, or the separate-but-equal position, situates black characters in domestically 'centered black worlds . . . that essentially parallel those of whites'. The multicultural frame appeals to themes of cultural diversity, mobility, and individualism, and privileges the 'upper-middle-class black family as the site of social life' (1995: 89).

4 Nike controls 29 per cent of the athletic shoe market. In 1997 its revenues were expected to exceed $8 billion. Its 1993 advertising expenditures ($132.5 million) place it in that elite group of advertisers whose advertising expenses exceed $100 million annually.

5 Because Nike has a product agreement with the NFL, these commercials, while ostensibly for Nike's $110 Air Veer football shoes, were also commercials for the NFL.

6 Hopper was selected for the series not because of this performance history, but because of the relatively normal character he played in *True Romance* (Magiera and Jensen, 1993), a film target for the male members of Generation X.

7 According to Magiera (1994), Hopper agreed to the series because he thought the character was 'very similar to the *Apocalypse Now*' character . . . [and] he loves sports and liked the fact 'that Spike Lee . . . directs and appears in Nike commercials'.

8 Lipsyle (1996) discusses the implications of this arrangement 'In a world where sports . . . is surpassing music as a currency of mass communications, this seems like a lot of cultural power, especially when there are messages in the commercials and when the major companies like Nike, Reebok and Adidas are replacing countries and professional teams as the centers of athlete loyalty.'

9 Nike engages in systematic market and product segmentation. Thus there are three basketball shoes: Air Jordan (for Michael), Flight (for Pippin), and Force (Barkley and David Robinson). To this list can be added Air Swoops, named after basketball player Cheryl Swoops (Cole and Hribar, 1995). There are also two tennis shoes: Challenge Court (McEnroe and Agassi) and Supreme Court (Knight in Batra et al., 1996: 379).

10 A 1988 advertisement for *Good Housekeeping* in the *New York Times* defined the new traditional woman as a woman who 'has a mission in life . . . a new kind of woman with deep-rooted values . . . market researchers call it "neo-traditionalism" . . . she has found her identity in herself, her home, her family' (*New York Times*, 1988).

11 But see Cole and Hribar (1996) on Nike's distinctly unfeminist production practices in Taiwan, Hong Kong and Singapore (see also Gargan, 1996).

12 West argues that the highly successful, assimilated black professional may 'put whiteness (in all its various forms) on a pedestal' (1993: 98).

13 In the 1960s, under pressure from Martin Luther King and other civil rights leaders, McDonald's began a minority ownership programme first in Cleveland, then in Chicago, Los Angeles, Washington, DC, Miami and New York City (see Love, 1995: 359–60).

References

Advertising Age (1994a) 'Letters to the editor'. 10 January.
Advertising Age (1994b) 'Editorial: Dennis Hopper, hero'. 17 January.
Andrews, D.L. (1995) 'The fact(s) of Michael Jordan's blackness: excavating a floating racial signifier', *Sociology of Sport Journal*, 13: 324–66.

Bakhtin, M.M. (1968) *Rabelais and His World.* Cambridge, MA: MIT Press.

Batra, R., Myers, J.G. and Aaker, D.A. (1996) *Advertising Management* (5th edn). Upper Saddle River, NJ: Prentice Hall.

Bird, L. (1993) 'Critics cry foul at Nike spots with actor', *Wall Street Journal,* 16 December.

Cole, C.L. and Andrews, D. (1996) '"Look – it's NBA Showtime!" Visions of race in the popular imaginary', *Cultural Studies Annual,* 1: 141–81.

Cole, C.L. and Hribar, A. (1995) 'Celebrity feminism: Nike style post-fordism, transcendence, and consumer power', *Sociology of Sport Journal,* 12: 347–69.

Cole, C.L. and Orlie, M.A. (1996) 'Hybrid athletes, monstrous addicts, and cyborg natures', *Journal of Sport History,* 22 (3): 229–39.

Couch, C.J. (1995) 'Oh, what webs those phantoms spin', *Symbolic Interaction,* 18: 229–46.

Denzin, N.K. (1995) '*White Man Can't Jump?* Race, gender and the postmodern emotional self', *Social Perspectives on Emotion,* 3: 33–54.

Denzin, N.K. (1996) 'Air Jordan: Michael Jordan on Michael Jordan', *Journal of Sport Sociology,* 15: 319–24.

Elliot, S. (1995) 'Super Bowl Campaigns Break Long Losing Streak', *New York Times,* 31 January.

Feagin, J.R. and Vera, H. (1995) *White Racism.* New York: Routledge.

Fiske, J. (1989) *Understanding Popular Culture.* Boston: Unwin Hyman.

Garfield, B. (1993) 'Nike goes Hopper mad with deranged ref ads', *Advertising Age,* 6 December.

Gargan, E.A. (1996) 'An Indonesian asset is also a liability', *New York Times,* 16 March.

Goffman, E. (1967) *Interaction Ritual.* New York: Doubleday.

Gray, H. (1995) *Watching Race: Television and the Struggle for 'Blackness'.* Minneapolis, MN: University of Minnesota Press.

Lipsyle, R. (1996) 'Knight: can a logo conquer all?', *New York Times,* 7 February.

Loro, L. (1994) 'Do MCI's ads offer a genius child? Ask a psychologist', *Advertising Age,* 14 March.

Love, J.F. (1995) *McDonald's: Behind the Arches* (rev. edn). New York: Bantam Books.

Magiera, M. (1994) 'Hopper labels "absurd" uproar over his Nike role', *Advertising Age,* 10 January.

Magiera, M. and Jensen, J. (1993) 'Dennis Hopper ads take Nike to edge', *Advertising Age,* 6 December.

New York Times (1988) 'The new traditionalist', advertisement for *Good Housekeeping,* 18 August.

Press, A.L. (1991) *Women Watching Television: Gender, Class, and Generation in the American Television Experience.* Philadelphia: University of Pennsylvania Press.

Price, S. (1993) *Media Studies.* London: Pitman Publishing.

Ritzer, G. (1993) *The McDonaldization of Society: An Investigation into the Changing Character of Contemporary Social Life.* Newbury Park, CA: Sage.

Schudson, M. (1984) *Advertising: The Uneasy Persuasion.* New York: Basic Books.

Scott, L.M. (1993) 'Fresh lipstick: rethinking images of women in advertising', *Media Studies,* 7: 141–55.

Seaman, W.R. (1992) 'Active audience theory: pointless populism', *Media, Culture & Society,* 14: 301–11.

Slowikowski, S.S. and Kohn, N. (1994) 'Look at us now: celebrity and the third space'. Presented to the 1994 Annual Meeting of the Society for the Study of Symbolic Interaction, Los Angeles, 8 August.

Smythe, D. (1994) *Counterclockwise: Perspectives on Communication* (ed. T. Guback). Boulder, CO: Westview Press.

West, C. (1993) *Race Matters*. Boston: Beacon Press.

Wieden, D. (1996) 'A sense of cool: Nike's theory of advertising', in R. Batra, J.G. Myers and D.A. Aaker, *Advertising Management* (5th edn). Upper Saddle River, NJ: Prentice Hall.

12 Theorizing/Resisting McDonaldization:
A Multiperspectivist Approach

Douglas Kellner

George Ritzer's *The McDonaldization of Society* has generated an unprecedented number of sales and amount of scholarly interest, as demonstrated by highly impressive sales figures, new editions of the book, and the growing critical literature dedicated to the phenomenon of which this book is a part (see also Alfino et al., 1998; Kincheloe and Shelton, forthcoming). Ritzer's popularization of Max Weber's theory of rationalization and its application to a study of the processes of McDonaldization presents a concrete example of applied social analysis which clarifies important developments in the present moment, calling attention to their costs and benefits, their positive and negative sides. The widespread reception – and the controversy it has evoked – suggests that Ritzer has touched upon some vital nerve centres of the contemporary era which I suggest have to do with discontents over modernity and ambivalent attitudes toward the rapid transformation of the present for which the term 'postmodernity' has been coined.

The choice of McDonald's restaurants as an example of defining problematical aspects of our contemporary world is a felicitous one. The phenomenon of 'McDonaldization' which Ritzer elicits from his analysis of McDonald's fast-food restaurants encompasses both production and consumption, and is applied to a broad scope of economic, political, social and cultural artefacts and mechanisms. Ritzer is able to apply his concepts to phenomena ranging from work to leisure, from food to media, and from education to politics. Encompassing such a diverse field of topics and artefacts exemplifies the sociological moment of illuminating abstraction, of generating a concept so broad as to conceptually grasp and interpret a wealth of data in a way that theorizes defining and constitutive features of the present moment. Such a mode of theorizing – now under attack by some modes of postmodern theory – helps us critically view key social dynamics, institutions and problems, thus exemplifying the major strength of classical social theory.[1]

In this study, I will attempt to illuminate both the strengths and weaknesses of Ritzer's theory of McDonaldization and will suggest some alternative perspectives. I will first discuss how Ritzer theorizes McDonaldization, focusing on his mode of social analysis, and will argue that Ritzer fails to adequately explicate its cultural dimensions. Drawing on contemporary cultural studies, I accordingly add a cultural perspective to Ritzer's analysis and discuss whether McDonaldization is properly a phenomenon of modernity or postmodernity, and whether it is better grasped by modern or postmodern theory. I then take on the issue of the standpoint and strategy of critique of key phenomenona like McDonald's, or McDonaldization, and sketch out some critical perspectives and strategies of resistance that explicate and supplement Ritzer's normative stance.

My argument is that Ritzer does not adequately distinguish between McDonald's and the broader phenomenon of McDonaldization, that his taking the infamous fast-food company McDonald's as the paradigm of McDonaldization skews his analysis negatively, missing the dialectics of McDonaldization, its positive and negative features. Yet I also want to argue that Ritzer does not develop an adequate standpoint of critique to evaluate either McDonald's or McDonaldization, that this problem results from excessive dependence on Weber's theory, and that a multiperspectivist method can overcome these problems. Accordingly, I argue for a multiperspectivist approach to capture the complexity of McDonald's and McDonaldization so as to better critically evaluate associated multifarious aspects and effects.

McDonaldization, Social Theory and Cultural Studies

The McDonald's fast-food restaurants certainly provide a useful example of a familiar sociological artefact that can be analysed to generate a more general and macro level of conceptualization. Few artefacts and institutions of the contemporary world are as well known and ubiquitous as McDonald's with its Big Macs, Golden Arches, and Ronald McDonalds, promotional tie-ins with popular films and toys, its charities, and saturation advertising. Both the rationalization of production and consumption in McDonald's is unparalleled in the contemporary era, and serves as a model for what Ritzer calls the 'McDonaldization of society', defined by increased efficiency, calculability, predictability and control through substitution of human labour power with technology, all of which constitute a quantitative and, to some, alarming growth of instrumental rationalization.

Ritzer's project combines use of Weber's sociological theory to generalize about McDonald's with a wealth of empirical data to illustrate and flesh out the points. His research method follows what Alvin Gouldner (1976) called 'newspaper sociology', assembling information and news on McDonald's through gathering and citing newspaper and periodical articles to illustrate his arguments – as opposed to historical sociology, ethnography, phenomenology, cultural studies, and so on.[2] This perspective combines a theoretical optic with empirical illustration to enable the reader to see how the general theoretical points are embodied in concrete phenomena that can be observed, confirmed and discussed.

Ritzer privileges Weber's conception of rationalization to theorize the phenomenon of McDonaldization, which he sees as 'coming to dominate more and more sectors of American society as well as of the rest of the world' (1996: 1). Ritzer extends Weber's analysis to a wealth of phenomena, demonstrating that the principles of McDonaldization are restructuring a vast array of fields, ranging from the food, media, education and health care industries, encompassing fundamental life processes from birth to death (1996: 161ff.). The strength of the analysis is the light that such strong perspectives shed on general social dynamics and the mapping of the macro structures of contemporary social organization. The limitation of the analysis is that the Weberian-inspired perspectives often generate a one-sided and limited optic that needs to be supplemented, corrected and expanded by further critical perspectives.

We might, for instance, deploy a Marx/Weber synthesis to theorize McDonaldization as a combination of instrumental rationalization of production and consumption with a sustained corporate attempt to increase profit.[3] Indeed, McDonaldization seems to equally involve commodification and rationalization, to commodify food production and to rationalize its production and consumption so as to increase profitability. While Ritzer applies the McDonaldization model to production and consumption, he largely emphasizes consumption and thus downplays the ways that McDonaldization has revolutionized production – despite some references to Taylorism and Fordism (Ritzer, 1996: 24–7, *passim*). Likewise, although he stresses the role of profit in driving McDonaldization (1996: 44, 62f, 87f, *passim*), Ritzer could better contextualize the phenomenon within the framework of globalization and a restructuring of capitalism, aiming at the increase of productivity and profit through rationalization of production and consumption. For in addition to being part of a rationalization process, McDonaldization is part of a new global form of technocapitalism in which world markets are being rationalized and reorganized to maximize capital accumulation.[4]

Equally, while Ritzer's largely sociological analysis illuminates key features of McDonald's fast-food chains and the applicability of its principles to a variety of other phenomena is striking, he neglects the cultural dimensions of the McDonald's phenomenon and in particular the ways in which the Corporation mobilizes advertising campaigns and promotional stunts to create an experience of fun, of family togetherness, and of Americanization itself which is associated with the McDonald's experience. Thus, when one bites into a Big Mac one is consuming the sign values of good times, communal experience, consumer value and efficiency, as well as the (dubious) pleasures of the product. McDonald's is selling not just fast-food, but a family adventure of eating out together, intergenerational bonding and a communal experience, as their advertising campaigns reiterate over and over in various ways. Purchasing and ingesting a specific food product is only one part of this experience, which includes the consumption of sign values such as inexpensive food, a family outing, Americana or modernity (see the detailed analyses in Goldman, 1992: 85ff.; Kincheloe, 1997: 249ff.).

McDonaldization is thus an ideology as well as a set of social practices, a cultural construct with its myths, semiotic codes and discourses. McDonald's itself projects an ideology of the USA as a melting pot in which all citizens participate equally in its democratic pleasures, regardless of race, class, gender and age. It furnishes a model of the USA as a land of consumer innovation and technical rationality which produces inexpensive and desirable goods for all, serving its customers' needs and providing a valuable product. McDonald's associates itself with traditions like the family, national holidays, patriotism, Christian charity and the icons of media culture. Going to McDonald's for denizens of the USA is thus joining the consumer society, participating in the national culture, and validating common values.

Ritzer thus underplays the ways that McDonald's is an ideological and cultural phenomenon, as well as an economic and sociological set of practices. Although he applies his analysis of McDonaldization to a wide range of cultural phenomena (the media, education, travel, food, and so on), Ritzer does not really engage the specifically cultural dimension of the operation. In Weberian terms, he neglects the charisma of the Golden Arches, Ronald McDonald and McDonaldland, the tie-ins and promotions, and the ubiquitous advertising, aimed at a variety of gender, race, class and national subject positions.[5]

Consuming McDonald's

Ritzer also excessively generalizes his analysis of the homogenization, massification and standardization of McDonaldization, neglecting the variety and diversity of consumer practices in different regions and parts of the world and the various uses to which consumers can put McDonaldization, using its products and procedures to serve their own needs. British cultural studies has stressed the importance of analysing the ways that audiences or consumers create their own meanings and experience. The McDonald's fast-food chains and other aspects of what Ritzer calls McDonaldization generate a variety of specific pleasures, meanings and effects which a micro analysis of particular forms and experiences of McDonaldization can interrogate. As I suggest below, people in different countries no doubt experience both McDonald's and McDonaldization in a variety of ways and there are gender, race, class and regional differences in the phenomena of fast-food and societal rationalization that Ritzer fails to explore in much detail.

By largely privileging Weber's theory of rationalization in his analysis of McDonaldization, Ritzer thus misses the subjective aspects of the process and the ways that various individuals and groups deploy McDonaldization to serve their own needs and interests. His privileging of the category of rationalization is thus too objectivistic and fails to articulate the subjective and cultural complex of McDonaldization. Indeed, I am not sure that Weber's metaphor of the 'iron cage' that Ritzer suggests, nor the alternative metaphors he proposes of the 'velvet' or 'rubber' cage, are the best ways to interrogate the McDonald's phenomenon. In the case of McDonald's – and many other fast-food emporiums, sites of mass entertainment and consumption, and media culture – perhaps something like 'the plastic fun house' is more appropriate. Whereas societal rationalization accurately describes aspects of the socio-economic roots of McDonaldization, there is a more hedonistic and fun-oriented cultural side that metaphors of a 'cage' do not adequately capture.

It is, for example, unlikely that many McDonald's customers see themselves as trapped in a cage, although no doubt most of its workers feel enclosed and encaged in their constrictive labour conditions, as evidenced by their especially high turnover rates (see below). On the cultural side, McDonaldization hides the conditions of rationalization with a colourful environment, often decorated with images from current films and icons of popular entertainment to provide a funhouse experience and to entertain customers as well as to fill their stomachs. Beneath the glitzy and kitschy appearance, inexorable conditions of rationalization (and attempts to maximize profits) work behind the backs of the customers, masked by the façade of the promised experience of McDonald's restaurants as providing fun and pleasurable fast eating for a fast-paced consumer society.

McDonald's Between the Modern and the Postmodern

Rationalization is itself equated with modernization in standard interpretations of Weber, and one might raise the question of whether McDonaldization is properly interpreted as an expression of modernity, as Ritzer (1996: 148f.) argues, or of postmodernity. Clearly, the rationalization or industrialization of food production constitutes a rupture with traditional life (for earlier analyses of the mechanization of agriculture, food, labour, house-cleaning, the objects of everyday life, and death, see Giedion, 1969). As Ritzer argues, following Weber's model, increased rationalization of everyday life involves ruptures with tradition and the substitution of new 'modern' forms, thus creating tensions between the modern and the premodern. Claims that we are now leaving modernity behind for a new postmodernity would suggest that we are leaving behind modern social and cultural forms like McDonaldization in favour of new postmodern conditions.

Against extreme binary either/or positions which would hold that we are within either modernity or a new postmodernity, I would argue that we are currently between the modern and the postmodern, in a liminal space between the two cultural and social paradigms (Best and Kellner, 1997; Kellner, 1995), and that there are identifiable features of both the modern and the postmodern involved in McDonaldization. In particular, McDonaldization as a rationalization of production and consumption is clearly modern in inspiration and form, whereas the proliferation of sign value in the McDonald's experience through advertising and publicity stunts has postmodern ramifications, as its consumers enter a quasi-mythical hyperreal world of Americana, family fun and good times.[6]

In other words, I would argue that whereas initially McDonaldization was pre-eminently an expression of modernity in its mass production and consumption of food, it crossed the postmodern divide through its phantasmagoric advertising and commodity spectacle, drawing its customers into a world of simulation, hyperreality and the implosion of boundaries, especially as it became globalized and part of postmodern hybridization that synthesizes signs of modernity with local traditions and culture. Thus, it seems to me a mistake to either insist that McDonaldization is primarily an expression of modernity or of postmodernity, for it is arguably both. Indeed, McDonaldization not only relates to both Weber's analysis of rationalization and Marx's theory of commodification, but also post-modern conceptions are involved in it. Thus, Baudrillard's investigations of implosion, hyperreality and simulation, as well as analyses of post-Fordist globalization, the hybridization of identity and semiotic practices that some see as central to the postmodern condition can usefully be deployed to analyse McDonaldization.

Interpreted from a Baudrillardian postmodern perspective, McDonald's cuisine can be seen as a simulation of food, since its artificial products, tastes and pleasures simulate such familiar products as burgers, fries and shakes. The products themselves are heavily dependent on chemical additives and artificial substances for their flavour, texture and materiality, and can thus serve as examples of artificially produced foodstuffs. McDonald's products thus constitute a technological model of fast-food production and consumption reconstituting food itself, using food technologies to produce novel substances, tastes and substitutions, and hence anticipating the artificial technofoods of the future.

The McDonald's experience is a hyperreal one, in which its model of fast-food consumption replaces the traditional model of home-prepared food with commodified food, which then becomes a model for food production, replicated through frozen and prepared food and the spinoff of countless other chain fast-food restaurant businesses. In other words, McDonald's provides a new hyperreal model of what food and eating are, mediated by its food technologies and organization of food production and consumption. As suggested earlier, McDonald's customers are also made to feel that they are especially virtuous and smart to take out their families, or to treat themselves or their friends to a fast, inexpensive and ready-made meal. And the advertising and promotion enables the McDonald's customer to participate in the hyperreal ideologies of Americana, family togetherness and social bonding. McDonald's also implodes boundaries between tradition and the contemporary, coding their advertisements with traditional images of Americana and family ideology, as it undermines family eating practices and redefines diet and culinary value, familial togetherness and communal experience.

Ritzer is thus mistaken to distance his analysis of McDonaldization from postmodern theory (1996: 153ff.), though he is certainly correct to see and emphasize the links with modernity and modernization. Ritzer's down-grading of the postmodern elements of McDonaldization are related to his failure to adequately theorize the cultural dimension of McDonaldization. And yet Ritzer does see how there is something like a McDonaldization of culture in the culture industry's rapacious lust for audiences and profits and rationalized cultural production. Likewise, it is clear that McDonaldi-zation can be linked with globalization, including its postmodern elements. Part of a postmodern globalized culture is the way that transnational cultural forms help produce a global culture, but one that is inflected by local conditions and practices (see the studies in Cvetkovich and Kellner, 1996, for examples of the dialectic between global and local).

McDonald's Between the Global and the Local

There is no doubt that McDonaldization is spreading as an international phenomenon. As the London *Economist* notes: 'the scale of the global Mac attack is impressive. The company, which has 18,700 McDonald's outlets serving 33 [million] people every day, will open up to 3,200 new restaurants both this year and next, compared with 2,430 in 1995 and 1,787 in 1994. About two-thirds of them will be outside America. By 2000, predicts James Cantalupo, president of McDonald's International, more than half of all the firm's restaurants will be abroad' (29 June 1996: 61). By 1985, some 22 per cent of units were located overseas accounting for 2.2 billion dollar (20 per cent of total) sales and 18 per cent of operating profit; by 1996 overseas sales reached 14 billion dollars constituting 47 per cent of total sales and 54 per cent of its 2.6 billion dollar operating profit: 'Overseas, then, is where burgers have become most bankable' (ibid.).

Ritzer is aware of the globalization of McDonald's and notes how it varies its product, architecture and atmosphere to local conditions, but does not adequately analyse the different meanings, social functions and experiences McDonald's generates in a variety of local conditions. Studies collected in James Watson's edited text *Golden Arches East: McDonald's in East-Asia* provide, for example, ethnographic studies of the ways that McDonald's is experienced by customers in China, Taiwan, Japan, Hong Kong and other East Asia sites (1998), though the studies are largely uncritical. I experienced its varied dynamics myself one night in Taichung, Taiwan, as I sought a restroom in the midst of the city. While wandering through the space of the local McDonald's – a three-storey building within a densely populated urban region – I noticed that the place was packed with students studying, young people talking and couples dating. My host said that in a crowded city, McDonald's was a good site for study and socializing, and the locals were taking advantage of this. Obviously, the social purposes and functions were quite different in Taiwan from those in the USA, which neither encouraged, nor in some cases did they even allow, hanging out and using the site as a study, or venue for courtship. The point is that McDonald's, or any global artefact, has very different meanings and functions in different regions and parts of the world, and a concrete analysis should interrogate local conditions in which consumers provide their own narratives of their site-specific and particular experiences to capture the variety and diversity of meanings of the McDonald's effect.

My Taiwanese host told me that it was especially young children who sought the McDonald's eating experience, demanding of their parents to take them to McDonald's for special treats or celebrations. For people in non-Western societies, McDonald's seems to signify Western modernity and to offer alternatives in terms of cuisine and social experiences. Yet no doubt it is also advertising and promotion that helps produce these meanings, providing a postmodern hyperreal and hybrid consumer experience for denizens of the many corners and crevices of the globe who consume Western modernity when they ingest a Big Mac. Moreover, McDonald's adapts to local cultures and cuisines, serving noodle dishes in Asian countries along with the Big Macs, and allows [regional] owners to vary the menu according to local tastes, Thus, while, on one level, McDonald's helps standardize and homogenize a global consumer culture, on another level it brings variety, diversity and novelty to many parts of the world, thus contributing to the creation of a hybridized postmodern global popular culture.

There are consequently both modern and postmodern aspects to the phenomenon of McDonaldization and the perspectives of both modern and postmodern theory can illuminate the phenomenon. In analysing a complex phenomenon like McDonaldization, it is important to focus on both production and consumption, grasping both the modern dimension of rationalized production and consumption, and the postmodern cultural dimension of hyperreal and hybridized consumption. Some of Ritzer's critics focus too exclusively on the domain of consumption, which often leads them to defend McDonaldization on the grounds that Ritzer overlooks the variety and diversity of consumer practices and the varied meanings and effects McDonaldization can have on different types of consumers (see Miles, 1998; Parker, 1998). While there is some validity in this criticism, it overlooks the extent to which McDonaldization constitutes a standardization and homogenization of production and consumption that is often highly dehumanizing and degrading to workers and consumers.

Thus, in my reading, McDonaldization is linked to the problematics of global capitalism and the project of rationalization of the labour process, markets and consumption to increase capitalist profitability and power. McDonaldization thus encompasses, from this perspective, both the forces of instrumental rationality and efficiency *and* a postmodern realm of hyperreality, simulation, implosion and hybridity. While it is perhaps the intensity and the relentlessness of his application of the Weberian optic that lends Ritzer's analysis both its power and limitations, other modes of interpreting McDonaldization could be deployed to supplement, complement and correct Ritzer's perspectives.

I would thus argue for what I call a multiperspectivist social theory (Best and Kellner, 1991, 1997; Kellner, 1995) to engage the phenomenon of McDonaldization and to provide a more contextual and multidimensional paradigm for analysing the multiplicity of economic, socio-political and cultural aspects of McDonaldization. This requires mobilizing the resources of both modern and postmodern theory, using not only Marx and Weber, but also Baudrillard, as well as the resources of cultural studies and a critical multiculturalism, to theorize the full range of the phenomenon of the global hybridization of McDonaldization, its cultural and ideological construction, and its complex effects. McDonaldization is a many-sided phenomenon and the more perspectives that one can bring to its analysis and critique, the better grasp of the phenomenon one will have and the better one will be able to develop alternative readings and generate oppositional practices.

Criticizing/Resisting McDonaldization

Ritzer's critics often complain that he is too pessimistic, does not adequately articulate resistance to McDonaldization, and/or is too totalizing in his criticism (Parker, 1998; Rinehart, 1998; Taylor et al., 1998). While Ritzer adds a list of the positive features of McDonaldization to the most recent edition of his book (1996: 12f.), on the whole his interpretation is primarily negative, although, as I argue, he fails to develop adequately a critical standpoint to take on his target. For the most part, Ritzer uses Weber's concept of the irrationality of rationalization, of the ways that it comes to contradict its own goals, to criticize McDonaldization, thus developing an immanent critique of the irrationalities that are produced by McDonaldization. In this section, by contrast, I will develop a multiperspectivist normative position to develop a more systematic and contextual critique.

Ritzer's critical optic is similar to some extent to the Frankfurt School critique of mass society that expands homogenization, standardization, commodification and instrumental rationality in such ways that precipitate a decline of individuality, freedom and, in Habermas's terminology, create a colonization of the life-world by the social system.[7] These critical perspectives on modernity and rationalization articulate people's fears of increased conformity, loss of freedom and diversity, and domination by external societal forces bound up with the evolution of modern societies. McDonaldization encapsulates in a provocative way these concerns and itself can thus serve as a target for the discontents with modernity and its problematical aspects.

On the whole, it is the merit of Ritzer's study to raise the question of the standpoint from which one can critique a popular phenomenon like McDonald's and how one can justify one's critique without falling prey to charges of elitism. Ritzer is to be commended for taking on a popular part of American and now global culture like McDonald's and generating a critical discussion. Ritzer's critics often accuse him of elitism (Parker, 1998; Rinehart, 1998; Taylor et al., 1998), but themselves often fall prey to an uncritical populism (Parker, 1998; Taylor et al., 1998), or fail to offer adequate responses or to articulate in more detail how one resists McDonaldization (Rinehart, 1998). Many of Ritzer's critics thus create apologetics and celebration of the mass culture he criticizes, thereby uncritically replicating a position increasingly widespread in cultural studies that puts all the weight of praxis and production of meaning on the side of the subject, thus effectively erasing the problematics of domination, manipulation and oppression from critical social theory (see the critique of this position in Kellner, 1995). Such positions put a positive gloss on McDonaldization, mass culture or consumerism in which moments of resistance and the construction of meaning are highlighted, as if these phenomena merely furnished resources to empower individuals and to resist dominant meanings or practices.

In general, it is a mistake to be overly abstract and one-sided in relation to a complex phenomenon like McDonaldization, or, for that matter, such things as mass culture, consumerism or the consumer society itself. Contemporary positions often are skewed into one-sided optics that primarily celebrate or denigrate the phenomenon under scrutiny, rather than providing a more contextual and dialectical approach that evaluates specific phenomena, articulates negative and/or positive dimensions, and then makes nuanced judgements. Perhaps Ritzer does not adequately appreciate or valorize the positive features of McDonaldization, but often his critics do not acknowledge the negative side, and are all too eager to defend mass culture, consumption or McDonaldization against Ritzer's often scathing criticisms.

In my own view, Ritzer's book is valuable for provoking a theoretical and practical debate concerning key novel and defining features of our contemporary world and forcing us to define our response to crucial aspects of our everyday life. Although many of Ritzer's critics chide him for being too pessimistic and negative, this dose of critical negativity is salutary in an age of positive thinking only too eager to embrace and celebrate the joys of consumer capitalism. Ritzer's analysis of McDonaldization is thus valuable for articulating discontents of critical individuals with relentless rationalization and accordant standardization, homogenization and massification of experience.

Indeed, in response to his many critics who argue that Ritzer is too hard on McDonaldization and rationalized consumer practices, I would argue that at least his sharp critique of McDonald's itself is perfectly justified and that there is little good which one can say of this particularly noxious institution.[8] Yet neither Ritzer himself nor many of his critics always adequately distinguish between McDonald's and the broader phenomenon of McDonaldization. Failure to make this differentiation often skews normative judgements and evaluations of the respective phenomena. In other words, one should distinguish between specific concrete examples of McDonaldization such as the McDonald's Corporation and the more general societal dynamics associated with rationalization and the application of instrumental rationality to social phenomena, relations and institutions.

For instance, I would not hesitate to develop a critique of McDonald's as a corporation and junk food emporium, while at another level, I would propose a more nuanced evaluation of McDonaldization as a social phenomenon. In the following analysis, I will accordingly articulate a multiperspectivist approach to criticize and resist McDonald's and McDonaldization, offering separate criticisms of these two phenomena. While I draw on Ritzer's appropriation of Weber's notion of the irrationality of rationalization in my critique, I argue that it does not provide an adequate standpoint to criticize either McDonald's or McDonaldization. Moreover, as my drawing on and expanding specific criticisms made by Ritzer of McDonald's suggests, he himself contributes aspects of a stronger evaluative position, which he does not, however, adequately articulate.

The Case Against McDonald's

I want to mobilize a variety of perspectives in this section to criticize the McDonald's Corporation and its product. This process is facilitated by the existence of a well-documented book by award-winning *Guardian* reporter John Vidal (1997) on a libel trial pitting McDonald's against two British activists, as well as an extremely impressive website which furnishes a vast amount of information about McDonald's and offers ample material for a substantive critique.[9] This site was developed by supporters of the two British activists, Helen Steel and Dave Morris, who were sued by McDonald's for distributing leaflets denouncing the Corporation's low wages, advertising practices, involvement in deforestization, harvesting of animals, and promotion of junk food and an unhealthy diet. The activists counter-attacked and, with help from supporters, organized a McLibel campaign, assembled a McSpotlight website with a tremendous amount of information criticizing the Corporation, and assembled experts to testify and confirm their criticisms. The five-year civil trial, Britain's longest ever, ended ambiguously on 19 June 1997, with the judge defending some of McDonald's claims against the activists, while substantiating other of their criticisms (Vidal, 1997: 299–315). The case created unprecedented bad publicity for McDonald's which was circulated throughout the world via Internet websites, mailing lists, and discussion groups. The McLibel/McSpotlight group claims that their website was accessed over 15 million times and was visited over two million times in the month of the verdict alone (Vidal, 1997: 326); the *Guardian* reported that the site 'claimed to be the most comprehensive source of information on a multinational corporation ever assembled' and was part of one of the more successful anti-corporate cam-paigns (22 February 1996; the website is at : http://www.mcspotlight.org/).

Building on material assembled in the libel trial, one can construct a very strong case against McDonald's. To begin, from a nutritional point of view, as Ritzer himself notes (1996: 126ff., 179f.), McDonald's food is overly saturated with salt, sugar and fats, producing high cholesterol and dubious nutrients. It is standardized and homogenized fare, providing a predictably bland and unexciting taste. As Joel Kovel remarks, the label 'junk food' is perfectly appropriate.

> in light of the fact that nutritional experts almost universally agree that the kind of food sold by McDonald's is bad for you. With 28 grams of fat, 12.6 of which are saturated, in a Big Mac, and 22 more grams in an order of French fries, along with 52 additives being used in its various food products, it is scarcely surprising that an internal company memorandum would state that: 'we can't really address or defend nutrition. We don't sell nutrition and people don't come to McDonald's for nutrition.' When the company's cancer expert, Dr. Sydney Arnott, was asked his opinion of the statement that 'a diet high in fat, sugar, animal products and salt and low in fibre, vitamins and minerals is linked with cancer of the breast and bowel and heart disease,' he replied: 'If it is being directed to the public then I would say it is a very reasonable thing to say.' (1997: 28)

Although the McDonald's Corporation defends its products as forming part of an overall 'balanced diet', Professor Michael Crawford, a con-sultant to the World Health Organization, testified at a public hearing:

> Not only are McDonald's encouraging the use of a style of food which is closely associated with risk of cancer and heart disease, whilst health professionals are trying to reduce the risks to Western populations, but they are actively promoting the same cultures where at present these diseases are not a problem. (McLibel Support Campaign, 1994; see also Vidal, 1997: 114)

In addition, in relation to the challenge of more health-conscious parents seeking better diets for their children, McDonald's is now heavily targeting advertising at children, aggressively using tie-ins with popular films and pop culture artefacts, and their Ronald McDonald clowns in order to attract younger customers who presumably will persuade their parents to take them to eat at McDonald's. Justice Bell, however, ruled in the McLibel trial, that McDonald's advertising practices 'exploits children by using them, as more susceptible subjects of advertising, to pressurize their parents into going to McDonald's' and that advertising which 'pretended to a positive nutritional benefit . . . did not match' (Vidal, 1997: 306–7).

Moreover, from the perspective of culinary taste, one could argue that McDonald's is regressive, even in terms of hamburgers and fast-food. I remember going to my first drive-in hamburger stand in Virginia in the 1950s and discovering the pleasures of a juicy cheeseburger with all the trimmings, a thick milk shake and crunchy French fries. I remember the introduction of McDonald's from this same era and how bland and boring its fare was in comparison with the rich and succulent burgers and shakes from the local hamburger joint. From my current perspective of concern with health and nutrition, I would not without guilt eat any fatty burger, but would argue that even within the range of possible burgers McDonald's is among the most mediocre and over-priced. And from the perspective of choosing from the possible range of health and gourmet foods open to us, I would say that from the standpoints of culinary taste and nutrition, McDonald's offers an obviously inferior option.

Ritzer uses Weber's theory of rationalization and argues that even from the standpoint of economic rationality, McDonald's does not provide the value that it promises. He suggests that there is a tremendous mark-up of profit in the fries, drinks, burgers and other products sold (1996: 60f.) and the multi-billion dollar profit margin every year would confirm that consumers are not getting good value from their product, but are enriching the Corporation at their own expense. In fact, McDonald's decline in sales during 1996–7 may in part be consumer recognition that they were getting ripped off, that McDonald's did not give good food value (see CNN, *Inside Business World*, 7 June 1997, and *Los Angeles Times*, 11 November 1997: D16, on McDonald's declining sales and consumer dissatisfaction with its products).

In addition, the McDonald's experience in eating is an example of assembly-line consumption that is hardly conducive to conversation and social interaction, and is thus rarely a quality family social experience or communal eating experience. The McDonald's goal is to guarantee a 10-minute eating experience (Love, 1986), and the production and consumption operation is geared to getting customers in and out of the restaurant as quickly as possible. As a corporation, McDonald's advertisements which celebrate traditional and family values, as well as good economic value, are thus highly misleading, and, as Ritzer points out, its practices often contradict the imperatives of value, efficiency and wholesomeness that its advertisements and corporate propaganda proclaim (1996: 121ff.).

From the standpoint of the production and consumption of food, McDonaldization articulates the tendencies toward conformity and massification noted by social theorists of the 1950s. The whole McDonald's experience forces one into the mould of preformed sameness and homogenization; one orders from a small range of choices and one must fit one's taste to the corporate experience. Whereas standard multipage menus address consumers as individual subjects, with their own complex likes and taste, in which one can privately contemplate the range of choices, the McDonald's marquee illustrates the product in a public space, fitting the individual into the slot of homogenized consumer subject. McDonaldization in this sense is essentially a phenomenon of rationalized modernization, part and parcel of the mass society with its frenzied pace and standardized consumption and production.

But McDonald's homogenization of food consumption went so far that it appears now as a caricature, a joke, the ultimate in kitschiness and trash. From a postmodern perspective that valorizes difference, otherness and variety, McDonald's is the paradigm of mass homogeneity, sameness and standardization, which erases individuality, specificity and difference. In this sense, McDonald's is thus profoundly out of synch with the post-modern turn, and if it survives, it is because of the weight of nostalgia, tradition and habit that will drive those previous consumers back to the site of earlier pleasant experiences. McDonald's advertisements indeed stress the continuity, stability, and tradition guaranteed by the Corporation, with one advertisement picturing a man returning to his town after many years away and finding that everything has changed, that much has disappeared, except for the good old McDonald's, still serving the same fare in the same place after all these years (see the detailed analysis in Goldman, 1992: 97f.).

Curiously enough, those who defend McDonald's, who are still attached to it, are nostalgic for those very institutions of modernity that destroyed tradition. Indeed, the paradox of McDonald's longevity is that an institution which destroyed tradition (that is, home cooking, individualized family restaurants, a balanced and healthy diet) has itself become tradition that accrues nostalgia and the aura of Americana – in part the result of McDonald's advertising campaigns. Yet nostalgia for McDonald's, continuing loyalty to its product and institution is in part the result of its longevity, of the fact that it has by now accumulated billions of consumers who return to the site of pleasant remembrances of when one was younger.

Architecturally, the McDonald's environment is a sterile and dehumanizing site of standardized and banalized design and structure signifying sameness, corporate homogeneity and artificial standardized space. As for its workers and conditions of labour, the McDonald's production mechanism is a conspicuous example of high-pressure, repetitive and low-paid labour, 'minimum wage from cradle to grave', generating extremely high turnover rates. McDonald's is notorious in resisting unionization and firing workers who try to create a union. Justice Bell ruled that McDonald's wages were extremely low and that many of its labour practices were unacceptable (see Vidal, 1997: 213–35, 309–10). Moreover, as the workers' solidarity network reported:

> Seventeen year old women are forced to work 9 to ten hours a day, seven days a week, earning as little as six cents an hour in the Keyhinge factory in Vietnam making the popular giveaway promotional toys, many of which are Disney characters, for McDonald's Happy Meals.
>
> After working a 70 hour week, some of the teenage women take home a salary of only $4.20! In February, 200 workers fell ill, 25 collapsed and three were hospitalized as a result of chemical exposure.
>
> Included in the Happy Meals sold at McDonald's are small toys based on characters from Disney films. According to McDonald's senior vice president Brad Ball, the Happy Meals characters from the '101 Dalmations' movie were the most successful in McDonald's history.
>
> Ball adds, 'As we embark on our new global alliance, we anticipate 10 great years of unbeatable family fun as customers enjoy "the magic of Disney" only at McDonald's'. (PR Newswire Associates, March 19, 1997)

Located in Da Nang City, Vietnam, the Keyhinge Toys Co. Factory employs approximately 1,000 people, 90 per cent of them are young women 17 to 20 years old. Overtime is mandatory: shifts of nine to 10 hours a day, 7 days a week. Wage rates average between six cents and eight cents an hour – well below subsistence levels.

Overcome by fatigue and poor ventilation in late February, 200 women fell ill, 25 collapsed and three were hospitalized as a result of exposure to acetone. Acute or prolonged exposure to acetone, a chemical solvent, can cause dizziness, unconsciousness, damage to the liver and kidneys and chronic eye, nose, throat and skin irritation.

All appeals from local human and labour rights groups continue to be rejected by Keyhinge management which refuses to improve the ventilation system in the factory or remedy other unsafe working conditions.

Along with demanding forced overtime, Keyhinge management has not made legally required payments for health insurance coverage for its employees, who now receive no compensation for injury or sickness.

Many of the young women at the Keyhinge factory making McDonald's/ Disney toys earn just 60 cents after a 10 hour shift. The most basic meal in Vietnam – rice, vegetables, and tofu – costs 70 cents. Three meals would cost $2.10. Wages do not even cover 20 per cent of the daily food and travel costs for a single worker, let alone her family. (http://www.ws51-vietnam.html)[10]

In addition, from an environmentalist perspective, McDonald's products are environmentally degrading and contribute to depreciation of the soil, rain forests, and grain and other resources that are used to make its beef and dairy products. Moreover, the production of beef in particular uses territory and resources that could produce more nutritious food and contributes to environmental pollution from excessive waste products involved in the production of beef. Cattle require a tremendous amount of resources to produce, with a single beefsteak requiring up to 1,200 gallons of water, up to 16 pounds of soybeans and grain are required to produce one pound of meat, and cow manure is a major source of pollution (see Rifkin, 1992). Whereas McDonald's initially denied that it imported beef from rain forest areas like Costa Rica and Brazil that were threatened by excessive deforestation, subsequent legal procedures revealed that McDonald's did receive supplies of meat from these areas (McLibel Support Campaign, 1994 and Vidal, 1997: 151ff). Thus, while McDonald's made concessions to environmental concerns – under intense public pressure – to substitute more biodegradable products for its previously non-biodegradable styrofoam cups and other packaging materials, on the whole its products and practices are environmentally harmful.[11]

Thus, I would strongly support Ritzer's concluding call for what amounts to a boycott of McDonald's in the interests of good health, quality eating experience, environmental matters and socio-political concerns with McDonald's labour practices and corporate policies. To critics who argue that such condemnation negates the popular pleasures of members of socio-economic groups other than one's own, I would argue that there are a variety of objective reasons devolving around health, environment, economics and politics that would justify critique of McDonald's and resistance to its products.

Evaluating McDonaldization

The phenomenon of McDonaldization, however, interpreted as a set of processes geared at increasing efficiency, calculability, predictability and control is more complex and ambiguous. There are times when one wants what Ritzer calls McDonaldization, when efficiency and various modes of instrumental rationality are particularly beneficial and when one desires to avoid their opposite. Rationalization/McDonaldization of labour might serve to de-skill labour and oppress the workforce, as Braverman (1974) and Ritzer remind us, but this same procedure might free workers from dehumanizing and alienating labour that is better done by machines and automation. Likewise, there are some products and services that one wants to be as rationalized, predictable and instrumental as possible, such as safe and efficient air travel and habitable hotels. Ritzer's celebration of such things as bed-and-breakfast establishments or the older forms of non-franchised motels could be the site of unpleasant surprises, as well as quirky and pleasing novelty or more customized service. When travelling, seeking food or shelter in unfamiliar environments, or utilizing machines and products, one often wants rationalized and predictable forms of goods and services, while other times one goes for the more novel and unpredictable experience.

The same dialectical analysis can be applied to Weber's analysis of bureaucracy and rationalization, as Gouldner (1976) and others argue. Whereas bureaucracies can be insensitive to individual differences and oppressive of particularity, highly rational and legally articulated rules and regulations can protect individuals against the excessive power of potentially oppressive institutions. Although within universities, all students and teachers have suffered from the oppressive force of bureaucracy, it is often useful to have articulated, calculable, efficient and controllable bureaucratic rules, procedures and practices. Thus, rationalization can promote the forces of domination and hierarchy, but it can also empower individuals against institutions via standardized practices and regulations.

In terms of resisting McDonaldization as societal rationalization, one needs to organize oppositional practices and subcultures that provide alternatives to more rationalized corporate forms of social and economic organization. Food co-ops, health food or ethnic restaurants, and growing and preparing one's own food generates alternatives to the sort of massified and standardized food that McDonald's offers, and in terms of health care, travel and a variety of other everyday practices one can often seek or devise alternatives to the corporate mainstream. In each case, it is a question as to whether corporate rationalization does or does not serve individual needs in a socially responsible manner, produce a useful product or service at a fair price, and proffer a reasonable product in comparison with other alternatives – and whether, in specific cases, one enjoys the luxury of choice.

On the whole, one might rationally choose to pursue alternatives to corporate rationalization and mass-produced goods and services, and to avoid McDonaldization at all costs. On the other hand, one is sometimes forced to utilize services or products from large McDonaldized corporations if there are no reasonable alternatives. Ritzer's critique, however, in some ways replicates the critique of mass society and culture produced by both the left and the right. Such critique bemoans the increase in the contemporary world of standardized sameness and homogenization, and the decline of individuality, diversity and multiple taste cultures. Ritzer also seems to assume that McDonald's is inexorably and relentlessly homogenizing the world, obliterating individuality and diversity. While there are undeniably tendencies toward homogenization, massification and globalization taking place for which the rubric McDonaldization provides a partial optic, there is also a proliferation of difference, diversity, variety and heterogeneity, as some forms of postmodern theory suggest. And while globalization partially involves the homogenizing of local culture and differences, it also involves proliferation of difference, hybridization and the expansion of consumer and lifestyle choices – at least for some privileged groups and individuals (see Watson, 1998).

Consequently, while Ritzer primarily focuses on the phenomenon from the vantage point of Weber's theory of rationalization, I have been arguing for what I call a multiperspectivist social theory to engage the phenomenon of McDonaldization in terms of theoretical analysis, social critique and resistance. While Ritzer's strong Weberian perspective calls attention to and illuminates key elements of what he calls the McDonaldization of society, I have proposed that adding other perspectives produces a fuller grasp of the McDonaldization phenomenon, thus supplementing Ritzer's analysis and critique. Which perspectives one deploys depends on one's own theoretical and practical projects and the specific contexts and extent of one's inquiry. In this chapter, I have obviously been limited to making a few theoretical and practical proposals which I hope facilitate critical discussion of the constitution and effects of the present organization of society.

Concluding Remarks

In sum and to conclude, Ritzer's study is valuable for helping us better understand important changes in the contemporary world that enable us to practically intervene and shape the social conditions that circumscribe our everyday experience and to empower us against oppressive forces. Ritzer's critical analysis calls attention to the dehumanizing and irrational sides of McDonaldization and forces us to articulate a standpoint of critique and to think of forms of resistance and alternatives. This involves producing individual and group strategies of resistance, as well as the production of viable and socially responsible alternatives. Perhaps Rinehart (1998) is right that Ritzer's approach is too individualistic and fails to articulate collective responses to McDonaldization, but most of his critics do not themselves spell out specific collective social alternatives and contestatory practices, projects that would have to be undertaken in any case by oppositional groups and social movements (see Vidal, 1997).

Yet Ritzer challenges us to consider precisely what form of society, values and practices we desire. There is no question that McDonaldization is here to stay and that we need to decide how social rationalization can serve individual and social needs *and* what sorts of alternatives we need to McDonaldization. I have suggested that we should simply refuse McDonald's (and other junk food sites) as a form of culinary practice, that we should exercise Herbert Marcuse's 'great refusal' (1964) and refuse to have anything to do with this highly objectionable form of assembly-line junk food. The social dynamics of McDonaldization are more complicated to evaluate, however, and Ritzer leaves us with the challenge to determine which forms of McDonaldization are positive and beneficial and which are harmful and destructive. It is the merit of Ritzer's book to force us to reflect upon these issues, and I have argued that thinking through McDonaldization from a multiperspectivist approach will help us to better understand the current form of contemporary society and to attempt to conceive of and create a better one.

Notes

1 Ritzer himself defines his project: 'As a theoretically based work in social criticism, this book is part of a historical tradition in the social sciences in which social theory is used to critique society and thereby to provide the base for its betterment' (1993: xiii). Thus, he situates his problematic in the tradition of classical social theory.

2 For an ethnographic account of McDonald's which draws on personal experience to analyse the menu, the line, the order and the dining, see Shelton (1996). Goldman (1992) and Kincheloe (1997) dissect the ideological and cultural meanings of McDonald's, while there are several histories that contain a wealth of stories, anecdotes and lore concerning the origins, history and dynamics of McDonald's as a corporate organization, and product of individuals (for example, Love, 1986). Ritzer, by contrast, uses grand theory to map the phenomenon of McDonaldization, and journalistic accounts to document its contemporary manifestations and effects.

3 For examples of the Marx–Weber dialogue and the issues involved, see Antonio and Glassman (1985) which contains my own take on the connections between Marx, Weber and critical theory are contained in this article (Kellner, 1985).

4 Offe (1985) and Lash and Urry (1987, 1994) describe this process as 'disorganized capitalism', while I would stress that capitalism is currently reorganizing itself on global and on what Ritzer describes as McDonaldized lines. See the discussion of globalization in the introduction to Cvetkovitch and Kellner (1996).

5 McDonald's has expanded its target audiences over the years, moving from family-oriented advertisements to targeting urban minorities and even GenXers (see Goldman, 1992: 89; Goldman and Papson, 1996: 11f., 237f.).

6 Ritzer emphasizes the former, but neglects the hyperreal cultural aspects of the McDonald's experience in which consumption of sign value is as fundamental as actually consuming the products in the act of eating. In other words, the McDonald's customer is not only chomping a burger, but gaining identity as a McDonald's consumer, participating in the communal experience of family fun or social belonging promised by the McDonald's ads and promotions. Or, alternatively, many McDonald's consumers may identify themselves as thrifty shoppers who are getting a good value for their money as they consume McDonald's products – a false conception, as I argue later.

7 For my take on the relation between Weber and the Frankfurt School, see Kellner (1985), and for my views on critical theory, see Kellner (1989). For Habermas's interpretation of the dialectic of system and life-world, which he relates to Weber's theory, see Habermas (1984, 1987).

8 Ritzer himself says that 'I bear no particular animus toward McDonald's' (1996: xix), though I am suggesting that McDonald's itself deserves a negative animus from many possible perspectives, while McDonaldization itself is more complex and must be judged in its particular manifestations in specific contexts in order to adequately appraise its effects, as I argue in the following pages. I also believe that Ritzer derives his predominantly negative evaluation of McDonaldization by taking McDonald's itself as the primary focus of his analysis.

9 For a more detailed account of the McLibel campaign, see Kovel (1997) and Vidal (1997). I might add parenthetically that computer databases and especially the World Wide Web supersede the sort of newspaper sociology that was widespread earlier and that Ritzer put to good use in his study. It used to be that one way to gather sociological data was through compiling newspaper articles on one's topic of inquiry. This was a highly specialized and time-consuming mode of research – that I myself engaged in for years – requiring access to a large number of newspapers, the ability to find material in periodic readers' guides, and the patience to search out the articles in question. Computer databases simplified this process and I was able to publish my book on the Gulf War the year after the event itself (Kellner, 1992), thanks to the use of Nexis-Lexis databases, as well as PeaceNet and alternative sources. This mode of research was even more costly and specialized, unless one had access to a free university account – as I did. But now the World Wide Web makes accessible a tremendous amount of information, collecting newspaper articles, scholarly studies and a wealth of other material. This source, of course, generates its own problems as well (reliability of information, information overload, learning how to access the most productive sites, and so on), but revolutionizes research and makes it relatively easy to track the fortunes and vicissitudes of a corporation like McDonald's.

10 On the importance of alliances between Disney, McDonald's and Coco-Cola, see 'The science of alliance', *The Economist* (4 April 1988: 69).

11 The McSpotlight website notes that despite lip service to environmental concerns, the actual impact of McDonald's on the environment is extremely harmful. As Kovel notes:

> Professor Graham Ashworth (director-general of the Tidy Britain Group sponsored by McDonald's) had to testify that McDonald's was in the 'top 1 or 2 percent' of all companies whose products end up as litter, it being estimated that on a given day in the UK, the company disgorges 7.9 million items as takeout that end up on the street. . . . When multiplied by the number of stores in the world the inhouse garbage is equivalent to over 1 billion pounds of waste every year. (1997: 30)

References

Alfino, M., Caputo, J.S. and Wynyard, R. (eds) (1998) *McDonaldization Revisited: Critical Essays in Consumer Culture*. Westport, CT: Praeger.

Antonio, R.J. and Glassman, R. (eds) (1985) *A Weber–Marx Dialogue*. Lawrence, KS: University of Kansas Press.

Best, S. and Kellner, D. (1991) *Postmodern Theory: Critical Interrogations*. London and New York: Macmillan and Guilford Press.

Best, S. and Kellner, D. (1997) *The Postmodern Turn*. New York: Guilford Press.

Braverman, H. (1974) *Labor and Monopoly Capital*. New York: Monthly Review Press.

Cvetkovich, A. and Kellner, D. (eds) (1996) *Articulating the Global and the Local: Globalization and Cultural Studies*. Boulder, CO: Westview Press.

Giedion, S. (1969) *Mechanization Takes Command*. New York: Norton.

Goldman, R. (1992) *Reading Ads Socially*. London and New York: Routledge.

Goldman, R. and Papson, S. (1996) *Sign Wars: The Cluttered Landscape of Advertising*. New York: Guilford Press.

Gouldner, A. (1976) *The Dialectic of Ideology and Technology*. New York: Seabury Books.

Habermas, J. (1984) *The Theory of Communicative Action: Volume One. Reason and the Rationalization of Society*. Boston: Beacon Press.

Habermas, J. (1987) *The Theory of Communicative Action: Volume Two. Lifeworld and System: A Critique of Functionalist Reason*. Boston: Beacon Press.

Kellner, D. (1985) 'Critical theory, Max Weber, and the dialectics of domination', in R.J. Antonio and R.M. Glassman (eds), *A Weber–Marx Dialogue*. Lawrence, KS: University Press of Kansas.

Kellner, D. (1989) *Critical Theory, Marxism, and Modernity*. Cambridge and Baltimore: Polity Press and Johns Hopkins University Press.

Kellner, D. (1992) *The Persian Gulf TV War*. Boulder, CO: Westview Press.

Kellner, D. (1995) *Media Culture*. London and New York: Routledge.

Kincheloe, J. (1997) 'McDonald's, power, and children: Ronald McDonald (aka Ray Kroc) does it all for you', in S. Steinberg and J. Kincheloe (eds), *Kinderculture: The Corporate Construction of Childhood*. Boulder, CO: Westview Press.

Kincheloe, J. and Shelton, A. (forthcoming) *The Sign of the Burger: Double Takes on McDonald's*. Boulder, CO: Westview Press.

Kovel, J. (1997) 'Bad News for fast food: what's wrong with McDonald's?', *Z Magazine*, September: 26–31.

Lash, S. and Urry, J. (1987) *The End of Organized Capitalism*. Cambridge: Polity Press.

Lash, S. and Urry, J. (1994) *Economies of Signs and Space*. London: Sage.

Love, J.F. (1986) *McDonald's: Behind the Arches*. New York: Bantam Books.

Marcuse, H. (1964) *One-Dimensional Man*. Boston: Beacon Press.

McLibel Support Campaign (1994) http://www.mcspotlight.org/people/witnesses/nutrition/crawford-michael.html.

Miles, S. (1998) 'McDonaldization and the global sports store: constructing consumer meanings in a rationalized society', in M. Alfino, J.S. Caputo and R. Wynyard (eds) *McDonaldization Revisited: Critical Essays in Consumer Culture*. Westport, CT: Praeger.

Offe, C. (1985) *Disorganized Capitalism*. Cambridge: Polity.

Parker, M. (1998) 'Nostalgia and mass culture: McDonaldization and cultural elitism', in M. Alfino, J.S. Caputo and R. Wynyard (eds) *McDonaldization Revisited: Critical Essays in Consumer Culture*. Westport, CT: Praeger.

Rifkin, J. (1992) *Beyond Beef: The Rise and Fall of Cattle Culture*. New York: Plume.

Rinehart, J. (1998) 'It may be polar night of icy darkness, but feminists are building a fire', in M. Alfino, J.S. Caputo and R. Wynyard (eds), *McDonaldization Revisited: Critical Essays in Consumer Culture*. Westport, CT: Praeger.

Ritzer, G. (1993) *The McDonaldization of Society: An Investigation into the Changing Character of Contemporary Social Life* (revised edition). Thousand Oaks, CA: Pine Forge Press.

Ritzer, G. (1996) *The McDonaldization of Society: An Investigation into the Changing Character of Contemporary Social Life* (revised edition). Thousand Oaks, CA: Pine Forge Press.

Shelton, A. (1996) 'Where the Big Mac is king: McDonald's, USA', *Taboo*, II (Fall): 138–56.

Taylor, S., Smith, S. and Lyon, P. (1998) 'McDonaldization and consumer choice in the future: an illusion or the next marketing revolution?', in M. Alfino, J.S. Caputo and R. Wynyard (eds), *McDonaldization Revisited: Critical Essays in Consumer Culture*. Westport, CT: Praeger.

Vidal, J. (1997) *McLibel. Burger Culture on Trial*. New York: The New Press.

Watson, James L. (ed.) (1998) *Golden Arches East: McDonald's in East Asia*. Palo Alto, CA: Stanford University Press.

13   The Moral Malaise of McDonaldization:
The Values of Vegetarianism

Keith Tester

Burger Chains and Bus Drivers

On 23 November 1996 the *Guardian* newspaper published a few 'News McNuggets' (Ritzer, 1993: 57). One of them can be quoted in full:

> A California bus company has agreed to pay $50,000 (£29,500) to settle a suit brought by a vegetarian bus driver sacked for refusing to hand out promotional hamburger coupons to passengers.

There are a number of ways in which this item can be read. First, it is a prime example of the McDonaldization of news. As Ritzer says of all 'News McNuggets', the story about the Californian bus driver has been ruthlessly edited so that it has no context and is, instead, just a statement of the bare facts (Ritzer, 1993: 57–8). A second reading would see the story as just the most recent example of the American fondness for litigation. But there is a third approach, an approach which highlights what the bus company did not see, what Ritzer's account of McDonaldization does not see, but what the bus driver was able to see very clearly indeed. This third approach emphasizes the moral questions which can be asked about McDonaldization. The bus driver saw that consuming burgers can be an immoral act and that, for a vegetarian, McDonaldization might need to be resisted even to the point of threatening one's own economic livelihood.

Presumably, the Californian bus company and the burger chain set up their relationship because it made good commercial sense for both sides. The bus company could subsidize the costs of its operations while the burger chain was able to target a desired market of consumers and attract them into the restaurants where they would spend money. For the bus company and the burger chain alike, this is a purely commercial issue. But the vegetarian bus driver saw the issue in much more moral terms. The bus driver realized that the bus passengers were being encouraged to eat parts of the corpses of dead (or, as most vegetarians would put it, murdered) animals. Through this moral approach to an otherwise straightforward commercial exchange, the bus driver was able to see that she or he had a responsibility or a right to stop others from indulging in immoral practices. The bus driver saw the blood and not the relish dripping from the burger. The bus company, the burger chain and George Ritzer never ever glimpsed the blood and flesh.

It is this question of the relationship between McDonaldization and morality which this chapter seeks to explore. Specifically, I want to propose that Ritzer's own account of McDonaldization mirrors the moral emptiness which rational organizations require and promote; Ritzer's account of McDonaldization is itself as morally empty as the world it seeks to describe. Yet more broadly, I use this chapter as an opportunity to examine whether vegetarianism is a viable way of resisting the rationalization of the world. This chapter is about whether the moral vacuum surrounding McDonaldization is inevitable or whether some individuals, through their own convictions, can enable us all to glimpse what we are really eating.

Rationality and Morality

Sociologists have long known that rationality and morality do not necessarily have any relationship whatsoever. And the point has recently been reinforced by Zygmunt Bauman. He says that the efficient operation of rational organizations presumes 'that all people involved in the work of the organization follow the commands they receive and are guided only by them . . . and that means that people should not be diverted by their personal beliefs and convictions or by emotions' (1994: 6). This is why the bus driver and the bus company entered into litigation. The bus company is a rational organization which cannot allow the personal preferences of its employees to get in the way of a quick buck. Business is about nothing more than the exploitation of resources to their maximum and, therefore, the maximization of profit: 'Other questions – moral questions prominent among them – are given short thrift in advance; they are dismissed on the grounds that they do not make good business sense, the only sense business may recognize' (Bauman, 1994: 11). Yet the bus driver saw her- or himself as a human being rather than an employee, and so personal beliefs about the immorality of burgers were most firmly brought to bear.

Moral value has become irrelevant or, perhaps more strongly, a problem to be overcome in the processes of rationality. Moral ties or relevances are denied any legitimate place because it is thought by the systems-managers that they might well get in the way of the efficient operation of the plan or the optimal exploitation of resources. These claims about rational organizations, which I have lifted from Bauman, are of course heavily indebted to the heritage of Max Weber. As Weber famously said in his essay 'Science as a vocation', ours is a world which is in many ways conditioned by the conceit that actually there are no mysterious forces worth bothering about and that, instead, everything can be mastered and dominated through the application of rigorous rational methods and procedures.

Weber explained that: 'This means that the world is disenchanted. One need no longer have recourse to magical means in order to master or implore the spirits. . . . Technical means and calculations perform the service. This above all is what intellectualization means' (1970: 139). Intellectualization means that rational technique, and technology in so far as it is the mechanism of rationality, becomes the principle and agent for the use of things. The chance of the moral relevance of things becomes, precisely, irrelevant. For the bus company the promotional coupon was a marketing matter. For the bus driver the coupon was an invitation to a slaughter.

Business rationality is deeply concerned with the question of the control of the working environment. Bauman stresses this aspect of rational organization and shows what it means for the individual: 'What counts is following the procedures to the letter. What is decried and punished more than anything else is twisting the procedure to suit individual preferences or affections' (1994: 6). Consequently, from the point of view of the bus company the driver had to be punished. Bauman goes on to clarify the stakes of this ejection of the personal: 'The most prominent among the exiled emotions are moral sentiments; that resilient and unruly "voice of conscience" that may prompt one to help the sufferer and to abstain from causing suffering' (1994: 8). To this extent, control involves the organizational construction of a rationalized environment in which the individual functionaries will act entirely predictably and without letting their consciences or emotions get in the way of the job in hand. This is precisely what the Californian bus driver refused to do.

Ritzer, meanwhile, emphasizes the relationship between technology and the control of individuals. According to Ritzer, the development of technology has been oriented towards the achievement of a clearly defined goal. He says that: 'The basic idea, historically, is to gradually and progressively gain control over people through the development and deployment of a wide variety of increasingly effective technologies. Once people are controlled, it is possible to begin reducing their actions to a series of machine-like actions' (Ritzer, 1993: 100), like handing out coupons with travel tickets. In the end, 'once people are behaving like human machines, then it is possible to replace them with mechanical machines, most recently and most notably, mechanical robots' (Ritzer, 1993: 100). Ritzer goes on to draw a clear moral message from this process: 'With the replacement of humans by machines, we have reached the ultimate stage in control over people – people can cause us no more uncertainty and unpredictability because they are no longer involved, at least directly, in the process' (1993: 101).

When he seeks to illustrate this process of the replacement of the emotional and unpredictable human with impersonal and impassive technology, Ritzer begins to explore the technologies of control which are exploited in food production. For example, bread production 'is no longer in the hands of skilled bakers, who lavish love and attention on a few

loaves of bread at a time' (Ritzer, 1993: 101 – was it ever?). Bread production has been taken away from the artisans because, as Ritzer rightly
points out, they cannot make bread in the massive quantities that are
required in the contemporary mass markets. But even if artisans could
produce quantity, they probably could not produce regular and predictable
quality. The artisan's loaf is unpredictable precisely because it is so
dependent for its production on the vagaries of human beings; one loaf
might be a slightly different shape or size from another, one might have
been baked for longer. Some loaves might even get wasted if they are left
to burn. Consequently: 'To increase productivity and to eliminate these
unpredictabilities, mass producers of bread have developed an automated
system in which, as in all automated systems, humans play a minimal role'
(Ritzer, 1993: 102). This kind of movement towards the technological
creation of a controlled, predictable, highly rational and profit-maximizing
environment also characterizes meat production. In particular, chickens
have long been bred according to the principles of 'factory farming'. On
the factory farm, the life of the chicken and the farm worker is controlled
by the technology. The breeding of the chickens is reduced to a series of
predictable steps which 'not only allows for greater control over individual
"farmers", but also the farmers in turn have greater control over the
chickens' (Ritzer, 1993: 103). For example, through the application of
carefully controlled factory techniques the farmer can add a measure
of predictability to the size of the chickens. The farmer can predict fairly
accurately the number of eggs the chickens will lay and the time they will
live. Ritzer also shows how the production of other meat has been
subjected to the control of technology and to the technology of control. He
concludes that 'the production of chicken, eggs, and meat has witnessed a
transition from more human small farms and ranches to nonhuman technologies. The technologies obviously lead to greater control over the
animals that produce the meat, thereby increasing the efficiency, calculability, and predictability of meat production' (Ritzer, 1993: 104).

McDonaldization and Morality

Ritzer gets his information about factory farming from the pages of Peter
Singer's book *Animal Liberation* (Singer, 1976; Ritzer, 1993: 198). But if
Ritzer uses Singer's book to help him construct his thesis of McDonald-
ization, it can also be said that Singer's book makes it quite clear that
Ritzer's story is itself McDonaldized. It is most certainly the case that Peter
Singer's book provides a lot of information which directly fits in with
Ritzer's concerns. But Ritzer misses the absolutely fundamental and crucial
aspect of Singer's argument. Singer does not provide all the information
about factory farming because he is writing a book about rational farming
techniques. Quite the contrary, Singer's overwhelming concern is to highlight the ethical and the moral vacuum which surrounds the contemporary

uses of animals and, in so doing, he hopes to inspire his readers to challenge rationalization through the adoption of a rigorous and coherent ethical conduct of life. Ritzer misses all of this. Instead of using Singer's book as a critique of rationality, he merely reads *Animal Liberation* as an account of rationality. A fine example of the difference between Ritzer and Singer is provided by the different ways in which they deal with the question of the methods of veal production. Ritzer says that: 'Calves produce veal . . . veal calves are immediately confined to tiny stalls where they cannot exercise and, as they grow in size, may not even be able to turn around. Being kept in stalls also prevents the calves from eating grass that would cause their meat to lose its pale color' (1993: 104). Ritzer then quotes Singer. Clearly, the story Ritzer is telling is one about how a calf is used in line with the demands of a controlled and controlling rational system which will produce the meat that consumers desire. Now Singer gives Ritzer the facts for his story about rationalization and control, but for Singer the facts carry with them an extraordinarily heavy moral baggage. Even before he cites the facts of veal production, Singer says that: 'Of all the forms of intensive farming now practiced, the quality veal industry ranks as the most morally repugnant, comparable only with barbarities like the force-feeding of geese through a funnel that produces the deformed livers made into *pâté de foie gras*' (1976: 127). At the end of his account of the methods of veal production, Singer leaves his reader in no doubt about the emotional and moral message which is to be learned. He asks the reader to bear it in mind that 'this whole laborious, wasteful, and painful process exists for the sole purpose of pandering to would-be gourmets who insist on pale, soft veal' (1976: 135).

Ritzer recites Singer's facts but without the vital added ingredient of the moral message. Ritzer talks about McDonaldization in its own, purposive and instrumental, terms alone. He sees animals only in terms of their use. His personal response to the situations of animals in factory farms is deemed irrelevant from the point of view of the rational construction of his story about McDonaldization. Contrary to Ritzer, Singer's argument is that the rational use of animals is not merely instrumentally and pro-cedurally interesting. Rather it is ethically and morally compelling. Singer discusses the rational use of animals because he wants to get them out of the literal iron cages; and he wants to encourage humans to get out of their metaphorical iron cages through the adoption of a vegetarian conduct of life.

Vegetarianism and Ethics

Although Singer's *Animal Liberation* did not meet with universal accept-ance even amongst those who were sympathetic towards it (see, for example, the friendly yet principled critiques in Clark, 1977; Regan, 1984), nevertheless it remains valid to contend that the book contained the most influential plea for vegetarianism to appear before the rather different wave of concern with healthy eating emerged in the 1980s. (It is certainly true to say that a rather corrupted reading of *Animal Liberation* has played a significant role in the development and the strategies of the movement for animals rights and liberation; see Tester and Walls, 1996.) *Animal Liberation* is a very powerful text which challenges its readers in a way that few other books about the treatment of animals manage to do. Briefly, Singer gives details about the treatment of animals in order to bolster his utilitarian argument that all sentient creatures prefer not to experience pain and suffering. Singer's possibly most radical claim was that this utilitarian calculation does not just apply to human beings. He expanded it to mean that all creatures who are capable of suffering demand the taking into account of their interests: 'If a being suffers there can be no moral justification for refusing to take that suffering into consideration' (1976: 9). Indeed, Singer contended that any refusal to take suffering into account simply on the grounds that the sufferer is, say, a cow and not a human being is nothing more than speciesism. According to Singer, the recognition of speciesist oppression requires us 'to attest personally to the sincerity of our concern for nonhuman animals' (1976: 175). The clearest and the most sincere form of that expression of concern is vegetarianism. This is because, according to Singer at least, vegetarians are not just practising a diet; they are also practising a much broader conduct of life which is organized around an appreciation of what is taken to be the moral fact that the human interest in eating meat is less important than the preference of the animal to live a life without the experience of unnecessary pain.

Singer's case for vegetarianism can be identified as a version of the asceticism which Weber saw running through the present thanks to the secularization of the Protestant ethic. Indeed, and at a purely anecdotal level, it is noticeable that vegetarianism tends to be much more widespread in predominantly Protestant cultural settings and situations than it does in predominantly Catholic ones; Britain and Germany more than France or Spain, the USA rather than Mexico, and so on. (Of course, I am not hereby saying that no Catholics are vegetarians any more than I am saying that no Protestants are meat eaters.) Just like Puritanism, Singer's vegetarianism involves conduct which requires the individual to choose certain values and construct her or his life around them. For Singer, vegetarianism is an 'ethos' which brings conduct and ethics together. As with Puritanism, the values associated with vegetarianism are concerned with the ethical meaning and the moral practice of life. Weber says that: 'For Puritanism, that conduct was a certain methodical, rational way of life. . . . The premiums were placed upon "proving" oneself before God in the sense of attaining salvation . . . and "proving" oneself before men in the sense of socially holding one's own within the Puritan sects' (1970: 321). In vegetarianism, the conduct is similarly methodical and the proof of the individual is to be found in the sincerity of her or his practical repudiation of speciesism. In these terms, vegetarianism might be identified as a form of secular salvation in which the individual does not prove her or his sincerity to other humans but, rather, to other suffering creatures. Moreover, Weber's Puritans turned away from the world even as they were forced to participate in it, and Singer's vegetarianism is a call to do something rather similar.[1]

Singer is quite clear that : 'Vegetarianism is a form of boycott. For most vegetarians the boycott is a permanent one, since once they have broken away from flesh-eating habits they can no longer approve of slaughtering animals to satisfy the trivial desires of their palates' (1976: 175). The Californian bus driver was practising the boycott when she or he refused to hand out the coupons for the burger chain. If this is right, for most vegetarians, then, McDonald's and its ilk are permanent no-go-areas and, indeed, most of the vegetarians who conduct their life according to the principle of boycott would be utterly unconcerned by the fact that most burger chains now offer vegetable-based products. That is, assuming that they were aware of such products in the first place. Furthermore, Singer says that: 'Until we boycott meat we are, each one of us, contributing to the continued existence, prosperity, and growth of factory farming and all the other cruel practices used in rearing animals for food' (1976: 175). This has an impact on the conduct of life. The conduct must be, in its own terms, quite methodical and indeed rational:

> To protest about bull-fighting in Spain . . . while continuing to eat chickens that have spent their lives crammed into cages, or veal from calves that have been deprived of their mothers, their proper diet, and the freedom to lie down with their legs extended, is like denouncing apartheid in South Africa while asking your neighbors not to sell their houses to blacks. (Singer, 1976: 175–6)

The boycott is not to be judged in terms of its universal success in encouraging everyone everywhere to condemn and avoid speciesism. According to Singer, it does not matter if the boycott which vegetarianism represents meets with global success and acceptance, since the secular salvation it implies is to be found elsewhere. The premium of the boycott is in what it does for the individual. It turns the individual into the self-aware author of her or his own moral integrity and ethical being. The individual becomes an inwardly glowing beacon of the possibility and viability of morality in an otherwise indifferent world; 'we ourselves set the example' (Singer, 1976: 176). After all: 'the vegetarian knows that he does, by his actions, contribute to a reduction in the suffering and slaughter of animals, whether or not he lives to see his efforts spark off a mass boycott of meat and an end to cruelty in farming' (1976: 177).

Care and Risk

Just as Weber's Puritan was able to know and gain some sense of an ascetic pleasure from the knowledge that God had been served, so Singer's vegetarian also gains certain satisfactions and a confidence born of the proof that the right has been done. If, as Weber might say, Puritanism brings a new relationship to self and possessions, then, as Singer sees it: 'Vegetarianism brings with it a new relationship to food, plants, and nature. Flesh taints our meals. Disguise it as we may, the fact remains that the centerpiece of our dinner has come to us from the slaughterhouse, dripping blood' (1976: 193). Weber's Puritans gained spiritual satisfaction; Singer's vegetarians gain a physical lightness of being which is itself an almost spiritual experience. Singer says that meat 'sits heavily in our stomachs, blocking our digestive processes until, days later, we struggle to excrete it'. He implies that this is a cause of the high incidence of intestinal cancers in those parts of the world which have the heaviest meat consumption levels. But: 'When we eat plants, food takes on a different quality. We take from the earth food that is ready for us and does not fight against us as we take it. Without meat to deaden the palate there is an extra delight in fresh vegetables taken straight from the ground' (1976: 193). Consequently, alongside ethical well-being and an almost spiritual unity with nature, vegetarianism is seen by Singer to bring with it benefits for physical health: 'Many vegetarians claim that they feel fitter, healthier, and more zestful than when they ate meat. Certainly your digestive system will find the new diet easier to cope with, and you will feel better after a big meal.' Singer goes on to contend that since a vegetarian diet draws on food which is ready to eat thanks to nature, it does not need to be subjected to treatment by pesticides and neither is it as likely as meat to have been contaminated by preservatives and other additives (1976: 195). This view was expressed quite clearly by Anna Thomas in a vegetarian cookbook of the 1970s. A significant part of her case for vegetarianism was based on the argument that 'more and more foods are being "processed", becoming the products of factories rather than farms. Chemical non-food "additives" alter the look of foods and prevent visible spoilage, but the nutritive value of treated foods is hugely diminished – and their cost to you is increased' (1973: 9). She went on to mention the presence of pesticide residues in food (and its higher concentration in meat) and the poison which is to be found in the sea and therefore fish. And so, in the end, vegetarianism for Anna Thomas could be commended because it is 'about joy, not pollution' (1973: 10).

Running through these claims is what might be called a dialectic of care. Singer and Thomas identify a powerful current in vegetarianism when they contend that there is some kind of connection between the boycott of meat and well-being. They are expressing the idea that there is a mutual reinforcement between care for the self and the care of others. As the thesis part of the dialectical equation it is stated that vegetarians care for animals because they recognize the deeply moral truth that animals have certain preferences and, perhaps, even rights which are infringed and ignored in factory farming. As the antithesis, it is stated that a vegetarian diet means that the individual ceases to ingest polluting chemicals and food additives (here, then, there is a blurring of the meaning of pollution: it can be moral and physical at the same time, and through the same practices; see Douglas, 1966, 1975). The synthesis is an ethic of care, in which care for animals is compatible with, if not indeed identical with, a care for self. Yet care is even wider than this. It goes beyond animals and individual vegetarians to include all human beings and, indeed, the earth itself. The vegetarian argument frequently makes the point that meat consumption is highly inefficient. First, the animals which are going to be slaughtered have to be fed; and they are fed food which could otherwise be given to starving humans. Second, the food which is given to the animals has to be pro-duced, and the land which is thus given over to animal food production could, otherwise, sustain sizeable human communities. (This dialectic of care is stated very clearly, and at its widest, in Wynne-Tyson, 1979.)

The implication of this dialectic of care is that the risks which are associated with certain forms of food consumption can be avoided through a vegetarian conduct of life. According to Ulrich Beck, the awareness of the risks surrounding certain foods is felt especially powerfully by con-sumers (and most people in the West are food consumers not producers). Beck talks about a 'double shock'. The first shock surrounds the realization that we might have been ingesting chemicals or viruses which are directly harmful to our own health and well-being; and this despite the fact that the food might have looked and tasted very good indeed. The second shock is derived from what Beck calls 'the *loss of sovereignty* over assessing the dangers, to which one is directly subjected' (1992: 54; original emphasis). This loss of sovereignty itself seems to have two aspects. On the one hand, it seems to imply for Beck the fact that actually the individual consumer, or for that matter any group of consumers, cannot know for sure whether any risk is involved in the consumption of any given food. Many risks surrounding contaminated food are beyond personal appreciation and experience: they cannot be seen, smelled or tasted. On the other hand, the truth that there is a risk gets caught up in the machinations of bureaucracy so that definite knowledge becomes more or less impossible to obtain. Beck's prose gets a little carried away in the shade of Kafka when he writes about what happens when a risk emerges: 'The whole bureaucracy of knowledge opens up, with its long corridors, waiting benches, responsible, semi-responsible, and incomprehensible shoulder-shruggers and poseurs' (Beck, 1992: 54).

Both of these aspects of risk ran through consumer reactions to the BSE scare in Britain in 1996. The panic emerged when the government reported the worry of its food scientists that there might be a direct link between a brain disease amongst cows and CJD, a fatal infection of the human brain. The link could be forged through the consumption of beef. In a newspaper article which was published a few months after the initial panic, Michael Jacobs pointed out that, according to most of the experts, the risks of contracting CJD from beef consumption were quite low. But Jacobs has obviously read Beck, and he asks his readers to look at the issue from the point of view of consumers: 'As an individual lay person, none of us has any idea what the statistical probability is of catching CJD. . . . We are not scientists conducting experiments or compiling statistics. All we have to go on is what the experts tell us.' Jacobs went on: 'So to the consumer, risk is not actually about probabilities at all. It's about the trustworthiness of the institutions which are telling us what the risk is. Do we believe them?' (1996). Of course, Jacobs' question is rhetorical: do we trust institutions? No. If these are the unanswerable and perplexing problems which meat consumption can raise, then vegetarianism is able to present itself as the safe, caring and ready answer. After all, we can all believe that vegetarians eat natural, unpolluted food and so they never run risks. Vegetarianism tells individuals that they do not need to trust the unreliable experts; they can trust their own emotions and their own bodies instead. Vegetarianism promises to offer a relatively easy and immediate solution to all of these shocks and confusions because of its experiential 'naturalness'.[2]

Vegetarianism and Risk Avoidance

It is largely beside the point whether the risks associated with certain foods are 'real' or not. What is all-important is the *perception* of the risk. Vegetarianism is able to play on this terrain of perception precisely because it is a conduct of life which is built around a perception of the healthy diet which individuals allegedly are able to know intuitively if they are left to make up their own minds. Jeremy MacClancy shows exactly how it is that a perception of risk might emerge. His argument is that the perception has little or nothing to do with scientific facts and research but that, instead, a food will be perceived to be risky to consume when it is identified as having been produced in a way which is 'unnatural'. Factory farming immediately falls into the area of the creation of perceived risks precisely because the words 'factory' and 'farming' rest together so uneasily; factories are places of mass production whereas farms, as Ritzer's nostalgic portrayal of them indicates, are perceived to be places of fields, meadows, happy animals and ruddy-faced humans. But, within this general situation, certain food products are likely to be held to be more risky to consume than others.

For example, MacClancy contends that the salmonella and 'mad cow' scares in Britain in the late 1980s (and, since MacClancy wrote his book, it is possible to add to his list the BSE panic of the mid-1990s) caused such worry because the eggs and beef were produced in 'unnatural' ways. MacClancy says that in the case of salmonella: 'Poultry and eggs, the public learnt, were being contaminated with salmonella because chickens were being fed the only partially sterilized carcasses of other chickens as a protein supplement' (1992: 156). Meanwhile, the 'mad cow' scare 'was caused by feeding cattle the remains of sheep, some of them infected with the spongiform disease "scrapie"' (1992: 157). The risks surrounding salmonella and 'mad cows' have two things in common. First, and certainly in the British context, they have been two of the most significant and widespread food scares of recent years. Second, in both cases, the perception of risk involved a sense of uneasiness that chickens and cows in factory units had been given animal products to eat regardless of the fact that they are naturally herbivorous. The perception and for that matter the experience of the risk was not necessarily the consequence of a causally direct linkage between animals forced to eat products from diseased animals and human death. Instead it owed a considerable part of its force to popular unease about the fact that, a vegetarian animal had been forced to become carnivorous . . . the meat produced had been sold to customers who do not believe that they should eat animals which eat other animals, even if they are not diseased' (MacClancy, 1992: 157; for more on this point about the inedibility of meat-eating animals, see Douglas, 1966). These are fears which vegetarianism is perceived to be able to overcome, precisely because it exploits nothing other than 'natural' food resources and 'natural' methods of production.

However, what is noticeable about the claims for vegetarianism on the grounds of health is that the ethical dimension becomes little more than an added extra. For example, Singer wants to make an ethical case for the refusal to eat meat. But his defence of that case forces him into a position in which an equally powerful argument in favour of vegetarianism can be made on the much more simple grounds of, as Anna Thomas put it, 'enlightened self-interest' (1973: 9). The argument which stresses enlightened self-interest is perhaps the aspect of vegetarianism least close to any criteria of an ethical standard of life. And perhaps it is for precisely that reason that the connection of vegetarianism to 'healthy eating' has come to be accorded such wide cultural acceptance. With the argument on the grounds of health, the ethical dimension of vegetarianism is cut away and all that remains is a dietary form which promises to offer some kind of insurance against the risks generated by factory farming and other technological processes.

McCartneyization

Without the crucial ethical dimension, which makes it the principle of a conduct of life rather than just an aspect of lifestyle, vegetarianism itself is liable to become McDonaldized. As its cultural penetration increases, vegetarianism becomes a technique with its own demands and criteria of calculability, efficiency, predictability and control. At this stage, it becomes important to distinguish between what might be called *ethical vegetarianism* and *lifestyle vegetarianism*. Ethical vegetarianism derives from a concern with the treatment of animals. It emphasizes an ethical conduct of life which is a repudiation and an active boycott of what is identified as the unethical treatment of animals in factory farms, laboratories, hunting, and so forth. Here, the argument about health and well-being is a consequence of the ethical position. Lifestyle vegetarianism derives from a concern with the risks associated with the consumption of certain foods which are produced in ways which are defined and perceived as being 'unnatural'. Here, the argument about health and well-being is primary and the ethical position about animals is a non-necessary addition. In these terms, the Californian bus driver is almost certainly an ethical vegetarian. Ethical vegetarianism paved the way for lifestyle vegetarianism when it sought to provide rational justifications for the avoidance of animal products. Lifestyle vegetarianism is presently the culturally dominant form in the West. It replaces the *being* of the ethical conduct of life with the *doing* of the consumer. It is in this way that lifestyle vegetarianism is easily compatible with the relationships and procedures of a McDonaldized environment.

A fine example of this is provided by *Seasonal Vegetarian*, a cookbook published by *Here's Health* magazine in the 1980s. According to the book: 'most people's first thoughts on becoming vegetarian, or simply on cutting down the amount of meat, fish and poultry in their diets are concerned with health' (Bounds, 1987: 6). This is already a long way from the position adopted by Peter Singer, whose first and recurrent thought was the ethical treatment of animals. Neither would Singer have seen vegetarianism as involving a simple reduction in the level of meat consumption. For Singer the boycott has to be total or it is nothing. According to *Seasonal Vegetarian*, the main problem for the vegetarian is nutrition, and so the book provides detailed information on the various types of proteins, fats, vitamins and minerals which together constitute a healthy diet. The book reassures its users that vegetarianism is not risky:

> cutting meat, fish and poultry from your diet does not mean that you will go short of vital nutrients. . . . In fact, research suggests that a vegetarian diet is positively healthier than a non-vegetarian diet and that common problems like obesity are less likely to occur for vegetarians than their meat-eating neighbours. (Bounds, 1987: 6)

In other words, lifestyle vegetarianism, at least in so far as *Seasonal Vegetarian* is typical of it, betrays many of the features of McDonaldization as Ritzer details them (Ritzer, 1993, 1995: 133–4). *Calculability* is demonstrated in the emphasis on nutritional content and quantifications of 'healthiness'. *Efficiency* involves the qualities of the food itself (the extent to which it supports a healthy body) and also its preparation. In this vein, *Seasonal Vegetarian* commends microwave cooking and deep-freezing. After all, thanks to microwaves: 'Cooking and reheating times are quicker, requiring smaller amounts of fluid and resulting in better retention of vitamins B and C, and vital minerals which are otherwise dissolved in cooking liquids' (Bounds, 1987: 9; cf. Ritzer, 1993: 87–8). *Predictability* is guaranteed by the highly rational recipes which detail quantities of raw materials, cooking times and the number of portions served. *Substitution of non-human for human technology* is represented in the role of the microwave. But Ritzer's point about the *irrationality of rationality* seems to be absent. Instead, according to lifestyle vegetarianism, irrationality is to be found elsewhere. Irrationality is identified as an aspect of the world of factory-farmed, salmonella-infected eggs and 'mad cows'; the world of the lifestyle vegetarian is safe, secure and risk-free. It is a world in which food is not risky; instead it is 'fun and full of variety whether it be the depths of winter or the height of summer' (Bounds, 1987: 6).

Lifestyle vegetarianism is also a world which makes money. In 1995, the meat-free frozen-food industry was worth £100 million in Britain alone. One third of this market was secured by the late Linda McCartney's own-name range, which had been launched in Britain in association with a subsidiary of the multinational United Biscuits. Indeed, by late 1995 the Linda McCartney range had sold 100 million meals and had its own dedicated factory in Norfolk, England, which could make a million meat-free meals every week. As Ritzer would almost certainly point out, such a factory is itself an exemplary example of McDonaldization. It is doing to vegetables and meat substitutes everything that the factory farm does to chickens and cows (but, of course, only instrumentally; once again, the ethical dimension which would stress the huge difference between a cow and a carrot has quite disappeared). There can be little or nothing 'natural' about the production processes which are relied upon by the plant in Norfolk. This is most definitely a long way from what Peter Singer undoubtedly had in mind when he made his call for vegetarianism. Moreover, whilst it would seem that Linda McCartney was herself a committed ethical vegetarian (see Barber, 1995), it is nevertheless the case that United Biscuits did not involve itself in this niche of the convenience food market because it makes good sense for the health of the nation. United Biscuits entered into a relationship with Linda McCartney only because it made good business sense. It made good sense because it generated more profits and lent United Biscuits a marketable 'green' profile. As Zygmunt Bauman says: 'The virtues of ethical investments or green products tend to be recognized only when the language of morality itself "makes good business sense", not when there are clear trade-offs to be made' (1994: 11).

Conclusion

There is, then, no simple answer to the question of whether vegetarianism can be taken to stand as a form and strategy of resistance to McDonald-ization. Part of the problem surrounds the split in the meaning of vegetarianism: the split between the ethical and the lifestyle strands. In principle, ethical vegetarianism can most certainly stand as a form of resistance. But the ethical case can only offer this alternative all the time it remains resolutely ethical and, therefore, wholly avoids any attempt to justify itself on rational grounds. The case for ethical vegetarianism can only offer a chance of resistance all the time that it refuses to answer the question of the cynic or cautious enthusiast: 'What's in it for me?' There was nothing in it for the Californian bus driver other than doing what she or he held to be the 'right thing'. In immediate, rational terms the bus driver carried out an immensely pointless deed, Yet the lifestyle argument does express good reasons for its embrace. These are reasons which resonate loudly and well with the emergence of risk perceptions around factory-farmed foods. As such, ethical vegetarianism has opened up the space for a more lifestyle-oriented version of vegetarianism in which the ethical case for animals (or the ethical case for the boycott of meat) becomes a choice rather than an essential and non-negotiable principle for the conduct of life. And thanks to the profits which can be made out of it, as well as its extreme easiness, the lifestyle strand has largely colonized what vegetarianism is popularly taken to mean and involve. What vegetarianism gains in profile and popularity, it loses in commitment and coherence. Lifestyle vegetarianism puts us back into the iron cages of the McDonaldized worlds. It makes meat avoidance totally rational. Meanwhile ethical vegetarianism makes us morally rigorous but, for the most part, utterly marginal. Or, at most, it makes us like the Californian bus driver: a character in a 'News McNugget'.

Notes

I would like to thank Barry Smart for helping me formulate some of the ideas explored in this chapter. However, he cannot be held responsible for my arguments.

1 When I make this connection between vegetarianism and Puritanism, I am seeking to explore the Western tradition of the kind of case Singer makes. I am not seeking to marginalize the role of meat avoidance in other, non-Western, religious traditions. These traditions have become increasingly significant amongst certain groups and individuals in the West and their Western adoption can be seen in terms of the *bricolage* of the 'New Age' sensibility. But I have not emphasized non-Western approaches, for two reasons. First, because, religious cases for meat avoidance are not at all necessarily the same as ethical pleas for vegetarianism. For example, the Book of Leviticus puts a taboo around the eating of pork, but the Book is not thereby a manifesto for the rights of pigs. Second, and this is a theme which runs through later arguments in this chapter, the Western moral *bricoleurs* are not necessarily engaging in ethical conducts of life when they construct their moral selves; they are, instead, playing with the ruins of conduct.

2 The McDonald's chain responded to the BSE scare in a leaflet which outlined why consumers could trust it. Interestingly, McDonald's did not rely on the experts. Instead it relied on the naturalness of the ingredients of a burger and the safety of predictability. It said that 'trust has never been more important'. It then gave three reasons why the chain could be trusted, First, its burgers are '100% pure beef – nothing else'. Second, 'McDonald's only use prime cuts of boneless beef. We add nothing to it.' Third: 'Our standards and controls are higher than you would ever expect. In fact, our hamburgers are given 40 quality control tests before they even arrive at the restaurant' (McDonald's, 1996).

References

Barber, R. (1995) 'Meet the McCartneys', *BBC Vegetarian Good Food*, November: 26–8.

Bauman, Z. (1993) *Postmodern Ethics*. Oxford: Blackwell.

Bauman, Z. (1994) *Alone Again: Ethics After Certainty*. London: Demos.

Beck, U. (1992) *Risk Society: Towards a New Modernity*. London: Sage.

Bounds, S. (1987) *Seasonal Vegetarian*. Twickenham: Hamlyn Publishing Group.

Clark, S.R.L. (1977) *The Moral Status of Animals*. Oxford: Clarendon Press.

Douglas, M. (1966) *Purity and Danger: An Analysis of the Concepts of Pollution and Taboo*. London: Routledge & Kegan Paul.

Douglas, M. (1975) *Implicit Meanings: Essays in Anthropology*. London: Routledge & Kegan Paul.

Jacobs, M. (1996) 'Sheepish about safety', *Guardian*, 24 July.

MacClancy, J. (1992) *Consuming Culture*. London: Chapmans.

McDonald's (1996) 'A message to our customers'. London: McDonald's Customer Services.

Regan, T. (1984) *The Case for Animal Rights*. London: Routledge & Kegan Paul.

Ritzer, G. (1993) *The McDonaldization of Society: An Investigation into the Changing Character of Contemporary Social Life*. Thousand Oaks, CA: Pine Forge Press.

Ritzer, G. (1995) *Expressing America: A Critique of the Global Credit Card Society*. Thousand Oaks, CA: Pine Forge Press.

Singer, P. (1976) *Animal Liberation: Towards an End to Man's Inhumanity to Animals*. London: Jonathan Cape.

Tester, K. and Walls, J. (1996) 'The ideology and current activities of the Animal Liberation Front', *Contemporary Politics*, 2 (2): 79–90.

Thomas, A. (1973) *The Vegetarian Epicure*. Harmondsworth: Penguin.

Weber, M. (1970) *From Max Weber: Essays in Sociology* (eds H.H. Gerth and C.W. Mills). London: Routledge & Kegan Paul.

Wynne-Tyson, J. (1979) *Food for a Future: The Complete Case for Vegetarianism*. London: Centaur Press.

14   McFascism?

Reading Ritzer, Bauman and the Holocaust

Peter Beilharz

What have we done? What have we achieved in the century of modernity, and what will we be remembered for? The hamburger has become a symbol of it all, the strength and the corruption of America and the West. Much craved and much despised, it now replaces the globe on the back of Atlas. Utopia, as I have argued elsewhere (Beilharz, 1992), has become a hamburger, an icon of satisfaction to the deprived, and a sign of global madness to ecologists and others on the left. George Ritzer's stroke of genius, in this, our, context, is to seize upon that symbol and use it as a way in to the labyrinth which we in the West inhabit. More than that, Ritzer employs the symbol as a way into classical and modern social theory. *The McDonaldization of Society* is indeed a remarkable achievement, and our students devour their copies, as we did. Does the book then satisfy? Here obviously views will differ. My own view is that the book works best as (to switch metaphors) a can opener. It is a way in, a beginning, an invitation to sociology.

In this chapter I want to pursue this theme through Ritzer's particular usage of the work of Zygmunt Bauman's equally celebrated book, *Modernity and the Holocaust*. In the second edition of *The McDonaldization of Society*, to anticipate, Ritzer (1996) installs a new section arguing that there are parallels between McDonaldization and the Holocaust, using Bauman's interpretation to support this claim. After contextualizing Ritzer's argument against the background of the renewed arguments concerning the Holocaust, I shall summarize this new turn in Ritzer's book before taking that thread into Bauman's labyrinth. Can we indeed speak of something like McFascism, or a genetic line from Hamburg to Pasadena via Auschwitz? Is there such a thing as McFascism?

Rediscovering Nazism

It could well be said, looking back on the twentieth century, that this thing called fascism has never really left us. How could this be so? Towards the close of the century it seems a little more apparent that fascism is less a premodern residual which blights modernity than a perennial current within modernity itself. For the most developed form of modern fascism, Nazism itself, was always an amalgam of modern and romantic motifs. Perhaps Jeffrey Herf captured these anomalies and contradictions best in categorical form in the title of his study of Nazi ideology and practice, *Reactionary Modernism* (Herf, 1989). Yet it is still arguably the case that fascism and communism alike are nevertheless viewed more generally as throwbacks rather than as alternative paths through modernity which failed (Arnason, 1993). With specific reference to the Hitler experience of Nazism, it is probably fair to suggest that when it is taken seriously outside continental Europe today, people still tend to puzzle abstractly over how it could be that such a civilized country as Germany could engineer such a project of barbarism as Nazism. How could it happen? Never again. But have we begun to understand it? Those who rediscover the brutal content of Nazism seem also often to behave as though it is they themselves who have discovered it. Thus, for example, Robert Young writes in *White Mythologies* that

> Horkheimer and Adorno [in their 1944 classic, *Dialectic of Enlightenment*] . . . pose the question: how has the dialectic deviated into fascism? Why has History gone wrong? [Their] project, therefore, was to return to the enlightenment in the wake of fascism . . . . (1990: 7)

This line of argument seems extraordinary coming from so sensitive a critic as Young. Horkheimer and Adorno did not subscribe to the dialectic in the standard Marxist sense, neither did they capitalize History, and neither their project nor even their hope was to return to an 'enlightenment' which could somehow miraculously be conceived outside of history. After Auschwitz, for the founders of critical theory, we can hardly return to enlightenment. The point is not that 'History' took a wrong turn; it is that (to put it differently) Europe has two histories, one of progress and one of domination, one of Beethoven and one of the pogrom (Horkheimer and Adorno, 1979). As Walter Benjamin and Freud and Weber all put it, in different ways, civilization depends upon violence – and Horkheimer and Adorno follow in this path. But once we agree, however tentatively, that the Holocaust in particular was perhaps less an 'accident' than an accident waiting to happen, then it becomes incumbent on us to offer something by way of explanation for this extraordinary occurrence.

'Never Again!' is too easy a slogan if it only implies as a result a modicum of practical vigilance against racism. Should we then blame the Germans as a people, as Daniel Goldhagen seems to imply in *Hitler's Willing Executioners*? Goldhagen's argument is compelling on one moral level at least, in as much as it indirectly draws attention to the sense that each of us is potentially capable of such evil. Only the line of his argument seems to corral Germans out, predisposed as it were by way of cultural genetics to such acts of barbarity (Goldhagen, 1996). Goldhagen's bibliography is otherwise scrupulous, but significantly he does not discuss Bauman's book, which is surprising given that *Modernity and the Holocaust* was published seven years prior to *Hitler's Willing Executioners*, given that Bauman's book was awarded the prestigious Amalfi prize for 1989, and given that Goldhagen, like Bauman, actually works in the kindred field to sociology called comparative politics. Whether or not Goldhagen can simply be said to be blaming the Germans, the appeal of his argument is certainly more publicly compelling than an argument for ambivalence might be.

Modernity and the Holocaust apparently works in the wake of *Dialectic of Enlightenment*, if more evidently it follows in the sober thought paths pioneered by Max Weber. Nazism, on Bauman's account, might be a reactionary modernism, but it is a modernism all the same and it stains the entire modern project; we never escape it altogether. Goldhagen's explanation for Nazism is a kind of cultural traditionalism; Bauman's, by comparison, rests on a sort of universalistic antimodernism or critique of modernity. With Bauman, we know that the Germans *did* it; but we also know emphatically that *we* could do it, perhaps even more readily within our locations in the cultural and technological matrices of late modernity. But where does McDonaldization fit into all this? Is it not trivial, or else somehow bizarre, to align the gates that told us 'Arbeit Macht Frei' with the Golden Arches that now reach across a thousand global suburbs? The sources of symmetry, however, also become apparent on a moment's reflection. If we step back to Weber's grander claims about the rationalization of the world, then perhaps Nazism and McDonald's have this much in common, that they are both perceptible expressions of this overarching trend. To question Bauman's case, or Ritzer's, from this perspective is also ultimately to question Weber's, or at least it is to question the dominant reading of Weber as a cultural pessimist, negative prophet of a real or imaginary 'iron cage' of which Auschwitz might be one sad realization.

McFascism?

Certainly Ritzer views Weber as the master theorist of rationalization. Ritzer tells us that Weber viewed bureaucracy as the paradigm case of rationalization. Although Weber on this account recognized the advantages of rationalization, he was most animated by its dangers, especially the possibility of what he (or Talcott Parsons) called the 'iron cage' of rationality (Ritzer, 1996: xvii). Ritzer constructs McDonaldization as a further expression of the imperative towards rationalization, that process '*by which the principles of the fast-food restaurant are coming to dominate more and more sectors of American society as well as of the rest of the world*' (Ritzer, 1996: 1; original emphasis). The imagery conjured up here is as implicitly Marxian as it is Weberian – this is an imperial logic, both within nations and across the world system. My purpose here is less specifically to engage with this more general argument than with its modified intersection with the Holocaust. Ritzer observes in the Preface to the revised edition that in addition to a new, kindred chapter on 'Birth, death and beyond' he has added a new section 'based largely on Zygmunt Bauman's excellent book, *Modernity and the Holocaust*' to the chapter on the precursors of McDonaldization. Here, to anticipate, 'I argue', says Ritzer 'that the Holocaust was driven by bureaucratization and was anticipated by Max Weber's theory of rationalization' (1996: xiv). Ritzer's argument, 'The holocaust: the end-product was death', seems to follow Bauman's book closely. Like Bauman, Ritzer argues that the Holocaust was a distinctive product of Western civilization, less a premodern or antimodern aberration than a specific result of modernity itself. For Ritzer,

> The Holocaust can be seen as an example of modern social engineering in which the goal was the production of a perfectly rational society. To the Nazis, this perfect society was free of Jews (as well as gypsies, gays, lesbians and the disabled). Bauman sees an analogy here to gardening. Just as a perfect garden is free of weeds, so a perfect Nazi society was one that was *Judenfrei* . . . The Holocaust had all the basic characteristics of rationalization (and McDonaldization). (1996: 22)

The Nazi system, that is to say, was guided by the same systemic imperatives as McDonald's – the obsession with efficiency, calculability and predictability, the latter choreographed by a huge non-human technology. The Holocaust simultaneously represented the apogee of social engineering and the ultimate irrationality of rationality – more specifically, it stood for the ultimate in dehumanization (Ritzer, 1996: 23).

Ritzer, too, twitches at the analogy which he has constructed. So he closes his section on the Holocaust and McDonald's as follows.

> Discussing the Holocaust in the context of the precursors of McDonaldization may seem extreme to some readers. Clearly, the fast-food restaurant *cannot* be discussed in the same breath as the Holocaust. There has been no more heinous crime in the history of mankind. Yet, there are strong reasons to discuss the Holocaust in this context. First, the Holocaust was based on the [same] principles of formal rationality, relying extensively on the paradigm of that type of rationality – the bureaucracy. Second, the Holocaust was also linked, as we have seen, to the factory system . . . finally, the spread of formal rationality today in McDonaldization supports Bauman's view that something like the Holocaust could happen again. (1996: 24)

So how are we to make sense of this? One reaction might be that these are entirely plausible as possible associations; but how compelling or persuasive are they? Another response might be to question the status of the entire McDonaldization thesis itself. For as Ritzer argues in the next pages of his book, McDonaldization sometimes looks more like a condensation than an exemplification of the rationalization in process – if the fast-food industry is highly rationalized, perhaps it ought really to be rationalization which is the core thesis. If 'McDonald's did not invent these ideas, but rather brought them together with the principles of the bureaucracy and the assembly line, thus contributing to the creation of McDonaldization', (Ritzer, 1996: 25), then perhaps we should be looking for the truth of McDonald's in further analysis of scientific management rather than the other way around. Not that this is news to George Ritzer, whose last lines on the subject are that like 'bureaucracy and the fast-food restaurant, even [like] the Holocaust, the automobile assembly line beautifully illustrates the basic elements of formal rationality' (1996: 25). But if this is Ritzer's line into the labyrinth of interpretation, what then of Zygmunt Bauman's story?

Modernity and the Holocaust

Like Ritzer, Bauman is a man with a mission. If Ritzer's is to provoke and to moralize via the image of rampant McDonaldization, Bauman's is to centre sociology and modernity on the Holocaust, to refocus vision upon it, shockingly, as 'normal' rather than pathological. Bauman seeks to expand its sphere of pertinence, outside the margin, beyond Jewish studies and German studies, into the mainstream of modernity's currents. The Holocaust, for Bauman, was a characteristically modern phenomenon that cannot be understood out of the context of the cultural tendencies and technical achievements of modernity. But it is not, was not, inevitable, as the expression of rationalization itself, for as Bauman proceeds to argue, it was an outcome of a unique, not routinized, encounter between factors themselves quite ordinary and common and caught up necessarily with the emancipation of the *political* state from social patterns of control (Bauman, 1989: xiii). Already some distinction in emphasis might be detected across Bauman's argument and the use to which Ritzer puts it. Bauman already implies here that the Holocaust was *political* and *contingent*; McDonaldization, in contrast, is not specifically political so much as it is economic, cultural and tendential.

The path of Bauman's argument in *Modernity and the Holocaust* is as obvious as it is compelling. Bauman's text opens with an attempt to identify dominant mythologies concerning the Holocaust, in order to transcend them. Bauman sets his own argument against the obvious competitors, those voices which would press upon us the view that the Holocaust ought be blamed either on the Germans (*qua* Goldhagen) or else on modernity as such, or at least on its insufficient development (a case that might be associated, for example, with Parsons). There are other variations, of course, including the claim that the Holocaust might represent *the* truth about modernity; contrary to Robert Young's reading of critical theory, this would be one way to interpret that lineage leading out of Adorno into the work of Herbert Marcuse, where it is modernity itself that is totalitarian. Against this latter reduction, Bauman wants to insist that the Holocaust is less the truth of modernity than a possibility within it, in which case the focus shifts appropriately to the conditions of its possibility. Normal, and yet not normal – this is the interpretative awkwardness that Bauman seeks to bridge. McDonald's, of course, we can by some observational criteria describe as normal; we normalize the institution, even if we do not frequent it. The Holocaust was normal in a different sense. 'The truth is that every "ingredient" of the Holocaust . . . was normal . . . not in the sense of the familiar . . . but in the sense of being fully in keeping with everything we know about our civilization' (Bauman, 1989: 8).

Certainly Bauman accepts the view that the Holocaust was also a product of industrialization, a kind of murderous Fordism bringing together a volatile mixture of technologies hitherto kept separate. Only here the difference between Fordism or McDonaldization and the Holocaust is clear. Fordism and McDonaldization become organizational forms and norms which may have unintended consequences or what economists charmingly call 'externalities'; the Holocaust was a rare, but programmatic, test of the hidden possibilities of modernity (Bauman, 1989: 12). Modern civilization was not the Holocaust's *sufficient* condition; it was, however, most certainly for Bauman its *necessary* condition. Without modernity as its condition of existence, the Holocaust would be unthinkable (Bauman, 1989: 13). This is, indeed, to point to the very facts which strike Ritzer in his borrowing of Bauman's analysis – the brute facts of modern civilization, like the factory system and the bureaucratic organization of society. Bauman's intellectual origins within Polish Marxism are evident here, in echo, for his has long been a kind of Weberian Marxism, here, perhaps, with the emphasis shifting more evidently towards the influence of Weber. Only the combination of bureaucratic culture and the logic of industrialization could produce this fatal outcome. So it was that it all fell into place. The emigration of German Jews which was chosen as a first practical solution to Hitler's objective of a *Judenfrei* Germany gave way to the larger and at the same time more localized ambition of a Jew-free planet and the Final Solution. Into late 1941 all the combined mechanisms of industrial society were thrown into action in order to achieve it. The diagnosis conforms with everything that Weber knew, and which Horkheimer and Adorno passed on – instrumental rationality has no goal or ethics of its own, except efficiency and calculability by default. Physical extermination of the Jews fulfilled both latter criteria. Thus the Holocaust is, strictly speaking, only loosely related to the localized European traditions of pogrom; they were spontaneous, often erratic outbursts, whereas the Holocaust was scientifically managed. Violence here was authorized, routinized, the victims dehumanized. The distinctions are telling, as Bauman sadly observes – in contrast to the Nazi formation of Jewish police, the very idea of cooperation of the victims with the perpetrators of a pogrom is inconceivable (Bauman, 1989: 23). Morality, or more properly ethics, both here become invisible.

But what is it, finally, that triggers the process whereby bureaucracy and industrialism result in something like the Holocaust? And what is it that makes us twitch at the connection which Ritzer then draws between one process of rationalization in McDonaldization and another, in the Holocaust? Bureaucratic processes, as we know well from Weber, cannot themselves think, or feed back; they are based on the systematic following of orders and rules or upon the extension of precedents. Judged by immanent criteria, the political economy of McDonald's viewed in this light is goal-rational, as well as instrumentally rational; all other things being equal, utopia is a hamburger, for producer and consumer alike. The Holocaust is also goal-rational, but from the Nazi perspective alone. The crucial distinction to be drawn here is that between an economic imperative driven by consumerism in the case of McDonald's and a political imperative driven by genocidal racism in the case of the Holocaust. Further, while McDonald's may well be licensed by the state in various global locations, it is not authorized by the state in the way the Holocaust was. McDonald's is not, yet, compulsory; for better or worse, it is mediated through markets. The Holocaust was compulsory, state-driven and underwritten by that legal monopoly of violence, and enforceable by death. The analytical and ethical or at least moral distinction which emerges between McDonald's and the Holocaust is substantial, and it cuts across the critical tendency throughout the West from Marcuse to Foucault (and in this context, at least, including Ritzer) to identify capitalist forms with totalitarianism of some kind. Capitalism is rapacious, imperial, consuming, the agent of creative destruction, but it is not totalitarian in the sense that the Nazis and the Soviets aspired to, for the 'dictatorships over needs' were primarily politically driven rather than profit-maximizing or seeking (Fehér et al., 1983). Fascism, in this optic, involved the identification not only of state and civil society but also of state and political society. The political imperatives of the Nazis became, by compulsion, both law and (in a special sense) social policy, the policy of society understood as the will of the state made manifest. McDonaldization is by these criteria a radically different phenomenon to the Holocaust, analytically as well as morally or ethically.

Stated in more pedestrian terms, the difference between McDonald's and fascism is that McDonald's is something we choose, and the aristocratic critics of consumer or mass society from Adorno on never seem quite to have accepted this, so to say, Tocquevillean sense that just as democracy may well generate mediocrity, consumer capitalism will inevitably encourage bad taste. But this does not entitle interpreters to become legislators of taste. Obviously we are not free to choose in any meaningful sense, as anyone with passing familiarity with Marxism or the market would agree. Only there is a massive, awesome distance between choosing to wheel by the Golden Arches and entering those other gates. As Bauman puts it, then, the significance of the Holocaust generically is that it underlines something about modernity and state violence which we, in the relative peace of Melbourne, Leeds or Maryland, are generally spared. For we need to take stock of the evidence that the civilizing process is, among other things, a process of divesting the use and deployment of violence from moral or ethical calculus, and of emancipating the desiderata of rationality from the interference of ethical norms or moral inhibitions (Bauman, 1989: 28). And in all this we need to remember that sociology, and its socio-logists, have been complicit in this too (Turner and Käsler, 1995).

The point is telling, for Bauman wants, I think, more than Ritzer to say that the problem, too, is us, is in us. The arrow points inward, and not only outward at the trends or patterns which we as sociologists read out of or project onto history. For there is a certain, stunning sense in which the logic of Bauman's case in *Modernity and the Holocaust* is that this was indeed an accident waiting to happen, innerly, that antisemitism was no more than an obvious convenience in its specifically anti-Jewish content. The Jews were, to cross vocabularies, a kind of floating signifier in a Nazi world-view for which fixity of place and boundary was central. Bauman employs various examples to make his case, but the single most obvious is that extraordinary amalgam of Jewish–Bolshevik–capitalist attitudes that turn the Jew into the universal enemy. As Bauman puts it, perhaps only the Jews could so easily be cast and resented as arrogant elites and unwashed masses simul-taneously (Bauman, 1989: 42). More modern, more mobile than other peoples, the Jews on this account were to be singled out and punished precisely by the traditionalists, the Nazi blood-and-soil types. The irony of history would allow these antimodernist phobias to be unloaded through channels and forms which only modernity could develop (Bauman, 1989: 45–6).

Reactionary Modernity?

For Bauman, then, this failure of the Jews neatly to fit into the ultimately murderous classificatory systems of traditionalized modernity made them its victims. He quotes Arendt:

> In contrast to all other groups, the Jews were defined and their position deter-mined by the body politic. Since, however, this body politic had no other social reality, they were, socially speaking, in the void. (Bauman, 1989: 30)

In the German case, the Jews were then destroyed by the body politic, by the state. Emancipation from the state – so it seemed – could come from the state alone. Only the Nazi state set out rather on a programme of genocide without precedent. Here, as Bauman observes, we see tradition and modernity folded into one another. The quest to eliminate the Jews was a hallmark of Nazi antimodernism; modernity, like Judaism, was inevitably constructed in this world-view as corrupting, alien, too mobile, too free. Yet as Bauman argues, what we today call racism is also a necessarily modern, ironically 'humanist' phenomenon, based as it is on the theory and practice of social engineering which is a defining characteristic of modernity. Racism, in short, is a thoroughly modern weapon used in the conduct of premodern or postmodern struggles (Bauman, 1989: 61). Racism, in the strongest sense, is therefore also a state regime or pro-gramme; it is a legal practice of violence, and not only a form of othering. It is an exterminatory state project of social engineering modelled, Bauman claims, after the rapacious models of gardening and medicine. The differ-ence between heterophobia and racism, according to Bauman, (1989: 81) is organized state violence. Totalitarianism, then, is the premodern fantasy of the single class or single race engineered by modern means into Stalinism or Nazism. Modernity, however, is not by definition totalitarian. The Holocaust was, and is, modern; but it does not follow that modernity is a Holocaust. Modernity is rather a field of tensions, where the totalitarian prospect coincides with and struggles against the pluralism of the human world (Bauman, 1989: 93). Modernity or the history of Western civilization might in this regard represent decline, but it does not add up to a single totalitarian solution to the field of tensions which holds it together. We do not yet all inhabit the iron cage.

To use the most conventional of sociological formulas, Bauman, then, is arguing in the tracks of Simmel and Weber that complexification and scale, the very characteristics of modernity, open us to the prospects of totali-tarianism as much as to pluralism. Opacity, complexity, invisibility, the absence of proximity, all make it easier for us in principle to harm others. The division of labour, *contra* Durkheim, makes the prospect of barbarism more straightforward, as no single actor in the line truly has to decide. Morality itself becomes traditionalized and therefore mechanical; efficiency and diligence become the leading values. This is the problem before us.

At times in Bauman's argument, too, it begins to seem as though it is bureaucracy which is the culprit in this scenario. Against the kind of street ordinary wisdom which tells us that luckily, perhaps, bureaucracy often simply fails to realize its goals, Bauman argues that 'Bureaucracy is programmed to seek the optimal solution. . . . *Bureaucracy which acquitted itself so well of the task of cleansing Germany made more ambitious tasks feasible, and their choice well-nigh natural*' (1989: 105). Elsewhere Bauman associates this with the sceptical common sense, articulated among others by Jacques Ellul, that the weakness at the heart of our culture lies in the inability to distinguish between what is possible and what we should do. Yet that latter arrogance is not itself bureaucratic. Bauman grants that the Holocaust 'needed visionaries, as bureaucracy picks up where visionaries stop. But bureaucracy made the Holocaust. And it made it in its own image' (1989: 105). This argument might prompt three different potential responses. One is that Bauman is simply here emphasizing bureaucracy contextually as a causal factor. A second response is that perhaps it is actually the case that bureaucracy was the vital factor. A third is to return the focus to what Bauman earlier singles out as decisive – Nazi politics itself. For if bureaucrats (and 'citizens') are people who do as they are told, then we must always return finally, in analytical terms, not to bureaucracy but to the politics and culture of the Nazi state and party. As Bauman (1989: 106) acknowledges, it is the coincidence of monomaniacal social-engineering will and bureaucratic forms which generates genocide. What allowed this to occur, in turn, was the pronounced supremacy of political over economic and social power, of state over society (Bauman, 1989: 112). McDonaldization, in contrast, might more adequately be explained as a capitalist strategy to establish economic hegemony through into the cultural sphere. The connections or implications then follow through all the way. Enslavement of the Jews was never the Nazi purpose; theirs was not, in this regard, a capitalist strategy. McDonaldization, by comparison, rests on the slavery of youthful part-time wage-labourers and the attempted enchantment of consumers.

The Jews had no option; those in the world of McDonald's still exercise choices, even if they are impoverished. This is not to say that the contemporary Western world of the Golden Arches, described so pitifully yet powerfully by Bauman, by Jeremy Seabrook and others, is not miserable by the criteria of critical theory, but it is at least to remind ourselves that suffering has other markings as well. And it is, as I have observed, to insist that we look inward as well as out, for, as Bauman (1989: 132) says, the most frightening aspect of the Holocaust was not the likelihood that this could be done to us, but the idea that *we* could do it. As against the Adorno-type case, then, in *The Authoritarian Personality*, or Goldhagen's logic in *Hitler's Willing Executioners*, the point is not that the world is divided into born proto-Nazis and their victims. Rather, the elongated message of the Holocaust for sociology is that we have now arrived at a moment in modern civilization in which it is possible that a particular combination of social arrangements can impinge upon human conscience to the point of nullity. Bauman's study is thus both a pinnacle of achievement for critical sociology and a missal for ethics, for the quality of inner life which makes solidarity durable or even possible. The moral is clear – in order to be good citizens, there need also to be good individuals. There need to be good persons, persons who can say no to moral injunctions based on the appeal to conformism. For the good or responsible citizen, on this interpretation of modernity, may well be she or he who defies social consensus. Moral capacity, as Bauman (1989: 179) puts it, must be sought not in the societal but in the social sphere, not in the sphere of the state but effectively in that of civil society.

Conclusions/Coda

Formally speaking, it may well be that Ritzer and Bauman start in similar places and end up in related conclusions. They each follow the pattern or trend or structural claims characteristic of the sociological classics, and end up with us, and our responsibility within these constraints. The implication of the interpretation I have put here is that what occurs in these two stories between beginning and end differs. My purpose is not to devalue Ritzer's contribution by comparing it to Bauman's; rather it is to suggest that a difference of emphasis yields a difference of results. *The McDonaldization of Society* works on that level of sociological abstraction close to the philosophy of history, where the object, as in Marx's *Capital* or Weber's *Protestant Ethic*, is to characterize the main or dominant trajectory of our times. McDonald's, in Ritzer's work, condenses or symbolizes the decline we live out through rationalization and commodification or reification. Bauman's project in *Modernity and the Holocaust* refers elsewhere, to the Marxian and Weberian sentiments in which he is steeped, but also, and deeply, to the theme of ambivalence which he follows out of Simmel. By virtue of its singularity in characterizing modernity, the logic of the McDonaldization argument necessarily appears to be one-dimensional. It represents a powerful trend which we are exhorted to stand against. Bauman's characterization of the Holocaust is similar to this, in some ways, but in others ambivalence is built into its structure. Even in the blackest of prospects, we know with Bauman that modern fate is also contingent and open.

Let me end on an anecdotal note. Like other teachers of sociology, I know of no book like *The McDonaldization of Society*; my own students consume it. Only every now and again I catch myself referring to the book as *The McDonaldization of the World*. In one sense, this is an understandable mistake, for Ritzer also wants and rightly to draw attention to the global aspect of consumption and its deleterious effects. But it has also occurred to me that, Freudian-wise, I associate Ritzer's book with another famous title, *The Bureaucratization of the World*. Its author, of course, was Bruno Rizzi (1985) – Ritzer, Rizzi, it all begins to make some kind of sense. Rizzi's great claim, successfully plagiarized later by James Burnham in *The Managerial Revolution* (1945), involved not only the emergence of a new ruling class of global technocrats, it also claimed – as did Burnham's book after it – that this process occurred uniformly, globally, across the combined experiences of fascism, Stalinism and the New Deal. Doubtless in my own mind the scope of the claim in Ritzer echoes the scope of the claims I remember in Rizzi, and I suppose that today I mentally connect both lines to the kinds of claims that view globalization primarily in terms of the homogenization of cultures, politics and economies on a world scale. The widely recognized problem with this kind of argument is not that it is wrong, but that it is one-sided. Viewed as a way in to understanding, it is as unobjectionable as any other such line in. The brilliance of George Ritzer's book is exactly as an interpretative line in to this world. *The McDonaldization of Society* is an invitation to thinking, and it should be celebrated as such. As to the spectre of McFascism, there is really no such thing. Fascism with a friendly face is a contradiction in terms. Fascism never smiles, at least not publicly. For the face of the other is beyond it. For us, as for our others, that is everything.

References

Arnason, J.P. (1993) *The Future That Failed*. London: Routledge.

Bauman, Z. (1989) *Modernity and the Holocaust*. Oxford: Polity Press.

Beilharz, P. (1992) *Labour's Utopias: Bolshevism, Fabianism, Social Democracy*. London: Routledge.

Burnham, J. (1945) *The Managerial Revolution*. Harmondsworth: Penguin.

Fehér, F., Heller, A. and Markus, G. (1983) *Dictatorship Over Needs*. Oxford: Basil Blackwell.

Goldhagen, D.J. (1996) *Hitler's Willing Executioners*. London: Little Brown.

Herf, J. (1989) *Reactionary Modernism*. New York: Cambridge University Press.

Horkheimer, M. and Adorno, T. (1979) *Dialectic of Enlightenment*. London: Verso.

Ritzer, G. (1996) *The McDonaldization of Society: An Investigation into the Changing Character of Contemporary Social Life* (revd edn). Thousand Oaks, CA: Pine Forge Press.

Rizzi, B. (1985) *The Bureaucratization of the World*. New York: Free Press.

Turner, S. and Käsler, D. (1995) *Sociology Responds to Fascism*. London: Routledge.

Young, R. (1990) *White Mythologies*. London: Routledge.

15   Assessing the Resistance

George Ritzer

Although it is embedded in a rich theoretical tradition and deals, I think, with a series of important social issues, *The McDonaldization of Society* was written, and originally was supposed to be marketed, as a book for the upper end of the trade market; that is, as a book for a general literate audience rather than an academic audience. I had previously published *Metatheorizing in Sociology* (Ritzer, 1991) and it, like some of my earlier books in metatheory, had sold less than a thousand copies and was promptly remaindered by the publisher. While it may have had an impact on a metatheorist here or there, it certainly had no effect on the larger society. There is undoubtedly a place for limited market, academic monographs, but there also has to be a place for efforts by sociologists to reach a larger audience; to have a broader impact. I resolved to have a go at writing such a book.

At about the same time, I had a conversation with a publisher of academic books. His company had for years been a major outlet for important sociological works. However, more recently he had published few, if any, books in sociology. I asked him why he had deserted sociology and he responded by saying that it was the other way around, sociology had deserted him. That is, sociologists had largely ceased to produce books that were of interest to anyone but a small number of other sociologists.

In the light of these events, I returned to an essay I had published almost a decade before (Ritzer, 1983) and decided to transform it into a book with the same title. The essay had elicited some interest, and enthusiasm for the topic had grown over the years whenever I discussed it in one type of academic forum or another. However, by the time the book was completed, its original publisher (Lexington Books) was out of business and I was casting about for an alternative. Some time passed and I finally reached an agreement with a new publishing company, Pine Forge Press (a division of Sage). Unequipped to market the book in the trade arena, Pine Forge marketed it as a supplementary text in a variety of courses, especially in sociology. This was not the market I had intended to reach, but much time had passed and I was anxious to get the book out so that I could move on to other projects. I did not have high hopes for the book marketed in this way. To my surprise, the book has already become one of the best-selling books of its genre in the history of sociology (Gans, 1997).[1]

Even more surprising was the fact that the book had a strong impact on the international intellectual community and that led, among other things, to a number of translations, citations in numerous books and articles in the social sciences, and volumes like this one. I regarded the book as a serious effort at theoretically based social criticism, but I worried that theorists and other sociologists would be put off by its casual style and popular subject matter. To my surprise, and joy, my fears proved ungrounded.

I recite all of this history because I think it relevant to an understanding of the chapters that appear in this book. In my view, a book should be judged by what it intends to do, not what a reviewer thinks it ought to have done. Relatedly, a book should be evaluated on the basis of what it includes and not the innumerable other things that it ought, in the opinion of reviewers, to include. Reviewers often end up outlining the book they would have written rather than reviewing the book that has been written. The relevance of all of this will become clear as this chapter proceeds.

With two exceptions, I found the chapters in this volume to be highly constructive. All offer criticisms, to varying degrees, of what in a more recent book I call 'the McDonaldization thesis' (Ritzer, 1998), but most do it in a constructive rather than a destructive way. They mainly assess what I tried to do and not what they think I should have done. It is certainly pleasing to have the work taken so seriously by such an esteemed group of authors. Interestingly, Bryan Turner (this volume) contends that *The McDonaldization of Society* and a similarly oriented book, Ulrich Beck's (1992) *Risk Society*, have been among the more influential books in the social sciences in the 1990s. It does seem as if there is an important place in the social sciences for works that address 'big' 'real world' issues and not just those of concern to a small number of like-minded scholars. Furthermore, the success of these works demonstrates that academic books do not need to be self-consciously heavy tomes in order to be of interest and relevance to the intellectual community.

With prefatory remarks out of the way, I turn to a discussion of the chapters organized under five basic headings. At the close I will offer some general conclusions on the McDonaldization thesis in light of these chapters.

The Need to Use Other Theories/Theorists

A number of chapters in this volume suggested directly or indirectly that it would be useful to draw on theoretical resources other than Weberian theory to analyse McDonaldization. In spite of the fact that many of these are, in effect, asking for a different book, I am generally sympathetic to such calls and have myself recently written an essay applying Mannheim's theory of rationalization to that topic (Ritzer, 1998). Obviously, I am more sympathetic to the use of some theorists than others, but as a general rule I think that the more theoretical lenses we aim at a topic, the more we are going to learn about it. I am not convinced that any of the theories to be discussed in this section offer a better optic than Weberian theory, but many certainly do offer additional insights.

I begin with Barry Smart's excellent introduction to the volume, in which one of his key points is that, in doing a Weberian analysis, I did not sufficiently pursue a more Marxian political economy approach which would have allowed me to better deal with the relationships between increasing rationalization and capitalism. Smart acknowledges that I do deal with the role of material interests in the spread of McDonaldization, but that discussion is too little and too late for his tastes. Smart makes a convincing case for the utility of Marxian theory in analysing the pressure toward McDonaldization in profit-making organizations. However, one of the reasons that I shied away from Marx is that I wanted a perspective that could account, as well, for the McDonaldization of non-profit organizations (some hospitals, many universities, the state, and so on). While Marxian theory is not silent on this issue, I felt that Weberian theory offered me a more wide-ranging theoretical perspective. I do find Marx useful in this context and would welcome more Marxian-oriented work on it, but for my tastes Weberian theory offered a more profitable return on my theoretical investment.

Smart also draws on the post-Fordists to argue that flexibility and reflexivity, rather than McDonaldized standardization, may now be the dominant model in society. As I sought to make clear in my discussion of post-Fordism (and post-industrialism), I think that *both* processes are occurring, although often in different sectors of society. I never argued that McDonaldization was the only contemporary trend of any importance. While post-Fordism and post-industrialism are advancing, I question Smart's assertion that they represent an alternative model to rationalization. If anything, it is here that we are undoubtedly in the realm, to coin a new term, of 'post-rationalization'.

Smart moves on to draw on more postmodern ideas (as does Kellner, below) to argue that I underplay the degree to which people are persuaded, seduced, by the signs of McDonaldization. I accept this as a friendly criticism; another issue worth further analysis. However, I wonder why Smart feels the need to choose between the images of seduction and entrapment? As I see it, signs are used to seduce people into becoming trapped in the iron cage of rationality.

John O'Neill attacks my theoretical orientation and instead states a preference for a Parsonsian approach to my Weberian orientation. This theme is picked up in the last section of his essay where Parsons's approach is described as sublime. This seems to be related to Parsons's 'pure' theory as opposed to my approach, and more generally American theory, where O'Neill argues 'theory is never served apart from the meat and potatoes of evidence, facts, data'. But my model *is* Weber rather that the (later) Parsons. As is well known, Weber never strayed very far from the 'meat and potatoes' of historical data when he theorized. While our data may be different, in *McDonaldization* (and related work of mine) I share the commitment to closely tying theorizing to empirical data.

Deena and Michael Weinstein get at the problem of humanism as a base to critique McDonaldization. They wonder what I mean by humanism (although the term is not explicit in the book), why I prefer it, and why my values are any better than anyone else's? To avoid what they see as a fruitless battle over values, they seek to re-analyse my perspective from the point of view of ideas derived from Heidegger. (Interestingly, they make it clear that such re-analysis will only add to our understanding and not have much practical effect on the continuing expansion of McDonaldization.) They base their approach on Heidegger's sense of technology as 'a comprehensive way of existing'. In contrast to bringing things forth that are not yet revealed through aware conduct, modernity is characterized by 'challenging-forth' through which 'things are now revealed by "setting upon" them and mobilizing them in a "standing reserve" so that they can be "challenged forth" to perform pre-designed operations'. It is the latter that the Weinsteins associate with my perspective of McDonaldization. However, since we are 'enframed' by challenging-forth, 'acting out a drama of revealing the world and ourselves as standing reserve, then it no longer makes any sense to speak about humanism, the idea that our destiny is to serve our needs and desires through the world'. The Weinsteins reinterpret many of my examples from this perspective and they conclude: 'McDonald's is a way of revealing the people who become implicated in its system as what they have been designed to be: elements of a reserve of customers who are challenged forth to be serviced properly for a price.' I regard this as a generally friendly amendment to the McDonaldization thesis interpreted within a different theoretical frame.

Doug Kellner's case for a multiperspectivist orientation is highly attractive at least in part because it resonates so well with a perspective I have championed since the publication of *Sociology: A Multiple Paradigm Science* (1975) and *Toward an Integrated Sociological Paradigm* (1981). I am a strong believer in a multiperspectivist approach, but it clearly is not employed in *The McDonaldization of Society*. I employed a singular theoretical approach in that work because it produces a more powerful document that is more likely to hold the interest of a wide range of readers. The problem with a book written from a multiperspectivist point of view is that it tends to be so splintered and complex that it rarely makes a 'good read'. The issues of concern in McDonaldization would lend themselves nicely to more academic treatises looking at the phenomena under consideration simultaneously using a number of different perspectives. Such works would probably not attract many readers, but they would greatly illuminate our understanding of the phenomena.

This lack of a multiperspectivist approach is linked to Kellner's criticism of the fact that I did not employ a postmodernist approach. This helped, in his view, to blind me to the cultural aspects of McDonaldization and such phenomena as signs, simulacra, hyperreality, and so on. I am sympathetic to this view, as well, and in fact my more recent work has moved in a postmodern direction. This perspective and the kinds of concepts delineated by Kellner take centre stage in my forthcoming book on the new means of consumption (Ritzer, 1999). However, it is a very different book from *McDonaldization*, which, needless to say, would, itself, have been a different book had I adopted a postmodern orientation. I think Kellner will be pleased with the new book since it integrates a modern, once again Weberian, perspective on disenchantment and enchantment with a postmodern orientation.

Kellner also believes that I do not do enough with the economics of McDonaldization, or with the way different people and cultures sub-jectively use McDonaldized systems. No doubt much more should be done on these issues, but had they all been done within the covers of *McDonald-ization*, I believe the result would have been a cumbersome and far less powerful product. What this seems to suggest is that *McDonaldization* is not the end point, but rather the base on which others can extend our knowledge of the process.

Extensions

Barry Smart challenges my contention that it does not make sense from the societal point of view to have the kinds of huge concentrations of fast-food restaurants and other McDonaldized systems that we now find throughout the USA, as well as in many other parts of the world. Smart's contribution here is to point out that with the increase in the global marketplace it makes no sense any more to talk of a societal level, at least in this context. It is the pressure to expand globally that makes for the over-concentration of McDonaldized systems around the world. While I accept much of this argument, Smart goes too far when he argues that it is this and *not* the fact that people have come to value McDonaldization in itself that accounts for the hyper-development of these systems. As I argue in *McDonaldization*, it is some combination of material and ideal factors, among others, that helps explain the process. Once again, Smart wants to push the argument too far in a Marxian direction, at least for my tastes.

However, Smart quickly reverses himself and seeks to include *both* economic and cultural factors as driving forces in McDonaldization. However, under the heading of culture Smart wants to focus on American cultural imperialism and not my argument that McDonaldization has come to be valued for itself. Yet there is no contradiction here. McDonaldization has come to be valued in itself throughout the world *because* of America's cultural imperialism. Smart clearly does not think McDonaldization has come to be valued and argues that there are still many people who do not appreciate the rationalization of food (and, presumably, everything else). This is certainly true, but their numbers are in my view shrinking steadily and dramatically in the face of the onslaught of McDonaldization.

The great merit of the chapter by Cristiane Bender and Gianfranco Poggi is to bring to the fore the fact that pre-McDonaldized systems were able to function at the expense of women who were locked into the home. They may not have been locked into the iron cage of rationality, but they were imprisoned in a sub-system that was instrumental to its functioning. Thus, while there are clearly costs associated with McDonaldization, what is ignored are the more indirect benefits to women. Tasks formerly performed in the home by women are now being performed by market or state-centred arrangements. They do bring with them dehumanization, but to eliminate them would mean that women would need to return to the home and perform those tasks with 'human warmth'. This is clearly an unacceptable alternative and an unacceptable human cost.

Bender and Poggi also make it clear that there are important national differences in this realm. In Germany, as compared to the USA, fast-food restaurants do not play as great a role. Fewer women are in the labour force; their main responsibility remains in the home. In the home, however, women have been confronted with technical rationalization, which has, for example, transformed the kitchen into a factory. Women in Germany do provide an alternative to the McDonaldization of the larger society, but it is not a humane and less alienating option, at least as far as women are concerned. Women need to continue their gains in the labour force, but men need to take more of a role in the family. However, all of this may be rendered less relevant by the fact, observed by Bender and Poggi, that fast-food chains and other McDonaldized systems continue to expand in Germany.

Joanne Finkelstein offers an interesting critique of the McDonaldization thesis based, in the main, on her work with restaurants. She argues that restaurants deliver not only oppression, but also foodstuffs and, more importantly, pleasure. She rightly contends that I ignore the pleasurable aspects of eating at McDonald's. Given my focus on the formal structures of the restaurant, I also ignore the novel social practices that arise in such settings. However, Finkelstein is talking about the rituals and codes associated with eating, while I am focusing on far more social structural constraints. Indeed, the existence of such structures is a crucial difference between McDonaldized restaurants and all others. I am not arguing, as Finkelstein suggests, that 'social rituals and human subjectivity are fully homologous', but I am arguing that rational social structures exert considerable control over human subjectivity. Violation and innovation are far more likely in settings constrained culturally than they are in those constrained structurally. Finkelstein describes a number of interests surrounding a meal, including 'the ethical training of the young, the negotiation of obligations in the gift exchange between a provider and receiver, the satisfaction of bodily appetites, the offering of hospitality, the enjoyment of play and physical intimacy'. (Of these, only the satisfaction of bodily appetites has much, if anything, to do with fast-food restaurants.) And it is these that 'provide sites for innovations in social practices'. While some innovations certainly take place in McDonaldized systems, I stick with my point that such innovations are far less likely there than in more traditional restaurants. Finkelstein may be right that 'the sharing of food is a generative and volatile social moment, capable of re-enacting the social repertoire but also igniting new social experiments', but the structural characteristics of McDonaldized restaurants (and other systems) make them far more resistant to such innovations. I am not sure that this suggests the end of the autonomous subject, but it certainly makes it much more difficult to manifest autonomy and individuality.

Finkelstein rightly argues that fast-food is nothing new, but I wonder how much the modern fast-food restaurant has in common with the seventeenth-century British coffeehouse. She emphasizes the conversational breakthroughs that took place in these coffeehouses. If there are any conversational breakthroughs in the fast-food restaurant, they relate either to the absence of conversation or its dominance by scripted routines.

While we have some differences, I appreciated Finkelstein's chapter. I especially liked her point that in order to create universal interest in mass products there has had to be a McDonaldization of tastes. This is traced to 'the universalization of an array of products, logos and images'. Another useful idea is the fact that, given its ubiquity, we now have come to recognize the fatuousness and emptiness of scripted interaction. Given this recognition, we are in a better position to resist such inauthentic interaction.

Bryan Turner contrasts my book with Beck's (1992) *Risk Society*. While I emphasize the centrality of predictability and standardization to rational societies, Beck points to the inherent risks in such societies. Turner discusses two ways of reconciling these perspectives. One is to argue that they represent two different historical epochs within modernity, with the earlier stage of McDonaldization to be replaced by the later, more reflexive, risk society. This suggests a decline in McDonaldization, but this conflicts with my fundamental perspective that McDonaldization is expanding, not declining. More promising is Turner's suggestion that the processes are occurring at two different levels, with risk prevalent on the global, macro level and McDonaldization predominant on the local, micro level. Drawing on my work on credit cards (Ritzer, 1995), Turner makes an excellent distinction between the riskiness of the global financial environment and the standardization of local banking.

I think that Turner is on track in the latter direction, but I don't think he has identified the correct levels. I would distinguish between the industrial (modern) and post-industrial (postmodern) sectors of society. McDonaldization is predominant in the industrial sector, while it is in the post-industrial sector that risks abound. There are few risks in the industrial sector, but such post-industrial sectors as genetic or nuclear research are rife with risk.

However we distinguish among levels, it remains my view that the non-McDonaldized sectors will increasingly come under the sway of rationalization. They may never become fully or even highly rationalized, but they will become far more rationalized than they are now. This suggests that the risks that Beck emphasizes will decline with increasing rationalization. Of course, such risks will never disappear completely and, in any case, new risks will arise in other sectors of society.

Turner's other main point is that the 'coolness' associated with participating in McDonaldized settings may be a model for the kind of political involvement required in the contemporary world. He contrasts this to the heat of non-McDonaldized nationalistic versions of political participation. The coolness and irony associated with McDonaldization may well be preferable to the possibilities of conflagration associated with nationalism. We are back to the choice between formal and substantive rationality and the reason for Weber's ambivalence toward both. The substantive rationality associated with nationalism may prove an antidote to formal rationality, but there is also the danger of a blow-up associated with substantively rational systems. Formally rational systems are not liable to such explosions, but they lack any heart. Rather than preferring the coolness of McDonaldized political participation, perhaps what we need is some of both. This follows Weber's suggestion for the need for both the ethic of ultimate ends and the ethic of responsibility.

Richard Münch positions McDonaldization in the antagonisms between authentic culture and the end of such culture, as well as between the debased middle class and the avant-garde. He identifies various advantages associated with the debased middle-class, end-of-authenticity position, including the fact that more of us now have access to more cultural products and that many of those who were previously isolated can now interact and produce new cultural products. However, he also identifies a classic middle-class culture which he sees being displaced by a culture of entertainment. The latter is critiqued from the classic middle-class position for producing superficial cultural products that are primarily deployed in the name of greater profits. To maximize profits in a global marketplace, cultural products must be standardized, that is, McDonaldized. Münch offers an excellent example of this – the musical productions of Andrew Lloyd Webber (there are others such as *Les Misérables*). Such cultural products are based on a limited number of recipes for success. However, because their life cycle is short, constant product innovation is needed. But as these cycles grow shorter, true innovation is increasingly less possible. Instead, 'old ideas are time and again packaged in a new way'. There is lots of movement impelled by technology and fashion cycles, but little that is new. In addition, there is a diversification and pluralization of products, but they are standardized products created by professionals. Thus we have lots of selections, but few, if any, that are truly new and authentic.

Münch does point to the fact that in the contemporary world we also have access to more authentic cultural attractions. He gives examples of a trip to Mexico to see Maya culture or to listen to Mexican street musicians. However, he fails to deploy Baudrillard's notion of simulations here and therefore neglects the fact that these, too, may be inauthentic and part of the global culture of the debased middle class. This calls into question Münch's assertion that classic middle-class, avant-garde and regional folk cultures have increased along with the increase in the commercial entertainment culture. It seems more likely that these types of culture are increasingly difficult to differentiate from one another.

While Münch is more ambivalent about the hegemony of the process of McDonaldization than I am, he offers a strong case that today's global diversity is different from the diversity associated with the products of relatively closed cultures:

> More and more, one can find in one place that which can be found in another until all places are alike, because they offer that which is offered everywhere. . . . When the same colourful diversity of Benettons, H&Ms and GAP accost us everywhere, the world seems more monotonous to us, although each individual town has become more diversified. (This volume, p. 141)

Of course, such a critical view is more associated with cosmopolitans, while for locals McDonaldization brings increasing diversification. However, in order to survive in the new global marketplace, the local culture must succumb and become just another set of wares to be sold on the cultural marketplace.

Münch also sees a struggle between 'historically evolved municipal structures' and 'artificially created entertainment centres'. In the terms of my forthcoming book (Ritzer, 1999), there is a struggle here between the old and the new means of consumption (for example, the shops in the downtown area of a small town versus the Wal-Mart that opens on its outskirts), a struggle that the latter is destined to win. Münch's discussion of the CentrO in Oberhausen offers an excellent example of one of the new means of consumption. Such settings can be anywhere with the result that the town is no longer the most important location, rather it is the roads, airports and railway stations that will take us to others of the interconnected set of entertainment centres.

Münch is concerned that this international market for cultural products causes the disappearance of culture as a medium of mutual understanding. What is 'in' or 'out', 'up' or 'down' becomes far more important than mutual understanding. The market devours our ability to decide among ourselves how to live on the basis of mutual understanding. Ever-faster changes in the global marketplace for cultural goods make it harder and harder for us to decide for ourselves what is in good taste. Yet we need such deliberations to help us define what is tasteful and, more importantly, what is likely to harm others. Münch concludes that the good life requires collective deliberation and 'cannot be left to the production machinery of a global fun industry in a completely McDonaldized world'.

To at least some degree, Norman Denzin appears to want me to attempt to extend McDonaldization to the media, advertisements and sports (see also Jary, below). However, while I appreciate the kind of analysis Denzin has undertaken here, I am hard-pressed to see what it has to do with McDonaldization. The kind of advertising campaigns analysed by Denzin certainly do further the interests of McDonaldized systems, but other kinds of systems could benefit as well. The real issue is what do such advertisements have to do with the elements of McDonaldization – efficiency, predictability, calculability, control and the irrationality of rationality. The fact is that they probably could be related in various ways, but Denzin does not make this linkage for us. Complicating matters is the fact that he chooses to focus on Nike rather than McDonald's, and while Nike unquestionably has its McDonaldized elements, the analysis would have been cleaner had he chosen to deconstruct a parallel set of McDonald's advertisements.

What Denzin says he is going to do is reveal the 'cultural logics of McDonaldization' through the analysis of Nike's advertisements. More specifically, he is going to show us 'how the non-rational, the emotional, and the personal have become rationalized', as well as how all of this relates to race and gender. The closest Denzin comes to directly engaging the McDonaldization thesis is in his discussion of the three cultural logics of the system of commercial discourse – late modern capitalism and its linkage to commodity consumption, emotional experience and its connection to such consumption, and reverse cultural racism and the use of blackness as a marketing category. (This seems to me to be a highly limited and selective list of cultural logics, but that is another matter.) In any case, Denzin does relate the second of these logics (emotional experience) by arguing that it 'personalizes the norms of efficiency, quantification and predictability . . . it turns non-human technology (exercise machines) into an extension of human agency'. Unfortunately, Denzin tells us nothing about *how* this cultural logic personalizes the 'norms' of McDonaldization, nor does he tell us *how* non-human technology is turned into an extension of agency.

More importantly, and perhaps the factor that lies at the crux of my differences with Denzin, Jary and others, is that I am far less interested in the 'norms' of McDonaldization than I am in its material realities, material structures and material effects on what people do. I recognize the significance of the cultural turn in sociology as well as what Durkheim called non-material social facts, but my main concern is material social facts and their practical impact on what people do. It is no accident that Weber used the imagery of an iron cage and his paradigm case was the bureaucracy. The fast-food restaurants, and their innumerable McDonaldized derivatives, are similarly material structures that have served to strengthen the bars of the iron cage. Saying this, I fully recognize that McDonaldization has affected the larger culture, which has not only been McDonaldized to some extent, but has in turn, as Denzin suggests, furthered the process of McDonaldization. Unfortunately, Denzin does not follow up on this insight by explaining just how these things have occurred.

The media will foster the interests of whoever pays the bills. To the extent that the commercial world has been McDonaldized, the media will support and extend it. Of perhaps greater importance is the fact that the media in general, and the advertising industry in particular, have been McDonaldized and, as a result, they will tend to be more supportive of McDonaldized than non-McDonaldized systems. At this level, it could be argued that the iron cage will be even stronger when the media, advertising and industry have McDonaldized equally; when there is a seamless web of McDonaldization across the full material–ideal spectrum.

Denzin suggests, quite correctly, that I (and Weber) do not devote sufficient attention to not only the media, but also race and gender (although I have given more attention to these issues in more recent work). My response, traceable back to my introductory comments to this chapter, is that one cannot do everything and critics should focus on what has been done, not what they would have done or would have liked to have seen done. More importantly, I do not think that Denzin has shown how 'nothing escapes the cultural logics of Weber's iron cage'. He may have demonstrated how commercial interests use and exploit race and gender to sell their wares, but he has offered no concrete linkages between McDonaldization and race and gender. I think those linkages are there, and recently I have tried to underscore some of them, but I do not think that Denzin has demonstrated these relationships.

Keith Tester argues that the *McDonaldization of Society* is 'morally empty', especially as it relates to McDonald's use of meat viewed from the vantage point of vegetarianism. He contrasts my position to that of a work I draw heavily upon, Peter Singer's *Animal Liberation*. I am admonished for missing Singer's argument that the contemporary use of animals is morally and ethically bankrupt and for simply using his work as a resource on the rationalization of the use of animals. Of course, I did not 'miss' Singer's argument; I simply do not accept it and did not find it relevant to my argument. (In using a resource, one is *not* obligated in my opinion to use all of its insights and orientations. Such an obligation would make academic work literally impossible.) I am not a vegetarian, and while I abhor the abuses of animals for food, I cannot condemn it the way Singer (and Tester) does. (I guess I am confessing to being guilty of 'speciesism'.) In any case, why should I abhor that any more (or less) than I abhor the way people are treated in McDonaldized systems? In fact, I'm morally outraged at Tester's apparent privileging of the animal over the human. Tester wants my 'personal response' to animal abuse, but if I had offered expressions of moral outrage at every point in the book that I felt it, the book would have been twice its current length. While criticism, even moral outrage, is implicit throughout, it is most explicit in the chapter on the irrationality of rationality, especially the dehumanization of contemporary life. Tester seems to be one of few readers who missed the implicit moral outrage throughout the book; in fact, the book is much more often criticized for being a one-sided critique of McDonaldization.

The bulk of Tester's chapter deals with vegetarianism as 'a viable [and moral] way of resisting the rationalization of the world'. The problem, of course, is that while vegetarianism *might* pose a threat to McDonald's, in itself it is of little significance to the broader process of McDonaldization. More importantly, Tester himself details the vulnerability of at least one form of vegetarianism, 'lifestyle vegetarianism', to McDonaldization. He shows how a cookbook, *Seasonal Vegetarian*, manifests each of the dimension of McDonaldization except for the irrationality of rationality. However, I see the latter in such cookbooks which replace human creativity with pre-set recipes. Interestingly, the only hope for resisting rationalization for Tester seems to lie in the moral rigour of ethical vegetarianism, but that also dooms participants to being 'utterly marginal'. This seems to support the iron cage thesis since vegetarianism either leads right back into the cage or into a marginal position that is no threat to the cage itself.

Tester does not explore why ethical vegetarianism avoids the iron cage, but I think the answer lies, once again, in Weberian theory and the distinction between formal and substantive rationality. It is the moral character of ethical vegetarianism that makes it an example of substantive rationality. For Weber, of course, substantive rationality represented an alternative form of rationality that in many ways was preferable to formal rationality. Yet, for Weber, substantive rationality was destined to be overwhelmed by the forward march of formal rationality. Thus, at least in these theoretical terms, ethical vegetarianism represents nothing more than a short-term impediment to McDonaldization in the food realm.

Peter Beilharz addresses the political implications of the McDonaldization thesis. He does this by building on the work of Zygmunt Bauman on the Holocaust, work that I had used as the basis for a discussion of the Holocaust as one of the precursors of McDonaldization. Beilharz goes back to Bauman and sees an important difference between the two books. He argues that while I see McDonaldization as economic/cultural and tendential, Bauman sees the Holocaust as political and contingent. Certain conditions had to be in place in Germany for the Holocaust to occur, but McDonaldization seems impervious to those conditions in its ability to sweep them aside effortlessly. Of course, as Weber detailed, a variety of conditions had to be in place before rationalization could arise in the Occident. Indeed, it was because those conditions did not exist in other parts of the world that those areas had, at least until that point in history, resisted the rise of rationalization.

Another distinction drawn out by Beilharz involves the fact that the Holocaust was instrumentally rational for the Nazis,[2] but clearly not for its victims. In contrast, Beilharz claims that McDonaldization is rational for producer and consumer alike. This is not wholly false, but much of my book deals with the ways in which McDonaldization is irrational for both workers and consumers, but especially for the latter. Following the logic of Tester's chapter in this volume, it might be that the only difference between McDonald's and a concentration camp is that the former is killing its clients more slowly than did the latter.

In a related point, Beilharz argues that 'the difference between McDonald's and fascism is that McDonald's is something we choose'. This, of course, is based on the view that consumers freely choose to go to McDonald's. There is no question that this is the case today, although we cannot ignore all of the subtle and not-so-subtle pressure brought to bear on consumers to lead them to go to McDonald's. Beilharz himself recognizes that the choices before people are 'impoverished'. More importantly, there is the issue of the future and its cage-like character; the expansion of McDonaldized settings will greatly reduce, or in some cases eliminate, non-McDonaldized alternatives. In that scenario, there will come a time when people are forced to go to McDonaldized restaurants if they want to eat. We already have locales (some small towns, highway rest stops) where the only alternatives are fast-food restaurants.

Beilharz also argues that 'Bauman wants, I think, more than Ritzer to say that the problem, too, is us, is in us'. The logic of the Weberian approach to this issue does lead me to focus on structures as the source of the problem. However, there are, at least by implication, problems in us. One relates to the economic and/or power needs of those individuals who push the process of rationalization to their own benefit. Another, is the willingness of consumers to accept these systems and not to support the non-McDonaldized alternatives. This brings us back to the Holocaust and questions about why the Jews allowed the Holocaust to happen: why they did not fight back even harder than they did? There are problems within us, but they are dwarfed by the problems that surround us. Nevertheless, at least some of the burden is on us, as Beilharz, following Bauman, says, to look inward, to be good persons, to say no to external pressures whether they emanate from Nazi headquarters or Oak Park, Illinois.

Applications

We can look at the chapters by Alan Bryman and Gary Alan Fine together since both involve an effort to apply the McDonaldization thesis to specific social phenomena. Bryman sticks close to my five dimensions in his application to the theme parks, especially those of Disney, while Fine does that as well as coming up with a more creative (and dubious) set of categories in order to think about the art world, especially Southern folk art, from the perspective of McDonaldization. Not surprisingly, Bryman finds that McDonaldization and its basic dimensions fit the theme park quite well, while Fine finds that Southern folk art is not well described by McDonaldization. What both are doing, and Fine makes this explicit, is using McDonaldization and its dimensions as a Weberian ideal-type in order to analyse these two phenomena. This is a very appropriate use of the idea, especially since I make it clear that McDonaldization is not an all-or-nothing phenomenon; there are degrees of McDonaldization. Thus, any social phenomenon can be analysed in this way in order to assess its degree of McDonaldization.

Bryman's use of McDonaldization in this way is not problematic, but Fine's is because, as mentioned above, he chooses, at least in the first part of his chapter, to derive his own set of dimensions from my work. If the ideal-type is to be used as Weber intended it as a kind of measuring rod, then it and each of its dimensions must be used consistently. If each analyst is free to create his or her own set of dimensions, then there can be no consistency from one analysis to another. In effect, Bryman is using my 'ruler', while Fine has gone off and created one of his own. Since Fine is using a different ruler from Bryman (and me), it is difficult to compare his work to Bryman's. Further complicating matters is the fact that I am not at all sure that Fine's dimensions are central to, or relate well to, McDonaldization. Fine's thinking (mass production, mass audience) seems to be tied to the mass culture thesis with which he begins his chapter. Furthermore, it seems to be more of a productivist orientation (not only mass production, but the production community and his orientation toward the 'production of culture' approach) than is inherent in my thinking on McDonaldization. I am not saying that Fine's dimensions are unrelated to McDonaldization, but I am wondering whether they are truly central to it today. More importantly, I am concerned about each analyst creating his/her own set of dimensions of an ideal-type such as McDonaldization.

Fine's basic conclusion is about the same in the second part of his chapter where he does use my dimensions of McDonaldization. I'm not sure I would say that McDonaldization is 'of limited relevance' to the art world, or that 'this ideal-type of McDonaldization does not adequately explain the dynamics of the art market'. (The ideal-type is not designed to explain such dynamics, but rather to allow us to engage in systematic comparative analysis of social structures or social processes.) However, I would say, following Fine, that the world of folk art exhibits McDonaldization to only a limited degree. Or, as Fine puts it, 'McDonaldization does not apply equally throughout all of society.' That is a perfectly acceptable conclusion from the perspective of the use of the Weberian ideal-type. In his work, Weber found, for example, that the organization formed by the disciples of the charismatic leader approximated the ideal-typical bureaucracy to a similarly limited degree. For his part, Bryman found a very high congruence (except, perhaps, in calculability) between the ideal-typical characteristics of McDonaldization and the nature of the contemporary theme park.

Given his productivist orientation, Fine concludes that it is possible to resist McDonaldization if we are willing to return to a system where 'small-scale, idiosyncratic, expressive production was dominant'. While he recognizes that there are various reasons why this will not happen, Fine holds this out as an alternative if we are willing to pay the additional costs associated with it. He concludes with the un-Weberian upbeat message that 'McDonaldization is only a brand name for a style of production that consumers can choose to reject, should they wish'. There are two major problems with this conclusion. First, it has the productivist bias that characterizes much of Fine's essay; McDonaldization has at least as much to do with consumption (and service work) as it does with production. Second, and more importantly, consumers do not really have the choice Fine suggests. His solution, which he recognizes is unlikely, represents an effort to return to some prior state. I have a hard time believing that the answer to the problems associated with McDonaldization, or any other large-scale social process, lies in the past. Here I side with Marx and the idea that we must look to the future, not to the past, for the solutions to contemporary problems.

Bryman's chapter is useful for its systematic application of the elements of McDonaldization to the theme park. I found a number of gems in this chapter, including, for example, the fact that in case of an accident Disney has 'a set of established procedures for making the person comfortable, minimizing damage to other people's enjoyment and to the company, and responding to suggestions that the company was at fault (for example, offering free tickets, meals)'. Bryman's main difference with me is over the issue of calculability, and whether the emphasis on quantity inevitably leads to a decline in quality. Bryman clearly finds quality at Disney and makes it clear that he is something of a fan and devotee. I found his discussion of dreams, fantasy and magic at Disney of great interest, especially since that is the theme of my new book (Ritzer, 1999) on the new means of consumption (two of which are the fast-food restaurant and the theme park). I argue that in order to compensate for their rationalized, disenchanted state, the new means of consumption have undergone a process, consciously and unconsciously, of enchantment or re-enchantment. Bryman's view is consistent with this thesis. However, I am not at all sure that that means that the experience offered is of high quality. In fact, enchanted experiences can, themselves, be McDonaldized. Indeed, it could be argued that that is the defining character of the Disney theme park.

Bryman concludes by warning that McDonaldization does not totally capture theme parks or exhaust their interpretative possibilities. I would certainly concur with that. McDonaldization for me is simply one important trend, one important way of thinking about contemporary developments.

Yet another application is found in the conclusion of the Weinsteins' essay which is primarily about the role of MTV in McDonaldizing rock music. As the Weinsteins conclude, 'Rock music has been McDonaldized. What it took to be its rebellious energy has been channelled into techno-logical entertainment systems eliciting standardized behaviour and attitudes available to anyone.'

Conceptual Issues

Perhaps Smart's most interesting contribution lies in his discussion of my use of the 'iron cage' metaphor to describe the impact of McDonaldization. For one thing, the cage idea communicates the sense of a burden, but fails in his view to communicate the fact that rationalized systems are also shelters that are impossible to live without. In Giddens's terms, rationalized systems are both constraining and enabling. This is certainly true, and I pointed out many of the advantages of McDonaldization early in my book, but I also make it clear that since those advantages were well known, I was going to focus on the negative aspects of McDonaldized systems. As Smart acknowledges at the close of his chapter, I am offering a work in social criticism, not a balanced portrayal of McDonaldization.

Smart also finds the 'iron cage' metaphor inappropriate because it suggests external constraint. He argues that for Weber Protestant asceticism did not seek external constraint, but to positively nurture a self-disciplined subjectivity. Smart is correct on the latter, but unfortunately it is an example of substantive not formal rationality. While the substantive rationality of Protestantism helped give birth to formal rationality, it was not itself formally rational. The fact that substantively rational Protestantism did not rely on external constraint tells us nothing about the formally rational systems which, for Weber, were literally defined by such external constraint. And it is these formally rational systems that lie at the core of the process of McDonaldization.

Smart discusses the interesting issue of whether, when resistance occurs, it is to Americanization or McDonaldization. This is not an easy matter since the two are so deeply intertwined. In my more recent work (Ritzer, 1998), I have sought to deal with the relationship between Americanization and McDonaldization (as well as globalization). I think it safe to say that both are being resisted, at least to some degree.

Smart accuses me of conceptual slippage – rationalization/its uneven consequences, McDonald's/McDonaldization; the impact of McDonald's on eating/as the overall model of rationalization. On the first, the uneven consequences (especially the irrationalities) are, as Smart acknowledges, part of the process of McDonaldization. On the second, McDonald's is discussed as the paradigm for the process of McDonaldization. Finally, I do believe, and I think amply demonstrate throughout my work, that McDonald's impact is not limited to the food industry; that it has had an impact on all modern rational systems. I will need Smart to better explain where precisely the slippage lies in these linkages.

Weinstein and Weinstein point to an interesting conceptual issue. They ask (as does Smart): is McDonaldization a synonym for rationalization, or do I have in mind 'specific recent developments in social organization that differ importantly from earlier forms and for which McDonald's serves as a paradigm or model'? The answer is both! McDonaldization is rationalization as it is manifesting itself today. And it does represent something new in comparison to predecessors like scientific management and the assembly line. While it builds upon and extends such predecessors, all continue to be deeply implicated in the process of rationalization.

Kellner makes a problematic distinction between McDonald's and McDonaldization. He has no problem being critical of McDonald's (a 'particularly noxious institution'), but feels the need to be more balanced in his approach to McDonaldization. I'm not sure why we need to be critical of one and more even-handed in dealing with the other, especially since McDonald's is the paradigm of the process and a near-perfect representation of it. Kellner is certainly correct that McDonaldization has its advantages and disadvantages, but as I point out in *McDonaldization*, McDonald's, too, has its pros and cons. Kellner argues that there are various objective problems associated with McDonald's, but those same problems are associated with the larger process. Conversely, the advantages he associates with McDonaldization can also be linked to McDonald's. In any case, while he says he is going to deal with it, Kellner still has the problem of the basis on which he can make positive or negative judgements about these phenomena. (For example, on what basis is he able to argue that 'McDonald's offers an obvious inferior culinary option'?) Kellner believes that some forms of McDonaldization are beneficial, others harmful, but my view is that in all of its forms McDonaldization has strengths and weaknesses. We need to articulate these for the process as a whole as well as for each and every specific form that it takes.

Inappropriate Criticism

Up to this point we have dealt with a variety of issues, including a number of criticisms of the McDonaldization thesis which, while I do not agree with all of them, were made in a highly constructive way. However, two chapters in this volume are, in the main, unfair and highly destructive. How am I to deal with such critiques? Among the alternatives are to ignore them, stoop to their level, or take the 'high road' and deal with them more seriously than they dealt with my work. While I am sorely tempted to stoop to their level, I will take the latter course.

John O'Neill has come up with a chapter that has a striking resemblance to a hamburger. The first and last sections of the paper are the top and bottom halves of the bun, while the middle sections offer some real beef. Oddly, the two halves of the bun are at odds with what is between them. The first and last parts are snide attacks on *The McDonaldization of Society* (and on me, in spite of an attempt to claim that their chapter does not constitute an *ad hominem* critique), but the middle sections, the vast majority of the chapter, generally involve a series of amplifications of the McDonaldization thesis. Let me begin with the criticisms associated with the first and last sections, and then turn to the more positive contributions of the chapter.

The chapter begins by accusing me of a lack of candour in arguing that the book is not about McDonald's, but McDonaldization. However, I reiterate that McDonald's (and the fast-food restaurant) is no more the focus of my book than that bureaucracy is the focus of Weber's work. In both works, they are the paradigms of the larger processes (and interests) of rationalization and McDonaldization. Given the thrust of his chapter,

O'Neill seems far more obsessed with, and bitter about, McDonald's itself than I am. Similarly, while I often critique Americanization, this chapter has a bitterness about things American that is not characteristic of my approach.

John O'Neill sees *McDonaldization* as a 'McText' and concludes his chapter by arguing that it is part of a 'parochial sociology whose evangelical success injures the mind as much as fast food injures the soul's body'. We are then treated to O'Neill's Warning: ONLY YOU CAN STOP TEACHING/READING RITZER! If that is not an *ad hominem* attack, then I have never seen one. John O'Neill's bitterness at McDonald's and things American is only exceeded by his bitterness at me (not unrelatedly an American social theorist) and my work. For example, early in the chapter I am described as an apparent 'prototype' of those who view McDonaldization as an iron cage. Rather than going mad or to prison, I am described as writing 'McCriticism' and 'McTexts' because they are 'profitable'.[3] Thus, I am depicted as having injured students' minds, of having trivialized sociological theory, and, worst of all, doing it for the money (the latter, of course, is just about the worst thing you can say about a scholar). I'm surprised that O'Neill did not hold my book responsible for 'mad cow disease' and the decline of Western civilization.

By the way, while I am the one accused of producing a McText, it is in O'Neill's chapter (not my book) that one finds the usual paraphernalia of a true McText – 'McCommunion' reduced to 10 easy steps, figures, boxes and graphics depicting the Marx, Weber, Durkheim and Ritzer 'burgers'. (If John O'Neill was doing a serious critique of my work, he would have tried to relate my earlier work [the 'toppings' on the 'Ritzer Burger'] on paradigm integration and metatheorizing to this one on McDonaldization.)[4] In contrast, *McDonaldization* offers old-fashioned pure text.

As I pointed out at the beginning of this chapter, I wrote a book that was oriented to bringing sociological theory and social criticism to a larger audience. It was *not* written as a text, let alone a McText; it was only after a series of missteps that it, or at least the US English-language version, came to be marketed as a text. The issue is not a McText, but whether we should be writing accessible sociological theory. The implied answer in O'Neill's chapter is that we should not. Rather, apparently, we should be writing the kind of obscure theorizing associated with the lionized Talcott Parsons and practised here, at least in the first and last sections, by O'Neill. There is little danger that such writing will injure very many people's minds because not many will bother to read it. I am not saying that there is not a place for Parsonian-style theorizing (to say nothing of my own metatheorizing), but I think there is *also* a place for accessible theorizing.

In any case, *McDonaldization* proved to be far more than a 'McText'; it has influenced scholars around the world. Indeed, in the body of his chapter, O'Neill treats it as a scholarly text by building upon its basic premises. The first part is a friendly addition to the McDonaldization thesis by focusing on the impact of the beef industry. The second part builds on ideas developed in *McDonaldization* on the impact of that process on the family and work. The third part develops my thinking on the impact of McDonaldization on the consumer, especially the turning of the consumer into an unpaid worker. The fourth part links, as do I, McDonaldization to Americanization. I found much of merit and of use in these sections. They seem disconnected from the first and last parts which are such acid critiques. If the McDonaldization thesis is so weak, if the book is a McText that should be shunned, then why is O'Neill devoting the bulk of his chapter to amplifying on some of its basic themes?

David Jary is repeatedly dismissive of the McDonaldization thesis. This position came as a surprise to me because Jary had invited me to give a keynote address on the McDonaldization of higher education at a conference at the university of which he is Dean, he included the term in his dictionary of sociology (Jary and Jary, 1995), and he even used it as the basis of a co-authored paper on McUniversity (Parker and Jary, 1995) (which he conveniently does not cite in his references). I wonder why Jary did all those things on the basis of, or with, a concept that he considers to be so limited?

Jary attempts to help by expanding on my model so that it more adequately deals with the phenomena of concern to me. First, he offers me a prehistory of the McDonaldization of sport and leisure, largely through the inevitable (in English sociology these days) idea of sportization derived from the work of Elias and his disciples. Now, while I do deal with sport and leisure, I deal with many other things as well (health, education, and so on) that have nothing to do with sportization. In addition, I am also urged to do a nuanced Foucaldian genealogy of sport and leisure, as well as a more neo-Gramscian analysis. Of course, had I done those things, I would have ended up with a very different book. Jary is describing a book he ought to write and not offering a valid or useful critique of my book.

Jary more or less begrudgingly accepts the McDonaldization thesis as a reasonably accurate portrayal of the first three stages of a six-stage process in the McDonaldization of sport and leisure. (I am not too happy with such a stage approach, but that is another matter.) Thus, Jary seeks to help me by adding three additional stages (as well as redefining at least two of the earlier stages in terms of signs, icons, spectacles, and the like). Jary's text on these stages is nearly incomprehensible, but we can gain some insight from his Figure 8.1. Stage 4 deals with the interaction between McDonald's and sports stars, sports teams and sports events in terms of signification and iconization. Unfortunately for Jary, McDonald's is not as active in the sports arena as, say, Disney or Nike. More generally, Disney and Nike are paradigms of something, but it is not McDonaldization (although they are certainly involved in the process). Stage 5 involves some sort of furthering of this process involving a set of well-known and accessible concepts like 'prolympism' and 'iconized sports stars'. In addition to having *nothing* to do with what I meant by McDonaldization, concepts like these would not have been very helpful to me in my effort to write an accessible piece of social criticism. Step 6 deals with sport and corporations, especially TV; Jary offers the reader no idea what that has to do with McDonaldization. I do not find Jary's six-stage approach helpful in conceptualizing McDonaldization.

There are many other problems in Jary's chapter. For example, he asks why I didn't choose Taylorism as my exemplar rather than McDonald's. Had Jary reread Chapter 2 of *McDonaldization*, he would have seen that I argue that Taylorism was only one of the factors that lay at the base of McDonaldization. Or he wonders whether McDonald's was only one of several organizations moving in a similar direction. Had Jary read the Preface to the first edition, he would have seen that I suggest that we could have talked in terms of things like 'Burger Kingization' or 'Seven Elevenization'. There is much more of this level of discourse in Jary's chapter, but it is time to move on.

Conclusion

In the main, what has been suggested by the chapters in this volume is that I should have drawn on other theoretical resources, made various extensions and applications, and clarified several conceptual issues. There are many useful ideas and suggestions here that are worthy of additional scrutiny and study. For example, it would certainly be useful to explore this issue from the perspective of other theoretical perspectives[5] – Marx, neo-Marxian theory, Parsons, Heidegger, Elias, Foucault, Gramsci, postmodernism and multiperspectivism. Similarly, we would profit from efforts dealing in greater depth with the relationship between McDonaldization and economic factors, culture, cultural imperialism, morality, the individual, subjectivity, self-discipline, seduction, gender, the family, the polity, societal differences, humanism, creativity, taste, risk, the city, the media, advertising, sports, resistance and fascism. In fact, in various essays over the last several years I have drawn on Mannheim and postmodernism as additional theoretical resources, extended the McDonaldization thesis to deal with such issues as Americanization and globalization (topics notable by their absence in this volume), and applied the concept to credit cards and the media. This kind of work, the kinds of suggestions offered in these pages, and this volume itself all suggest that a topic that was intended for a broader audience has become an issue that is not only of interest to academics, but one that is linked to a wide variety of their theoretical and empirical concerns. In fact, there is a nearly endless list of theoretical resources and social issues that can be related to the McDonaldization thesis. Indeed, it may be the openness of the McDonaldization thesis, rather than the thesis itself, that will prove to be its most enduring quality. As Rorty (1979) has argued, the point is to keep the intellectual conversation going. The chapters in this volume have certainly done that and, more importantly they have suggested a wide range of future directions for conversations about the McDonaldization of society.

Smart's original call for this volume suggested that authors deal with both their resistance to the McDonaldization thesis as well as additional thoughts on resisting the process of McDonaldization. What is surprising is how little of this volume deals with resistance to the process. While there are hints in other chapters, the major exceptions are Tester (vegetarianism as a mode of resistance), Fine (the return to small-scale, idiosyncratic expressive production) and Bender and Poggi (the state as a force capable of resisting McDonaldization). While this comparative lack of attention could be taken to mean a number of things, it may well indicate implicit recognition of the power of the process of McDonaldization, if not its inexorability. I would like to see more scholarly attention devoted to resisting the process and, more generally, more resistance throughout the world to the spread of McDonaldization. I do not think McDonaldization will be stopped, but I do think that greater resistance will allow us to maintain more ways of escaping the process and more domains that are relatively free of McDonaldization.

The most optimistic scenario, extending a point made by Finkelstein, is that the likely further proliferation of McDonaldization may lead to a greater realization of the emptiness at the heart of the process and thereby to greater resistance to it. Thus, in a bizarre sense, the hope for resistance lies, dialectically, in a society and world saturated by McDonaldization. We can only hope that McDonaldization proves more vulnerable than has capitalism (at least thus far) to the dialectical contradiction that is embedded in the continuing success of both.

Notes

I would like to thank Doug Goodman for his very useful suggestions on the structure of this chapter.

1 *McDonaldization* does not appear in Gans's list of best-sellers. Sales as of this writing would put the book well up on Gans's list.

2 One could question this by arguing that the Holocaust hastened the defeat of the Nazis by robbing them of the contributions of a large and well-educated group, as well as because of the great resources needed to maintain the enormous system for rationalized death.

3 I am also described as 'performing' skunk works. However, in but one of many sloppy components of the chapter, O'Neill misses the point that skunk works are created, not performed.

4 By the way, O'Neill appears to misinterpret my work on paradigm integration by labelling it 'nirvana'. To me, the integrative paradigm was designed to supplement extant paradigms and was not seen as some sort of ideal sociological position designed to supplant all others. Similarly, he uses the seemingly ludicrous idea of meta-metatheorizing (which occupies a minor place in my metatheoretical work)

rather than the focus of my concern – metatheorizing. In having a little fun at my expense, O'Neill is systematically distorting my thinking.

5 In fact, I have recently explored Karl Mannheim's thinking on rationalization as an alternative theoretical resource (Ritzer, 1998).

References

Beck, U. (1992) *The Risk Society*. London: Sage.

Gans, H. (1997) 'Best-sellers by sociologists: an exploratory study', *Contemporary Sociology*, 26: 131–5.

Jary, D. and Jary, J. (1995) *Collins Dictionary of Sociology* (2nd edn). Glasgow: HarperCollins.

Parker, M. and Jary, D. (1995) 'The McUniversity: organization, management and academic subjectivity', *Organization*, 2: 1–20.

Ritzer, G. (1975) *Sociology: A Multiple Paradigm Science*. Boston: Allyn & Bacon.

Ritzer, G. (1981) *Toward an Integrated Sociological Paradigm: The Search for an Exemplar and an Image of the Subject Matter*. Boston: Allyn & Bacon.

Ritzer, G. (1983) 'The McDonaldization of Society', *Journal of American Culture*, 6 (1): 100–7.

Ritzer, G. (1991) *Metatheorizing in Sociology*. New York: Lexington Books.

Ritzer, G. (1995) *Expressing America: A Critique of the Global Credit Card Society*. Thousand Oaks, CA: Pine Forge Press.

Ritzer, G. (1998) *The McDonaldization Thesis: Explorations and Extensions*. London: Sage.

Ritzer, G. (1999) *Enchanting a Disenchanted World: Revolutionizing the Means of Consumption*. Thousand Oaks, CA: Pine Forge Press.

Ritzer, G. (forthcoming) *Cathedrals of Consumption*. London: Sage.

Rorty, R. (1979) *Philosophy and the Mirror of Nature*. Princeton, NJ: Princeton University Press.

Index

Adorno, T. W., 23, 71, 137, 223
advertisements for Nike, 166–9, 174–5, 182, 243; racial and cultural logics of, 171–3; responses to, 169–71
advertising, 128, 130, 172, 242–3; of McDonald's, 76, 77, 191, 198–9
Albrow, M., 3
alienation, 36–7, 39n
alternatives to McDonaldization, 201–2
Americanization, 1–2, 17, 80–1, 129–30, 188, 249
Americans, and McDonald's, 33–4, 48–51
Andrews, D., 125
Animal Kingdom (Disney World), 108
anxiety, social relations and, 86
art galleries, 149–51; *see also* folk art
Asian cuisine, 75
athletes, and emotional bond with consumers, 175
Australia, sport in, 127
authentic culture 139, 241
avant-garde culture, 140, 141

banking, 93
Barthes, R., 75
Baudrillard, J., 63, 67, 130, 191
Bauman, Z., 11, 208, 209, 219; *Modernity and the Holocaust*, 222, 224, 225, 226–9, 230–1, 245
Baumol, W. S., 25
Baxter, Richard, 10
Beck, U., 16, 85–91, 94–5, 215, 240
beef, 42–3, 14–15, 200
beefburgers, 43, 45
Beilharz, P., 245–6
Bell, D., 118
Bender, C., 239
benefits of McDonaldization, 14, 131, 239
Berger, P. L., 90
bio-medicalization of life, 66
birth and death, McDonaldization of, 23, 65–6
blackness, as spectacle, 180–1
Bourdieu, P., 91

boycott, 213, 218
brand names, 124
bread production, 209–10
Brillat-Savarin, J. A., 74
'bringing-forth', 61
Bryman, A., 246, 248
BSE crisis, 14–15, 215–16, 220n
BSkyB, 126
Buckingham, D., 102
bureaucracy, 3, 9–10, 31, 34–5, 37, 201; Holocaust and, 228, 230–1
Burnham, J., 232
Burns, T., 34
Busch Gardens, 103, 108, 109, 117
business rationality, 208, 209

calculability, 4, 9, 16, 65, 91, 225; of culture, 137; of folk art, 158; of sport, 117, 123; of theme parks, 108–10, 113; vegetarianism and, 218
capital accumulation, 6, 7; flexible, 12; Fordist, 11–12
capitalism, 11, 24–5, 64–5, 228; Foucault and, 85; globalization of, 1, 7, 193; Marx and, 5, 83–4; science and, 5–6; Weber and, 84
care, risk and, 214–16
casualization, 93, 94
celebrity endorsement, 172
celebrity-hood, 177–9; race and, 179
CentrO project, 142–3, 242
'challenging-forth', 61–2, 65, 66, 237
charismatic leadership, 101–2
children, at McDonald's, 46
citizenship, 83, 94, 97–8, 99
classic middle class culture, 136–7, 139, 140–1, 241–2
Coca-Cola, 1, 122, 124
coffeehouses, 78–9, 240
Cole, C., 125
collecting, 153–4
commodification, 188–9, 191, 194; of culture, 137–8
communication, 139, 143
computerization, 45, 120

consumers, 22–3, 59, 128, 129, 203–4n; choice for, 228, 248; control of, 59; persuasion of, 12–13, 63–4, 77; satisfaction of, 65; self-service, 13, 47–8; as sporting commodity, 173–5
consumption, 13, 96, 188, 193, 198
control, 4, 16, 23, 59, 91, 225; culture and, 137; in folk art, 159; of leisure, 123; and power, 31; sport and, 117, 123; technology and, 209; in theme parks, 104–7, 108
Cooley, C. H., 77–8
coolness of commitment, 96–7, 98–9, 241
corporate sport, 127, 129
Crawford, M., 197
Cross, G., 129
cultural imperialism, 2, 8, 130, 238; resistance to, 17, 18
cultural logics, 165, 243; of Nike advertisements, 171–3
cultural pessimism, 23–4, 36–7
cultural products, 137–8, 139, 148; standardization of, 241
cultural risk, 94–5
cultural studies, 187–9
culture: of entertainment, 136–41, 241; globalization of, 135–6, 137–8, 139–40, 144; standardization of, 94, 137–8, 139, 140, 189, 192; and understanding, 144, 145, 242; see also classic middle class culture
cycles of popular culture, 138–9, 140–1, 144, 241

de-humanization, 3, 16, 17, 201, 225, 239; critique of, 36–7; McDonaldization as, 23, 35–6, 59, 79, 80, 202
democracy, 65
democratic state, political power of, 37–9
Denzin, N., 242–4
deregulation, 92–3
deskilling, 12, 33, 91, 93–4
diet, 15; American, 43; Asian, 43
discipline, 85
Disney, Walt, 101–2, 109–10
Disney cast members, control and, 105–6, 106–7
Disney gaze, 106
Disney hotels, 112
Disney World, 103, 105, 110, 111, 112
Disneyland, 101, 102, 103; quality in, 109–10
diversification of culture, 139, 140, 141–3, 242
diversity, 11, 12, 189, 193; in art world, 160, 161
domination, 31, 201

Donnelly, P., 130
Douglas, M., 89
Dunning, E., 123
Durgnat, R., 125

eating, 96, 189–90; American, 33–4, 47, 50; pleasure of, 75, 76, 239; see also food
Eco, U., 72, 77
economic rationalization, 11–12, 15; irrationalities of, 15–16; resistance to, 17
economics of fast food, 6
education, 63, 64
efficiency, 4, 6, 9, 16, 65, 91, 201, 225; in art, 157–8; of culture, 137; of sport, 117, 123; of theme parks, 102–4, 111; of vegetarianism, 218
Elias, N., 72, 74, 75, 123
Ellul, J., 230
emotional experience, 165, 243
employment at McDonald's, 45–6, 180, 199–200, 201
entertainment, 76, 136–41, 241
environment, McDonald's and, 177, 200
Environmental Defense Fund, 177
environmental pollution, 86, 88–9
epidemics, history of, 88
ethical vegetarianism, 217, 218, 219–20, 245
Euro Disney, 15, 112, 128

factory-farming, 210–11, 216
Falk, P., 96
family, 26–7, 28, 30; McDonald's and, 50, 80, 191
fascism, 222–3, 228, 245
fast food, 3, 8, 47–8, 98, 240; as hyperreal experience, 77, 191–2, 203n; industrialism and, 79–80, 91–2; irrationalities of, 15, 16; production of, 5–6; proliferation of, 7; resistance to, 17; and social practice, 76, 78
Fine, G. A., 246–8
Finkelstein, J., 239–40
Finster, Howard, 152–3, 157, 158
flexible specialization, 93–4
folk art, 150, 154, 155, 156, 246–7; production of, 157–9; Southern contemporary, 154, 156, 159–61
folk culture, 140
food: and modernity, 71–4; preparation of, 28; rationalization of, 4–8; as a social code, 74–9, 80; and social practices, 75, 78, 96, 239; see also eating; fast food
food/merchandise outlets, in theme parks, 105
food scares, 216–17; see also BSE crisis
football, BSkyB and, 126

Fordism, 11–12, 59, 91, 92, 94, 227
formal rationality, 4, 9, 91, 249
Foucault, M., 71, 85
France, 8, 18
franchising, 35, 39n; of art galleries, 151
Frankfurt School, 85, 194

Gans, H., 148
Garfield, B., 111, 169, 171
gender relations, 25–6, 30
General Motors, 34
Generation X, 174
Germany: fast food in, 28, 29, 239;
    households in, 28–9
Gershuny, J. J., 25
global marketing, 19, 137–8, 144, 145
globalization, 129, 135, 192, 232; of
    capitalism, 1, 7, 193; of culture, 135–6,
    137–8, 139–40, 144; local and, 7, 33,
    141–2, 160, 192–4, 202; in sport, 130
Goffman, E., 178
Golden Arches, 14, 63, 76, 77, 92
Goldhagen, D., 223–4
Goldman, R., 130
Gray, H., 179
Gross, Otto, 84

Habermas, J., 23, 58
Halle, David, 153
Hampstead (London), McDonald's in, 18
Hargreaves, J., 123
Harvey, D., 118
Harvey, J., 130
hegemonic distribution system, art galleries
    and, 150–1
Heidegger, M., 237; 'The question concerning
    technology', 61–2, 66
Heller, A., 78
Herf, J., 223
higher education, 3, 32–3, 36
Holocaust, 65, 66, 225–6, 245–6; modernity
    and, 226–9
homogenization, 12, 72, 194, 198, 202
Hopper, Dennis, 164, 166–9, 171, 175, 176–9,
    182
Horkheimer, M., 137, 223
Houlihan, B., 130
households, technical rationalization of, 29,
    30
Hribar, A., 125
humanism, 60, 62, 72, 77, 237
hypersignification of products, 122

iconization, 124–5, 252
ideology, 189

imitation of cultural products, 138
individualism, 11, 72, 78; risk society and,
    87
individualization, 87, 89–91, 92
industrialism, 79, 80, 118, 228, 240; service
    society and, 24–30
innovation, 239–40, 241; cultural, 138–9;
    technological, 135–6
instrumental rationality, 193, 194, 227–8
intrinsic value, 5, 78
iron cage 84, 85, 163, 248–9; family as, 26;
    of McDonaldization, 9–14, 23, 79, 190,
    243
ironists, 97–8
irrationality of rationality, 15–16, 34, 102,
    110–11, 194, 218–19

Jacobs, M., 215–16
Japan, sport in, 127
Jary, D., 252–3
Jerusalem, McDonald's in, 18
Jews, 227, 229, 231
Jordan, Michael, 125, 165, 180
Judge, J., 111
junk food, 197
Jurassic Park, 137

Kellner, D., 237–8, 249–50
Kern, R. M., 153
Knight, Phil, 173, 175, 176
Kottak, C. P., 14
Kovel, J., 197, 204n
Kroker, A., 12, 16
Kundera, M., 78

labour relations, at McDonald's, 45–6
Lash, S., 7
Law, J., 3, 8, 12
law, 35
leisure: McDonaldization of, 117–19, 120–8,
    130–1, 252–3
leisure products, 119
Lévi-Strauss, C., 71
life course, 90
lifestyle vegetarianism, 217–18, 219, 220
Lipsyle, R., 173
local culture, and global diversity, 141–3
Love, J. F., 180
Luckmann, T., 90
Lynes, R., 148

MacCannell, D., 112
MacClancy, J., 6, 8, 216
market globalization, 19, 137–8, 144, 145
market segmentation, 148–9, 153, 154–5

marketing, 139, 207–8; of McDonald's, 12–13, 63
Marx, K., 5, 39n, 57, 83–4, 236
mass audience, for art, 153–4, 247
mass consumption, 11, 198
mass culture, 148
mass production, 11; of art, 151–3, 247
material interests, 5, 6, 7
McCartney, Linda, 219
McDisneyization, 101, 109; resistance to, 111–13
McDonald's, 3–4, 45–51, 63; American ideology and, 189; expansion of, 2, 22, 192; food at, 15, 196–8; marketing, 12–13, 63; race and, 179, 180–1; sport and, 124; see also fast food; McDonaldization
McDonald's Consumer Care Culture, 177
McDonaldization, 2–4, 5, 6, 7–8, 32, 57–60, 116–17, 186–7; critique of, 14–20, 196–200; iron cage of, 9–14, 23, 79, 190, 243; as a policy, 31; resisting, 200–2; Ritzer's social theory of, 187–94; see also rationalization, McDonaldization as
McJobs, 180
McKay, J., 127
McLibel, 18–19, 196
McMasters, 180
McNews, 92
McSpotlight, 19, 196, 204n
McText, 53–4, 251–2
media, 181–2, 243–4; race and, 164–5
medicine, 63, 64, 86–7, 92
Millar, S., 6
Miller, T., 127
Mills, C.W., 19–20
modernity, 8–14, 70–1, 79, 80, 92; constraints of, 9–11, 37; food practices and, 71–4; Holocaust and, 226–31; and postmodernity, 119–20, 128, 190–2, 193; risk society and, 85–7
modernization, 190, 198; as standardization, 94–5
Moog, Carol, 171
morality: McDonaldization and, 207–8, 210–11, 244; rationality and, 208–10; vegetarianism and, 211–13, 214–15, 217–18, 220
Morris, David, 18
MTV, 67–8, 248
multiperspectivist social theory, 194, 202, 237–8
Münch, R., 241–2
music videos, 67–8

nation-state, 37, 38, 97
nationalism, 97, 98, 241
Nazism, 65, 66, 223–4, 229–30
'News McNuggets', 80, 207
NFL, and Nike adverts, 169, 170, 172
Nike, 1–2, 125–6, 163, 165, 176–7; Dennis Hopper and, 165–7; and race, 179; see also advertisements for Nike
non-human technology, 35, 36, 159, 218

objective culture, 64–5
occupation, differences in, 37–8
O'Neill, J. & G., 236, 250–2
order, 37, 71, 85

Packard, V., 132n
pan-capitalism, 67–8
Papson, S., 73, 130
parking, at theme parks, 102–3, 104
Parsons, T., 236
passes, at theme parks, 103, 111
Peterson, R. A., 153
pleasure, pursuit of, 76–7
Poggi, G., 239
political action, 95, 241
political domination, and social change, 37, 38
popular sociology, 58
post-Fordism, 94, 118, 236
post-industrialism, 236, 240
Postman, N., 23, 26
postmodernity, 98–9, 118, 144, 186; and modernity, 119–20, 128, 190–2, 193
power, 31
predictability, 4, 9, 16, 65, 91, 201, 225; of culture, 137; of folk art, 158–9; of sport, 117, 123; of theme parks, 107–8; of vegetarianism, 218
premodern agriculture, 61
Preston, P., 6
production, 188, 193, 198; of art, 157–9; of culture, 137–8, 139, 148
production community, 154–7, 161
profits, 137, 198, 219, 241
Protestant ethic, 11, 26, 37, 212–13, 249
public relations, 86
public sphere, 145
Puritans, 212, 213, 214

quality, in Disneyland, 109–10
queues, at theme parks, 105, 110–11

race, 179, 181–2; media and, 164–5
racism, 229–30

rationalization, 8–14, 26, 245; iron cage of, *see* iron cage; irrationality of, *see* irrationality of rationalities; McDonaldization as, 2–3, 58–9, 91–4, 188, 189–91, 201, 202, 224, 225–6, 249; morality and, 208–10; risk and, 85, 240–1; Weber and, 2, 3, 26, 84, 224
recreation, rationalization of, 117
reflexivity, 87, 88
regulation, 84
Reich, R. B., 37
relative effort, in acquiring a burger, 44
restaurants, 73–4, 75–6, 239–40; in theme parks, 103
reverse cultural racism, 165–6
Rifkin, J., 43
Rinehart, J., 202
risk, 14, 16, 84–7, 85–91, 240; care and, 214–16; McDonaldization and, 92–4; social, 89–91, 93, 94–5; traditional and modern, 87–8; vegetarianism and, 215–17
ritual eating, 96, 239
Ritzer, G., 2, 41, 57–60, 74, 109, 116–17, 118, 186, 202–3, 222; critique of, 31–6, 98, 119, 127–8, 194–5; and factory farming, 210–11; and fast food, 5–6, 6–7, 8, 12, 15, 77, 78; food as a social code, 74, 75, 76; and the Holocaust, 224–6, 228; and irrationality, 15–18, 102, 218–19; and modernity, 70–1, 72, 91–2, 94;and rationalization, 2, 3, 4–5, 9, 10, 14, 26, 190; and resistance, 128–9; sociological theory of, 187–9; and technology, 209–10; Weber's influence on, 23–4, 34–5, 53, 163, 164, 189–90
Rizzi, B., 232
Rock & Roll McDonald's, 69
rollercoasters, 109
Ronald McDonald's Children Charities, 180
Rorty, R., 97–8
Rugby League (UK), 126–7
Rugby Union (UK), 127
rule specification, 123

safety/security, 14, 15–16, 93
salmonella, 216
sameness in art, 153
Sayer, D., 10
science, 5–6, 86–7
Seasonal Vegetarian, 218
seduction of consumers, 12, 13, 63
self-servicing work, 16, 59, 122
self-taught art, 149–50, 152–3, 155
service society, industrialization of, 24–30, 34

Sheard, K., 123
Shearing, C. D., 105
signs, 124, 125, 191
Simmel, G., 64
Singer, P., *Animal Liberation*, 210–13, 214, 218, 244
Smart, B., 236, 238, 248–9
Smythe, D., 173
social change, 6, 7, 26–7, 28, 90
social code, food as, 74–9, 80
social exchange, 79
social practices, food and, 75, 78, 96, 239
socio-cultural risk, 89–91, 93, 94–5
sociological theory, 51–2, 85
sociology, 95; of risk, 83–5
sponsorship of sports, 116, 124, 125–6
sport: McDonaldization of, 117–19, 120–8, 130–1, 252–3; and racial order, 165–6, 169
Stalker, G. T., 34
standardization, 11, 12, 23, 45, 94, 98, 193; of culture, 94, 137–8, 139, 140, 189, 192; in sport, 119
standing reserves, 61, 62, 63, 65, 237
Steel, Helen, 18
Stenning, P. C., 105
subjectivity, 9, 10, 11, 77, 239

Taiwan, McDonald's in, 192–3
taste, 144, 153; construction of, 73–4, 240; homogenization of, 154
Taylor, Rogan, 126
Taylorism, 12, 79, 91, 92, 122, 253
technological innovation, 135–6
technology, 65, 66, 70; and control, 209; Heidegger and, 61–2
television, sport and, 125–6
Tester, K., 244–5
theatre lighting, 33
theme parks, 101; McDonaldization of, 102–11, 113, 246, 248
Thomas, A., 214, 217
Tolliver, Mose, 152
totalitarianism, 228, 230
tourism, McDonaldization of, 112, 117–18
towns, 142–3, 242
transportation, 139, 143
trust, 216, 220n
Turner, B., 240–1

uncertainty, 89, 92–3
understanding, 143; culture as medium of, 144, 145, 242
United Biscuits, 219
United States of America, beef in, 42–3

universalizing discourse, 80, 81
Urry, J., 7
USSR, McDonald's in, 129
utopianism, 132n

Van Maanen, J., 107
Vatican, 31
Vattimo, G., 74–5
veal production, 211
vegetarianism, 18, 207–20, 244–5; *see also*
    ethical vegetarianism; lifestyle
    vegetarianism
Vidal, J., 14, 15, 19

Wall, The (Pink Floyd), 57
Warde, A., 13
Waters, Roger, 57, 67

Webber, Andrew Lloyd, 138, 241
Weber, M., 26, 30, 58, 208–9, 224–5, 245; and
    bureaucracy, 9–10, 34–5; and capitalism,
    84–5; and Protestant ethic, 11, 26, 37,
    212–13, 249; Ritzer's use of, 23–4, 34–5,
    53, 163, 164, 189–90
Weinstein, D. M., 237, 248, 249
'What's wrong with McDonald's?', 18, 19
Wieden, Dan, 171, 172
Williams, J., 125, 127, 130
women: benefits of McDonaldization for,
    239; as housewives, 29; and the service
    sector, 26, 27, 28, 30
workers, *see* employment at McDonald's
Wright, Ian, 125

Young, R., 223